Explorations in Economic Anthropology

Explorations in Economic Anthropology

Key Issues and Critical Reflections

Edited by
Deema Kaneff and Kirsten W. Endres

berghahn
NEW YORK · OXFORD
www.berghahnbooks.com

First published in 2021 by
Berghahn Books
www.berghahnbooks.com

© 2021, 2023 Deema Kaneff and Kirsten W. Endres
First paperback edition published in 2023

All rights reserved. Except for the quotation of short passages for the purposes of criticism and review, no part of this book may be reproduced in any form or by any means, electronic or mechanical, including photocopying, recording, or any information storage and retrieval system now known or to be invented, without written permission of the publisher.

Library of Congress Cataloging-in-Publication Data

Names: Kaneff, Deema, 1962- editor. | Endres, Kirsten W., editor.
Title: Explorations in economic anthropology : key issues and critical reflections / Edited by Deema Kaneff and Kirsten W. Endres.
Description: New York : Berghahn, 2021. | Includes bibliographical references and index.
Identifiers: LCCN 2021005182 (print) | LCCN 2021005183 (ebook) | ISBN 9781800731394 (hardback) | ISBN 9781800731400 (ebook)
Subjects: LCSH: Economic anthropology. | Equality.
Classification: LCC GN448 .E97 2021 (print) | LCC GN448 (ebook) | DDC
 306.3--dc23
LC record available at https://lccn.loc.gov/2021005182
LC ebook record available at https://lccn.loc.gov/2021005183

British Library Cataloguing in Publication Data
A catalogue record for this book is available from the British Library

ISBN 978-1-80073-139-4 hardback
ISBN 978-1-80073-911-6 paperback
ISBN 978-1-80073-140-0 ebook

https://doi.org/10.3167/9781800731394

Contents

Acknowledgements   viii

Introduction. Chris Hann and the Anthropological Study of Economic Life   1
Kirsten W. Endres and Deema Kaneff

Part I. Reconsidering (Post)Socialist Spaces

Chapter 1. Civilizations and Economies: Notes on a Neglected Theme   19
Johann P. Arnason

Chapter 2. From Halecki to Hann: The Historiography of Historical Regions   35
Stefan Troebst

Chapter 3. Out of the Frying Pan and into the Fire, or Modernization Forever? Economic Strategies in the Transformation of Peasant Societies   52
Mihály Sárkány

Chapter 4. Something to Be Nostalgic About? Goulash Socialist and Postsocialist Rural Society in Hungary   64
Nigel Swain

Chapter 5. Man Does Not Live by Bread Alone: The Indivisibility of Economic and Discursive Aspects in Neoliberal and Populist Regimes in Poland 76
Michał Buchowski

Chapter 6. Making a Reality of Other People's Fictions: A Smithian Critique of Post-Marxian and Polanyi-ite Accounts of Exploitation
Michael Stewart 89

Chapter 7. Resilience and Surveillance in Hann's Eurasia 102
Steven Sampson

Part II. Economic Anthropology in a Changing World

Chapter 8. Hijra, Port and Market: Pre-Ottoman Economies in Southwest Arabia's Zaydi Realm 121
Andre Gingrich

Chapter 9. From Social Norms to Legal Norms: Regulating Work in Postneoliberal Political Economies 134
Ruth Dukes and Wolfgang Streeck

Chapter 10. The Moral Economy of Anthropological Scholarship 145
Monica Heintz

Chapter 11. Some Thoughts on Embeddedness, Value and the Moral Dimension in the Work of Chris Hann 157
Frances Pine

Chapter 12. Property, Resources and Gauging Social Change 169
Deema Kaneff

Chapter 13. Birth, Property and the Male Descendant: Some Evidence from India 182
Chris Gregory

Chapter 14. What Has Happened to Turkish Tea? Thoughts on a Cash Crop, the Turkish State and Society in This Millennium 194
Lale Yalçın-Heckmann

Part III. Economies of the Sacred and Secular

Chapter 15. Economy Is a Ritual 209
Stephen Gudeman

Chapter 16. The Rice, the Rice Goddess and the Sickle: An Agricultural 'Revolution' among the Bru of Khe Sanh, 1989 219
Gábor Vargyas

Chapter 17. The Dharma and the Dime: Money and Buddhist Morality 232
Christoph Brumann

Chapter 18. Stealing Goddesses: The Political Economy of Kingship in Premodern India 243
Burkhard Schnepel

Chapter 19. Dalits and the Market: Liberation or Oppression? 255
David N. Gellner

Chapter 20. Polanyi Goes to Mauritius: Economy and Society in the Postcolony 267
Thomas Hylland Eriksen

Publications by Chris Hann 278
Index 299

Acknowledgements

The editors wish to express their gratitude to the contributors of this volume for their willingness to engage in this project and for the hard work they put into their respective chapters. We are also deeply appreciative of the collective effort that was made to get everything to us within a tight schedule. We very much value the assistance received from Ildikó Bellér-Hann, Berit Eckert and Anke Meyer, who helped us with valuable information during the book's secretive planning and writing. Your input made the whole process so much easier and added to the pleasure!

We would like to acknowledge Steve Gudeman for his support from the beginning of this endeavour and for his ongoing interest. Our sincere thanks to John Eidson for his continued support in a variety of ways, one of which was the reading of the introduction and providing us with much appreciated and valued comments. We also would like to thank the two anonymous reviewers of the manuscript for their insightful and constructive feedback.

Our gratitude goes to everyone at Berghahn Books who saw the book through to publication. In particular, we wish to thank Marion Berghahn for her enthusiasm and commitment to the project, and to Anthony Mason, Tom Bonnington and Caroline Kuhtz for their patient guidance during the review and production process, as well as to Jon Lloyd for copy-editing the final manuscript.

Finally, we would like to thank Chris Hann for inspiration, and for giving us a reason to work together – a task we very much enjoyed – and also for the opportunity to collaborate with all the wonderful people mentioned above.

Introduction
Chris Hann and the Anthropological Study of Economic Life

Kirsten W. Endres and Deema Kaneff

In an era of rising global precarity and social inequality, the field of economic anthropology is pertinent in terms of the questions it raises, the debates it engenders and the solutions it offers through in-depth ethnographic studies of local and contextualized economic practices. Chris Hann's published work has substantially contributed not only to shaping the subdiscipline, but also to raising awareness of what anthropology can contribute to broader debates on economic transformations and their social consequences. This book honours his achievements with a collection of chapters authored by leading scholars in the field of (economic) anthropology, as well as related disciplines such as sociology and history. It is organized around three interrelated research areas, each engaging with issues central to Hann's own investigations over the past decades. Before moving on to these three areas, which highlight both key issues and critical reflections in economic anthropology, it seems appropriate to begin this introduction with a short account of Chris Hann's academic life and work.

From Cardiff to Halle: Reflections on an Academic Journey

Schooled in Wales, where he was raised, Chris Hann embarked on his undergraduate studies in 1971, in 'Philosophy, Politics and Economics' at Jesus College, Oxford University. Travelling through continental Europe

---

Notes for this chapter begin on page 14.

during the summer vacation months sparked a curiosity about Eastern Europe that would have a lasting impression. It influenced Hann's choice for an area specialization that would later distinguish him as an anthropologist of (post)socialism. After graduating with a first-class degree in 1974, he decided to continue his academic education by taking a course in social anthropology at Cambridge University. It was here that he met the distinguished anthropologist and historian Jack Goody, who would eventually become his Ph.D. supervisor and a lifelong intellectual mentor. Goody encouraged Hann to undertake ethnographic field research in Eastern Europe for his Ph.D. dissertation, an idea Hann found attractive because he thought that 'the anthropologist, using the methods of participant observation, could generate fresh kinds of knowledge about what was really going on in those societies that would go beyond the stereotypes of totalitarianism' (Hann 2010). Hann completed his dissertation in 1979, which came out as a book the following year with the title *Tázlár: A Village in Hungary*. It was the first published monograph on rural Eastern Europe by a British anthropologist.

In 1978–79, Hann started new fieldwork in the Carpathian mountain village of Wisłok Wielki in southeastern Poland. In contrast to other Soviet Bloc countries, peasant farming in Poland had not been collectivized and appeared 'extremely unproductive' in comparison to Hann's previous experience in Hungary (Hann 2016a). Hann's fieldwork took place in the midst of Poland's national political and economic crisis in the early 1980s. The resulting monograph, *A Village without Solidarity: Polish Peasants in Years of Crisis*, came out in 1985. By this time, Hann had already opened up a third fieldsite, this time in Turkey, with the aim of expanding his comparisons 'to include developing countries of the capitalist world' (Hann 1985: vii). This provided an important counterbalance to the previous two (post)socialist fieldsites.

After more than a decade in Cambridge, where he lectured in the Department of Social Anthropology and was a Fellow of Corpus Christi College, Hann took up a Professorship of Social Anthropology at the University of Kent in 1992. His teaching commitments and administrative tasks did not prevent him from publishing extensively over these years, but he nevertheless welcomed the opportunity to prioritize writing when he joined the Wissenschaftskolleg zu Berlin as a Fellow in 1997 (Hann 2000). At that time, the Max Planck Society (the central organization which maintains over eighty institutions that conduct scientific research across the physical and social sciences) was already hatching plans for a new Institute for Social Anthropology, to be located in one of the Neue Bundesländer, or new federal states in the territory of the former German Democratic Republic (GDR), with Hann designated as one of the founding Directors. The Institute was established in the city of Halle/Saale in 1999. Hann placed his initial research focus on 'Property Relations' (1999–2005), a theme that had gained much momentum following the 1989–91 collapse of the socialist states. It was the topic studied by the first research team in the Department.

In the following years, while at the Max Planck Institute for Social Anthropology (MPI), Chris Hann established a fourth fieldsite – with Ildikó Bellér-Hann – in the Xinjiang Uyghur Autonomous Region, northwestern China. Despite the particular challenges of carrying out research in this part of China, the material also held considerable comparative value in giving Hann yet another field location from which to explore 'postsocialist' questions. The expansion of research activities into an additional region, of what was once viewed as the socialist world, provided a final piece of the puzzle, allowing him to develop a concept of Eurasia that became fundamental to his thinking. 'Composed primarily of the landmass that is conventionally divided into the two continents of Asia and Europe' (Hann 2016b: 1), Eurasia has become a major organizing principle of his work that is founded on viewing the interconnectedness of the landmass. 'Eurasia' also unifies a number of research themes – civilizational analysis, the relationship between religion and economy, and economic embeddedness more generally, as well as (post)socialism. Conceptually, Hann reconciles influences from Goody and Polanyi in order to develop his own notion of Eurasia: drawing on Goody's concept of Eurasia as a structural unity (that in turn Goody had adopted from Childe; see Hann (2016b: 3)), while adding a particular unifying and historically rooted force to the concept, based on an understanding of embedded economy drawn from Polanyi. This has enabled Hann to 'recentre' the Western tradition of scholarship away from Europe and an 'Atlantic' bias, instead putting Eurasia centre stage as the locus for the generation of historical development (Hann 2016b: 7). At the same time, the mixed forms of economic practices exemplified by Eurasia provide a platform from which a contemporary critique of neoliberalism and market dominated economics can be conducted.

The thematic unity provided by the concept of Eurasia is reflected in the research groups Hann established at the MPI. A series of studies focused on the links between religious phenomena and new forms of capitalist economy, such as the focus groups 'Religion and Civil Society' (2003–5), 'Religion and Morality' (2006–8) and 'Economy and Ritual' (the latter headed jointly with Stephen Gudeman, 2009–11). The group 'Social Support and Kinship in China and Vietnam' (2006–10) set out to investigate the distinctive features of 'socialism with neoliberal characteristics' (Endres and Hann 2017). Research themes relating to economy and social change were further pursued in the focus groups 'Industry and Inequality in Eurasia' (with Catherine Alexander and Jonathan Parry, 2012–14) and 'Financialisation' (with Don Kalb, 2015–17). The ERC-funded project *Realising Eurasia: Civilisation and Moral Economy in the 21st Century* (REALEURASIA, 2014–20) paid particular attention to the embeddedness of the economy in religion, polity and society, and emphasized the commonalities across various civilizational traditions in Eurasia with regard to the moral norms governing economic relations and practice. A project group focusing on the post-Soviet transformation of Siberia was established initially in Hann's department in 2000, but it gained status as an interdepartmental research unit two years later.[1]

Despite expanding his scope of research areas, Hann has maintained and closely followed developments in the four Visegrád states (Poland, Slovakia, the Czech Republic and Hungary). In 2017, he initiated the Visegrád Anthropologists' Network (V4 Net) with a twofold aim: to contribute to a deeper understanding of the social processes emerging out of the gradual 'deepening of neoliberal structural peripheralization' (Hann 2019a: 301) in these countries; and to consolidate the standing of anthropology in the region. Under his leadership, the department, named 'Resilience and Transformation in Eurasia', has grown and flourished. It has expanded to include several additional groups led by established senior researchers who both complemented and extended his research trajectories. These included the topics of citizenship from below, lifestyle plurality, tradition and urban modernity, markets and infrastructure, and ethnic minorities and the state.[2]

The contributors to this volume are part of the extensive and multidisciplinary network of research collaborators, senior colleagues and academic friends who have worked with Hann over the years and have engaged with his ideas and arguments on numerous occasions.[3] The chapters are arranged into three parts, which are organized around the interrelated themes of rethinking postsocialist developments, global economic and social transformations, and the economy's relationship to the sacred world. They reflect the wide range of topics on which Hann has researched and written during his – to date – four-decade engagement with anthropology. The themes also represent the important ways in which Hann has helped extend the frontiers of the discipline: not only in terms of regions that have gained the focus of anthropological interest (postsocialist Eurasia), but also intellectually in terms of broadening our understandings of economic activities and critically engaging with capitalism from the perspective of former socialist arrangements. We feel the best way to highlight Hann's contribution to the discipline and beyond is through the chapters that make up this book by colleagues stimulated by his work. The chapters also provide testament to Hann's impressively rich set of intellectual interests.

Reconsidering (Post)Socialist Spaces

> The point of the Eurasian perspective is to escape from the binary of Europe and the rest of the world. It is to declare Yes, we are the children of the past 500 years, but we are also heirs of much older interactions between the human economy and the religious-political nexus, dating back in the Old World at least 3,000 years. (Hann 2016b: 7)

As noted above, the theme of Eurasia is prominent in Hann's large-scale vision, presumably triggered by his initial interest in 'postsocialist' states that served as a lever for critical thinking about civilizational centres, market economies and embeddedness. 'Eurasia' stands in contrast to the North Atlantic world as the global centre of the market and of disembedded economic activity. It is a means to move beyond potential Eurocentric biases and boundaries through providing a broader and recentred conceptual framework. Hann's intellectual goal in adopting the 'Eurasia' terminology was to synthesize on a macro-scale while at the same time providing a concept that accommodates modern world changes from a long-term historical perspective. In Hann's (2016b: 9) conceptualization, the Eurasian landmass is characterized by a 'unity-in-civilizational-diversity' that presents a potentially important antidote to the socially disintegrating effect of neoliberal capitalism. As he puts it: 'The study of civilizations in Eurasia draws our attention to functional adaptations of many kinds, but also to the persistence of values that cannot be reduced to any materialist calculus' (Hann 2012a: 120). Elaborating on Jack Goody's thesis of Eurasian commonalities and Karl Polanyi's 'substantivist' approach to the study of economic history, Hann reminds us that both of them 'together enable us to recognize that Eurasia, from the Axial Age civilizations to the mixed economies of the post-war era in Western Europe, offers an alternative to the liberal and neoliberal nightmares' (Hann 2015: 319).

The contributions in the book's first part engage with these ideas from different disciplinary backgrounds. Johann P. Arnason's chapter links up with the big question of 'whether social and cultural anthropology has a contribution to make to civilizational analysis' (Hann 2018c: 339). This is also the subject of debate in a recent book he coedited with Hann (Arnason and Hann 2018). In his chapter in this volume, Arnason recognizes a major weakness of contemporary work by civilizational analysts, namely that economic considerations are not given sufficient attention. Arnason's chapter takes up this challenge by returning to classical sources in order to explore ways in which 'the economy' has been treated, and what lessons can be learnt from the comparative and embedded approach offered by economic anthropology.

In chapter 2, Stefan Troebst scrutinizes five concepts of historical meso-regions (East-Central Europe, the Balkans, the Black Sea Region, Europe and Eurasia) for their value as both heuristic devices and investigative frameworks. In so doing, he highlights the importance of Hann's development of 'Eurasia' as an analytical framework. Troebst argues for an intensification of interdisciplinary and transnational cooperation to create a transregional perspective that spans several centuries and ties several historical meso-regions together.

Modernization agendas, Mihály Sárkány reminds us in his chapter, formed the backdrop to all of the fieldsites where Hann has worked. Sárkány looks at the mixed activities of rural communities in two locations – former socialist Hungary and Kenya – borne out of a necessity for survival. In both cases, local economic strategies amount to the prioritization of households' survival above the supposed lure of market engagement (whether state-driven or otherwise). As Sárkány notes, 'poverty hinders modernization'. He therefore not only underlines the ongoing relevancy of mixed economic activities, but at the same time questions 'modernization' programmes and the nature of the economic transformations in both capitalist and socialist systems.

A consistent finding of researchers working in 'postsocialist' states, also evident in Hann's own work, is the acknowledgement that socialism offered many sections of the population a high degree of social and economic security. It is this security that has been eroded since the reforms of 1989/91, which is especially evident in the case of those who have been economically marginalized through the 'shock therapies' of neoliberalism. Often, voices that express former socialist arrangements in a positive way have been dismissed or trivialized as 'nostalgia'. At the same time, such views do not necessarily imply that postsocialist citizens wish to return to a past of collective property and central planning. Rather, as Hann holds, 'their sentiments must be understood as commentary on the present, and even as a form of resistance to the prevailing order, with implications for future alternatives' (Hann 2012b: 1127). 'Nostalgia' is a perspective that has gained currency with hindsight.

In his chapter, Nigel Swain contends that postsocialist nostalgia also has a 'real' basis, at least in rural Hungary where he, much like Chris Hann, has conducted fieldwork over the past four decades. The mutual dependency of the 'first' (formal) and the 'second' (informal) economy provided a material security that enabled many rural communities to live comfortably and prosper. It is this material security under Hungary's system of 'goulash socialism', Swain argues, that rural dwellers miss the most in the contemporary era.

Disenchantment with the inequalities produced by neoliberal market capitalism has not only triggered longing for bygone times in the former socialist countries of Europe, but has also produced a turn to right-wing populism and nationalism. These tendencies may not be unique to Eastern Europe, but, as Hann notes: 'Populist *ressentiments* in Hungary and the other Visegrád states are not difficult to understand when one recognizes the failure to bridge the economic gulf separating them from the West' (Hann 2019b). In the fourth chapter, Michał Buchowski explains the mechanisms that have promoted right-wing and nationalist tendencies in the case of Poland. He takes a Gramscian approach to highlight the role of public discourses in co-shaping social images and practices, and shows how various populist narratives have contributed to the discursive creation of an 'internal Other' that, in addition to external Others, is deemed to threaten the moral (and physical) integrity of the nation.

The consequences of postsocialist marginalization, and the rise of inequalities, is tackled from a different angle by Michael Stewart in his chapter, who takes the example of Romany money lenders in rural Hungary to address the question: 'When do people feel exploited?' Rather than applying a Marxian perspective, Stewart suggests that the complex phenomena of money lending may best be understood through the lens of Adam Smith's Theory of Moral Sentiments.

The present desperate situation of large sectors of the populations of the former socialist states lends support to Hann's view that: 'Neither the militant post-socialist liberals nor today's populist power holders in Hungary and Poland can dismiss the accomplishments of their Marxist-Leninist predecessors' (Hann 2019a: 327). Yet can Hann's results from the Visegrád-based ethnographies also be applied more broadly to other socialist and postsocialist systems? This is the question Steven Sampson pursues in his chapter by looking at the case of Romania. He argues that repression and surveillance were more extreme than in the Hungarian case, and people's coping strategies were less successful both before 1989 and afterwards. A key concept discussed in this context is 'resilience' – a term that appears in the name of Hann's department at the Max Planck Institute, but has largely remained untapped in his work, both theoretically and analytically.

Economic Anthropology in a Changing World

> The larger question at issue is whether, in the globalized world of the twenty-first century, it is still possible to organize the economy according to principles other than those of neoliberal market capitalism. (Hann 2018a: 1717)

Socialism's appeal in terms of the greater security – economic and social – that it offered its citizens, which is evident in cases observed by Hann (amongst others), has provided a means from which to critically evaluate capitalism. In other words, the search for a human face of capitalism, and a critique of its worst economic extremes, has provided a backdrop from which to explore the alternate political economy of socialism, a central concern of much of Hann's work. Nor does Hann subscribe to the common interpretation of the collapse of the Soviet Bloc 'as proof that there can be no alternative to private property as the most basic organizing principle of human economy, or at least of those economies which have reached a high degree of complexity and technological sophistication' (Hann 2019a: 101). Hann's engagement with Polanyi, amongst other economic historians, is precisely centred on the intricate interconnectedness of economic activity within society. Polanyi's concept of embeddedness offers ways of exploring economic relations from a broader context than the approaches traditionally used in other disciplines.

Andre Gingrich's chapter argues that a Polanyi-inspired approach in economic anthropology, as advocated and elaborated by Hann, may be usefully applied to the precapitalist economies in Southwest Arabia during the centuries preceding Ottoman rule. In particular, Gingrich focuses on the ritual and nonritual exchanges in the Zaydi realms of the northern Yemeni highlands from the twelfth to fifteenth centuries. He shows that Karl Polanyi's triad of forms of economic integration – reciprocity, redistribution and market exchange – helps us to grasp and explain the pre-Ottoman social, political and economic constellations along the Indian Ocean's northwestern shorelines.

Whereas in the 1960s and 1970s, Polanyi-inspired anthropologists considered embeddedness as a characterizing feature of premarket or precapitalist societies, current perspectives advocate that all economies are inextricably embedded in social structures, norms and power relations. This view also appeals to sociologists concerned with labour law. As Ruth Dukes and Wolfgang Streeck argue in their chapter, economic anthropologists have much to offer to an institutional analysis of law and society. More specifically, they hold that insights gained through in-depth anthropological studies of work and employment are crucial for understanding the normativity of working life as well as for the making and remaking of labour law under contemporary, post-industrial conditions.

A salient concept that Hann and others have critically engaged with over the years is the concept of the moral economy (see e.g. Hann 2018b). First advocated by E.P. Thompson (1971) and later developed by James Scott (1976), it has been most usefully deployed in analysing reactions to the expansion of the market principle and the threat it posed to 'a normative consensus among certain groups concerning basic entitlements' (Hann 2018b: 230). In her chapter, Monica Heintz applies the concept of 'moral economy' in a very different way from how it is conventionally understood in anthropology. For Heintz, moral economy gains relevance by way of the idea of an open science where data and results are freely accessible and there is a sharing and collaboration of knowledge. She explores the issue of access with respect to the anthropological discipline and more specifically acknowledges Hann's role in promoting Eastern European scholarship in a number of ways, not least through facilitating exchanges between scholars of Eastern and Western Europe. In other words, Heintz reads Hann's endeavours through the lens of the economy of sharing and collaboration that characterizes open science – a movement that aims to make research and its results more widely accessible and inclusive.

The theme of moral economy (and embeddedness) is also taken up by Frances Pine in chapter 11 in a very different context. In her critical appraisal of how E.P. Thompson's term has been overused and sometimes misused, Pine reinforces and expands upon how the economic field can be better understood when examined from a broader perspective that includes the moral dimension (as termed by Hann). She shows how in arguing for embeddedness and the widening of the definition of economic practices, Hann is implicitly – if not always explicitly – taking into account kinship/gender/generational factors, which are intricately entangled in notions of labour, morality and economic practices.

Hann's interest in the complexities of economic life has gone beyond the specific topic of moral dimensions. In the first years of the Max Planck Institute for Social Anthropology, with the research group 'Property Relations', he set out 'to reach inside local understandings of particular property systems, as well as to enhance comparative analyses of property systems generally' (Hann 2001: 76). In her chapter, Deema Kaneff takes stock of Hann's contribution to the anthropological study of property and highlights the continuing influence of his work on the topic. Some two decades after the original work on this subject, Kaneff suggests a shift in perspective, taking the powerful ideas about property – reconceptualized as resources – in order to build a model of social change. She argues that the mobilization of resources, as they move between use and/or exchange value, can be developed as an analytical tool for understanding processes of social change.

In chapter 13, Chris Gregory is concerned with both property and labour, or what Polanyi called 'special' (or fictitious) commodities. He draws on his own fieldwork in the central Indian town of Kondagaon to conclude that these special commodities require special methods of investigation. While he emphasizes the importance of ethnographic fieldwork in determining the relationship between kinship, economy and religion, he also sees the need to locate these studies in their broader cultural-geographical and historical contexts.

The relationship between the state and the economy is a relevant theme beyond former socialist Europe. The tea-producing smallholders on the Black Sea coast of Turkey, a developing capitalist location and thus with comparative value when considered against the previous socialist fieldsites, provided an opportunity for Chris Hann and Ildikó Bellér-Hann to explore the theme of economic relations and the state (Bellér-Hann and Hann 2001; Hann 1990). Lale Yalçın-Heckmann takes up this theme in her chapter on tea production. She carries the story forward to the current millennium and investigates the ongoing role of the Turkish state, focusing on how global competition and continuing modernization have been affecting Turkish tea and the tea-growing region of the Black Sea since the early 2000s.

Economies of the Sacred and the Secular

> We must attend to the common-sense meaning of economy, i.e. the production, distribution and consumption of goods and services, involving markets, money and material technologies. These modern analytic categories can be applied to any human economy, including those in which people do not themselves recognize 'economy', do not distinguish between practical work and ritual (or between the work of men and the work of Gods). (Hann 2018b: 250)

The relationship between religion and economic activities – a position from which to explore the embeddedness of economic practices – has been an important theme in Hann's work. His interest in the study of religious communities harks back to the 1980s, when he studied the tensions between Greek Catholics and the dominant Roman Catholic Church in southeastern Poland (e.g. Hann 2002; Hann and Goltz 2010). During the first two decades at the MPI, Hann and several of his research groups devoted considerable attention to investigating the dynamics of changing religious practices under postsocialist conditions. Rituals, it was argued, often 'represent a reaffirmation of the connectedness of socialism vis-à-vis the divisive individualism of market economy' (Gudeman and Hann 2015: 7). However, the research has gone further, including several countries in Europe and Asia that have not been subject to socialist economic principles and that had been substantially influenced by one of the 'world religions', as identified by Max Weber in his comparative studies of religions and civilizations. One of the main questions driving this research pertained to the relationship between changing economic conditions and religious observances and practices. How does the sacred – and its entanglement with the secular – reflect the impositions of the market?

In the spirit of this thematic direction, the chapters in the last part look at the economy's relation to the sacred and the secular. In his chapter, Stephen Gudeman revisits 'economy and ritual' (a topic he had worked on with Hann a decade earlier) and takes the argument one step further; suggesting that all economies can be seen as rituals imbued with beliefs concerning human practices relating to livelihoods. Importantly, he argues this case across a range of locations, showing the relevancy of such a position 'across the board'.

The remaining chapters in this part focus on different dimensions of economy and ritual in the specific context of Asia. In his chapter, Gábor Vargyas examines the relationship between popular religious tradition and technological innovation among the Bru ethnic minority in the Central Highlands of Vietnam. He shows that while the production of rice is intricately linked to ritual, ritual 'accommodations' are found when new methods for harvesting and threshing are made available. Despite these adaptations of customary beliefs and practices, Vargyas argues that in the course of agricultural modernization in the past three decades, religious considerations have ultimately lost out to an overwhelming desire for innovation.

The relationship between economy and ritual is scrutinized by Christoph Brumann in chapter 17, who asks how contemporary Buddhist religious specialists in East and Central Asia handle economic and financial questions. He argues that money matters have remained a constant concern for both the clergy and the laity across Buddhist societies, and much effort goes into symbolically marking the boundaries between 'Buddhist businesses' and ordinary market transactions. Brumann concludes that from a Buddhist emic perspective, the desire is to keep the two domains of religion and economy separate from each other; in so doing, he reappraises the relationship of interconnectedness discussed by Gudeman and Hann (2015).

Also inspired by the complex relationship between ritual and the economy, and the work carried out by Gudeman and Hann (2015), Burkhard Schnepel looks at the interface of ritual and political economy. His chapter takes the reader to east India, where he investigates the circulation of goddess idols in the politico-economic context of Hindu kingship. Despite their commodity potential, these idols circulate not by exchange, but by theft. However, these thefts are not considered illegitimate; on the contrary, as Schnepel shows, they add authority and legitimacy to the thief's power and thus create what Appadurai (1986) has termed 'tournaments of value'.

David N. Gellner's chapter looks at the Indian *jajmani* system, a system of ritual and occupational obligations practised in traditional Indian communities that has been romanticized in the literature as a morally embedded and sanctified way of organizing the division of labour in the caste-based village social structure. In line with Hann (2018b), Gellner argues that it is pertinent to trace moral reconfigurations through social relations. More recent research has shown that many contemporary Dalits (formerly untouchables) in fact prefer the uncertain and risk-driven market relations to the 'value-laden hierarchies of prestige and contempt' that characterize the *jajmani* system. In this case, the socially embedded form of the economy seems incompatible with the principles of equality and liberty that underlie the modern world.

During the early nineteenth century, many Hindus were recruited from British India to work as indentured plantation labourers in colonial Mauritius, where they joined descendants of European settlers, African slaves, Creoles and Chinese traders. Thomas Hylland Eriksen shows that a Polanyian lens can be fruitfully applied to study the structural differences that remain among the various ethnic and religious groups constituting the multicultural tapestry of contemporary Mauritian society. In his chapter, Eriksen discusses to what extent Hann's Eurasian perspectives can shed light on one of the major social, economic and cultural faultlines that cuts across the island, namely that between Hindus and Creoles.

Concluding Thoughts

Few anthropologists can claim the degree of ethnographic adroitness that is evident in Chris Hann's scholarship: research based on four quite different sites spanning Eurasia – Hungary, Poland, Turkey and China – which is always solidly informed by an excellent grounding in, and appreciation of, the relevant (theoretical) literature. The three themes under which the 20 chapters that make up this volume are organized bear witness to the breadth of Hann's intellectual capacities, developed over a lifetime of research based on detailed ethnographic accounts. The chapters highlight his endowment to the anthropological discipline and indeed beyond. His promotion of 'Eurasia', which enables practical and ideological engagement with former socialist states while recentring 'European' or 'Western' (scholarly) conceptual frameworks; his concern with embedding economic activities in wider social contexts and practices (in rejection of the dehumanizing capitalist processes); and his ongoing concern to engage, more specifically, with the relationship between religion and economy, are all themes which feature in his lasting intellectual contribution to anthropology.

In closing, we also wish to highlight the more practical support that Hann has given to the discipline. In his role as a director of the Max Planck Institute for Social Anthropology, he has built an academic infrastructure that reaches far beyond the actual Institute in Halle that has grown, in its first two decades, to become arguably the largest research centre for anthropological study in the world. It is an infrastructure that has made it possible for scores of Ph.D. students, postdoctoral researchers and senior scholars from around the world to benefit from training, networks, conferences and opportunities to visit. Beyond its 'practical' value, such institutional building has created a global anthropological community. Hann has also been instrumental in sponsoring and developing anthropology in Eurasian countries, where local scholars have gained from support, and anthropological departments have been strengthened through joint collaboration. At the same time, he has enriched the scope of German anthropology, taking it into hitherto less-explored territorial directions, while facilitating exciting interdisciplinary exchanges.

As evidenced in the following chapters, many of us have been inspired by Chris Hann's ongoing intellectual projects. We express our gratitude through these contributions, which engage with his ideas. It is our gift offered with thanks and appreciation.

Kirsten W. Endres is Head of Research Group at the Max Planck Institute for Social Anthropology and Adjunct Professor at the Martin Luther University in Halle/Saale, Germany. She has worked in Vietnam on sociocultural transformation processes that arise from the dynamic interplay between state, society and market. Her books include *Performing the Divine: Mediums, Markets, and Modernity in Urban Vietnam* (2011) and *Market Frictions: Trade and Urbanization at the Vietnam-China Border* (2019).

Deema Kaneff is Reader in Social Anthropology at the University of Birmingham, United Kingdom, and Research Partner at the Max Planck Institute for Social Anthropology in Halle, Germany. She has worked in Bulgaria and Ukraine, and her research interests and publications focus on property/resources and social change, global capitalism and inequalities, and the anthropology of postsocialism. Her books include *Who Owns the Past? The Politics of Time in a 'Model' Bulgarian Village* (2004) and the forthcoming monograph *Resources and Reforms: Everyday Conflicts and Social Change in Rural Ukraine*.

Notes

1. The Siberian Studies Centre (2002–12), jointly led by Chris Hann and Günther Schlee and coordinated by Otto Habeck, addressed a variety of themes related to social processes and technical changes in Siberia.
2. These research groups were: Lale Yalçın-Heckmann's group 'Caucasian Boundaries and Citizenship from below' (2004–9); Christoph Brumann's group on the interplay between tradition and urban modernity; Kirsten Endres' research on markets and infrastructure in mainland Southeast Asia; and Dittmar Schorkowitz's historical anthropological perspectives.
3. The editors sincerely thank John Eidson for his helpful comments on an earlier version of this Introduction.

References

Appadurai, Arjun. 1986. 'Introduction: Commodities and the Politics of Value', in Arjun Appadurai (ed.), *The Social Life of Things: Commodities in Cultural Perspective*. Cambridge: Cambridge University Press, pp. 3–63.

Arnason, Johann, and Chris Hann (eds). 2018. *Anthropology and Civilizational Analysis: Eurasian Explorations*. Albany: SUNY Press.

Bellér-Hann, Ildikó, and C.M. Hann. 2001. *Turkish Region: State, Market and Social Identities on the East Black Sea Coast*. Oxford: James Curry.

Endres, Kirsten W., and Chris Hann (eds). 2017. *Socialism with Neoliberal Characteristics*. Halle/Saale: Max Planck Institute for Social Anthropology. Retrieved 2 December 2020 from https://www.eth.mpg.de/cms/de/publications/institute-reports/institute_report_2017-dep-hann.

Gudeman, Stephen, and Chris Hann. 2015. 'Introduction: Ritual, Economy, and the Institutions of the Base', in Stephen Gudeman and Chris Hann (eds), *Economy and Ritual: Studies of Postsocialist Transformations*. New York: Berghahn Books, pp. 1–30.

Hann, C.M. 1980. *Tázlár: A Village in Hungary. Changing Cultures*. Cambridge: Cambridge University Press.

———. 1985. 'Rural Transformation on the East Black Sea Coast of Turkey: A Note on Keyder', *Journal of Peasant Studies* 12(4): 101–10.

———. 1990. 'Second Thoughts on Smallholders: Tea Production, the State and Social Differentiation in the Rize Region', *New Perspectives on Turkey* 4: 57–79.

Hann, Chris. 2000. 'Time's Catapult or Besonders schwerer Fall der geistigen Überfüllung', in Wolf Lepenies (ed.), *Jahrbuch 1998/99*. Berlin: Wissenschaftskolleg zu Berlin, pp. 56–60.

_____. 2001. 'Department II: Property Relations', in *Max Planck Institute for Social Anthropology Report 1999–2001*. Halle/Saale: Max Planck Institute for Social Anthropology, pp. 74–128. Retrieved 2 December 2020 from https://www.eth.mpg.de/pubs/institute-reports/pdf/mpi-eth-institute-report-2001-de.

_____. 2002. 'The Development of Polish Civil Society and the Experience of the Greek Catholic Minority', in Peter G. Danchin and Elizabeth A. Cole (eds), *Protecting the Human Rights of Religious Minorities in Eastern Europe*. New York: Columbia University Press, pp. 437–54.

_____. 2010. 'Interview of Chris Hann' (video file). Retrieved 2 December 2020 from http://www.dspace.cam.ac.uk/handle/1810/229720.

_____. 2012a. 'Civilizational Analysis for Beginners', *Focaal* 62: 113–21.

_____. 2012b. 'Transition, Tradition, and Nostalgia: Postsocialist Transformations in a Comparative Framework', *Collegium Antropologicum* 36(4): 1119–28.

_____. 2015. 'Goody, Polanyi and Eurasia: An Unfinished Project in Comparative Historical Economic Anthropology', *History and Anthropology* 26(3): 308–20.

_____. 2016a. 'The Wisłok Project, 1978–1985', *Lud* 100: 83–92.

_____. 2016b. 'A Concept of Eurasia', *Current Anthropology* 57(1): 1–10.

_____. 2018a. 'Economic Anthropology', in Hilary Callan (ed.), *The International Encyclopedia of Anthropology* Vol. 4. Hoboken, NJ: Wiley-Blackwell, pp. 1708–23.

_____. 2018b. 'Morality and Economy: Work, Workfare, and Fairness in Provincial Hungary', *Archives Européennes de Sociologie* 59(2): 225–54.

_____. 2018c. 'Afterword: Anthropology, Eurasia and Global History', in Johann P. Arnason and Chris Hann (eds), *Anthropology and Civilizational Analysis: Eurasian Explorations*. Albany: SUNY Press, pp. 339–53.

_____. 2019a. *Repatriating Polanyi: Market Society in the Visegrád States*. Budapest: Central European University Press.

_____. 2019b. 'A Betrayal by the Intellectuals', *Eurozine*. Retrieved 2 December 2020 from https://www.eurozine.com/betrayal-liberal-intellectuals.

Hann, Chris, and Hermann Goltz (eds). 2010. *Eastern Christians in Anthropological Perspective*. Berkeley: University of California Press.

Hann, Chris, and Keith Hart (eds). 2009. *Market and Society: The Great Transformation Today*. Cambridge: Cambridge University Press, pp. 1–16.

Hann, Chris, and Keith Hart. 2011. *Economic Anthropology: History, Ethnography, Critique*. Cambridge: Polity.

Scott, James C. 1976. *The Moral Economy of the Peasant: Rebellion and Subsistence in Southeast Asia*. New Haven: Yale University Press.

Thompson, Edward P. 1971. 'The Moral Economy of the English Crowd in the Eighteenth Century', *Past & Present* 50: 76–136.

Part I

Reconsidering (Post)Socialist Spaces

Chapter 1

Civilizations and Economies
Notes on a Neglected Theme

Johann P. Arnason

Classical Beginnings

If the dominant ideology of the post-Cold War world is to be challenged at its most fundamental level, a critique of economic reductionism is vitally important. To put it another way, relativizing *homo oeconomicus* is an urgent and demanding task. In this regard, a comparative analysis of civilizations, with particular emphasis on their varying visions of the human condition, would seem a promising road to explore, but the results so far are less than conclusive. One of the shortcomings to be corrected by civilizational analysts is their retreat from the economic sphere, which is all the more striking since the pioneering formulations of the civilizational approach were focused on or at least fully aware of the economic field. Max Weber's civilizational studies took off from the question of modern capitalism and its sources; his French contemporaries, Emile Durkheim and Marcel Mauss, did not share that orientation, but as Richard Swedberg (2010) rightly underlines in his reflections on classical beginnings of civilizational analysis, their conceptual preliminaries indicate technology, commerce and money as civilizational phenomena. What this view would have meant for comparative inquiry remains speculation. A certain shift of the comparative focus is already evident in Weber's analyses of China and India. The initial emphasis on economic ethics and their religious foundations is not abandoned, but it is relativized to a significant degree by a growing interest in the different constellations of religious and political power (in this regard, the contrast between

China and India is fundamental). However, this line of thought was not taken to its systematic conclusions. In Durkheim's case, the specification of the civilizational approach in the final chapter of *The Elementary Forms of Religious Life* left economic issues aside, except for a short remark on the sacral origins of money, and, as later readings of this work have shown, the idea of religion as a meta-institution – in other words, a civilizational framework – is primarily relevant to politics.

At a later stage, the concern with interrelations of religion and politics was renewed by S.N. Eisenstadt; the religio-political nexus is the central theme of his comparative civilizational studies, although when it came to general formulations, he preferred to subsume religion under a more comprehensive category of ontological or cosmological visions. By the same token, the economic dimensions and specificities of civilizations became less important for his purposes; in particular, the problematic of capitalism and its varieties is strikingly underrepresented in his writings on multiple modernities.

A closer look at Eisenstadt's general theoretical stance may clarify the reasons for this distantiation from the economic domain. His approach to sociological analysis was anti-reductionistic, and more precisely opposed to all ways of naturalizing social phenomena. This implied the rejection of materialist views on the primacy of the economy, as well as of the functionalist assimilation of society to an overall model of living systems. In the latter case, the stress on systemic reproduction suggests affinities with economic reductionism. If the rationale for the civilizationist turn was, as Eisenstadt saw it, to strengthen the case against reductionist claims, the obvious line to take was a strong focus on the historical interplay of culture and power; this entailed, in the most prominent cases, a particular emphasis on the intertwining of religious and political patterns. A further factor may have been the increased prestige and influence of economics as a discipline, resulting in widespread attempts to impose or imitate its approaches in other fields, but also provoking resistance and a search for counterweights. This development was particularly pronounced in the 1970s and 1980s, at a time when civilizational analysis was re-entering sociological debates. In such circumstances, economic sociology found it difficult to establish its own credentials, and the integration of its problematic into a civilizational frame of reference was an even more challenging task, understandably reserved for later.

If we want to bring the economic sphere and its capitalist version back in, it seems advisable to begin with another look at the classical sources, and more substantive indications are to be found in Weber's writings than in those of the French classics. As Swedberg (2010) notes, the question of capitalism, which had been somewhat overshadowed by a broader field in the comparative studies, comes back in force in the 1920 introduction to Weber's essays on the sociology of religion (Weber 2002). Modern capitalism is discussed at much greater length than other products of the world-historical rationalizing process, which now becomes more explicitly central to Weber's line of argument than before, but it is also shown to be dependent on a complex constellation of other historical forces and patterns related to the same pattern. The upshot is a conception of capitalism as a civilizational phenomenon, a part of a *'cultural order, to which actors orient themselves and which consists of economic, religious, political, artistic and scientific elements'* (Swedberg 2010: 25, emphasis in original). This cultural order is supposed to provide a general meaning. That claim raises two questions: what is the spatio-temporal scope of the meaningful orientations? And how do we define the unity of the order that is obviously supposed to be more than the sum of its parts? Swedberg neutralizes the first question by positing – without further justification or demarcation – a Western civilization, older than modern capitalism but otherwise of uncertain duration. He seems to assume that Weber's references to the Occident denote a single and continuous civilization, but that is far from self-evident. The phenomena and processes characterized as Occidental, beginning with developments in ancient Greece and ancient Israel, are so different in kind and distant in time that we can more plausibly speak of a long-term multicivilizational sequence. Moreover, the opening sentence of the summary refers to the 'modern European cultural world', and hence to an epoch and a region more circumscribed than the *longue durée* and the geocultural trajectory of the Occident. If civilizational terminology is to be used, Weber's remark can be taken to foreshadow the conception of modernity as a new civilization, emerging in Europe with more transformative force and a stronger global impact than elsewhere (which does not exclude parallel or related beginnings). That is the view adumbrated but not elaborated by Eisenstadt, overshadowed by his much more detailed analyses of multiple modernities.

If this line of interpretation is pursued, the second question – left completely open by Swedberg – must be tackled. The idea of a distinctive civilization presupposes a central and defining constellation of meanings, and enough work has been done on comparative studies to support the point that such cultural cores should be understood as problematics rather than as programmes or principles; in other words, they are contested horizons of significance, open to selective emphases, conflicting interpretations and divergent traditions. The varying balances between unity and diversity are a matter for comparative studies.

Perspectives on Modernity

Eisenstadt's understanding of modernity as a new civilization clearly centres on a notion of human autonomy, but he never spelled it out in a way that would both demarcate it from more restrictive versions of the concept and map out the expanded dimensions. Drawing on his indications, multiple fields of the modern turn to enhanced autonomy may be distinguished. It changes human relations with nature, practical as well as theoretical; new perspectives open up for the interpretation and transformation of social-historical life; and the human ability to lend meaning and significance to the world (to use Weber's terms) finds more articulate expression. The obverse of this enlarged scope for action and imagination is a development that was already central to Weber's vision of modern times (from the *Protestant Ethic* to his final statement in the introduction to his collected essays on the sociology of religion): human agency, empowered by rationalization, is for that very reason enmeshed in structures and processes that unfold their own dynamics and impose their logic on the actors. Eisenstadt adds another complicating factor, which is less visible from the Weberian viewpoint. The problematic of autonomy gives rise to rival interpretations, individualistic as well as collectivistic, particularistic as well as universalistic, and they enter into the making of different modernities. Finally, there is a dimension briefly but very suggestively explored by Weber and rethematized but too narrowly defined by Eisenstadt. Specific orientations, visions and problems of autonomy develop in different spheres of social life; the distinction between economic, political and cultural domains is not exhaustive, but can at least serve as a provisional framework. Eisenstadt links this issue to the question of specific rationalities, which he opposes to constructions of totalizing reason. However, each domain constitutes a broader context, irreducible to a type of rationality and involving a plurality of world perspectives and human self-images. As will be seen, this has some bearing on the question of *homo oeconomicus*.

It is not being suggested that autonomy, in the broad sense assumed here, is a uniquely modern trait; rather, it is the epoch-making extension of its scope, across multiple sociocultural spheres and adding up to a major overall transformation, that marks a historical divide. This view aligns with the well-established finding that structural components of modernity – be it capitalism, democracy or nation formation – have premodern roots and antecedents; their distinctively modern reach and role are due to new dimensions and combinations. The concept of modernity is, in short, a historical one rather than a building block for general theory; it refers to the driving forces and long-term dynamics of multilinear but culturally interconnected transformations.

If autonomy as an imaginary signification (Castoriadis 1987) is open to divergent conceptions with developmental consequences, closer analysis of modern formations must deal with the interpretations that have dominated in different contexts. A survey starting from recent and contemporary conditions would inevitably begin with notions of economic action, rationality and self-regulation as models of autonomy. During the heyday of neoliberalism, notions of the market taking over the roles of government flourished, and market mechanisms were supposed to provide a master key to the workings of institutions, including religion. Although the financial crisis dealt a major blow to these ideological constructs, the resilience of neoliberalism has prompted some analysts to describe it as a broad civilizational shift, beyond the absolutization of economic rationality or the apotheosis of economic man. Marcel Gauchet (2017: 738) refers to a 'juridico-technico-economic complex' that has, as he sees it, become a dominant model of rationality, with disruptive implications for democracy.

If neoliberalism has civilizational dimensions, obscured by its primary focus and by the rhetoric of advocates as well as critics, comparative approaches may throw light on that part of the story, and a brief glance at the sociological classics can serve to frame the problem. They were not confronted with problems of the kind now attracting comment, but their perceptions of an economy-centred society and their attempts to relativize that state of affairs through better understanding are still relevant. Marx is commonly criticized for leaning towards economic reductionism, due to his theorizing of production as a founding and formative component of social life; however, in his most interesting text (the *Grundrisse*, unfinished and unknown to a broader public until almost a century later), the paradigm of production acquires historical and futurological dimensions that take it beyond received notions of the economy. As Marx presents it, the history of human societies begins with a primordial unity of producers and natural as well as social preconditions; the resulting patterns of quasi-natural (*naturwüchsig*) order, varying according to circumstances, set limits to the extension and autonomy of economic activities. Such limits were definitively overcome by the capitalist mode of accumulation. Marx's speculations about the future of this megamachine of unending growth led him to hypothesize a situation where the application of scientific knowledge to production would have reduced human involvement to mere supervision, and thus liberated time and energy for the free development of human abilities in other fields. The ultimate triumph of economic man, the harnessing of cognitive progress to productive gain, would result in an anthropological mutation. Marx obviously retreated from this ultra-utopian vision, and later writings suggest a more moderate horizon of expectations, but the effort to portray capitalist development as a road to the revolutionary sublation of economic reason persisted.

Other major classics opted for different ways to relativize the centrality of the economy. Weber saw capitalism as the dominant force of modern life and hence – on the anthropological level – the main influence on the model of the *Berufsmensch* that had become an irresistible norm. However, his genealogy of modern capitalism highlighted the religious background to upgraded economic behaviour of the kind that had transformed social life. Later mutations were less about a 'new spirit of capitalism', a change to human mainsprings of the economy, than about a shift towards systemic constraints. Economic actors became increasingly subordinate to economic mechanisms. Weber's comparative studies, meant to throw more light on the specific trajectory of the Occident, did not do much to diversify or contextualize the image of *homo oeconomicus*. The emphasis was on cultural (most fundamentally religious) obstacles to an autonomous emergence of modern capitalism, but on a more marginal note, Weber suggested that the major non-European civilizations might vary in their ability to import ready-made capitalism from elsewhere (this seemed easier to achieve in East Asia than in India, and more so in Japan than in China). Creative reinventions of capitalism are not envisaged. In both the European and the extra-European contexts, the long-term perspective is thus focused on adaptation to systemic patterns that have gained the upper hand over action, culture and history, but this very strength of capitalism as a caging frame is also a weakness in relation to its twin other: bureaucratic domination. If there is a Weberian prospect of moving beyond the reign of *homo oeconomicus*, it is the very ambiguous possibility of capitalism retreating before bureaucracy.

Durkheim's approach to the economic determinants of modern society and the question of their preconditions was more attuned to reformist aims. The first major instalment of his project focused on the division of social labour, at first sight a primarily economic phenomenon, and led to the conclusion that neither the emergence nor the functioning of this complex and quintessentially modern structure could be explained without reference to moral aspects of the social bond. The economic rationality of social organization had to be sustained by a more elementary level of solidarity. However, the social pathologies due to a weakening of this connection were significant, and the cure proposed by Durkheim was based on a reformist version of socialism, which in turn could only be implemented within the framework of democratic institutions. Durkheim's theory of democracy, centred on a communicative relationship between state and society, was left unfinished and remained unpublished for a long time. In that double sense, his critique of the excessive but at the same time unbalanced economy-centredness of modern societies was inconclusive.

Before moving on to broader comparative views, a fourth classic deserves at least a brief mention. In Simmel's *The Philosophy of Money*, the intention to cut *homo oeconomicus* down to size is clear from the beginning. Simmel proposes relativizing historical materialism by uncovering a spiritual (*geistig*) infrastructure beneath the economic foundations emphasized by the materialists (Simmel 2011). Moreover, he focuses on an economic factor inadequately understood by both Marxists and their 'bourgeois' critics: the institution of money. His analysis of this phenomenon, and particularly of its modern ramifications, throws doubt on his own introductory claim to the effect that the book contains no 'economically meant' statement. This was obviously written to block criticism from professional economists, who would not have understood Simmel's agenda. In fact, his clarification of the cultural significance of money throws new light on the whole economic sphere. But this breaking of new ground did not open up any vistas on life beyond the reign of economic man; rather, the whole problematic of a monetarized society was – with due notice taken of its achievements – subsumed under a 'tragedy of modern culture', from which there was no exit.

Lessons from Economic Anthropology

The above observations should suffice to show that an effort to denaturalize *homo oeconomicus* (Caillé and Laville 2008: 565) is integral to the legacy of classical sociology, but the formulations found in key texts of the classics are incomplete, ambiguous and divergent. For further exploration of the issue, it seems advisable to broaden the frame of reference. As noted at the beginning, civilizational analysis has hitherto not done much to develop comparative approaches to economic practices and institutions. Anthropologists have dealt much more extensively with such questions; there is both a wealth of evidence from the tribal societies once seen as the defining domain of anthropology and a complex of questions raised when the discipline crossed into historical and sociological fields. Here I will start with the critical survey of economic anthropology undertaken by Chris Hann and Keith Hart, and more specifically with their description of a 'golden age' in the history of that subdiscipline.

The golden age was characterized by a clear-cut distinction between two ways of conceptualizing the economic dimension of human societies

(Hann and Hart 2011: 55–71). The formalist approach, following the lead of mainstream economics, emphasized the supposedly universal human effort to economize the means–end relationship, thus fuelling 'ideologies that reduce human societies to utility-maximizing individuals' (Hann and Hart 2011: 56). By contrast, the substantivist approach, striving for an equally universal focus, was 'concerned with the general provisioning of material wants in society' (Hann and Hart 2011: 56). These polarized viewpoints had not been formulated with such clarity before. Neither the formalist nor the substantivist paradigm came from within anthropology, at least not in their exemplary versions (the formalists took their cue from Lionel Robbins and the Austrian School, while the substantivist position was first defined by Karl Polanyi), but both struck a chord with anthropologists (the substantivist view more legitimately so, according to Hann and Hart) and they drew on anthropological sources.

But if the golden age achieved a landmark clarification of terms and issues, Hann and Hart also show that – like many other golden ages – it foreshadowed its own demise. The formalist-substantivist debate fizzled out, at first sight for different reasons on each side, though the underlying problem of a shared overpolarization may, as will be seen, have weighed more heavily. Polanyi and his followers concentrated on the case for non-market coordination in historical societies, especially the early empires, but their critics could show that they seriously underestimated the role of markets, money and exchange in these premodern settings. As a result, the substantivists lost ground, largely because of unguarded ambitions to expand their argument beyond the stateless societies that had been the first port of call for scholars in search of economic otherness, and 'Polanyi's conceptual framework had already gone out of fashion' (Hann and Hart 2011: 126) when fundamental questions about the changing roles of exchange, reciprocity and redistribution had to be raised again, in connection with the new 'great transformation' that began with the apparent triumph of global capitalism. No widely accepted reformulation of the substantivist approach has emerged, but there are significant attempts to reformulate the underlying conceptual distinctions and historical frames of reference. Stephen Gudeman's model of five economic spheres that 'grow, shrink, overlap and conflict' (Gudeman 2016: 14) is one such proposal, designed to correct Polanyi's overpolarized contrasting of embedded and disembedded structures. Gudeman distinguishes between 'house, community, commerce, finance and meta-finance sectors of economy'; these 'range from the less to the more abstract and encompassing' (2016: 14). Another example, more open to alternative views, is a collection of papers on market and society, edited by Chris Hann and Keith Hart (2009), but here we must differentiate the arguments of various contributors. Jens Beckert (2009: 38–55) notes the radical redefinition of the concept of embeddedness in contemporary economic sociology. The most influential approach 'restricts embeddedness to the investigation of social network structures' (Beckert 2009: 50), thus abandoning Polanyi's concern with the broader problematic of social integration and – a fortiori – his normative agenda.

Philippe Steiner (2009: 56–71) suggests a way to re-activate Polanyi's ideas without losing sight of advances in economic sociology. The key move is a reappraisal of the French sociological tradition, from Durkheim's work on the division of labour to Mauss' study of the gift: this school of thought worked towards a better understanding of social life as a state of tension between the core norms of social integration and the utilitarian activities that tend to impose their own logic. The interplay of embedding and disembedding thus became a recurrent feature of human societies, assuming different forms and dimensions in successive historical stages. Theorizing along these lines avoids Polanyi's stark dichotomy of traditional embeddedness and modern market-driven disembeddedness, but allows for more nuanced views on the novelty of modernity. Finally, Chris Hann (2009: 256–71) goes further and highlights fundamental ambiguities of embedding and disembedding, as well as basic differentiations on both sides. His starting point is the experience of Soviet-type societies and the light that it throws on more general questions. As he sees it: 'Marxist-Leninist-Maoist socialism promoted a non-market disembedding of the economy from social relations, with social consequences no less devastating than the market-driven processes analyzed by Polanyi' (Hann 2009: 258). The role of politics in the capitalist context had not gone unnoticed; Polanyi was well aware of the political pressures involved in the triumph of economic liberalism, as well as in the so-far limited attempts to create counterweights. However, the political component of Soviet-type societies (contrary to Hann's preference, I would not call them socialist) is both more central and more paradoxical. Politically enforced imperatives disconnect the economy from social needs and priorities, and, as Hann notes, this is achieved through mechanisms that correspond to Polanyi's concept of redistribution, with the specific twist that resources and outputs are redistributed in favour of accumulation, but the primacy of the latter is masked by ideological claims to long-term social utility.

This point can be taken further. If the command economy imposed by the political centre is disembedded, the same can in a sense be said about the political order: the omnipresent party-state monopoly outlaws contestation and suppresses the dialogue between power and society that is essential to democratic integration. Last but not least, the closure of the official ideology, self-promoted to the status of a sole scientific worldview, amounts to insulation from social experience and cultural innovation, and hence to a disembedding shift. The whole constellation suggests that the Soviet model was not, as has often been suggested, fatally weakened by its incapacity to differentiate social spheres, and thus to match a general modern pattern; rather, the core problem was a paradoxical and in the long run self-destructive combination of one-sidedly political integration and a disconnective differentiation (for further discussion of this aspect, see Arnason 2000).

Hann's emphasis on political factors is not meant to close the book on Polanyi's problematic. He proposes distinguishing the ambiguous political dynamics from a 'generalized moral disembedding' (Hann 2009: 257), a dislocation that affects social cohesion and ethical life. However, it would seem reasonable to broaden the spectrum beyond the dichotomy of moral and political frameworks. The above-mentioned example of Soviet-type societies raises the question as to whether they represent a specific civilizational project or a variation of general modern trends. The issue of civilizational embedding and disembedding can also be linked to historical examples. For instance, social action in general and its economic dimensions in particular were framed differently in the Indian caste order and in the much more inclusive Chinese pattern of hierarchy, decisively influenced by Confucian social ethics. Another case in point is the ongoing debate on the 'ancient economy': so far, the results indicate a tension between the household (*oikos*) conception of economic life, to some extent applied at the level of the city-state, and the disembedding dynamics of commercial and military capitalism.

Further reflections on these problems are beyond the scope of the present chapter. To conclude, I will outline a perspective that would complement rather than oppose the views discussed above. First, however, we must briefly consider the formalist side. Its troubles have more to do with overstretch and backlash than with scholarly controversy. The school of thought known as New Institutional Economics is aligned with the formalists in spirit if not in the letter; its focus is on the rules of interaction between utility-maximizing individuals, without regard to the sociological and historical dimensions recognized by older institutionalist approaches, and its general logic is not alien to the neoliberal vision of business making and remaking its own rules as it goes along. The neo-institutionalists may therefore be seen as formalists setting out to occupy the territory that the substantivists had not been able to defend in an effective fashion. If this expanded approach has nevertheless faced mounting criticism, which is mainly due to the financial crisis; it discredited the belief in economics as an exact science with a correspondingly solid consensus and prompted a new search for alternative paradigms. In the wake of this chastening experience, interest in lessons from anthropology has grown, but no new divide comparable to the debate between formalists and substantivists has emerged.

Wealth as a Historical Category

Another look at the formalist-substantivist controversy may help to identify and conceptualize a starting point for moves beyond it. The task would be to resuscitate and redefine the category of wealth, essential to classical economic thought (from Smith to Marx) and revived by some contributors to current rethinking (e.g. Mistral 2019). It can be understood in a way that would highlight a blind spot on the frontier between formalists and substantivists.

There is no doubt about the individualistic premises of the formalists, and the interactionist approach to institutions does not alter that background. As for the substantivist position inaugurated by Polanyi, the emphasis on reciprocity and redistribution as alternative modes of coordination implies an underlying focus on the reproduction of society. It would obviously not be justified to rank Polanyi among the straightforward functionalists, but we can speak of a residual functionalism, and to that extent link the controversy to the polarization of individualist and functionalist approaches in twentieth-century social theory. The proposed exit from this dilemma is loosely linked to the Marxian paradigm of production, but goes beyond it by pointing to social and cultural differentiation. In a paradoxical sense, the productivist approach, conducive to reductionism when taken to be self-contained, reveals its potential when aligned with the critique of Marx advanced by a later generation of classical sociologists (Durkheim, Weber and Simmel) who insisted on the radical autonomy of culture and politics.

The key point is the centrality of wealth, which is defined in terms of the ability to produce a surplus, over and above the requirements of simple reproduction, with broader implications than those commonly acknowledged in economic thought. Marx noted several aspects of this sociocultural capacity: the growth of the surplus product goes hand in hand with the diversification of human needs and the development of human abilities, but it also opens up possibilities of unequal control and appropriation, and it gives concrete content to a notion of wealth that can be subsumed under a general symbol. Marx notes this meaning of money in the *Grundrisse*, whereas *Capital* contains a more reductionist theory, equating money with an embodiment of abstract labour.

This reductionism is backed up by two complementary claims. On the one hand, the potentiality of surplus is portrayed as a natural endowment of human labour, open to different social uses and orientations; on the other hand, Marx tries to reduce the complex surplus production of modern capitalism to the expenditure of labour power in general and to measure the product on this elementary basis. In the latter regard, Marx's posthumously published texts hint at an alternative view: capitalist development appears as an ongoing subsumption of material, social and cognitive resources under the logic of accumulation, geared towards the maximization of monetary wealth (Marx 1969).

Before moving on to turn Marx's fruitful intuitions against his reductionist arguments, the relationship to the formalist-substantivist debate should be clarified. If the formalists rested their case on the means-ends scheme as a model of action, the link between production and wealth can – as I will try to show – enable a connection with the attempts to move beyond means and ends towards a better understanding of the creativity of action (see especially Joas 1996). The idea of action as an opening of horizons, engagement with problems and invention of solutions (and therefore more embedded in interpretive frameworks and more exposed to their inbuilt conflicts than the most influential theories of action have wanted to admit) will prove relevant to questions about the economic sphere. The issue is not whether we can apply the means-ends scheme beyond modern forms of economic life (we obviously can), but how far we can get with it in different contexts that always involve creative action, but not to the same degree or with the same implications. As for the substantivist side, the idea of creative action implies a transformative capacity that takes us beyond the structures and dynamics of reproduction. The functionalist barrier to full recognition of history is thus overcome.

The core point of a substantivist approach, however reformulated, is the emphasis on what Polanyi called human livelihood and Marx had described as a metabolism between society and nature: the extraction and transformation of natural objects in order to satisfy human needs. But to grasp the dynamic character of this relationship, as well as its connection to surplus and wealth, we must see it as a long-term process accompanied by a broadening of horizons. To posit the ability to produce a surplus as an aspect of human nature is to go beyond empirically meaningful claims; what can be maintained is that it was already evident in prehistorical times and has unfolded throughout history. This is not to suggest a return to the notion of 'productive forces' in continuous progress. For one thing, Lévi-Strauss' analysis of the 'savage mind' leads him to conclude that this mode of thought was rational enough to enable cognitive progress and growing mastery over natural resources, without any significant technological change, but in the long run leading to the historical breakthrough of the Neolithic revolution. For another, and with closer reference to later history, growth is not the only modality of change affecting the surplus; varying and sometimes competing cultural definitions and ways of appropriation also shape the social meaning of surplus, work and wealth.

The broadening of horizons entailed by the production of surplus involves the elementary levels of time and space. Marshall Sahlins (2017) argues that hunters and gatherers had devised a way of life that enabled them to maximize free time; at the imagined other extreme of human development, Marx's vision of a technologically ultra-advanced postcapitalist society presupposes a fundamental change to the balance between work and free time that will allow the humanization of wealth. Spatial expansion is part and parcel of the quest for resources (distance is a major factor in the construction of prestige goods) and so is migration. Control of enlarged spaces can be a triple asset: it means access to wealth, evidence of power, and support for claims to higher legitimacy; all three aspects are taken to further lengths by historical empires.

That said, the production and acquisition of objects – for purposes of use, exchange or prestige – is central to the constitution of an economic sphere and to its demarcation through the category of wealth. At this point, it seems appropriate to turn to Marcel Mauss, the most iconic pioneer of economic anthropology and most invoked ancestor of the substantivists; we can also link the themes at issue to the loose ends of his reflection on civilizations, which was noted at the beginning of this chapter.

Mauss insisted that 'markets and money are universal, though not in their current impersonal form' (Hann and Hart 2011: 50); this sets him apart from the substantivists who took their cue from Polanyi, but his admittedly incomplete analysis of money foreshadows an alternative formulation of their concerns, with stronger emphasis on the basic autonomy of the economic sphere and a broader view of its historical metamorphoses than the Polanyi school could accommodate. Mauss' approach can only be understood as a critical reception of Durkheim's ideas. Towards the end of his work on elementary forms of religious life, Durkheim outlined an argument about religion as a generative framework of other institutions; he noted that the connection might be harder to trace in the case of the economy than in other domains, but singled out the category of value as a promising starting point. Mauss retained a strong sense of the sacral context, but went beyond Durkheim in emphasizing the plurality of symbolic orders and the specific meanings at work in each of them.

Where Durkheim had envisaged a one-sided derivation, Mauss saw an interconnection, which was asymmetric because of the undoubted centrality of religion, but multidimensional because of the involvement of other orders. In his two most succinct statements on the subject of money (Mauss 2015: 48–50 and 51–52), he underlines the sacral and magic meaning essential to the emergence of money and retained in less overt form during its later history, but also the connection to operative categories of the economic domain. The notion of value is necessary to mediate between the spheres of production and consumption, and value is measured by money (Mauss 2015: 51). But there is more to money than an economic function guaranteed by a religious source: 'As soon as money exists, exchange exists, and a dynamic and psychological element enters the picture' (Mauss 2015: 51). The term 'psychological' may be read as a shorthand reference to subjectivity and creativity; the point is that the scope for action, enlarged by money and exchange, opens up different directions. It can lead to the integration of exchange into complex and extensive networks of social interaction on multiple levels. In such formations, analysed by Mauss in *The Gift*, the economy is doubly embedded: in constellations of ritualized but also purposive and mutually constitutive interaction, and in a universe of collective representations with a sacral core. However, the dynamism in question can, in the much longer run, culminate in a disembedding of the economy, sustained by monetary structures; that process is never complete, always being dependent on some political and cultural preconditions, and periodically exposed to interventions backed up by political power and ideological projects.

Mauss' ethnographical notes stress both the diversity of objects assuming the function of money and the varying degree of their dependence on religion. That line of thought can serve to develop the missing perspective on economic life in his general comments on civilizations (Mauss saw no problems with applying the latter concept to tribal societies). As for the question of lasting sacral connotations, recent analyses of capitalist accumulation and its 'promise of absolute wealth' (Deutschmann 2001) lend support to the claim that such implicit meanings are operative in modern economies. But the concept of wealth also has other points of contact with the civilizational approach. As I have argued, its reference to broader horizons takes it beyond the means-ends scheme of action and, by the same token, it is open to divergent interpretations. Civilizational traditions can be compared from that point of view. Aristotle's much-quoted distinction between two kinds of wealth reflects a tension between *oikos* and market within Greek civilization. Comparing the cultural and institutional frameworks of wealth in the Chinese imperial order and the Indian caste regime is a rewarding topic and is far from exhausted. Marx's vision of an affluent future society with a new understanding of wealth aimed at a civilizational reorientation of modernity, but the influence of this part of his work was at best indirect and mixed. Other civilizational challenges to really existing modernity are likely to emerge from our present crisis.

Johann P. Arnason is Emeritus Professor of Sociology at La Trobe University, Melbourne, Australia, and an associate of the Department of Historical Sociology in the Faculty of Human Studies, Charles University, Prague, Czech Republic. His research interests centre on social theory and historical sociology, with particular emphasis on the comparative analysis of civilizations.

References

Arnason, Johann P. 2000. 'Communism and Modernity', *Daedalus* 129(1): 61–90.
Beckert, Jens. 2009. 'The Great Transformation of Embeddedness: Karl Polanyi and the New Economic Sociology', in Chris Hann and Keith Hart (eds), *Markets and Society. The Great Transformation Today*. Cambridge: Cambridge University Press, pp. 38–55.
Caillé, Alain, and Jean-Louis Laville. 2008.'Actualité de Karl Polanyi', in *Essais de Karl Polanyi*. Paris: Seuil, pp. 565–85.
Castoriadis, Cornelius. 1987. *The Imaginary Institution of Society*. Cambridge: Cambridge University Press.
Deutschmann, Christoph. 2001. *Die Verheissung des absoluten Reichtums*. Frankfurt am Main: Campus.
Gauchet, Marcel. 2017. *Le Nouveau Monde*. Paris: Gallimard.
Gudeman, Stephen. 2016. *Anthropology and Economy*. Cambridge: Cambridge University Press.
Hann, Chris. 2009. 'Embedded Socialism? Land, Labour, and Money in Eastern Xinjiang', in Chris Hann and Keith Hart (eds), *Markets and Society: The Great Transformation Today*. Cambridge: Cambridge University Press, pp. 256–71.
Hann, Chris, and Keith Hart (eds). 2009. *Markets and Society: The Great Transformation Today*. Cambridge: Cambridge University Press.
Hann, Chris, and Keith Hart. 2011. *Economic Anthropology*. Cambridge: Polity.
Joas, Hans. 1996. *The Creativity of Action*. Cambridge: Polity.
Marx, Karl. 1969. *Resultate des unmittelbaren Produktionsprozesses*. Frankfurt am Main: Verlag Neue Kritik.
Mauss, Marcel. 2015. *Schriften zum Geld*. Berlin: Suhrkamp.
Mistral, Jacques. 2019. *La Science de la Richesse : Essai sur la Construction de la Pensée Économique*. Paris: Gallimard.
Sahlins, Marshall. 2017. *Stone Age Economics*. London: Routledge.
Simmel, Georg. 2011. *The Philosophy of Money*. London: Routledge.

Steiner, Philippe. 2009. 'The Critique of The Economic Point of View: Karl Polanyi and the Durkheimians', in Chris Hann and Keith Hart (eds), *Markets and Society: The Great Transformation Today*. Cambridge: Cambridge University Press, pp. 56–71.

Swedberg, Richard. 2010. 'A Note on Civilizations and Economies', *European Journal of Social Theory* 13(1): 15–30.

Weber, Max. 2002. 'Prefatory Remarks' to *Collected Essays in the Sociology of Religion*, in *The Protestant Ethic and the Spirit of Capitalism*. Oxford: Blackwell, pp. 149–64.

Chapter 2

From Halecki to Hann
The Historiography of Historical Regions

Stefan Troebst

What Is a Historical Region?

The research design of historical (meso-)regions is a transnationally comparative approach, resembling a middle-range theory, developed by historians of, in and from East-Central Europe. Approaches relying on historical regions are also employed by historians of art and of literature dealing with this part of Europe. In addition, such historical regional concepts have attracted sporadic interest in general history, historical sociology and social anthropology. Meso-regionalizing historical concepts ranging from 'East-Central Europe' and 'the Balkans' to a 'Monde méditerranéen' and a 'Black Sea World', even to historical macro-regions like 'Eurasia', an 'Atlantic World' or 'the Indian Ocean', are constructions that identify nonterritorialized units connected by time that cross the boundaries of state, society, nation and sometimes even civilization. They provide a working hypothesis for a comparative historical analysis that aims to detect and delineate specific clusters of structural characteristics over longer periods. Constructs of this type are constituted by specific combinations of a larger number of markers rather than by one or a few individual characteristics. They are 'fluctuating zones with fluid borders' and can be structured into centres and peripheries (Strohmeyer 1999: 47). Here, too, the specific is unimaginable without the surroundings; one historical region can only be understood in the context of others. Correspondingly, transregional relations and interregional interactions complement the internal structure of any particular historical meso-region. Thus, a meso- or macro-regional historical concept can be defined as a research strategy with built-in control mechanisms arising from a solid foundation in the sources and an empirical dimension. The concept is at the same time an investigative framework as well as a heuristic artifice, both dialectically related to real-time historical processes.

In the following, I will look at some examples of concepts of historical regions developed and applied in the humanities and social sciences starting with Oskar Halecki's 'divisions of Europe' of the 1950s and ending with Chris Hann's (2016) recent plea for a transcendent historical macro-region called Eurasia.

Five Concepts of Historical Regions: East-Central Europe, the Balkans, the 'Black Sea World', Europe and Eurasia

(1) East-Central Europe

Although the concept of historical meso-regions is of universal applicability, it is the product of a transnational discussion of Polish, Czechoslovak and German historians in the 1920s and 1930s, first on 'Slavdom' and 'the Slavs' and then on 'Eastern Europe' (Wandycz 1992; Troebst 2013). After the Second World War, the Polish historian Oskar Halecki, now an émigré in the United States, turned his views into a model that covered all of Europe. In his book *The Limits and Divisions of European History* (Halecki 1950), he differentiated not only between an 'old Europe' based on the ancient world and a 'new Europe' beyond the historical boundaries of the Imperium Romanum, but also between four modern European historical meso-regions with roots in the Middle Ages: Western Europe (France, Spain, Great Britain and Italy), West-Central Europe (Germany, Switzerland and Austria), East-Central Europe (Poland, Ukraine, Hungary and the Balkans) and Eastern Europe (Muscovy/Russia/the Soviet Union). His main goal was to mark out a cultural boundary between Western, West-Central and East-Central Europe on the one hand, characterized by the Western churches, and on the other hand of an Eastern Europe dominated by the Orthodox Church. Simultaneously, he attempted to relativize the dividing line between East-Central and West-Central Europe, a theme to which he gave greater emphasis in his broad study *Borderlands of Western Civilization: A History of East-Central Europe* (Halecki 1952). Halecki's influence shaped the development of West German research on East European history, which to a certain extent also drew on earlier concepts such as that of (more localized) 'historical landscapes' and indirectly the (highly ideologized) 'culture areas' (Jordan 2005; Schultz

2013). The result was the development of the meso-regional historical categories of 'East-Central Europe', 'Southeastern Europe', 'Northeastern Europe' and 'Eastern Europe'; the latter was used both to refer to the East Slavic realm and as an overarching supracategory (Zernack 1977, 1993; D. Müller 2003). Just as Halecki was being read in the new German Federal Republic, his ideas were also beginning to exert a subcutaneous influence on the Soviet Bloc (Małowist 1973; Kula 1983; Sosnowska 2004; Marung, Müller and Troebst 2019).

In Hungary, the historian Jenő Szűcs adopted Halecki's concept of 'East-Central Europe' in a modified form (Szűcs 1983). Like Halecki, he sought to identify structural factors that remained influential over a longer period, normally for several centuries. In reference to the Middle Ages, Christianization, the creation of medieval *nationes*-states, the Magdeburg Law, Ashkenazi Jewish settlement and German internal colonization are highlighted. For the early modern period, Szűcs and West German historians of Eastern Europe focused on the high percentage of nobles, the potential of the triad diocese-university-court as metropolis, libertarian corporate societies and refeudalization. In reference to the nineteenth century, they all chose great power domination and linguistic nationalism, and for the twentieth century, a 'realm of petty states', National Socialist domination and occupation, Soviet hegemony, mass movements of refugees, deportations, expulsions, ethnic cleansing, Holodomor, Holocaust, Porajmos and Sovietization. There was also Catholic and proletarian opposition, political-intellectual dissent and, ultimately, the epochal turning point of 1989 with its genuinely East-Central European innovations such as the Round Table, the Velvet Divorce and the cooperation of the Visegrád Group (Poland, Hungary and Czechoslovakia or rather the Czech Republic and Slovakia). Most importantly, Szűcs simplified Halecki's model by combining West-Central and East-Central Europe into what he again called (somewhat incongruously) East-Central Europe. His own pattern of the 'three historical regions of Europe' – Western, East-Central and Eastern – remains influential today. Like Halecki, Szűcs used the division between Orthodoxy and Catholicism to separate Eastern Europe (i.e. Russia) from East-Central Europe. However, the Hungarian historian saw an obvious socioeconomic and cultural dividing line between the latter and Western Europe; in his view, this cleft exerted an influence from the beginning of the 'second serfdom' in the early modern period up to the Cold War. 'East-Central Europe' quickly received wide acceptance as a meso-regional historical concept in the context of the East-West conflict, both in a narrower Polish-Bohemian-Hungarian sense and in a broader perspective including Byzantium, the Ottoman Empire and the post-Ottoman Balkans (Janowski et al. 2005)

(2) The Balkans

The meso-regional concept of 'Southeastern Europe' and the overlapping term 'the Balkans' became the subject of fierce debate as a result of the wars arising from the dissolution of Yugoslavia in the 1990s. The German historian Holm Sundhaussen disputed Maria Todorova's rejection of a regional concept of 'the Balkans' and her 'revelation' of it as an exclusionist stereotype. This provoked an intense discussion, as a result of which the differences between the positions reduced noticeably: while Sundhaussen continued to speak of the Balkans as a 'historical meso-region' (*Geschichtsregion*) (Sundhaussen 1999, 2003), Todorova offered the compromise formula of a region with a common 'historical legacy' (Todorova 2002, 2005a, 2018: 90–92). By this she meant the long-term impacts by Byzantium and the Ottoman Empire, which shape the European territories of these sunken empires up to the present day and make them into a historical meso-region.

Alongside regionalizations, which refer to historical, cultural, economic, religious, social, linguistic and political geography, mental maps heavily intrude upon meso-regional historical concepts (D. Müller 2015). In this vein, Holm Sundhaussen warned against the 'intermixture of mental map and historical region' (Sundhaussen 2005: 30). Thus, 'the Balkans' is on the one hand the designation of a historical meso-region and on the other the label of a negative cultural stereotype. The same goes for 'Eurasia' (Hann 2016) or 'the Levant' (Schwara 2003), but this dual mechanism can also work the other way round – e.g. the historical meso-region 'Northern Europe' or rather 'Scandinavia' carries positive connotations associated with the welfare state, egalitarianism, consensus-orientation in politics, high educational standards, etc. (Götz 2003; Stråth 2010).

(3) The 'Black Sea World'

The concept of historical meso-regions, developed by German-speaking historians of Eastern Europe, has been *avant la lettre* employed by a number of authorities in the field of the history and culture of the Black Sea Region – Arnold Toynbee (1922), Mikhail Rostovtzeff (1922) and Gheorghe Ion Brătianu (1969), and implicitly also by Fernand Braudel (1949). Following in their footsteps, Neal Ascherson (1995) and Charles King (2004) wrote their popular monographs while Eyüp Özveren (1997) elaborated a historical 'Framework for the Study of the Black Sea World, 1789–1915'. In his view, in the 'long' nineteenth century, mercantile *longue durée* effects from ancient and Byzantine times were stronger than the political division of the region between the empires of tsars and sultans

(Özveren 2001). Nevertheless, research results on the Black Sea as a historical meso-region remain mostly in the regionalist community (Bellér-Hann and Hann 2001) and are rarely perceived in fields such as Middle Eastern, Mediterranean, Balkan, East European, Eurasian or West Asian history (Troebst 2007, 2019). However, the recent resurfacing of the Black Sea Region in international geopolitics seems to bring about a change:

> With the annexation of Crimea by Russia in the spring of 2014, 150 years after the Crimean War, the Black Sea has returned to the center of world history. Again the Black Sea Region has become the arena of shifts in Europe's basic order. It proves the geopolitical significance as well as the strong symbolic and affective connotations of the Black Sea. (Berlin Center for Cultural and Literary Research 2016, my translation)

Currently, an international handbook on the history and culture of the Black Sea Region, edited by historians from Vienna and Leipzig, is in the making.

(4) Europe

It is obvious that 'Europe' is an implicit historical macro-region that requires no less critical reflection (Mishkova and Trencsényi 2017). At the same time, a study of the subregions of Europe's East, above all of Northeastern Europe, Southeastern Europe/Balkans and Russia, would carry additional importance as they share boundaries with other historical meso-regions not only within 'Europe' but also beyond, including with 'Eurasia' and 'the Arctic' as well as with the 'Black Sea World', the 'Levant' and the 'Near East'. One can therefore agree with Jürgen Kocka, who perceives 'East-Central Europe as a challenge for a comparative history of Europe' (Kocka 2000: 166); this is true for both the historical meso-region of East-Central Europe as well as, more generally, for meso-regional historical concepts. Thus, the restriction of the analytical framework of the historical meso-region to a single historical subdiscipline has recently weakened; this approach is becoming increasingly attractive for historians outside the field of East European history. For example, Jürgen Osterhammel, a German global historian, in a survey of seven historiographical 'models of Europe', presented a 'model of cultural spaces' that incorporated a 'model of historical regions' (Osterhammel 2004: 167–68), with explicit reference to Halecki and Szűcs. Similarly, the cultural historian Hannes Siegrist talks of 'historical spaces' as the central object of study for comparative history, alongside 'cultures', 'societies' and 'paths of development' (Siegrist 2003). In an essay on 'regions and worlds', Johannes Paulmann tried to bring together regional and global history by leaving out the levels of national and European history. While he rejects the political notion of a 'Europe of regions', he considers the concept of historical meso-regions helpful for analysing not only the history of Europe but also of other parts of the world:

> The analytical frame of historical meso-region (*Geschichtsregion*) offers connecting possibilities for the study of regional relations on a global scale as transitions to other 'meso-regions' are perceived as being fluid. Historical meso-regions are to be understood as exclusively context-bound, internal relations and external ones are considered to be constitutive for them. So far, historical meso-regions of this type are studied primarily in the *European* context. Yet since in principle they are relational to other regions, not only to neighbouring regions but also to ones that are more distant, other parts of the world should be also taken into account. (Paulmann 2013: 666, my translation).

A similar perception of 'regional history' – as applied by Paulmann and others – figures in a recent article by Diana Mishkova, Bo Stråth and Balász Trencsényi (2013) on the impact of meso-regional historical concepts on the national historiographies of Central, Southeast and Northern Europe. However, in looking at discourses of historians from the mid-nineteenth century to the post-1989 period, the three authors include not only 'supranational/ transnational regional history' whose 'narratives ... try to subsume the competing national vision under a common macro-regional umbrella', but also a 'subnational regional history' of 'micro-regions that were eventually nationalized' (Mishkova, Stråth and Trencsényi 2013: 257). They demonstrate that historiographic concepts like 'Scandinavia', '*Norden*', '*Mitteleuropa*', 'the Balkans' and 'Southeastern Europe' are more often than not (geo)politically connotated and thus become influential particularly in times of crisis. At the same time, the authors stress that concepts of this type are among 'the most important and promising tools of historical projects trying to question or relativize the nation-centric narrative' (Mishkova, Stråth and Trencsényi 2013: 304).

A recent phenomenon is the interest of historically inclined sociologists in 'the historical regions of Europe'. Johann P. Arnason, whose field of research is the comparison of civilizations, has given increasing interest to meso-regional historical concepts in the context of the debate on the 'unique course' (*Sonderweg*) of European history: 'Regional divisions have probably been more salient and their meaning more contested in Europe than in any other part of the world' (Arnason 2005: 387).

Arnason makes use of the publications by Szűcs, Troebst, Zernack and particularly Halecki, as the 'Haleckian' title of a collected volume coedited by him proves: *Domains and Divisions of European History*. In

Arnason's view, however, 'Oskar Halecki's seminal reflections on "limits and divisions" ... do not go far enough':

> They do not do justice to the domains or dimensions within which the dividing lines are drawn. If we pursue this line of reflection and link it to available concepts, we encounter categories open to differentiation, but at the same time grounded in specific patterns of unity and adaptable – albeit in varying degrees – to perspectives on Europe as a whole. Four main foci of this kind have served to make sense of European unity and divisions: *civilizations, religions, regions* and *nations*. (Arnason and Doyle 2010: 2)

Most recently (and inspired by Arnason), Gerard Delanty, another sociologist also interested in intercivilizational comparisons, discovered the concept of historical meso-regions. In his article 'The Historical Regions of Europe: Civilizational Backgrounds and Multiple Routes to Modernity' of 2012, he comes up with 'a six-fold classification ... to capture the diversity of Europe's historical regions':

> [T]hese [European historical regions] should be seen in terms of different routes to modernity and have broad civilizational backgrounds in common. The forms of modernity that constitute Europe as a world historical region correspond to North Western Europe, Mediterranean Europe, Central Europe, East Central Europe, South Eastern Europe, North Eastern Europe. (Delanty 2012: 9)

After going through the history of his six historical regions of Europe, Delanty arrives at a far-reaching conclusion:

> The six historical regions ... are historically variable and overlapping. They do not simply overlap with each other, but are also closely linked spatially and culturally with areas that lie outside the European region as a whole. The paper has stressed in this regard the formative influence of the east in the west, and the importance of the Russian and Ottoman-Islamic worlds in the making of Europe. This serves in part to correct the older eurocentric view of the making of Europe that tended to see Europe as shaped by itself and to define all its regions in terms of their relation to the North West ... The emphasis on a plurality of regions with their own civilizational backgrounds and routes to modernity does not, it must be noted, mean that there is no unity since all these regions interacted with each other and ultimately such interaction made possible the genesis of modernity and the formation of Europe as a world historical region. (Delanty 2012: 23)

In Delanty's as well as Arnason's view, from a historical perspective the meso-regional structure of Europe is one of the unique characteristics of the half-continent in comparison with other parts of Eurasia and the world (Arnason 2010; Delanty 2013: 195–214) – a perception also shared by social anthropologists such as Christian Giordano. Giordano defines 'Europe as a system of historical regions: Centre, peripheries and external regions' (Giordano 2003: 121) and he lists, in much the same way as Delanty, 'Northwestern Europe', 'Mediterranean Europe', 'Central-Eastern Europe', 'Southeastern Europe' and 'Eastern Europe' (Giordano 2003: 123–30; Giordano 2010; Delanty 2013: 197) The historicity of this meso-regional structure, according to him, explains Europe's 'present socio-economic gradient' (Giordano 2003: 130).

(5) Eurasia

Being originally a geopolitical term (Hancock and Libman 2016), 'Eurasia' has been applied by the social anthropologist Chris Hann in his research on postsocialism (Hann 2002). In 2006, he defined Eurasia by the fact that its national units had been shaped by what he called cryptically 'MLM socialism' (i.e. 'Marxist-Leninist-Maoist socialism'). Thus, it reaches from post-GDR Thuringia over the Russian Federation and China well into the Mekong Delta. In historical terms, however, Hann perceived Eurasia as a world civilization whose roots go back to the agrarian empires of earlier millennia, even to the Paleolithic (Hann 2006: 3–4). At the same time, he saw the concept of a 'postsocialist Eurasia' as a corrective to Eurocentrism in general and to 'nauseating ... self-congratulatory proclamations about the alleged uniqueness of "European values"' in particular. Instead, 'more attention to the "big history" of the landmass should help us to see the parochialism of such claims and to expose the hubris behind them' (Hann 2006: 245).

In 2016, Hann became more explicit on the *longue durée* of his Eurasia by describing it as 'a spatio-temporalization with a reference in materialist realism, a thing ... that has existed in the world for a very long time' (Hann 2016: 1; cf. also Cohen 2012; Witzenrath 2015). Similarly, he outlined in detail the geographical extent: Eurasia is 'a "supracontinental" unity forged over the past three millennia' consisting of 'the largest landmass of the planet', 'i.e. Europe + Asia', 'including large islands such as Great Britain and Japan' as well as 'the southern shores of the Mediterranean, in other words, the northern zones of the continent known as Africa' (Hann 2016: 2). Again, he perceived 'Eurasia' as a sort of panacea against Eurocentrism:

> To imagine Europe and Asia as constituting equivalent 'continents' has long been recognized as the ethnocentric cornerstone of a Western, or Euro-American, world view. The amalgam Eurasia corrects this bias by highlighting the intensifying interconnectedness of the entire landmass in recent millennia. (Hann 2016: 1)

Despite 'a distinguished academic pedigree' claimed by Hann (2016: 9), his concept of a Eurasian *longue durée* that reaches well into the present and thus his hope, into the future, has been met with severe criticism, as being a scholastic 'utopia' (Schlee 2016: 18; Schlee 2015; Testa 2015; 2017; cf. also Hann 2015), as well as by constructive critique: 'What's Good to Think May Not Be Good to Build' (Pomeranz 2016).

Instead of a Conclusion: Terms, Trends and Transregionalism

The conceptualization of historical regions, as well as their practical application of models of this type in research, are in the ascendant in several disciplines in the humanities and social sciences – and this independently from 'the spatial turn'. Terminological interferences from the political or cultural realm do not stop this trend, which encompasses alongside the intraregional focus increasingly also interregional or transregional comparison.

Terms

Like mental maps, (geo)political terminology too can produce confusing effects on the humanities and social sciences when it comes to historical meso-regionalizations. For example, in 1990, the political scientist and expert on communism Charles Gati published an article on the events of 1989 in the authoritative journal *Foreign Affairs*, metaphorically entitled 'East-Central Europe: The Morning after'. The first sentence read somewhat enigmatically 'Eastern Europe is now East-Central Europe' (Gati 1990: 129). What Gati meant was the end of Soviet hegemony over the satellite states – from Poland to Bulgaria. While the then still existing USSR was labelled 'Eastern', the European Warsaw Pact member states were terminologically moved from the very East to an east-of-centre position – in line with Halecki's divisions. An even more drastic example, combining mental maps and political language, is Paul R. Magocsi's seminal *Historical Atlas of East Central Europe* of 1993. When the second edition was published in 2002, the title was changed to *Historical Atlas of Central Europe*. In the preface, Magocsi explained this change in the following way:

> It has ... become clear since 1989 that the articulate elements in many countries of the region consider eastern or even east-central to carry a negative connotation and prefer to be considered part of Central Europe ... If Central Europe responds to the preference of the populations of the countries in question, this would seem to lend even greater credence to the terminological choice. (Magocsi, 2002: xiii)

However, it would be rash to assume that all historians dealing with the region succumb to political or populist pressure. Quite a number of them have tried to make a distinction between the use of one and the same regional term in politics and history, and thus to avoid the dilemma of multiple connotations. In 1990, Michael G. Müller declared the German equivalent to East Central Europe (*Ostmitteleuropa*) to be an exclusively academic term by labelling it 'an artificial terminological creation – a synthetic term to be applied most of all by scholars' (M. Müller 1990: 2). And in 2004, the Polish-British art historian Katarzyna Murawska-Muthesius turned to an even more radical terminological measure by replacing the denomination 'East-Central Europe' with the fantasy term 'Slaka' (Murawska-Muthesius 2004) – the name of a fictitious COMECON country in Michael Bradbury's novels *Rates of Exchange* of 1983 and *Why Come to Slaka?* of 1986. His 'Slaka' combines typical features of Poland, Bulgaria and Vietnam.

Trends

Notwithstanding the danger of terminological and conceptual mingling, and even collusion, geography-based regionalizations still seem apt as a means of referring to historical meso-regions. This is even more true due to the heuristic value the concept has in academia. The German historian of Russia Frithjof Benjamin Schenk has set out five innovative benefits of meso-regional historical concepts that reveal the possible uses and insights to be gained for the historian's trade. According to Schenk, these are:

1. overcoming the limitations of national history through transnational comparison;
2. the dynamism and flexibility of such concepts over time;
3. the approach's 'clinically pure' character and its comparative and analytical framework largely (though of course not completely) free of contamination by 'historical reality';
4. the term's immanent self-critical reference to the self-fulfilling prophecy of concepts of region;
5. the term's applicability to Europe as a whole, i.e. that implicit historical region which is so often seen as written in stone. (Schenk 2004: 23–24)

Schenk's second point, the factor of 'time', requires further explanation, or indeed expansion. Despite concentration on the specific and structural references to space by the different meso-regional historical concepts, one cannot ignore their chronological nature and thus the dimension of time. The historian Wolfgang Schmale therefore suggested incorporating

Reinhart Koselleck's model of 'temporal layers' (*Zeitschichten*) and in so doing adopting Norman Davies' concept of a 'tidal Europe' – a Europe whose form and content from the ancient world to the present has pulsed, sometimes becoming larger, sometimes smaller (Davies 1996: 9; Schmale 2003: 196; Koselleck 2004). Using the example of nation-building processes in East-Central Europe, Maria Todorova has demonstrated that the use of a *longue durée* timeframe relativizes the *differentia specifica* of the historical meso-regions under study when compared to the 'genuine' Europe, i.e. 'Western Europe', even if it does not remove them entirely (Todorova 2005b). In referring to the philosopher Ernst Bloch's figure of thought of a nonsimultaneity of the simultaneous (*Gleichzeitigkeit des Ungleichzeitigen*), Todorova argues that by comparing nonsimultaneous historical processes – e.g. developments in the Balkans in the twentieth century with developments in nineteenth-century Northern Europe – notions of backwardness can be levelled up. This seems to be a particularly promising dimension for a future approach to meso-regional historical concepts – to undertake an intraregional, but above all an *interregional* comparison not, as in the past, primarily synchronically, but diachronically, along parameters such as modernization or state- and nation-building, but also others that are less well-tested, such as legal culture, political culture, industrialization and urbanization.

Transregionalism

The fact that one historical meso-region is constituted, among other factors, by 'neighbouring' historical meso-regions is only one of several transregional features. The others are flows of ideas, people, goods, etc. from one historical meso-region to another (Troebst 2018). For example, the process of adopting constitutions in the newly founded states of Southeastern Europe in the nineteenth and early twentieth centuries was strongly influenced by West European models, in the case of Greece also by the Greek diaspora in the United States (Spiliotis 1998: 211–314). In the same way, 'socialist' Eastern Europe under Soviet hegemony left visible traces in the infrastructures, agricultures, industries, education systems, etc. in the Global South and China. Furthermore, postsocialist East-Central Europe witnessed a remigration of political émigrés who shaped the newly emerging political landscapes of Poland, Ukraine, Latvia and other countries of the region. And the very term 'Iberoamérica' for those parts of the Americas that had been colonies of Spain and Portugal stands for transregional influence.

Nevertheless, research combining two or more historical meso-regional concepts in a transregional perspective is only a beginning. Of course, there is Jack Goody's by now 'classical' *The East in the West* (Goody 1996), in fact the blueprint of Hann's timeless macro-region 'Eurasia' as well as an 'anti-Eurocentric' (and anti-Wallersteinian) contribution to the debate on the divergence between 'Western Europe' and 'East Asia' (Pomeranz 2000; cf. also O'Brien 2010; Rössner and Middell 2016; Wallerstein 2011 [1974]). Moreover, there are seminal case studies taking on networks that tie historical meso-regions together, such as Sebouh David Aslanian's (2011) monograph on the economic activities of the Armenian merchants of Isfahan between Amsterdam and Manila from the beginning of the seventeenth to the middle of the eighteenth centuries. Furthermore, Maria Todorova and Karl Kaser recently claimed that 'Europe' in general and 'the Balkans' in particular are bound together by 'historical legacies' due to a 'shared history' with the Near East (Todorova 2007; Kaser 2011); Marie-Janine Calic set out to write 'the global history of a region' called 'Southeastern Europe' (Calic 2016); and recently 'a transnational history of East-Central Europe' was also published (Hadler and Middell 2017). Yet a transregional history that combines, say, East-Central Europe with the Indian Ocean, or the Black Sea Region with the 'Atlantic World' is still missing. In this respect, Hann's concept of 'Eurasia' appears to be an attractive research design in sociocultural anthropology, and this despite the fact that 'recognition and realization of pan-Eurasian affinities continues to be impeded by geopolitics' (Hann 2016: 1) – one may cite, for example, the Russian Federation's proposal of 2010 for 'a common economic space from Vladivostok to Lisbon', the US 'New Silk Road Initiative' of 2011 or the Chinese 'Belt and Road Initiative' of 2013.

Bringing together the concept of historical meso-regions and transregionalism is an intriguing challenge that is yet to be mastered by scholars in the humanities and social sciences. Endeavours in this field require interdisciplinary and transnational cooperation as well as a historical depth of focus of several centuries, if not – as Chris Hann reminds us (Hann 2016) – millennia. The first steps in this direction have already been taken.

Stefan Troebst is a Slavicist and historian specializing in Eastern Europe. Since 1999, he has been Professor of East European Cultural Studies at Leipzig University, Germany, and Deputy Director of the Leibniz Institute for the History and Culture of East-Central Europe (GWZO), also in Leipzig. His fields of research are international and interethnic relations in modern Eastern Europe as well as the comparative cultural history of contemporary Europe.

References

Arnason, Johann P. 2005. 'Introduction: Demarcating East Central Europe', *European Journal of Social Theory* 8: 387–400.
_____. 2010. 'Interpreting Europe from East of Centre', in Johann P. Arnason and Natalie J. Doyle (eds). *Domains and Divisions of European History*, Liverpool: Liverpool University Press, pp. 139–57.
Arnason, Johann P., and Natalie J. Doyle. 2010. 'Introduction: European Perspective on Unity and Division', in Johann P. Arnason and Natalie J. Doyle (eds), *Domains and Divisions of European History*. Liverpool: Liverpool University Press, pp. 1–17.
Ascherson, Neal. 1995. *Black Sea*. New York: Hill & Wang.
Aslanian, Sebouh D. 2011. *From the Indian Ocean to the Mediterranean: The Global Networks of Armenian Merchants from New Julfa*. Berkeley: University of California Press.
Bellér-Hann, Ildiko, and Chris Hann. 2001. *Turkish Region: State, Market & Social Identities on the East Black Sea Coast*. Oxford: James Currey.
Berlin Center for Cultural and Literary Research. 2016. *Batumi, Odessa, Trabzon. Cultural Semantics of the Black Sea in the Perspective of Eastern Port Cities*, project description, http://www.zfl-berlin.org/projekt/batumi-odessa-trabzon.html, accessed 11 February 2021.
Brătianu, Georges I. 1969. *La Mer Noire des Origines à la Conquête Ottomane*. Munich: Societas Academica Dacoromana.
Braudel, Fernand. 1949. *La Méditerranée et le Monde Méditerranéen à L'Epoche de Philippe II*, 2 vols. Paris: Colin.
Calic, Marie-Janine. 2016. *Südosteuropa: Weltgeschichte einer Region*, Munich: C.H. Beck.
Cohen, Walter. 2012. 'Eurasian Literature', in David Porter (ed.), *Comparative Early Modernities 1100–1800*. New York: Palgrave Macmillan, pp. 47–72.
Davies, Norman. 1996. *Europe: A History*. Oxford: Oxford University Press.
Delanty, Gerard. 2012. 'The Historical Regions of Europe: Civilizational Backgrounds and Multiple Routes to Modernity', *Historická Sociologie* 3(1–2): 9–24.
_____. 2013. *Formations of European Modernity: A Historical and Political Sociology of Europe*. Basingstoke: Palgrave Macmillan.
Gati, Charles. 1990. 'East-Central Europe: The Morning after', *Foreign Affairs* 69(5): 129–45.
Giordano, Christian. 2003. 'Interdependente Vielfalt: Die historischen Regionen Europas', in Karl Kaser, Dagmar Gramshammer-Hohl and Robert Pichler (eds), *Europa und die Grenzen im Kopf*. Klagenfurt: Wieser, pp. 113–35.
_____. 2010. 'Südosteuropa – eine Region eigner Art?', in Joachim J. von Puttkamer and Gabriella Schubert (eds), *Kulturelle Orientierungen und gesellschaftliche Ordnungsstrukturen*. Wiesbaden: Harrassowitz, pp. 19–39.
Goody, Jack. 1996. *The East in the West*. Cambridge: Cambridge University Press.
Götz, Norbert. 2003. '*Norden*: Structures That Do Not Make a Region', *European Review of History* 10(2): 323–41.

Hadler, Frank, and Matthias Middell (eds). 2017. *Handbuch einer transnationalen Geschichte Ostmitteleuropas*, Vol. 1: *Von der Mitte des 19. Jahrhunderts bis zum Ersten Weltkrieg*. Göttingen: Vandenhoeck & Ruprecht.
Halecki, Oscar. 1950. *The Limits and Divisions of European History*, London: Sheed & Ward.
———. 1952. *Borderlands of Western Civilization: A History of East Central Europe*. New York: Ronald Press Co.
Hancock, Kathleen, and Alexander Libman. 2016. 'Eurasia', in Tanja A. Börzel and Thomas Risse (eds), *The Oxford Handbook of Comparative Regionalism*. Oxford: Oxford University Press: pp. 202–24.
Hann, Chris (ed.). 2002. *Postsocialism: Ideals, Ideologies and Practices in Eurasia*. New York: Routledge.
———. 2006. 'Not the Horse We Wanted!' *Postsocialism, Neoliberalism, and Eurasia*. Münster: LIT.
———. 2015. 'Declining Europe: A Reply to Alessandro Testa', *The Anthropology of East Europe Review* 33(22): 89–93.
———. 2016. 'A Concept of Eurasia', *Current Anthropology* 57(1): 1–10 (with comments by M. Benovska-Sabkova, A. Bošković, T.H. Eriksen, D.N. Gellner, A. Gingrich, N. Kradin, J. de Pina-Cabral, G.L. Ribeiro, D. Robert, G. Schlee, P. Skalník and D. Wengrow, ibid., 10–28).
Janowski, Maciej, Constantin Iordachi and Balázs Trencsényi. 2005. 'Why Bother about Historical Regions? Debates over Central Europe in Hungary, Poland and Romania', *East Central Europe* 32: 5–58.
Jordan, Peter. 2005. 'Großgliederung Europas nach kulturräumlichen Kriterien', *Europa Regional* 13: 162–73.
Kaser, Karl. 2011. *The Balkans and the Near East: Introduction to a Shared History*. Berlin: LIT.
King, Charles. 2004. *The Black Sea: A History*. Oxford: Oxford University Press.
Kocka, Jürgen. 2000. 'Das östliche Mitteleuropa als Herausforderung für eine vergleichende Geschichte Europas', *Zeitschrift für Ostmitteleuropa-Forschung* 49: 159–74.
Koselleck, Reinhart. 2004. *Futures Past: On the Semantics of Historical Time*. New York: Columbia University Press.
Kula, Witold. 1983. *Historia, zacofanie, rozwój*. Warsaw: Wydawnictwo Naukowe PWN.
Magocsi, Paul R. 2002. *Historical Atlas of Central Europe*, 2nd edn. Seattle: University of Washington Press.
Małowist, Marian. 1973. *Wschód a Zachód Europy w XIII–XV wieku: Konfrontacja struktur społeczno-gospodarczych*. Warsaw: Wydawnictwo Naukowe PWN.
Marung, Steffi, Uwe Müller and Stefan Troebst. 2019. 'Monolith or Experiment? The Bloc as a Spatial Format', in Steffi Marung and Matthias Middell (eds), *Spatial Formats under the Global Condition*. Berlin: De Gruyter, pp. 275–309.
Mishkova, Diana, Bo Stråth and Balázs Trencsényi. 2013. 'Regional History as a "Challenge" to National Frameworks of Historiography: The Case of Central, Southeast, and Northern Europe', in Matthias Middell and L. Roura Aulinas (eds), *Transnational Challenges to National History Writing*, Basingstoke: Palgrave Macmillan, pp. 257–314.

Mishkova, Diana, and Balázs Trencsényi (eds). 2017. *European Regions and Boundaries. A Conceptual History*. Oxford: Berghahn Books.
Müller, Dietmar. 2003. 'Southeastern Europe as a Historical Meso-region: Constructing Space in Twentieth-Century German Historiography', *European Review of History* 10(2): 393–408.
⸺. 2015. 'Geschichtsregionen und Phantomgrenzen', in Béatrice von Hirschhausen, Hannes Grandits, Claudia Kraft, Dietmar Müller and Thomas Serrier (eds), *Phantomgrenzen. Räume und Akteure in der Zeit neu denken*. Göttingen: Wallstein, pp. 57–83.
Müller, Michael G. 1990. 'Ostmitteleuropa: Begriff – Traditionen – Strukturen', unpublished manuscript of a lecture given at Freie Universität Berlin, 25 April.
Murawska-Muthesius, Katarzyna. 2004. 'Welcome to Slaka: Does Eastern (Central) European Art Exist?', *Third Text* 18(1): 25–40.
O'Brien, Patrick K. 2010. 'The Divergence Debate. Europe and China 1386–1846', in Gunilla Budde, Sebastian Conrad and Oliver Janz (eds), *Transnationale Geschichte: Themen, Tendenzen und Theorien*, 2nd edn. Göttingen: Vandenhoeck & Ruprecht, pp. 68–82.
Özveren, Y. Eyüp. 1997. 'A Framework for the Study of the Black Sea World, 1789–1915', *Review: A Journal of the Fernand Braudel Center* 20: 77–113.
⸺. 2001. 'The Black Sea World as a Unit of Analysis', in Tunç Aybak (ed.), *Politics of the Black Sea: Dynamics of Cooperation and Conflict*. New York: I.B. Tauris, pp. 61–84.
Osterhammel, Jürgen. 2004. 'Europamodelle und imperiale Kontexte', *Journal of Modern European History* 2(2): 157–81.
Paulmann, Johannes. 2013. 'Regionen und Welten: Arenen und Akteure regionaler Weltbeziehungen seit dem 19. Jahrhundert', *Historische Zeitschrift* 296: 660–99.
Pomeranz, Kenneth. 2000. *The Great Divergence: China, Europe, and the Making of the Modern World Economy*. Princeton: Princeton University Press.
⸺. 2011. 'The Great Divergence Debate at 10 – and at 250', *Historically Speaking* 12(4): 20–25.
⸺. 2016. 'Eurasia as Scholarship and Politics: What's Good to Think May Not Be Good to Build', unpublished manuscript.
Rössner, Philipp R., and Matthias Middell (eds). 2016. *Great Divergence Revisited*. Leipzig: Leipziger Universitätsverlag.
Rostovtzeff, Micheal I. 1922. *Iranians and Greeks in South Russia*. Oxford: Clarendon Press.
Schenk, Frithjof B. 2004. 'The Historical Regions of Europe – Real or Invented? Some Remarks on Historical Comparison and Mental Mapping', in Frithjof B. Schenk (ed.), *Beyond the Nation: Writing European History Today*. St Petersburg: European University, pp. 15–24.
Schlee, Günther. 2015. *Civiliations, Eurasia as a Unit and the Hochkulturgürtel: An Essay about How to Subdivide the World in Terms of Cultural History and What to Explain with the Units Thereby Created*. Halle: Max Planck Institute for Social Anthropology.
⸺. 2016. 'Comment', *Current Anthropology* 57(1): 18–19.

Schmale, Wolfgang. 2003. 'Die Europäizität Ostmitteleuropas', *Jahrbuch für Europäische Geschichte* 4: 189–214.
Schultz, Hans-Dietrich. 2013. 'Europa als kultur-räumliches Projekt', in Hans Gebhardt, Rüdiger Glaser and Sebastian Lentz (eds), *Europa – eine Geographie.* Berlin: Springer, pp. 132–35.
Schwara, Desanka. 2003. 'Rediscovering the Levant: A Heterogeneous Structure as a Homogeneous Historical Region', *European Review of History* 10(2): 233–51.
Siegrist, Hannes. 2003. 'Perspektiven der vergleichenden Geschichtswissenschaft. Gesellschaft, Kultur und Raum', in Hartmut Kaelble and Jürgen Schriewer (eds), *Vergleich und Transfer. Komparatistik in den Sozial-, Geschichts- und Kulturwissenschaften.* Frankfurt am Main: Campus, pp. 304–38.
Sosnowska, Anna. 2004. *Zrozumieć zacofanie. Spory historyków Europę Wschodnią (1947–1994).* Warsaw: TRIO.
Spiliotis, Susanne-Sophia. 1998. *Transterritorialität und Nationale Abgrenzung: Konstituierungsprozesse der griechischen Gesellschaft und Ansätze ihrer faschistoiden Transformation, 1922/24–1941.* Munich: R. Oldenbourg.
Strohmeyer, Arno. 1999. 'Historische Komparatistik und die Konstruktion von Geschichtsregionen: der Vergleich als Methode der historischen Europaforschung', *Jahrbücher für Geschichte und Kultur Südosteuropas* 1: 39–55.
Stråth, Bo. 2010. '"Norden" as a European Region: Demarcation and Belonging', in Johann P. Arnason and Natalie J. Doyle (eds), *Domains and Divisions of European History.* Liverpool: Liverpool University Press, pp. 198–215.
Sundhaussen, Holm. 1999. 'Europa balcanica: Der Balkan als historischer Raum Europas', *Geschichte und Gesellschaft* 25: 626–53.
_____. 2003. 'Der Balkan: Ein Plädoyer für Differenz', *Geschichte und Gesellschaft* 29: 642–58.
_____. 2005. 'Die Wiederentdeckung des Raums: Über Nutzen und Nachteil von Geschichtsregionen', in Konrad Clewing and Oliver Jens Schmitt (eds), *Südosteuropa: Von vormoderner Vielfalt und nationalstaatlicher Vereinigung.* Munich: R. Oldenbourg, pp. 13–33.
Szűcs, Jenő. 1983. 'The Three Historical Regions of Europe: An Outline', *Acta Historica. Revue de l'Academie des Sciences de Hongrie* 29: 131–84.
Testa, Alessandro. 2015. 'On Eurasia and Europe', *The Anthropology of East Europe Review* 33(2), 60-88.
_____. 2017. 'A Utopia of Eurasia: The Uses and Abuses of a Concept – A Counter-reply to Chris Hann', *The Anthropology of East Europe Review* 35(1), 64–79.
Todorova, Maria. 2002. 'The Balkans as Category of Analysis: Border, Space, Time', in Gerald Stourzh (ed.), *Annäherungen an eine europäische Geschichtsschreibung.* Vienna: Österreichische Akademie der Wissenschaften, pp. 57–83.
_____. 2005a. 'Spacing Europe: What Is a Historical Region?', *East Central Europe* 32(1–2): 59–78.
_____. 2005b. 'The Trap of Backwardness: Modernity, Temporality, and the Study of Eastern European Nationalism', *Slavic Review* 64: 140–64.

———. 2007. 'Historical Legacies between Europe and the Near East', in *Carl Heinrich Becker Lecture der Fritz Thyssen Stiftung 2007*. Berlin: Fritz Thyssen Stiftung, pp. 57–80.
———. 2018. *Scaling the Balkans. Essays on Eastern European Entanglements*. Leiden: Brill, pp. 83–92.
Toynbee, Arnold J. 1922. *The Western Question in Greece and Turkey: A Study in the Contact of Civilizations*. London: Constable.
Troebst, Stefan. 2003. 'What's in a Historical Region? A Teutonic Perspective', *European Review of History* 10(2): 173–88.
———. 2007. '*Le Monde méditerranéen – Südosteuropa – Black Sea World*. Geschichtsregionen im Süden Europas', in Frithjof B. Schenk and Martina Winkler (eds), *Der Süden: Neue Perspektiven auf eine europäische Geschichtsregion*. Frankfurt am Main: Campus: pp. 49–73.
———. 2010. 'Meso-regionalizing Europe: History Versus Politics', in Johann P. Arnason and Natalie J. Doyle (eds), *Domains and Divisions of European History*. Liverpool: Liverpool University Press, pp. 78–89.
———. 2012. '"Historical Meso-region": A Concept in Cultural Studies and Historiography', *EGO – European History Online*, March. Retrieved 8 December 2020 from http://www.ieg-ego.eu/en/threads/crossroads/the-historical-region.
———. 2013. 'Sonderweg zur Geschichtsregion. Die Teildisziplin Osteuropäische Geschichte', *Osteuropa* 63(2–3): 55–80.
———. 2017. 'European History', in Diana Mishkova and Balázs Trencsényi (eds), *European Regions and Boundaries: A Conceptual History*. Oxford: Berghahn Books, pp. 235–57.
———. 2018. 'Historical Mesoregions and Transregionalism', in Matthias Middell (ed.), *The Routledge Handbook of Transregional Studies*. London: Routledge, pp. 169–78.
———. 2019. 'The Black Sea as Historical Meso-region: Concepts in Cultural Studies and the Social Sciences', *Journal of Balkan and Black Sea Studies* 1(2): 11–29.
Wallerstein, Immanuel M. 2011 [1974]. *The Modern World-System*, 4 vols. New York: Academic Press; Berkeley: University of California Press.
Wandycz, Piotr S. 1992 'East European History and Its Meaning: The Halecki-Bidlo-Handelsman Debate', in Pál Jónás, Peter Pastor and Pál Péter Tóth (eds), *Király Béla emlékkönyv. Háború és társadalom: War and Society. Guerre et Société. Krieg und Gesellschaft*, Budapest: Századvég – Centum, pp. 308–21.
Witzenrath, Christoph (ed.). 2015. *Eurasian Slavery, Ransom and Abolition in World History, 1200–1860*. Farnham: Ashgate.
Zernack, Klaus. 1977. *Osteuropa: Eine Einführung in seine Geschichte*. Munich: C.H. Beck.
———. 1993. *Nordosteuropa: Skizzen und Beiträge zu einer Geschichte der Ostseeländer*. Lüneburg: Nordostdeutsches Kulturwerk.

Chapter 3

Out of the Frying Pan and into the Fire, or Modernization Forever?
Economic Strategies in the Transformation of Peasant Societies

Mihály Sárkány

Chris Hann is a unique scholar in many respects.

To mention one: he is perhaps the only person who has carried out fieldwork in villages in three different socialist countries (Hungary, Poland and China) as well as in a nonsocialist country, Turkey, where, as in Xinjiang, China, he conducted research together with his wife. The results were published in monographs and long studies, which describe and discuss socioeconomic and political conditions, changes and certain elements of social consciousness such as religion and ethnicity. In addition, Hann presented his empirical knowledge within a comparative perspective, tackling socioeconomic problems in the contemporary world after the collapse of existing socialism. He did this within the European context, with an eye on Eurasia as a whole, and relying on the theoretical inspiration of Karl Polanyi's approach to economy.[1]

A common feature of the four fieldwork sites was that the modernization of the rural sector was on the agenda at the time of Chris Hann's research (Hann 2006: 115–17). In the socialist contexts, there was also an ambiguous effort to change the mentality of people from individualism to developing a stronger concern for social cohesion.[2]

Sharing Bellér-Hann and Hann's view that social identities depend on both public and private spheres (Bellér-Hann and Hann 2001: 22), I make a brief comment on this process from the point of view of the individual based on my fieldwork carried out in Hungary, from the 1970s up until

Notes for this chapter begin on page 61.

the last decade, and on additional fieldwork that I conducted in Kenya in the 1990s.

As modernization is a vague and confrontational concept because too many authors have used the term in different ways and with different emphases, in the following discussion I invoke ideas, organizational forms, practices and broad historical problems encapsulated in, and connected with, the term. In the second part of the chapter, I turn to a discussion of its applicability in two cases.

Broadly speaking, two major groups of opinions can be distinguished concerning modernization.[3]

One group is formed from those who connect modernization to the modernity of thinking, which is rational, not bound by dogmas and traditions, and therefore accumulates knowledge with a confidence that everything is cognizable. This type of thinking advocates education as a means towards human improvement. There is a belief that autonomous personalities can be formed, and they consciously build their relations to others beyond the familial-kinship-local bonds in an awareness of their liberty and equality in the legal sense of the word. This is achieved within democratic political frameworks amongst individuals who have open minds for novelties (Knight 1956: 1097–98; Eisenstadt 2000: 4–7).

The other group is formed by those who focus on the relevance of the Industrial Revolution, on its technical and organizational aspects and on its social consequences. This stance, moreover, relies on the formation of nation-states with their educated and trained professionals in civil and military service, supposing that these transformations lead to a 'replacement of an entire way of life by another way of life' (Apthorpe 1979: 108–109; Tipps 1973: 199).

The common feature of the two approaches was the confrontational intention: to compare the new with an obsolete past.

The elements noted above, which appeared from the Renaissance in European history, were accumulated and associated together with an emergence of a world market. Scientific revolution in agriculture preceded the Industrial Revolution, but it was the Industrial Revolution that created the material basis in the form of commodities and incomes on which the outlined concept of modernity became a *Zeitgeist* in Western Europe in the last decades of the nineteenth century. This was reflected in the phraseology of economic historians, who spoke about 'modern' capital in opposition to 'age-old' or 'antideluvian' capital, like Karl Marx (1972 [1867]), Werner Sombart (1902) or Max Weber (2001 [1905]). Max Weber even used the term 'modernization' in connection with changes in Turkey and Japan in the second part of the nineteenth century (Weber 1927: 96, 380).

The whole process has been a product and a producer of the urban world with its factories in industrial and intellectual life (universities), with class struggle expressed in organized forms in political parties, with sophisticated social stratification and individualism in mass societies, with an increasing circle of goods for consumption, and with various occupations and activities leading to a multitude of life modes. An opposition based upon a division of labour existed between town and countryside since the dawn of civilization. It was a driving force of European history, as was emphasized by Marx (1972 [1867]: 373), but this relationship changed its character as the urban market economy started to conquer the rural economy with its supply and demand of commodities on a hitherto unimagined scale. As the commerce renders 'the superfluous useful, and the useful necessary' (Montesquieu 2001 [1748]: 359), the circle of wants increased and so agrarian producers had to satisfy new needs within their own families (and beyond). Equipped with new technologies, they were able to provision more and more others, which led to a decline in the overall number of agrarian producers within the active population. Economists found this figure a good marker of economic development when making comparisons between countries (Baade 1965: 74–106; Jánossy 1966: 41).

The Great Transformation (Polanyi 1944) of society as a whole was a long process, and the rural followed the urban example with a considerable delay in Europe before it was fully integrated. This fact was reflected in the sociological depiction of the ideal types of 'community' and 'society' by Tönnies (1887), who generalized certain features of the pre-industrial village and the industrial town, which were placed on a rural-urban continuum by Redfield (1960: 141), who separated them from their historical context.

This process was even more elongated in the eastern part of Europe than in the western part. The economic transformation followed the same pattern (Hobsbawm 1987: 49), but there was a thirty to fifty-year delay in the decline of the agricultural labour force ratio within the total labour force and a delay in eradicating illiteracy through the school system between 1850 and 1945 (Berend and Ránki 1969: 41; Grigg 1975). Moreover, there was a mentality that evaluated the individual according to his or her social status, as well as behavioural manifestations that were viewed as rooted in a feudal past that had survived the legal liquidation of serfdom in the second part of the nineteenth century. Taking these facts into account, it is not surprising that in order to follow the attractive example presented by the West, the term 'modernization' popped up as a demand in the Soviet Union for a short period in the 1920s, although it was soon superseded by the program of building socialism (Davies 2006: 72). Such development aimed to 'catch up' with the West, but in a different way that rejected a Western model of society and human existence: the objective was economic progress and an improvement of life conditions on the basis of collective property and with an emphasis on collective interests, which involved the limitation of individual liberty.

The peak of the term 'modernization' came in the 1950s and 1960s, when former colonies became independent in South Asia and Africa and the new states sought the most appropriate form of development on the one hand, and powers involved in a Cold War struggled for dominating them on the other hand. One option was socialism, as it existed in the Soviet Union, Mongolia, China and in East and Central Europe with attractive programmes of industrialization and full employment, but also with a limitation of individual freedom and wealth. In contrast, the *theory of modernization*, which flourished in the sociological and political thinking of the Western world in those years, promised transformation through engagement with a market economy that was connected to the (capitalist) world and with a pluralistic democracy. With a small initial investment in the form of support, it was believed that a society of affluence and freedom would develop, as exemplified by the United States and the former colonial powers in Western Europe (Gregory and Altman 1989: 34–35; Wolf 1982: 12–13). The application of the *theory of modernization* had dubious results. It has been successful, or at least has had a limited success, in some countries in East and South Asia, but did not have the expected results in Africa south of the Sahara. The widespread use of the word 'modernization' meant that it lost its connectedness with a capitalistic market economy and also found a place in the conceptual toolkit of the social sciences in socialist countries (Kulcsár 1982: 12–13).

To sum up: the different applications of the term 'modernization' included oppositions of new and old, urban and rural, West and East in Europe, centre and periphery in a transforming world, and in all applications, there was a connotation of the opposition of rich and poor, and the promise of development. Anthropologists who carried out fieldwork in the 1970s had to face one or more of these oppositions even if they formulated their research targets with other words and with a focus on certain aspects of a process of transformation of a whole way of life.

In this second part of this chapter, I reflect on one constituent of the modernization process on the basis of my fieldwork in villages in Hungary and Kenya. This constituent is the relevance of a combination of self-sufficiency and commodity production.

Certain forms of self-sufficiency and exchange are practised in every society, but their relevance varies quite significantly. The subordination of agrarian production to the rule of the market was a slow and long process, so self-sufficiency and commodity production, or more accurately participation in the market economy, was combined in many 'intermediate forms' (*Zwitterformen*). Thus, Marx, a contemporary of the Industrial Revolution on the Continent, realized that 'surplus labour is not extorted by direct compulsion from the producer, nor the producer himself yet formally subjected to capital', that is, 'capital has not yet acquired the direct control of the labour-process. Alongside independent producers who carry on their handicrafts and agriculture in the traditional old-fashioned way, there stands the usurer or the merchant' with his capital 'feeding on them ... The predominance, in a society, of this form of exploitation excludes the capitalist mode of production', but 'may serve as a transition' to it (1972 [1867]: 533).

In France, in the first decades of the nineteenth century, 69 per cent of the population lived in settlements with fewer than 2,000 inhabitants – that is, in villages – and the ratio of agrarian producers in the active population decreased from 51 per cent in 1872 to 10 per cent in 1975, by which time the producers had become fully integrated into the market economy and the peasantry had vanished (Mendras 2002; Vivier 2006: 1).

In Hungary, the similar ratios were 69 per cent in 1880, 44.8 per cent in 1941, 22.8 per cent in 1970 (Sárkány 1983a: 34), 17 per cent in 1990 and 6.2 per cent in 2001 (Csapóné 2005: 190). Ferenc Erdei, a great sociologist often referred to by Chris Hann (Hann 1980, 2006, among others), understood agricultural producers to be an underclass under a doubled social structure between the two World Wars. He thought that a historical-national structure preserved feudal traits alongside, and in combination with, a bourgeois structure during this time (1942) and he saw the future of agrarian producers in their embourgeoisement (Erdei 1980). The history created different opportunities and I suggest that the word 'peasant' lost its meaning in the era of socialism in the decade following the collectivization of agriculture that was completed by 1962 (Sárkány 1983a: 35). Yet the terminology was preserved in the official ideology; the government, controlled by the Hungarian Socialist Workers' Party, was called the 'government of workers and peasants'.

In Kenya, where I carried out fieldwork studying coffee production by smallholders in Kikuyu villages in the Nyeri District, mainly in Rititi in 1993 and 1995,[4] the rural population constituted more than two-thirds of the rapidly growing population of the country in 2019.[5]

Coffee was a cash crop; the people did not drink it in the villages. It was marketed through cooperatives, the people bought the chemicals through cooperatives, obtained loans from the Bank of the Cooperatives and were paid for their coffee in a complicated system of four instalments during the year. I conducted research in a period when the production of coffee rapidly fell as a consequence of decreasing coffee prices in the years leading up to my research, and my task was to find an explanation for the decline in production. As there was a state ban on the cutting down of the coffee trees, I observed the techniques people adopted when making use of the land on which the coffee trees stood. The land was cultivated using a horticultural method, with intercropping and with manual labour. The coffee tree plantations, though seemingly separated from other cultivated lands, were used by many for producing food crops, or the territory was treated as a pasture for cattle while neglecting the coffee trees. Most people knew very well how to take care of the coffee trees in order to obtain a greater yield, but very few put more effort into doing this, since the prospect of a good income was small. It happened that food plants, like beans, were planted between and under the trees, and this actually increased the yield of the coffee trees, because the smallholder added the necessary dung to the beans, which had a positive effect on the coffee trees. The harvest from the food plants could have been sold on the market too, but this rarely happened. It was obvious that having food for the domestic unit was the priority for the majority of the smallholders, who had very small holdings: 0.24 hectares per head, 1.36 hectares per family, while the range of the farms was between 0.02 and 8.5 hectares in the sample that I collected (with the help of local teachers) from a total of 164 households.

A particularly good example of avoiding the risk of not having sufficient food was presented by two sisters, who had a relatively big farm of 2.9 hectares. They had coffee trees on 1.2 hectares and as their late father had had entrepreneurial foresight, they also had seventy-seven macadamia nut trees, which brought in an annual income twenty-five times higher than that of their coffee trees. Despite this value, when I asked whether they would like to plant more macadamia trees, the answer was no, because other plants, food plants, do not grow under a nut tree. Other smallholders had a more entrepreneurial outlook in Rititi. One of the residents had a large farm and also a workshop for producing beds. The latter even employed a number of local people. Another man established a tree nursery and many tried to find jobs in addition to cultivating their gardens, which was mainly done by women in accordance with a traditional division of labour in the homestead (Kenyatta 1978: 53–55). Forms of – to quote a Hungarian saying that describes mixed activities – 'standing on several legs' were numerous and could include commuting to Nairobi as wage labourers working on construction sites or elsewhere. To see it from the other perspective: everyone in Rititi, including teachers, had and cultivated holdings.

It was possible to see a correlation between the use of a smallholding and its size, and the size of the family as well, but it did not explain everything.

It was obvious that the inspiring ideas of Karl Marx or Karl Polanyi are not sufficient for interpreting the variations of mixed economies, and the proposition of Pierre Bourdieu (1986) concerning three types of 'capital' (material, social and cultural) have a relevance when searching for an explanation. The market, I suggest, lies behind the decisions in the case of 'intermediate forms', even if the effort is to avoid the market where possible. The three types of 'capital' are rarely together in the desired quantity and quality in all the village cases, where adaptation to the encompassing economic relations was an imperative. To put it bluntly, poverty hinders modernization even if the state promotes it, as in the case of Kenya, where, for example, children learn a world language (English) and an East African regional language (Swahili) besides receiving education in their mother tongue during eight years in compulsory elementary schools. Education in the elementary school is free of charge in principle, but as a school uniform is compulsory and has to be bought by the parents, it contributes to the mounting costs, which must be covered. In villages of the Nyeri District, the educational level is high. In my sample, boys achieved an A level in two-thirds of the families and girls achieved an A level in one-third of the families in 1993 (as revealed in my questionnaires from the 164 households). Four children from Rititi went on to study at a university in 1993, which I knew, because I had the opportunity to contribute to their studies. The exchange was a kind of moral economy. Their mothers visited those in the village whom they presumed to be well-to-do persons in order to ask for contributions to the studies of their children, and I was classified in this category. Donations had a compensation: invitation for a lunch cooked by the mothers or by another female member of the family.

As I had no opportunity to continue my work in Rititi, I cannot say anything about changes since the mid-1990s, but as coffee production in Kenya has decreased since the years of my research (Karanja and Nyoro 2002: 29) and the mentioned proportion of agrarian producers within the active population is very high, it is most probable that the majority of inhabitants in villages in Nyeri continuously practise one or another 'intermediate form' of 'getting' a living.

Many features of this form of livelihood resonated with Varsány, Hungary, where people in 1972 remembered well the presocialist conditions, when 80 per cent of families were unable to survive from cultivating their holdings without another source of income, if they had any land at all. Many people would leave the village in late spring (May) in order to seek work in another part of the country, not returning until early November. The work was usually contract work on estates, agricultural wage labour in the village on estates, or working on construction sites. 'Standing on several legs' was a well-known form of living in rural settlements in a country where industrialization had a 100-year history, where obstacles to a market economy had been removed 80 years earlier, yet 72.4 per cent of agrarian producers' households had less than 3 hectares in 1935 (Oros 2002: 675), which was insufficient for earning a living. The state administration provided work for a few craftsmen who also lived in villages, but a desire to become self-sufficient was manifested in 1945, when the redistribution of the lands of the large estates was implemented. This was evident from the documents of land redistribution in Varsány (Sárkány 1983b, 1991).

During the Varsány project carried out by the Institute of Ethnology of the Hungarian Academy of Sciences, we hired a house from an old lady, whose family belonged to the rich 20 per cent before socialism, but not to the exceptional 6 per cent, who also had wage labourers and produced for the market. She summarized the image of a good life using a phrase of the socialist times: 'In those reactionary times we wanted to have a granary full, a stable full ... When we sold and bought animals at fairs the aim was that the number of legs [of the horses, cows, etc.] should be the same.' There was no cash crop in Varsány, which played a similar role to that of the coffee in the smallholders' economy in Kenya, but everything that was produced in agriculture was marketable. The main products were cereals, maize and fodder plants. However, there was widespread anxiety in engaging in the impersonal market forces, as was expressed in the following saying: 'If the weather is good and the harvest is abundant, the prices will be low. If the weather is bad the prices will be better, but we have nothing to sell.'

These conditions changed during the socialist period, when the farming cooperative absorbed the majority of agrarian producers. It was also true that others (first of all men) left the village for wage labour in industry or in the service sector, while women remained in the cooperative. However, a certain space was opened up for private agricultural production on household plots left for the use of members of the cooperative; in principle at least, household plots were 0.57 hectares in size and every family had gardens too. In practice, by the 1970s, the household plots were cultivated by the cooperatives and their owners received their yields after the harvest. Maize was given by the cooperatives and used to feed the pigs, of which one or two were bred and slaughtered at home. A few people used their possibilities for producing something for the market, for example, a bull calf for export to Italy, which was fattened with fodder from the cooperative (which also provided the market). However, such market-oriented private production did not reach the same level as that of the inhabitants of Tázlár, who worked in another type of cooperative

(Hann and Sárkány 2003). As industrial and service incomes were united in the households, they provided a chance for improving one's life conditions. Elderly people, who retired from the farming cooperatives, received a pension from 1966 onwards if they worked at least ten years in the cooperative. New houses, household utensils and factory-made dresses proved that village life was similar to or even better than life in the city. This was a real modernization with a socialist attribute (Hann 2013: 185). However, the perceived backwardness of the rural region was repeated again and again at Congresses of the Hungarian Socialist Workers' Party; village society and the general outlook on life has approached those of the city, but it has not yet caught up (Orbán 1983: 38). This was an ideological stance, proving the strength of those in the socialist party leadership who preferred to coordinate the economy as a whole in a similar manner to the way in which they coordinated industrial factories (that is, a bureaucratic rather than market coordination). Market coordination characterized agricultural production in cooperatives and in private production as well (Kornai 1992: 91–108).

A well-functioning, export-oriented agricultural system based upon the production of state farms and cooperatives was dissolved with a reprivatization of the lands after 1990, which again led to a size of holdings that was reminiscent of the situation in the presocialist conditions (Hann and Sárkány 2003: 133), though the rates have improved somewhat in the last few decades. Only a handful of farmers have been able to become agricultural entrepreneurs and many people have totally given up working on the land. The majority have combined entrepreneurial activities with wage labour and the cultivation of their lands, and the proportion of unemployed has been fairly high in the village (133 persons from a village of 1,691 inhabitants in 2011; this number has decreased due to state workfare programmes in recent times).[6]

The conditions of life were further 'modernized'. Tap water is available in houses, the aqueduct was finished by 1990 and a construction of channels followed it. As the borders are open, people may travel to Germany in order to work seasonally on asparagus farms, or travel to London to be waiters or servers in coffee houses while holding diplomas in European studies (in one case that I know well). They usually return and invest their earnings in order to improve their life conditions in Varsány or in its vicinity, because familial bonds remained strong in the village.

Focusing on the many individual variations in which farming activities can be combined with the ongoing relevance of non-agricultural activities, it is perhaps pertinent to finish with a question: is this the end of modernization or an ongoing delay?

Mihály Sárkány is Senior Honoris Causa at the Institute of Ethnology, Research Centre for the Humanities of the Eötvös Loránd Research Network (MTA Institute of Excellence) and a retired associate professor at the Department of Cultural Anthropology, ELTE University, Budapest, Hungary. His main research fields are economic anthropology, peasant studies, history and theories of sociocultural anthropology, and the transformation of contemporary rural economy and society both in Hungary and Africa.

Notes

1. In addition to his remarkable organizational and editorial achievements, Chris Hann is a very prolific author; therefore, I mention here only some of his major works (Hann 1980, 1985, 2019a; Hann and Bellér-Hann 1999; Bellér-Hann and Hann 2001; Hann and Hart 2011). His full bibliography is available on the webpage of the Max Planck Institute for Social Anthropology/Max-Planck-Institut für Ethnologische Forschung: http://www.eth.mpg.de/hann (retrieved 7 December 2020). It is also available at the end of this volume.
2. Chris Hann continues his research in the region of Hungary, where he carried out his first fieldwork and also extended his interest to a town, Kiskunhalas, near Tázlár (Hann 2019b).
3. There is a huge literature on modernization. I refer here to those authors whose formulations I found particularly apt.
4. The IFRA, Nairobi, made the research possible and I would like to express my gratitude to Mme Le Cour Grandmaison, the director of the institute in those years, and to her colleagues, especially to Bernhard Calas.
5. Retrieved 7 December 2020 from http://www.new-ag.info/en/country/profile.php?a=1787.
6. Népszámlálás 2011: 147, 167. Szenográdi 2020.

References

Apthorpe, Raymond. 1979. 'Peasants and Planistrators in East Africa, 1960–1970', in Bernardo Berdichewsky (ed.), *Anthropology and Social Change in Rural Areas*. The Hague: Mouton, pp. 89–120.
Baade, Fritz. 1965. *Versenyfutás a 2000 évig*. Budapest: Közgazdasági és Jogi Könyvkiadó.
Bellér-Hann, Ildikó, and Chris Hann. 2001. *Turkish Region: State, Market & Social Identities on the East Black Sea Coast*. Oxford: James Currey.
Berend, T. Iván, and György Ránki. 1969. *Közép-Kelet-Európa gazdasági fejlődése a 19. században*. Budapest: Közgazdasági és Jogi Könyvkiadó.
Bourdieu, Pierre. 1986. 'The Forms of Capital', in John G. Richardson (ed.), *Handbook of Theory and Research for the Sociology of Education*. New York: Greenwood Press, pp. 241–58.
Csapóné, Riskó Tünde. 2005. 'Agrárfoglalkoztatási helyzet Magyarországon, illetve az észak-alföldi régióban', *Competitio* 4(1): 189–200.

Davies, Robert W. 2006. 'The Modernisation of the Soviet Economy in the Interwar Years', in Markku Kangaspuro and Jeremy Smith (eds), *Modernisation in Russia since 1900*. Helsinki: Finnish Literature Society, pp. 71–83.
Eisenstadt, Samuel N. 2000. 'Multiple Modernities', *Daedalus* 129(1): 1–29.
Erdei, Ferenc. 1980. *A Magyar Társadalomról*. Budapest: Akadémiai Kiadó.
Gregory, Chris, and Jon Altman. 1989. *Observing the Economy*. New York: Routledge.
Grigg, David B. 1975. 'The World's Agricultural Labour Force 1800–1970', *Geography* 6(3): 194–202.
Hann, C.M. 1980. *Tázlár: A Village in Hungary*. Cambridge: Cambridge University Press.
———. 1985. *A Village without Solidarity*. New Haven: Yale University Press.
Hann, Chris. 2006. *'Not the Horse We Wanted!' Postsocialism, Neoliberalism, and Eurasia*. Münster: LIT.
———. 2013. 'Still an Awkward Class: Central European Post-Peasants at Home and Abroad in the Era of Neoliberalism', *Praktyka* 3(9): 177–98.
———. 2019a. *Repatriating Polanyi: Market Society in the Visegrád States*. Budapest: Central European University Press.
———. 2019b. 'Azok a 90-es évek Kiskunhalason – külföldi szemmel', in József Ö. Kovács and Aurél Szakál (eds), *Kiskunhalas története 4. Tanulmányok Kiskunhalasról a 20. század második feléből*. Kiskunhalas: Kiskunhalas Város Önkormányzata; Halasi Múzeum Alapítvány: Thorma János Múzeum, pp. 551–65.
Hann, Chris, and Ildikó Bellér-Hann. 1999. 'Peasants and Officials in Southern Xinjiang', *Zeitschrift für Ethnologie* 124(1): 1–32.
Hann, Chris, and Keith Hart. 2001. *Economic Anthropology*. Cambridge: Polity Press.
Hann, Chris, and Mihály Sárkány. 2003. 'The Great Transformation in Rural Hungary: Property, Life Strategies, and Living Standards', in Chris Hann and the "Property Relations" Group, *The Postsocialist Agrarian Question: Property Relations and the Rural Condition*. Münster: LIT, pp. 117–41.
Hobsbawm, Eric J. 1989. *The Age of Empire*. New York: Vintage Books.
Jánossy Ferenc. 1966. *A gazdasági fejlődés trendvonalai és a helyreállítási periódusok*. Budapest: Közgazdasági és Jogi Könyvkiadó.
Karanja, Andrew M., and James K. Nyoro. 2002. *Coffee Prices and Regulation and Their Impact on Livelihoods of Rural Community in Kenya*. Nairobi: Tegemeo Institute of Agricultural Policy and Development, Egerton University.
Kenyatta, Jomo. 1978. *Facing Mount Kenya*. Nairobi: Heinemann Kenya.
Knight, Frank H. 1956. 'The Responsibility of Freedom (Contribution to a Discussion: Man's Self-Transformation)', in William Thomas, Jr. (ed.), *Man's Role in Changing the Face of the Earth*. Chicago: University of Chicago Press, pp. 1096–102.
Kornai, János. 1992. *The Socialist System*. Oxford: Clarendon Press.
Kulcsár, Kálmán. 1982. 'A magyar falu és a magyar parasztság', in András Vágvölgyi (ed.), *A falu a mai magyar társadalomban*. Budapest: Akadémiai Kiadó, pp. 11–39.

Marx, Karl. 1972 [1867]. *Das Kapital. Kritik der politischen Ökonomie*, Vol. I. Berlin: Dietz Verlag.
Mendras, Henri. 2002. 'The Invention of the Peasantry: A Moment in the History of Post World War II French Sociology', *Revue Française de Sociologie* 43: 157–71.
Montesquieu, Charles de Seconda, Baron de. 2001 [1748]. *The Spirit of the Laws*. Kitchener: Batoche Books.
Népszámlálás 2011. 2013. *2011. Évi Népszámlálás. Vol. 3. Területi adatok. 3.13. Nógrád megye*. Miskolc: Központi Statisztikai Hivatal.
Orbán, Sándor. 1983. 'Átalakuló parasztság – változó parasztpolitika', *Társadalomtudományi Közlemények* 1: 36–42.
Oros, Iván. 2002. 'A birtokszerkezet Magyarországon', *Statisztikai Szemle* 80: 674–97.
Polanyi, Karl. 1944. *The Great Transformation: The Political and Economic Origins of Our Time*. Boston: Beacon Press.
Redfield, Robert. 1960. *The Little Community and Peasant Society and Culture*. Chicago: University of Chicago Press.
Sárkány, Mihály. 1983a. 'Parasztság és termelési viszonyok', *Népi Kultúra – Népi Társadalom* XIII: 21–35.
──────. 1983b. 'Economic Change in a Northern Hungarian Village', in Marida Hollos and Bela C. Maday (eds), *New Hungarian Peasants: An East-Central European Experience with Collectivization*. New York: Brooklyn College Press, pp. 25–55.
──────. 1991. 'Documents of Land Redistribution as Ethnographic Sources', in Timo Yliaho (ed.), *The Third Finnish-Hungarian Symposium on Ethnology in Konnevesi 20-25. 8. 1989*. Vol. I. Historical Sources. *Ethnos* 8(1): 119–24.
──────. 1992. 'Modernization, Cultural Pluralism and Identity. An Approach from Cultural Anthropology'. *Prospects* 22(1): 21–30.
Sombart, Werner. 1902. *Der moderne Kapitalismus*. Leipzig: Duncker & Humblot.
Szenográdi, Ferenc. 2020. 'A munkahelyteremtésre koncentrál
Varsány vezetése', *NOOL a Nógrád megyei hírportál* 2020. 06. 09. Retrieved 7 December 2020 from https://www.nool.hu/kozelet/ helyi-kozelet/a-munkahelyteremtesre-koncentral-varsany-vezetese-3272004.
Tipps, Dean C. 1973. 'Modernization Theory and the Comparative Study of Societies: A Critical Perspective', *Comparative Studies in Society and History* 15: 199–226.
Tönnies, Ferdinand. 1887. *Gemeinschaft und Gesellschaft*. Leipzig: Fues.
Vivier, Nadine. 2006. Agriculture and Economic Development in Europe. IEHC Helsinki Session 60. Retrieved 7 December 2020 from http://www.helsinki.fi/ iehc2006/papers2/Vivier.pdf.
Weber, Max. 2001 [1905]. *The Protestant Ethic and the Spirit of Capitalism*. New York: Routledge.
──────. 1927. *General Economic History*. New York: Greenberg.
Wolf, Eric R. 1982. *Europe and the People without History*. Berkeley: University of California Press.

Chapter 4

Something to Be Nostalgic About?
Goulash Socialist and Postsocialist Rural Society in Hungary

Nigel Swain

Chris and I go back a long way. We drove together to Hungary in the autumn of 1976 to begin our research: he ultimately to Tázlár, me to Budapest. We wild-camped a few miles short of the Austro-Hungarian border, crossed it at dawn and were in Budapest for breakfast. Thereafter I drove down to Tázlár roughly once a month until I left Hungary, to compare developments in his *szakszövetkezet* (specialist cooperative) village with the national picture that I was investigating. Chris has remained faithful to anthropology and, indeed, to Tázlár throughout his career. Amongst so much else in his oeuvre, he has produced a priceless chronicle of Tázlár from a workaholic to a TV-and-benefits-dependent community (Hann 2016a: 48). I have been more promiscuous academically and moved between sociology and social history, dabbling in economics, economic history, politics and latterly memory studies. It was in the context of teaching South Korean graduate students about postsocialist nostalgia that I came across Chris's podcast that serves as the starting point of this chapter (Hann 2016b). It is almost unique within the academic discussion of postsocialist nostalgia in arguing that valuable things were actually lost, that nostalgia has a real-world basis and that is not merely a regret for an imagined past, or an ironic reimagining of that past.[1] His podcast focuses in particular on how their loss of security deprived citizens of time for cultural activities. This chapter too places security centre stage, but it engages more with the material resources lost as socialist security disappeared, to be replaced by postsocialist insecurity and then widespread precarity.

Notes for this chapter begin on page 73.

Chris and I were of the generation that 'discovered' the 'second economy' in the planned economies of 'actually existing' socialism; we experienced it constantly in our everyday interactions; it stood at the heart of my first monograph (Swain 1985), and Chris wrote an important essay on it in his edited collection on market economy and civil society that appeared just as socialism was collapsing (Hann 1990). At the time, what we stressed – certainly what I stressed – was the mutual dependence of the 'second economy' on the first and vice versa: they were interrelated, not independent economies; the second provided income and commodities that the first could not, yet those active in the second depended on the first for basic income and social security benefits. Hungarian agriculture, and Hungary's variant of 'actually existing socialism', which was widely characterized as 'goulash socialism' (after the dish) because it was 'soft' and prioritized wellbeing, 'worked' because of the 'second economy' and its quasi-institutionalization within the first, that is, within the agricultural cooperatives (Swain 1985). But what I did not emphasis sufficiently at the time, because it was not an issue, was its security aspect. Security of employment in the 'first economy' was central to this symbiotic relationship. The 'second economy' provided much-needed additional income, but it was rarely more than that; it could not provide sufficient to substitute for the first economy income or pay for social insurance, certainly not at the high rate that the full-time self-employed would be expected to pay. It could not exist without the first, yet because of the generalized shortage characteristic of actually existing socialism (Kornai 1980), demand on the second economy was constant, so there was security from the second economy too. The first and second economies combined to give a security on which, by the second half of the 1970s, many rural communities were building, if not prosperity, then certainly new and more comfortable houses.

The consequence for enterprises of socialism's generalized shortage was that labour was always in short supply. Partly as a consequence, labour discipline was relatively lax and all sides (government, party, managers, unions and workers) valued workplace community identity, even if it was of a rather formulaic kind (Bartha 2013; Kott 2014; Scheiring 2020). In agriculture, the situation was slightly different. The dominant enterprise form was the producer cooperative in which members were obliged to work, so the management was duty bound to provide them with employment where possible. Yet a combination of the intrinsic seasonality of agricultural production and the increasing mechanization of parts of it made the provision of year-round employment problematic. This was a particular concern for women because, in the gendered employment structure of socialist farming, they figured highly amongst the 'unskilled' manual field labour workforce that was being replaced by machinery, while they did not qualify for the new, 'skilled' machine driving and controlling jobs because these were considered in legislation to be damaging to the female constitution (Asztalos Morell 1999: 336, 354).

Agricultural producer cooperatives in Hungary's goulash socialism took the task of providing out-of-season employment for their members, and particularly their female members, very seriously. On the Red Flag cooperative near Szolnok on the Hungarian Great Plain just east of the River Tisza that figured in my first monograph (Swain 1985), this was to be achieved by building greenhouse complexes for vegetable production. The managers concerned stressed to me on numerous occasions that they did not expect the venture to make much money, but they had a duty to provide employment. The economics were indeed complex. The venture was certainly economically worthwhile, because on my last visit in 1978, a second complex, doubling the capacity, was underway, and there were plans for adding a processing plant because their customers locally could not process the vast number of cocktail onions that the farm produced, a venture that engaged mainly women on a subcontracting basis. They received government subsidies for both investments, but these subsidies were dependent on the produce being exported. Presumably, whatever the short-term profitability of the venture, the fact that it opened access to government funding and perhaps channels to export marketing, while serving the socially desirable goal of providing jobs for the female membership, made the project worthwhile overall. Economic considerations were important, but the 'cash nexus' did not dominate.[2]

In the village of Lillavertes, further into the Great Plain than the home of the Red Flag farm, the cooperative had a pasta unit that employed some women, but the farm devoted more attention to social activities outside the farm: its sports group, the village House of Culture (community centre) including a significant library, the fire brigade and its financial contribution to the crèche and kindergarten. In the deep southwest of Hungary, in the ethnically Croatian village of Dravanova, the farm had a bottling and processing unit that employed women. In a neighbouring ethnically Hungarian village, the farm could not come up with a solution of its own, but subcontracted marrow processing to a local food industry enterprise, thus providing employment for women outside the high season from August to October, a deal that was beneficial for the women because their income from the marrow processing was approximately 50 per cent higher than their income from farm work. Thereafter, employment until the spring was found for some by contracting labour to a sugar enterprise where the women packed sugar.

A central feature in Hungary's quasi-institutional integration of the second economy in agriculture was the promotion and integration of both household-plot farming and subcontracted family-based farming on communal land. The Red Flag cooperative organized cocktail onion production on this kind of subcontracting basis on a large scale, as alluded to above. In Székhely the cooperative implemented such policies so extensively that in 1993, a villager noted ruefully to me that: 'The golden age of the coop organizing everything for the members has gone.' A similar echo of a 'golden age', when cooperatives had organized household plot fodder then vegetable production, then milk and animal sales for members, can be found in the qualitative research report from the 2010s by Gyöngyi Schwartz (2016: 309). In the Noble Grape cooperative, whose transformation into a holding company I followed in some detail (Swain 2000), household plot production was supported in the normal way, but there were no schemes to support family-based farming on communal land. Rather, it concentrated on first economy security and was amongst the first to introduce the payment of regular monthly incomes and paid holidays; it also supplemented family allowances and provided sickness payments before these became a legal requirement.

Despite goulash socialism's first and second economy security and congenial working conditions, it was popular discontent with its performance in the later 1980s that forced it into history. Pressure from below in 1988 and 1989 on the part of grassroots social entities that some labelled 'civil society' – a term Chris consistently criticized (Hann 2019) – became unstoppable, triggering factionalism within the party's once-united leadership, 'reform circles' within its grassroots, and ultimately its abdication from power (O'Neil 1998; Swain 1989, 2006a, 2006b). Kotkin's assertion that the Hungarian roundtable negotiations were merely a party 'self negotiation' and that elements in the party worked to 'fortify the loose anti-Communist opposition' is an ill-informed distortion (2009: 10, 11), as is Mark's claim that negotiated revolution in Hungary was accomplished 'almost entirely without popular participation' (2010: 3). Hungarian citizens demanded more democracy and a better life than goulash socialism could offer.

It is important to recognize, as has been demonstrated by Adam Fabry in particular (2019: 39–72), that in response to this manifestation of popular dissatisfaction with the achievements of goulash socialism, neoliberalism was not simply imposed on Hungary from outside, but had indigenous roots (in particular in Financial Research Plc., the successor to the Financial Research Institute). But that there was a meeting of minds and neoliberalism arrived in part 'by invitation' should not obscure the fact that no alternative was on offer other than joining the

European Union (EU) and adopting its increasingly neoliberal policies. Alice Amsden, Jacek Kochanowicz and Lance Taylor advocated a South Korean solution (1994), but their arguments went against the conventional wisdom of international financial organizations and found no support in the policy community. Chris notes that at the time, he was more attracted by the 'soft nationalism' of the Hungarian Democratic Forum with its more muted market rhetoric (2016a: 40). I was closer to friends in the Alliance of Free Democrats and trusted that the social liberalism of their sociologists would win out over the neoliberalism of their economists. Neither expectation was realistic. The postsocialist world would be a capitalism moulded by neoliberal priorities, which became, over time, a form of 'dependent capitalism' (Scheiring 2020; Swain 2011).

The 1990s were a time of momentous change in the countrysides of Central and Eastern Europe. I spent many years investigating those changes and then far too many more writing them up. I was perhaps over concerned with the big, 'world historical' question: what does the transition from socialism to capitalism look like, and which social groups emerge as the new postsocialist bourgeoisie? It was the managers, of course, or rather some managers, those with sufficient human, social and cultural capital (including market nous) to restructure, reorient and buy out the enterprises that they once managed (Swain 2000, 2011, 2013b). However, my focus on winners resulted in insufficient attention being paid to the losers, of which there were many. The standard response to market pressures of market-aware farm managers was to follow the solution suggested to the rural sociologist Pál Juhász by one of their ilk back in the 1970s: lease the land and sack two-thirds of the workforce (Swain 2013b: 92). Farm workforces did indeed fall rapidly by between a half and two-thirds. In some villages in the region (especially in Bulgaria), the impact of postsocialist transition was mitigated for a time by the continuation of a paternalistic mindset on the part of more traditional cooperative leaders, who attempted to offer some employment and continued to provide the services that the cooperative had offered in the past (Swain 2013b: 116–17, 127–31). Such paternalism was less common in Hungary, where much cooperative transformation took place in the context of bankruptcy.

In a traditionally industrial region in northern Hungary, the agricultural cooperative in Dombház (unusually) folded immediately, and postsocialist reality rapidly became apparent. State-sector, heavy-industry jobs quickly disappeared. One of the mayor's responses was the standard one of replacing socialist-era first-economy security with small-scale job-creation schemes, which could only benefit a minority of the newly unemployed. In parallel, a seemingly more innovative strategy was adopted in the form of creating a village dairy. But this attempt to create a commercial market business out of, in essence, 'second economy' dairying suffered from the evaporation of second-economy security: persistent market demand. Demand for their milk disappeared or, to be more precise, in a marketized economy with intense competition for a commodity as basic as raw milk, there was no demand at the price that these undercapitalized, small-scale producers were willing to accept. Events in Dombház well illustrate the disappearance of the dual security provided by Hungary's goulash-socialist integrated first and second economies: the loss of first-economy jobs on the one hand and the disappearance of second-economy demand on the other (Swain 2013b: 209–13).

The disappearance of security from the market coincided with the emergence of new market actors, driven by supply and demand, but also ready, as market actors are, to exploit a monopoly where they could. Chris has written about the term 'moral economy', categorizing it as a 'clumpish' concept of no contemporary resonance in Hungary (Hann 2018: 230). I share his reservations concerning 'moral economy' as an analytical concept, but the way in which some of our interviewees, particularly but not exclusively in Bulgaria (Swain 2013b: 118,132–33), referred to the new generation of 'middle men', who either refused to buy or paid insultingly low prices, echoed the complaints about 'Regrators, Engrossers, Forestallers, Hawkers and Jobbers' that Thompson described in eighteenth-century England (1971: 95). In both situations, a new and aggressive market logic was being imposed on producers who had been accustomed to certainty and security.

With the disappearance of employment and a secure market for household production, people had little choice but to retreat to self-provisioning and near-subsistence production. A pensioner couple from the northern Hungarian village of Tabar typified this approach. Regular purchases were restricted to basic items such as bread and cooking oil, while butter and sour cream were irregular luxuries. Meat came from the two pigs slaughtered each year and their 80–100 chickens, which also produced eggs, some of which were sold. The kitchen garden produced vegetables, some of which were eaten fresh, while the remainder were pickled for the winter. Similarly, some fruit was eaten fresh, while the remainder was turned into jams or syrups. Other articles came where possible from the secondhand 'Polish market', still the term used in Hungary for informal, car boot sale-type markets, a legacy of the socialist years when Poles were renowned for their long-distance informal trading (Swain 2013b: 93–94).

Many in the Eastern European countryside were fearful of EU membership and the prospects of increased competition from the West. What they did not appreciate sufficiently was that EU membership meant the extension to the new Member States of the Common Agricultural Policy (CAP) and its system of subsidies. Our research during the early years of transformation found that 1992 (the year in which the necessary legislation was passed in most countries) was a short-lived window of opportunity for those who wanted to create a farming venture from the remains of socialist agriculture, whether cooperative managers or small-scale private farmers. This changed with EU membership. Its accompanying generous subsidies produced renewed security, and farming, on what by Eastern European standards was still a modest scale, but would count as large-scale on the western side of the continent, became a viable option. Existing farmers breathed a sigh of relief and a new cohort could enter the fray (Hamar 2016: 371–72; Megyesi 2016: 295–96; Schwartz 2016: 318).

In 2014, I had the opportunity to meet some new and newly prosperous farmers from the same district in the deep south of Hungary to the west of the Danube. Simplifying greatly, they could be characterized as follows: Balázs was prospering because of EU subsidies; Feri's farm was only viable because of them; Pisti could embark on part-time farming because of them, with prospects for further development; while, thanks to them, the pensioner Laci had transformed a struggling chicken farm, which he had run since 1993, into a prosperous arable farm after 2007. Balázs could prosper on 20 hectares of vineyard, although an elderly couple with a well-established vineyard in a neighbouring village felt 40 hectares were essential. Pisti only had 20 hectares of arable land, hence his retention of a full-time job in a local German-owned company, but he dreamed of acquiring 100 hectares like a former colleague of his who had just given up his day job for full-time farming. Feri, a dairy farmer with 35 hectares, found them just sufficient to feed his herd. EU hygiene requirements had caused him serious problems, but the subsidies kept him afloat. Laci now had 80 hectares, but, despite living well from them, had ambitions to make it a round ton.

But the bulk of EU subsidies do not go to this new sector; rather, they go to the big farms that emerged from the postsocialist transformation process. The well-known distortions of the CAP that privilege already large-scale farmers have been amplified in Eastern Europe. In 2010, according to European Commission data, the 0.57 per cent of farms with incomes of over €100,000 annually received 34.56 per cent of direct payment subsidies, while the 95.39 per cent of farms with incomes under €20,000 annually received 40.17 per cent of them, and the 61.42 per cent of farms with incomes under €1,250 received just 6.72 per cent (Swain 2013a: 379). In 2014, according to the EU's Farm Accountancy Data Network survey, which intentionally excludes small farms, the 7 per cent of farms with incomes of over €100,000 received 55.3 per cent of decoupled subsidies, while 74.8 per cent of farms with incomes of under €25,000 received 20.7 per cent of them.³ These distortions would be less of a problem if the farms that benefited from them were major village employers, but they are not. In fact, farms employ fairly few villagers. By the 2010s, only 7.7 per cent of farms surveyed by Csurgó, Kovách and Megyesi employed more than five people, and 43 per cent of them supported no full-time employee at all (2016: 67), while generally the number of full-time employees in agriculture fell in the decade between 2003 and 2013 (Koós 2016: 90). Agriculture is prospering because of subsidies, and businesspeople and politicians alike are investing extensively in land and farming businesses (Swain 2016: 579), but agriculture is increasingly divorced from villages and their economies. What is more, the polarization between rural communities that exists throughout Europe, from peri-urban suburban villages clustered around the capital or regional centres on the one hand to isolated poverty-stricken peripheral communities on the other, is much starker in the eastern half of the continent (Swain 2016: 585–87). Postsocialist industry is heavily dependent on Western investment (Swain 2011) and tends to be located within easy reach of the West. Beyond that belt, which includes Noble Grape village – which, an easy commute from Veszprém, is experiencing an influx of townies in search of affordable and spacious housing – there is much less scope for the development of non-agricultural employment. The consequence for Hungary is extreme deprivation in some rural areas, in particular in the northeast and southwest.⁴

In the more than a quarter of a century that has elapsed since the main legislation for agricultural restructuring in Central and Eastern Europe was implemented, social scientists have discovered the 'precarity' of labour in the neoliberal order (Standing 2011). In Hungary, the key policy tool introduced to address precarity has been a variant of workfare schemes, which have existed in the United States since the 1970s and became increasingly common across Europe as neoliberal policies were adopted (Keller et al.: 13). Reading some of the literature on rural workfare, my initial response was déjà vu, for little has changed since the 1990s: mayors, made impotent by reduced revenues, using their best and perhaps prejudiced judgement about who exactly are the deserving poor, dispense a small amount of largesse together with some job-creation schemes. The difference is that, a quarter of a century on, there is both a little less and a little more: local authorities now have even less revenue for their own largesse, but there is a rather more generous and systematic job-creation option in the form of state-supported workfare.⁵

My second reaction to Hungarian workfare, in particular to the Start Model Programme version of the schemes, which allows for the creation of social agricultural cooperatives, growing mainly fruit and vegetables for local, predominantly noncommercial outlets, was a profound sense of irony: a quarter of a century after the collapse of socialism and the introduction of the all-pervasive marketplace of neoliberalism, policy-makers have rediscovered agricultural producer cooperatives as a means of addressing rural poverty. This irony is not lost on the participants either. Tázlár has one such venture, and Chris refers to 'wry comments to the effect that *közmunka* (the Hungarian term) was becoming a new form of collective farming' (Hann 2018: 243). Monika Váradi similarly notes that mayors complain they are being obliged to become 'collective farm chairmen' (2015: 87).

Hungary's rural workfare schemes have been much analysed. They began in 2009 and developed significantly in 2011 and 2013; there is overwhelming evidence that they are not good at creating 'real jobs', and the tensions that inevitably develop between existing farmers and subsidized social producers remain unresolved (Keller et al. 2016: 15–18). Nevertheless, there can be no denying that they have become well established and locally embedded. In the absence of anything else, they provide security, admittedly low-paying, but secure – the bottom line of socialism. They restore that measure of security above the poverty line that the cash nexus removed, acting, perhaps, as a 'moral economy'. Chris prefers 'moral community' (2018: 249) and elsewhere describes them as a 'benign aspect of a counter movement to the rise of a capitalist market society in Hungary since the end of the Kádár era' (2016a: 54). My verdict is less positive. The conditions attached to the benefits, the substance of much liberal criticism, really are intrusive. Not only are welfare benefits dependent on taking part in the schemes, but the conditions attached also include requirements that, though apparently trivial, are profoundly influenced by racial stereotyping, such as insisting that the recipient's children not miss 50 days of schooling (Keller et al. 2016: 14) and keeping their gardens tidy (Asztalos Morell 2014: 5). More importantly, the schemes' state-controlled yet devolved structure makes them entirely dependent on local mayors, their personalities and experience. Not only has the current Hungarian government rediscovered agricultural producer cooperatives, it has also reintroduced the omnipotent 'small kings' (*kis királyok*) of socialist-era local administration. Inclusion in or exclusion from the schemes is a local decision: whether they operate to help the Roma (as in Uszka studied by Ildikó Asztalos Morell (2014)) or exclude the Roma (as was the case in some villages studied by Judit Keller and her colleagues (Keller et al. 2016: 21)), and whether they distinguish between 'deserving and undeserving' or 'capable and incapable' (Kovai 2016: 148) depends on mayors alone.

The cover of my book on Central European rural restructuring in the 1990s shows the never-used office building of a Czech agricultural producer cooperative, which was completed as socialism ended – a symbol of collectivization's over ambitious project to industrialize agriculture (Swain 2013b). Concluding this chapter, the image of another socialist-era building comes to mind – that of a friend's parental (peripheral) village home, built at the beginning of the 1970s rural housing boom, empty now and unsold because it is worth so little, a symbol of the demise of something altogether more precious: a working community. Eastern European socialism was flawed: it could not have survived in the long term; it ignored too many market signals. However, systemic ignoring of the market was replaced by neoliberal subordination to it. In consequence, many in rural Hungary, when looking back from the precarity of the postsocialist present to the security of the goulash socialist past, really do have something to be nostalgic about.

Nigel Swain is Honorary Senior Research Fellow in the Department of History at the University of Liverpool, United Kingdom, where he taught until 2016. He has published extensively on the political, economic and social history of Eastern Europe since 1945, on the 'change of system' and early postsocialism in Hungary, and on rural society in Hungary and Eastern Europe in both the socialist and postsocialist years.

Notes

1. For postsocialist nostalgia, see, for example, Luthar and Pušnik (2010); and Todorova and Gille (2010).
2. This paragraph and the next one are based on research notebooks from 1976–78.
3. Author's calculations. For the FADN, see https://ec.europa.eu/agriculture/rica/database/consult_std_reports_en.cfm (retrieved 7 December 2020).
4. For a graphic illustration, see Keller et al. (2016: 12).
5. Ildikó Asztalos Morell's study (2014) is unusual in analysing the importance of public works from as early as 1994.

References

Amsden, Alice H., Jacek Kochanowicz and Lance Taylor. 1994. *The Market Meets Its Match: Restructuring the Economies of Eastern Europe*. Cambridge, MA: Harvard University Press.

Asztalos Morell, Ildikó. 1999. *Emancipation's Dead-End Roads? Studies in the Formation and Development of the Hungarian Model for Agriculture and Gender 1956–89*. Uppsala: Uppsala University.

_____. 2014. 'Workfare with a Human Face: Innovative Utilizations of Public Work in Rural Municipalities in Hungary', *Metszetek* 3(4): 3–20.

Bartha, Eszter. 2013. *Alienating Labour: Workers on the Road from Socialism to Capitalism in East Germany and Hungary*. New York: Berghahn Books.

Csurgó, Bernadett, Imre Kovách and Boldizsár Megyesi. 2016. 'Fölhasználat, Üzemtípusok, Gazdálkodók', in Katalin Kovács (ed.), *Földből Élők: Polarizáció a Magyar Vidéken*, Budapest: Argumentum, pp. 37–68.

Fabry, Adam. 2019. *The Political Economy of Hungary: From State Capitalism to Authoritarian Neoliberalism*. Cham: Palgrave Pivot.

Hamar, Anna. 2016. '"Itt . . . mezőgazdaság . . . ?!"', in Katalin Kovács (ed.), *Földből Élők: Polarizáció a Magyar Vidéken*. Budapest: Argumentum, pp. 359–84.

Hann, C.M. 1990. 'Second Economy and Civil Society', in Chris Hann (ed.), *Market Economy and Civil Society in Hungary*. London: Frank Cass, pp. 21–44.

Hann, Chris. 2016a. 'Cucumbers and Courgettes: Rural Workfare and the New Double Movement in Hungary', *Intersections: East European Journal of Society and Politics* 2(2): 38–56.

_____. 2016b. 'How Is Nostalgia Felt in Post-Socialist Hungary?', Latest Thinking Podcast. Retrieved 7 December 2020 from https://lt.org/publication/how-nostalgia-felt-post-socialist-hungary; https://www.eth.mpg.de/cms/en/media/latest_thinking_hann_hungary.

_____. 2018. 'Moral(ity and) Economy: Work, Workfare, and Fairness in Provincial Hungary', *European Journal of Sociology* 59(2): 225–54.

_____. 2019. *Repatriating Polanyi: Market Society in the Visegrád States*. Budapest: Central European University Press.

Keller Judit, Katalin Kovács, Katalin Rácz and Nigel Swain. 2016. 'Workfare Schemes as a Tool for Preventing the Further Impoverishment of the Rural Poor', *Eastern European Countryside* 22: 5–26.

Koós, Bálint. 2016. 'A Földből Élők – A Mezőgazdaság Foglalkoztatási Funkciója', in Katalin Kovács (ed.), *Földből Élők: Polarizáció a Magyar Vidéken*. Budapest: Argumentum, pp. 69–96.

Kornai, János. 1980. *The Economics of Shortage*. Amsterdam: North Holland.

Kotkin, Stephen. 2009. *Uncivil Society: 1989 and the Implosion of the Communist Establishment*. New York: Random House.

Kott, Sandrine. 2014. *Communism Day-to-Day: State Enterprises in East German Society*. Ann Arbor: University of Michigan Press.

Kovai, Cecília. 2016. 'Önellátó Függőség', in Katalin Kovács (ed.), *Földből Élők: Polarizáció a Magyar Vidéken*. Budapest: Argumentum, pp. 137–60.

Luthar, Breda, and Maruša Pušnik. 2010. *Remembering Utopia: The Culture of Everyday Life in Socialist Yugoslavia*. Washington DC: New Academic Publishing.

Mark, James. 2010. *The Unfinished Revolution: Making Sense of the Communist Past in Central-Eastern Europe*. New Haven: Yale University Press.

Megyesi, Boldizsár. 2016. 'A Zalaszentgróti Kistérség', in Katalin Kovács (ed.), *Földből Élők: Polarizáció a Magyar Vidéken*. Budapest: Argumentum, pp. 281–304.

O'Neil, Patrick H. 1998. *Revolution from Within: The Hungarian Socialist Workers' Party and the Collapse of Communism*. Cheltenham: Edward Elgar.
Scheiring, Gábor. 2020. *The Retreat of Liberal Democracy: Authoritarian Capitalism and the Accumulative State in Hungary*. Cham: Palgrave Macmillan.
Schwartz, Gyöngyi. 2016. 'A Böhönyei Mikrotérség Agrárfolyamatai', in Katalin Kovács (ed.), *Földből Élők: Polarizáció a Magyar Vidéken*. Budapest: Argumentum, pp. 305–30.
Standing, Guy. 2011. *The Precariat: The New Dangerous Class*. London: Bloomsbury Academic.
Swain, Nigel. 1985. *Collective Farms Which Work?* Cambridge: Cambridge University Press.
_____. 1989. 'Hungary's Socialist Project in Crisis', *New Left Review* 176: 3–29.
_____. 2000. 'From Kolkhoz to Holding Company: A Hungarian Agricultural Producer Co-operative in Transition', *Journal of Historical Sociology* 13(2): 142–71.
_____. 2006a. 'The Fog of Hungary's Negotiated Revolution', *Europe-Asia Studies* 58(8): 1347–75.
_____. 2006b. 'Negotiated Revolution in Poland and Hungary, 1989', in Kevin McDermott and Matthew Stibbe (eds), *Revolution and Resistance in Eastern Europe: Challenges to Communist Rule*. Oxford: Berg, pp. 139–55.
_____. 2011. 'A Post-Socialist Capitalism', *Europe-Asia Studies* 63(9): 1671–95.
_____. 2013a. 'Agriculture "East of the Elbe" and the Common Agricultural Policy', *Sociologia Ruralis* 53(3): 369–89.
_____. 2013b. *Green Barons, Force-of-Circumstance Entrepreneurs, Impotent Mayors: Rural Change in the Early Years of Post-Socialist Capitalist Democracy*. Budapest: Central European University Press.
_____. 2016. 'Eastern European Rurality in a Neo-liberal and European Union World', *Sociologia Ruralis* 56(4): 574–96.
Thompson, E.P. 1971. 'The Moral Economy of the English Crowd in the Eighteenth Century', *Past and Present* 50: 76–136.
Todorova, Maria, and Zsuzsa Gille (eds). 2010. *Post-Communist Nostalgia*. New York: Berghahn Books.
Váradi, Monika Mária. 2015. 'Szegénység, Projektek, Közpolitikák', *Tér és Társadalom* 29(1): 69–96.

Chapter 5

Man Does Not Live by Bread Alone
The Indivisibility of Economic and Discursive Aspects in Neoliberal and Populist Regimes in Poland

Michał Buchowski

In this chapter, I address the issue of Central European economic and political transformation that started in 1989 in the former communist polities and socialist societies. In the process, the Cold War global order has been transformed into a post-Cold-War one (Chari and Verdery 2009). It involved multidimensional and interrelated reconfigurations in the economic, political and social domains. These reconfigurations were inherently intertwined with the images present in collective consciousness that shaped public discourses, and in which certain narratives managed to gain hegemonic status. In other words, I argue that the post-1989 transformations were grounded in economic, social and political conditions, but that the role of cultural aspects should not be neglected. Combining the material and the mental aspects helps us to understand why in some postsocialist societies, many people became so keen on right-wing populism and nationalism. In order to present my argument, first I paint, with a broad brush, the structural framework in which transformation processes took place and social actors played their part. Next, I cite some selected data showing how, measured by pure economic indexes, an escape from the dire communist economic results was efficacious. Finally, I seek mechanisms that, despite economic growth in postsocialist countries, have brought about populism and nationalism. Although several statements have greater relevance for the whole Central Europe, my focus here is on the case of Poland.

Notes for this chapter begin on page 86.

(Post)Communism and (Post)Socialism

Communism was an authoritarian *political regime* in which, in principle, the monopoly of one party was a dogma. *Socialism* was *a socioeconomic-cultural system* in which *societies ruled by communist authorities* lived and functioned.[1] This conceptual distinction by no means implies that the political regime was separate from society or that political and social actors did not comprise an integrated whole. Under the pressure of rebelling populations that became tired and weary of an inefficient economy, in some cases a permanent shortage economy (Verdery 1996: 19–37), and a rigid political regime called 'socialist democracy',[2] political alliances in Central Europe were reshuffled within the period of less than half a year. If one accepts Zygmunt Bauman's distinction of 'political' and 'systemic' revolutions, the first being just a makeshift of political arrangements and the second a change of governance reshaping the political, economic and social order (Bauman 1992: 156–57), then, in hindsight, the 1990s was a systemic revolution. As a result, a new *postcommunist political regime* with principles of liberal democracy has been accepted and, by analogy, a complex socioeconomic-cultural system we call *postsocialism* has emerged.

A globally framed historical contingency that led to the end of the Cold War resulted in a specific variant of capitalism called *neoliberalism* – known as Thatcherism in the United Kingdom and Reaganomics in the United States – introduced in the former Communist Bloc after 1989. As Joseph Stiglitz admits: 'The heyday of the neoliberal doctrine was probably 1990–1997 after the fall of the Berlin Wall' (2001: xv). Implementation of neoliberalism in postsocialist societies was known under the guise of *shock therapy*,[3] advocated, among others, by Leszek Balcerowicz in Poland.[4] This economic project was sponsored by several Western governments and international institutions, such as the World Bank, the International Monetary Fund, the Paris Club and the London Club, and later the European Union. This process was highly complex and painstakingly documented, including in anthropological literature (e.g. Buchowski et al. 1999; Berdahl et al. 2000; Burawoy and Verdery 2000; Hann 2002; Kürti and Skalník 2009).[5] Experts flooded capital cities and advised local governments how to run companies without knowing a lot about local specificities. Since experts usually did not see much outside of the hotel premises where they stayed, they earned the label of 'Marriott Brigades' (Wedel 1998). It is symptomatic that this tag was named after the luxurious hotel chain.

One of the tenets of the postcommunist 'new deal' accepted at the top political level was an extraordinarily rapid privatization of state-owned companies. David Harvey (2004) describes this as accumulation through dispossession, by which wealth is concentrated in the hands of a small number of capitalists who acquire it by privatizing public property. In public eyes, and as many court documents reveal, it was carried out by partly corrupt and criminal elites. The restructuring of the economic system ensued enormous social changes. Several thousand industrial plants across Central and Eastern Europe were shut down, inevitably inflicting growing unemployment, a phenomenon unknown in the communist past. Industrial devolution was so hasty and widespread that as late as the early 2000s, a quarter of the working-age population in Poland was jobless; in some desolated regions of Poland, the unemployment rate reached 50 per cent. Simultaneously, agricultural land was privatized. Although in Poland in this sector, privatization was applicable to only one-fifth of the tilled land – due to the fact that during socialist times almost 80 per cent of the land remained in private ownership – this comprised an enormous property stretching over four million hectares. Many of the two million farmers felt threatened by the sudden reassessment of interest rates of their bank loans and widening price scissors. Disbanded almost overnight in 1993, state farms left at least 200,000 agricultural workers unemployed and without any serious prospects for supporting their families. In many dilapidated rural areas, one could see people picking mushrooms and berries in the forest and then trying to sell them on roadsides to travellers, as if they were returning to a gathering type of economy.

Therefore, the social dissatisfaction of vast groups of society was a result of unemployment resulting from the closure of huge industrial plants in big cities that were once former 'Solidarity' movement strongholds, while the forlorn situation in small towns was due to the closure of local industries after decades of operation, as well as the miserable situation of countryside manual workers and farmers. Many protested against such a sweeping disordering of their lives (see Ekiert and Kubik 1999), but their protest was fragmented, dispersed and quelled. Even trade union leaders supported the reform. As Janusz Steinhoff, a minister in the former government, admits, 'we have to realise that at that time "Solidarity", as a trade union and social movement ... supported these reforms. At that time all felt responsibility and necessity to take decisions that were controversial in the public perception' (Sandecki 2020).

The invention and circulation of discourses legitimizing these reforms played a significant role in making shock therapy possible. To say that discourses alone govern social processes privileges culturalist explanations to an extent that I do not support. In general, I opt for seeking reasons for the implementation of neoliberal reforms, and the ensuing resistance to it, from a globalization perspective. Accepted in Central Europe, economic neoliberalism[6] has transformed the region into a semi-periphery in relation to the most advanced economic countries (Shields 2009). This had an effect on class relations (Buchowski 2017). My stance dovetails with 'relational realism', which 'concentrates on the situated social mechanisms and spatiotemporal sequences of capital, labor, states, and social reproduction' (Kalb 2018: 305). In my view, an interpretive framework should not just consider but should also emphasize the role of public discourses in co-shaping social images, political and economic ideologies and practices. Discourses are an inseparable part in establishing complex and hierarchical relations between both global and local capital, and between owners of transnational capital, wealth and resources and their local compradors. Discourses are inherent in struggles between conflicting classes realizing their egoistic interest, and between political classes and states competing for investments or seeking to control production, consumption, flows of capital and labour. In order to wield respective populations' imagery and, at least in liberal democracies, win voters' support, dominant classes – operating in accordance with rules identified by Antonio Gramsci (1994) – participate in a production and circulation of discourses that assume hegemonic status. This implicates that certain worldviews, images about the 'natural order of things', power, hierarchy and social relations dominate collective consciousness. Counterdiscourses were always proposed, but were dwarfed by neoliberal ones. The latter were fortified by many academics – not only economists, but also political scientists and sociologists, intellectual compradors of neoliberalism.

How was it possible that neoliberal discourses could gain an upper hand and become so influential? Two main causes for this can be noted. First, there is an *ideological* reason. In the anti-communist impulse, a decisive majority of postsocialist societies rejected the past and embraced the promise of the affluent future. 'Catching up with the West' was one of the driving forces of the reforms. Knowledge of the essentialized West among people was typical to outsiders who had never lived in it. It was a myth about Western lifestyles and high standards of living. Reformers received advice from the experts recruited from the ranks of neoliberal economists. Decisions and actions were aimed at building instant capitalism and new agile, entrepreneurial, mobile subjects, as opposed to stagnant 'socialist dinosaurs'. Imminent wealth would come to those eager to join a middle class. All in all, most decisions and actions were driven by a desire to break away from communism and join the privileged Western club. The second reason is more *theoretical*: 'The neoliberal programme tends to construct in reality an economic system corresponding to the theoretical description, in other words a kind of logical machine, which presents itself as a chain of constraints impelling the economic agents' (Bourdieu 1998: 96). In other words, economic practices and their elucidations, or the material and mental aspects of the social reality, comprise a tightly integrated whole that is difficult to challenge. An extension of this machine, or rather its inexorable part, were discourses sanctioning social shifts that accompanied economic transformations. Creating a class of postcommunist orphans, living skeletons of the past, of losers, of people unable to adapt and also of those who stay on the way to 'capitalist normality' and 'European modernity', was a necessity. Often referred to as 'lost in transition', people were presented in dominant discourses not as entrapped in a structural framework brought about by neoliberal reforms, but as victims of their own mental and cultural vices. An image of social classes of losers presumably 'unable to adapt' to the new 'natural' socioeconomic and political order appear as an inevitable cog in the functioning of Bourdieu's logical machine.

Impressive Economic Performance: Some Data

The first difficult years of transformation passed and the restructured economy slowly recuperated. Joining the European Union in 2004 gave additional impulse for further development. Indeed, in economic terms, the results look good. Let me provide some data.

If 1989 is taken as the baseline (= 100), then gross domestic product, consumption and accumulation in Poland by 2013 almost doubled. The cumulative real increase in gross domestic product in the years 1996–2016 reached 119 per cent, with an average annual growth rate of about 4 per cent. Systematically, starting from 1994, real gross disposable income in the household sector increased, and in 2013 reached almost 160 per cent of income from 1989, and in 2014 increased to the level of US$18,000 per capita. Gross monthly salaries reached 130 per cent. The average value of household assets since the mid-1990s has more than doubled to almost US$15,000. The average annual salary measured in purchasing power parity increased from US$16,000 in 1996 to US$24,000 in 2015. In the same period, the real annual salary increased by approximately 59 per cent. Contrary to popular opinion, income inequality decreased in the period 2004–13, and officially the Gini coefficient[7] dwindled from 37.6 to 30 per cent. Total agricultural production increased to 130 per cent, and goods produced from industry, construction and assembly production increased threefold (all data: *Polska* 2014, 2016).

Similar improvements are evident in the social welfare sector. Life expectancy increased by over five years, from 72.2 years in 1996 to 77.3

years in 2014. The enrolment rate (i.e. the proportion of students in the population between nineteen and twenty-four years old) at the higher education level increased from below 10 per cent in the early 1990s to over 50 per cent today. Poland belongs to the group of Organisation for Economic Co-operation and Development (OECD) countries with the highest share of people aged twenty-five to sixty-four having at least basic vocational education (90.8 per cent). In the period between 1996 and 2015, the employment rate of the adult population increased by 4.5 per cent to 62.9 per cent, but it was still one of the lowest among OECD countries. High unemployment in the first decade of transformation, which – as mentioned above – at the beginning of this century exceeded 20 per cent, decreased in 2015 to 7.5 per cent and at the end of October 2019 was just above 5 per cent.

Impressive economic results have to be put in a comparative perspective. Fulfilling consumption and lifestyle aspirations is relativized to other social groups or countries. For example, the average annual per capita salary was almost half the average for OECD countries, which was US$41,000. The increase in wages was accompanied by an increase in the price of consumer goods and services – by 1996, it had reached 157 per cent; in the meantime, in the OECD countries, it rose on average 'only' by 73 per cent. The fertility rate in Poland decreased from 1.59 in 1996 to 1.29 in 2014, which, of course, does not ensure a simple generational reproducibility (*Polska* 2016). The lowering of the unemployment level was partly due to ample emigration. It was estimated that at the end of 2015, about 2,397,000 inhabitants of Poland lived at any given moment either as permanent or temporary residents in other countries. Most of them – 2,098,000 – were in Europe; of them, around 1,983,000 resided in EU Member States (Notka informacyjna 2016: 2). This means that over 6 per cent of the country's inhabitants had migrated.

These positive statistical data are in contradiction to the increasingly widespread rejection of neoliberalism. Economically successful reforms undeniably improved average living standards, especially if one compares these results to the communist past as well as to the hard times in the 1990s. Thus, one might ask the following question: why did a large section of the population show dissatisfaction with and vote for political forces that criticize a neoliberal economic set-up and a social pecking order based on values implied by neoliberalism? Relativizing material upgrade to other social groups and nations only partly explains the negative critical perception of neoliberal reforms by so many social strata in Poland.

Social Hierarchy, Identity and 'Populism'

As mentioned above, in the newly established neoliberal order of things and people, social hierarchies have been redefined. Workers, agricultural workers, small farmers, 'hopeless' sectors of the communist intelligentsia incapable of transforming into 'experts' or entrepreneurs were condemned and dubbed as legendary *Homo sovieticus*, people exhibiting a passive, lazy, irresponsible, envious and demanding post-Soviet mentality (Sztompka 1993). It became a derogatory descriptor of all people seen as underdogs. It also acquired a status of an analytical category used widely by philosophers, political scientists and sociologists (Buchowski 2006). Those who hold a socialist mentality could not match their mirror image of the self-acclaimed elites, who put themselves at the top of the social ladder. Elites were comprised, on the one hand, by intellectuals, supposedly intrinsically Westernized and unspoiled by the *Homo sovieticus* syndrome, and, on the other hand, by the crème de la crème of the new economic and political order, inventive entrepreneurs and pro-Western politicians.

Over time – a changing economic situation and generational change – the category of *Homo sovieticus* exhausted its elucidatory power and no longer spoke to people's imagination. In order to render the ongoing processes, to capture social relations and to legitimize exclusion of some groups from society's 'civilizationally correct' mainstream, new categories were invented. The criteria for internal social divisions shifted from those based on the image of the 'post-Soviet mentality' to cultural features ascribed to classes defined by elites as plebeian. In the process, some characteristics associated with the old derogatory categories melted into the new label. Compatibility with the West, which involves living a liberal lifestyle and sharing cosmopolitan cultural values, started to serve as criterion for classification. The category of *mohair berets* gained popularity. The term refers to a specific head cover made of knitted mohair commonly used by older, often devout ladies. It describes social groups primarily associated with Radio Maryja, a Catholic radio station, now a media conglomerate, higher education institution and religious centre, established by Redemptorist Father Tadeusz Rydzyk, closely tied with the Law and Justice party that has been in power in Poland since 2015. Rydzyk is famous for his anti-European, conservative Catholic views with respect to moral norms and right-wing rhetoric. After some years, *mohair berets* morphed into the following, partly related categories. The first of them is *Janusze i Grażyny* (literary Januses and Graces, metaphorically Bills and Suzys). In this new distinction, a distance between older people – who still recall communist times – and the younger generation is emphasized. *Janusze i Grażyny* represent a lower-middle class still sharing some cultural habits perceived as reaching back to the communist past. The second and subsequent incarnation, invented by a new middle class of youngsters, who feel some kind of superiority towards (what they perceive as) less cultured peers is *Sebas and Karynas* (literally, Sebastians and Carinas, metaphorically Chads and Stacys). It stands for a lower-middle class, *parvenue*, relatively young people behaving boorishly, wearing tracksuits in public and going for all-inclusive holidays to resorts filled with people similar to them, spending most of their time by a hotel pool and consuming alcoholic drinks. The invention of such culturally inferior groups again reveals a pertinent social problem. The self-nominated elites create groups sharing cultural values that they perceive as tasteless. Invented uncultured groups are ridiculed and presented as inferior. An opposition between 'modern' and 'cosmopolitan' elites and a 'backward' and 'parochial' underclasses, analogical to the former opposition between 'progressive neoliberals' and 'staunch dinosaurs of socialism', is re-created and reproduced. The mechanisms are similar, only the organizing idioms and contents have been changing over time. In any case, it is a differently articulated *classism*.

The relationship between dominating and dominated classes is dialectical. Discriminatory practices inevitably generate resistance on the part of social classes made inferior. One may say that those wielding public discourses impose their view upon groups constructed as subalterns who do not necessarily subscribe to this kind of hierarchy. Discredited classes oppose their sociosymbolic subjugation. Political movements appear voicing concerns of condemned people. Politicians merely facilitate the transformation of anger and feelings of inferiority into a defiance of economic and cultural domination. They coordinate and coagulate dispersed anxieties into political action and transform subalterns from a class 'in itself' into a class 'for itself'. Resistance to hegemonic neoliberal and cosmopolitan discourses surfaced and prevailed in Poland in 2015, a year of presidential and parliamentary elections that brought right-wing politicians to power.

Upheaval of the Disdained

Sensing the tiredness of several social groups after two and a half decades of disparaging discourses, as well as resentment of elite's groups' haughtiness, right-wing politicians offered a political programme ennobling 'parochial' identity, lifestyle and cultural traditions, and blaming elites for all misfortunes of 'ordinary people'. Pitting 'the people' and 'the elites' against each other is a crucial part of the populist ideology that one can find in handbooks (see Mudde and Rovira Kaltwasser 2017). In Poland, as in many other countries, the division has been combined with other populist ideas about a coherent nation, a myth of the existence of a homogenous people – in this case a Catholic Polish nation – who rightly fear the external world, immigrants and multiculturalism, as well as with a nostalgia towards the past. The dichotomy also relies on the wisdom of 'the people', references to a conspiracy theory about the intricate globalized world, which should be explained in simple terms and repaired by application of a direct and straightforward politics bringing eternal *law and justice* (see Rydgren 2017: 488–92). The latter, I think not coincidently, is the name of the main right-wing party led by Kaczyński.

One might say that tables have been turned. In the now dominating – at least in the public media – discourses, formerly degraded groups are called the proud and undivided 'sovereign'. Anti-neoliberalism is translated into slogans about the renationalization of economic assets appropriated by the international and local oligarchs. Condescending elites are accused by 'the people' of corruption and promoting liberal values about gender, abortion and sex, which is alien to the traditional Christian and Polish culture. They are loathed for their *lewactwo* (a pejorative term derived from the word *lewicowy* or leftist). In the same way that derogatory concepts were used to describe the outcasts of transformation by the groups shaping public discourses up to 2015, so now the very same groups are presented as 'unfitting people', as redefined internal Others. A general comparison of the two discriminatory narrative schemes – concerning *Homo sovieticus* and *Homo cosmopoliticus*, a person accepting the Western lifestyle and liberal values – leads to the conclusion that in the distinction between the 'proper Us' and the 'improper internal Them', emphasis has shifted from mental and behavioural habits purportedly threatening modernization, or seen as discordant with a progressive lifestyle, to the attributes characterized as the Western rotten values that threaten a nation's existence and its morale and integrity.[8]

Not by Bread Alone

The processes described in this chapter result from various factors operating at the global, regional and local levels. Neoliberalism as a theory and practice can indeed be identified as the main cause for the rise of populist movements in Central Europe and in Poland in particular. (However, one should also bear in mind that this is a global phenomenon.) Historical conjuncture brought a neoliberal economy to the region in which an authoritarian political regime and command economy were rejected. Meanwhile, as Polanyi (2001) argues, capitalism has an inherent contradiction. A regulatory force of the *invisible hand* of the market is irreconcilable with *social justice*, since the latter cannot be done by blind market forces. In Polanyi's framework of the double movement (Hann 2019a), 'populism' represents a countermovement to neoliberalism (Cayla 2019; Hann 2015, 2019b). At the rhetorical (and sometimes practical) level, populists attempt to snatch wealth from the hands of the few and redistribute it among the many.

However, these abstract terms cannot explain why people whose average standards of living rose steadily, if slowly and unevenly, since 1993 have dumped the system that brought them prosperity, at least in relation to the past. In order to understand this phenomenon, cultural factors need to be brought into the picture. First, the Other appears as an inherent part of socioeconomic processes. Neoliberals discursively create internal Others by domesticating orientalizing discourses; populists make the internal Others by negative Occidentalism discourses, often also by repatriating past nationalist ideas. Second, both socioeconomic and political regimes – neoliberalism and populism – are ethically highly ambivalent. The 'actually existing neoliberalism' focused on establishing a hegemonic discourse, legitimizing a radical restructuring of economy that produced 'human waste' (Bauman 2004) whose appearance had to be conceptually contained. 'Actually-existing right-wing populisms' focus on political strategies aimed at winning and retaining power. They often entail exclusion of the Others, both external and internal, which leads to anti-elitism on the one hand and xenophobia on the other. Third, and most importantly for my argument, socioeconomic processes cannot be adequately interpreted and understood without serious consideration of discourses that assist these processes, especially in a world in which the media are so important. Without discursive, culturally conditioned creations of the Others, economic and political practices are impossible. Discourses grease social practices and are an inherent part of the socioeconomic reality that we merely conceptually abstract from it for analytical purposes. They are, like Godelier's (1984) *L'Idéel et le Materiel*, possible to disentangle, but immanently interlaced.

Michał Buchowski is a professor and Head of the Department of Anthropology and Ethnology at Adam Mickiewicz University, Poznan, Poland, as well as a professor and Chair of Comparative Central European Studies at European University Viadrina in Frankfurt/Oder,

Germany, and an Honorary Fellow of the Royal Anthropological Institute of Great Britain and Ireland. He has authored and edited several books, most recently *Purgatory: Anthropology of Postsocialist Neoliberalism* (2017, in Polish) and *Twilight Zone Anthropology: Voices from Poland* (ed., 2019).

Notes

1. For a justification of this distinction, see Buchowski (2017: 26).
2. A popular joke illustrates how people perceived the decades long political system:
   – What's the difference between 'democracy' and 'socialist democracy'?
   – It is the same as between a chair and an electric chair!
3. Champions of the new deal denied that it was a shock therapy. Janusz Lewandowski, a former member of the Polish Parliament, former Minister of Privatisation and now Member of the European Parliament, said recently that 'I disagree that the reform itself was shock in its character' since the 'visible hand of the state belonging to reformers' was involved (Sandecki 2020).
4. Balcerowicz organized a think-tank of the shock-therapy plan consisting of Jeffrey Sachs, Stanisław Gomułka and Jan-Vincent Rostowski. The latter two worked at the London School of Economics, the institution famous at that time for its neoliberal profile, and at which Robbins and von Hayek taught. Rostowski and Gomułka served as economic advisors to subsequent governments. The former was an fiscally rigid Minister of Finance in the last government, both considered politically liberal and economically neoliberal, before the populist Law and Justice party (PiS) led by Jarosław Kaczyński took power. PiS implemented some welfare programmes, with its flagship project called 500+, a distribution of a 500 zloty (c. €115) allowance for each child under eighteen years of age a month. It was immediately hailed by former leaders as a populist agenda and destructive to the economy. However, after more than four years of PiS rule and until the COVID-19 pandemic, economic indexes were still good.
5. For a succinct account of these anthropological descriptions, see Brandstädter (2007); Buyangelderiyn (2008); Horschelmann and Stenning (2008); Buchowski (2012).
6. Neoliberalism refers to such commonly known and interrelated policies such as: economic liberalization (which implies austerities in the domain of social welfare); deregulation of the markets; globalization and the free flow of capital and goods (as well as highly skilled professionals); and, all-important in the postsocialist context, (re)privatization (see Springer, Birch and MacLeavy 2016: 2).
7. The index of social inequality, which numerically expresses the uneven distribution of goods in a given society; the lower its value, the less diverse the income; a ratio of 0 per cent would mean absolute equality, and 100 per cent would mean that all wealth is acquired by a single family.
8. Several features indicated in this section are constitutive of the so-called thin populist ideology, including: 'a harmonious and homogenous people', 'the conception of a "sacred heartland"', 'dislike [of] the present world in which ... people are uprooted and alienated, and they long for a return to the "rootedness" of an integrated and coherent "community of the people"'. Populists also speak 'in the name of "the people"' and 'present a dualism by pitting "the people" against "the elite"', which they portray as corrupted (Rydgren 2017: 3–4). This understanding of populism also emerges from the Polish case discussed in this chapter.

References

Bauman, Zygmunt. 1992. *Intimations of Postmodernity*. London: Routledge.
_____. 2004. *Wasted Lives: Modernity and Its Outcasts*. London: Polity Press.
Berdahl, Daphnie, Matti Bunzl and Martha Lampland (eds). 2000. *Altering States: Ethnographies of Transition in Eastern Europe and the Former Soviet Union*. Ann Arbor: University of Michigan Press.
Bourdieu, Pierre. 1998. 'Neo-liberalism, the Utopia (Becoming a Reality) of Unlimited Exploitation', in *Acts of Resistance: Against the Tyranny of the Market*. New York: New Press, pp. 94–105.
Brandtstädter, Susanne. 2007. 'Transitional Spaces: Postsocialism as a Cultural Process', *Critique of Anthropology* 27: 131–45.
Buchowski, Michał. 2006. 'The Specter of Orientalism in Europe: from Oriental Other to Stigmatized Brother', *Anthropological Quarterly* 79(3): 463–82.
_____. 2012. 'Anthropology in Postsocialist Europe', in Ullrich Kockel, Máiréad Nic Craith and Jonas Frykman (eds), *A Companion to the Anthropology of Europe*. Oxford: Wiley-Blackwell, pp. 68–87.
_____. 2017. *Czyściec. Antropologia Neoliberalnego Postsocjalizmu* [Purgatory: Anthropology of Neoliberal Postsocialism]. Poznań: Wydawnictwo Uniwersytetu im. Adama Mickiewicza w Poznaniu.
Buchowski, Michał, Edouard Conte and Carole Nagengast (eds). 1999. *Poland Beyond Communism: 'Transition' in Critical Perspective*. Fribourg: Fribourg University Press.
Burawoy, Michael, and Katherine Verdery (eds). 1991. *Uncertain Transition: Ethnographies of Change in the Postsocialist World*. Lanham, MD: Rowman & Littlefield.
Buyandelgeriyn, Manduhai. 2008. 'Post-post-transition Theories: Walking on Multiple Paths', *Annual Review of Anthropology* 37: 235–50.
Cayla, David. 2019. 'The Rise of Populist Movements in Europe: A Response to European Ordoliberalism?', *Journal of Economic Issues* 53(2): 355–62.
Chari, Sharad, and Katherine Verdery. 2009. 'Thinking between the Posts: Postcolonialism, Postsocialism, and Ethnography after the Cold War', *Comparative Studies in Society and History* 51(1): 6–34.
Dunn, Elizabeth. 2004. *Privatizing Poland: Baby Food, Big Business, and the Remaking of Labor*. Ithaca: Cornell University Press.
Ekiert, Grzegorz, and Jan Kubik. 1999. *Rebellious Civil Society: Popular Protest and Democratic Consolidation in Poland, 1989–1993*. Ann Arbor: University of Michigan Press.
Godelier, Maurice. 1984. *L'Idéel et le Matériel: Pensée, Economies, Sociétés*. Paris: Fayard.
Gramsci, Antonio. 1994. *Letters from Prison* (ed. by Frank Rosengarten; trans. by Raymond Rosenthal). New York: Columbia University Press.
Hann, C.M. (ed.). 2002. *Postsocialism: Ideals, Ideologies and Practices in Eurasia*. New York: Routledge.
Hann, Chris. 2015. 'Backwardness Revisited: Time, Space and Civilization in Rural Eastern Europe', *Comparative Studies in Society and History* 54(4): 881–911.

———. 2019a. *Repatriating Polanyi. Market Society in the Visegrád States*. Budapest: Central European University Press.
———. 2019b. 'Anthropology and Populism', *Anthropology Today* 35(1): 1–2.
Harvey, David. 2004. 'The "New" Imperialism: Accumulation by Dispossession', *Socialist Register* 40: 63–87.
Hörschelmann, Kathrin, and Alison Stenning. 2008. 'Ethnographies of Postsocialist Change', *Progress in Human Geography* 32: 339–61.
Kalb, Don. 2018. 'Upscaling Illiberalism: Class, Contradiction, and the Rise and Rise of the Populist Right in Post-socialist Central Europe', *Fudan Journal of Humanities and Social Sciences* 11: 303–21.
Kürti, László, and Peter Skalník (eds) 2009. *Post-Socialist Europe: Anthropological Perspectives from Home*. Oxford: Berghahn Books.
Mudde, Cas, and Cristóbal Rovira Kaltwasser. 2017. *Populism: A Very Short Introduction*. Oxford: Oxford University Press.
Notka Informacyjna. 2016. *Informacja o rozmiarach i kierunkach czasowej emigracji z Polski w latach 2004–2015 [Information about the Size and Directions of Temporary Migration from Poland, 2004–2015]*. Warsaw: Główny Urząd Statystyczny.
Polanyi, Karl. 2001 [1944]. *The Great Transformation: The Political and Economic Origins of our Time*. Boston, MA: Beacon Press.
Polska. 2014. *Polska 1989–2014 [Poland 1989–2014]*. Warsaw: Główny Urząd Statystyczny.
———. 2016. *Polska w OECD, 1996–2016 (Poland in OECD, 1996–2016)*. Warsaw: Główny Urząd Statystyczny.
Rydgren, Jens. 2017. 'Radical Right-Wing Parties in Europe: What's Populism Got to Do with It?', *Journal of Language and Politics* 16(4): 485–96.
Sandecki, Maciej. 2020. 'Leszek Balcerowicz w 30. rocznicę swojego planu: Nikt nie zrobił tego lepiej' [Leszek Balcerowicz at the 30th Anniversary of His Plan: Nobody Has Done It Better], *Gazeta Wyborcza*, 24 January. Retrieved 7 December 2020 from https://trojmiasto.wyborcza.pl/trojmiasto/7,35612,25628096,leszek-balcerowicz-na-30-rocznice-swojego-planu-gospodarczego.html.
Shields, Stuart. 2009. 'CEE as a New Semi-periphery: Transnational Social Forces and Poland's Transition', in Owen Worth and Phoebe Moore (eds), *Globalization and the 'New' Semi-peripheries*. Basingstoke: Palgrave Macmillan, pp. 159–76.
Springer, Simon, Kean Birch and Julie MacLeavy 2016. *The Handbook of Neoliberalism*. London: Routledge.
Stiglitz, Joseph E. 2001. 'Foreword', in Karl Polanyi 2001 [1944]. *The Great Transformation: The Political and Economic Origins of our Time*. Boston, MA: Beacon Press, pp. vii–xvii.
Sztompka, Piotr. 1993. 'Civilizational Incompetence: The Trap of Post-Communist Societies', *Zeitschrift für Soziologie* 22(2): 85–95.
Verdery, Katherine. 1996. *What Was Socialism, and What Comes Next*. Princeton: Princeton University Press.
Wedel, Janine. 1998. *Collision and Collusion: The Strange Case of Western Aid to Eastern Europe*. New York: St Martin's Griffin.

Chapter 6

Making a Reality of Other People's Fictions
A Smithian Critique of Post-Marxian and Polanyi-ite Accounts of Exploitation

Michael Stewart

It is hard, in a short rejoinder to a body of work as wide-ranging as that produced by my friend and colleague Chris Hann, to do any justice to the contributions to knowledge emerging from his research, even if we only consider the field of economic anthropology. In this short chapter, I take one institution associated with my own ethnographic work and use this to reflect on a much larger notion – an idea that lies at the centre of some forms of economic theory. In this way I hope to contribute to the large-scale comparative endeavour that Chris' teacher and mentor, Jack Goody, transposed into anthropology and that Chris has championed since. This chapter is also a response to Chris' interest, inspired by the work of Karl Polanyi, in the nature of 'market society'.

Place, Time, Person

Chris and I started our lifelong engagement with Hungary in what felt like very different places and times. He arrived at the height of 'goulash socialism', when the trauma of the 1956 Revolution and its bloody aftermath were apparently being laid to rest. A robust social calm was being fostered, sweetened by fresh access to international banking loans that buoyed up the leaden state socialist economies of the 1970s. I arrived eight years later – but it was a generation apart. My mentors were the rebellious students of Chris' friends, and my fieldsite could not have

Notes for this chapter begin on page 100.

contrasted more with his: an exemplary case of 'market socialist' innovation among the socially favoured (and 'productive' farmers) versus Roma who felt that they only got to lick the bowl of the goulash after everyone else had had their turn. Both Chris' viticulturalists and my Roma benefited hugely from the redistributive logic of state socialism – his through the improbable preservation of wine-making on the sandy soils of mid-Hungary and mine through the equally unlikely preservation of 'cotton wool' labour in underproductive factory production lines.

Our engagements, over the course of thirty or more years, have followed each other on something like parallel tracks, never allowing us to move so far apart as to prevent friendly conversation and exchange. Chris has promoted the work of Karl Polanyi and, on and off, I have engaged with the tradition of work going back to Adam Smith, notably Smith when seen as the progenitor of Austrian economics with its interest in individual agency and action under conditions of uncertainty. Looking at Hungary with 'Austrian' eyes made sense to me, for the idea of an ever-evolving 'commercial society' spoke more to the experience of my informants than Polanyi's moral critique of 'market society' and its various 'fictional commodities'. For better or worse, the Rom I know have been rather good at making realities out of other people's fictions.

In this chapter I will take one controversial, rather visible phenomenon that has emerged since the collapse of the state socialist regime amongst the Rom-Gypsies, which is mostly presented in the media as an acute social sickness: so-called 'usury' or informal money-lending. This activity is held in general disgust in Hungary and the broader postsocialist region, but within Roma communities, the practice is accepted, indeed morally normalized. This chapter tries to understand this disjunction. Beyond this particular investigation lies a broader issue. Which of the two traditions helps us to better understand the phenomenon that has been postsocialism? Is it that line of thinking associated with Karl Marx, which sees 'exploitation' at the heart of the dynamic and revolutionary system that he calls 'capitalism'? Or is a better account provided by the tradition deriving from the radical politics of Adam Smith, who characterized our distinctive social order as a 'commercial society'? Smith placed the purely commercial contract at the heart of the dynamism of 'commercial society', locating it as both the source of extraordinary new freedoms and the many hazards that went hand in hand with the new order.

Usury

In the spring of 1988, I returned to Hungary with a Granada film crew to make a *Disappearing World* film about the Rom I had lived with from 1984 to 1985. One day we filmed Gypsy women scavenging on a giant industrial rubbish tip for piles of nylon thread, which they would later sell to viticulturalists in the wine-producing area of Gyöngyös – the thread being used to tie vines to the trellises. As we started filming, the tip's administrator approached and ordered us to put down the equipment. The official explained to me: 'In this country the Party and the People do not allow this to be shown ... We consider this to be usury [*uzsorás*].' With neither mental nor physical labour involved, the turning of rubbish into profit, the making of 'easy money' was not to be shown – especially not by a film crew from the (still) enemy/capitalist West!

I remember this incident so vividly because 'usury' was not a term that had any currency in daily life in Hungary during the 1980s (though it was historically part of Party discourse). Thirty years later, the picture is very different. Across the postsocialist space in towns and villages, from the mid-1990s onwards, informal forms of money-lending emerged, often with very high interest rates. Under socialism, bank loans had been widely available to the poor, notably through the Takarékszövetkezet – the mutual savings' bank, for whom the regular and predictable wages of the Roma provided sufficient collateral. However, with the collapse in Romany employment in the late 1980s, the Takarékszövetkezet's client base had become 'unbankable'. Markets, like nature, abhor a vacuum and pawn shops sprung up offering short-term access to liquidity to the Roma. Then came Provident,[1] a bank offering a 'door-to-door' service of 'instant cash for those without a bank account'. Stung into action, the Takarékszövetkezet, having realized that with no Gypsy borrowers in much of the country its business model would collapse, came back into the loans market. It was in this context of multiple agents trying to monetize the financial needs of the long-term poor – above all their need for continuous financing of their everyday expenditure on food and utilities under conditions of irregular income – that Romany people too stepped into the market. Inevitably, since the more 'consolidated', who at the very least were employed through the local government in public work schemes, could borrow from the bank or even the Mayor (both of whom could secure their income by taking deductions at source from welfare payments), the Roma lenders found themselves contracting the utterly 'unbankable', that is, people (Roma and non-Roma alike) with almost no collateral. Consequently, the price of this money was high – 'exorbitant' some said. For example, in the village of 'Lápos' studied by my UCL colleague, the rural socioanthropologist Judit Durst, the established rate of informal interest in 2014 (when base bank rates were around 3 per cent) was 70 per cent. In neighbouring, more prosperous, villages, money was lent at 50 per cent to nonrelatives and 25 per cent to people acknowledged as part of one's 'banda' or wider, extended family.

In public commentary on the new banking arrangements in these increasingly desperate villages, it was the private money-lenders who provided the touchstone for moral soul-searching (Varró 2008). Interestingly, several of these 'usurers' studied by Durst were themselves former or current debtors. One of her main informants used a Provident loan to start his own money-lending enterprise (Durst 2015). Tellingly, little of the public moralizing commentary attacked Provident, hire-purchase companies or other formal actors: it was the Roma lenders who were condemned. In the wake of a tide of 'moral anxiety' after the global financial crash, in 2011 the Hungarian government introduced a Usury Act, tightening previous criminal law and promising 'zero tolerance' towards usury. Since then, even first-time offenders can face imprisonment and significant prison terms have been handed down. Those who borrow money under such arrangements are represented as the helpless victims of organized larceny (Ritok 2011).

Yet, on the ground, ethnographic reports – drawing on the kind of local expertise and engagement that Chris has promoted across his teaching career – indicate that villagers take a much more nuanced line and do not in general judge the providers of 'kamatos pénz' (money with interest) harshly. One of Judit Durst's informants in an impoverished Borsod (north Hungarian) village told her about a local money-lender whom she had thought of as particularly aggressive in his demands for repayments: 'Actually he is a good-hearted man. If the electricity company wants to turn off the light in your house or they want to take somebody to prison, he helps; he always pays up for them.' Another money-lender took the family home of a debtor in lieu of massive unpaid debts and handed it over to one of his own children, though he did 'help' (according to his own account) the debtor by renting him his other house in the village for a low sum. Durst was told: 'You've got to make living somehow. And hats off to him, he is looking after his kids with his profit' (Durst 2016: 60). Villagers in this region were careful to make a distinction between people who do 'fair lending with interest' and the 'vultures' (*dögös*) who lend and spend without any social considerations. The distinction is contextual – while the commercial loan to a stranger just mentioned is accepted (and the 'foolish' family who lost their home condemned) a mayor, whose moral role entails protecting and helping his villagers, was unable to even enforce full repayment of informal loans with no interest, without being painted as a vulture. In this case, the mayor had to accept his own bankruptcy in order to continue to operate politically in the area. In summary, the main criteria by which an informal money-lender is thought to be 'proper' or fair is that they, unlike their vulturous counterpart, keeps the appearance of solidarity by representing themselves as the protector/helper of the helpless (cf. Waters' (2018) fine discussion of the 'financialization of help' in Mongolia).

So, villagers make normative judgements about informal money-lending, just not the same as those of outsiders. Durst provides an account of one informal money-lender who, despite rapidly building up a loan of 140,000 Hungarian Forints (HUF) (and receiving 36,000 HUF in interest repayments), was forced to 'close' the debt and accept only repayment of the principal over 14 months, with no further interest (Durst 2015: 50). Such a person is talked about as 'proper', as a 'helper' who operates a 'fair' system. Other money-lenders who apply, say, compound interest on the full debt at each pay point rather than treating the loan as a one-off 'payday loan' are judged harshly. Durst gives an example of one such individual who doubled an original debt of 25,000 HUF each month until it reached the value of the debtor's house (400,000 HUF) in the fourth month (Durst 2015: 37). This kind of money-lender stands in danger of being denounced to the police – a sanction that, as we have seen, has offered real power to debtors since 2011.

Outsiders, however, continue to denounce all informal money-lenders as rapacious. Sociologists, human rights activists and others anathematize it – and ethnicize it – as an 'exploitative' practice that is all the more incomprehensible in that Roma appear to exploit their fellow Roma. The exploitative nature of the interest appears as self-evident proof of this due to the great gap between the official bank and the informal money-lenders' *requested* rate of return. In some sense, or such is the official view, there is an act of theft in informal lending (though once you include the fee for 'express loans' and those for weekly payment at the front door, real Provident costs match those of informal lenders). Against this officially sanctioned discourse, the Roma assert that the local lenders are wholly within their rights and are simply 'cleverer' than their borrowers. Is it time to re-examine our notions of 'exploitation'?

Exploitation at Issue

The concept of exploitation lies at the heart of Marxist and Marxian theories and explanations of the economic arrangements of class societies. As

Chris Hann notes in his book on Polanyi (Hann 2019), the coherence of Marx's 'Kapitalismuskritik' lies in its focus on 'capitalist exploitation'.[2] The core idea here – that one social class lives off the unpaid, 'the stolen' – labour of another is immensely powerful. Proudhon made a name for himself telling the world that property is theft, but Marx told a much simpler and more compelling story: the whole unequal social order is based on theft; the domination of one class by another rests, in the last analysis, on the unpaid labour of the former.

What I want to do here, in line with the call for this volume to approach broad questions of economic anthropology in a comparative manner, is to shift the focus away from Hungarian villages to consider 'exploitation' in the wider context of the anthropology of modern market transactions. In particular, I want to cast a sceptical eye over the literature where the language of exploitation has been invoked most consistently and received its greatest theoretical underpinning: the world of modern work, where, as Marilyn Strathern once put it, 'exploitation [is] at issue' (1988: 133–69). More specifically, I want to examine the distinctiveness of the labour process in market societies. How far does Marx's underlying and 'coherent' conception of exploitation take us in this paradigmatic case?

Readers may recall that Marx's basic question was to ask how exchanges that produce unequal returns, with the owner of capital taking a greater share of the output than the sellers of labour, seem fair to both? As Marx presented matters, drawing deeply on Smith, Locke and others, 'value' could only derive from labour and the mechanism of the wage contract allowed the value of workers' output to be greater than the value required to reproduce their ability to work (what Marx called their *labour power*) without it appearing that anything unfair had taken place. So, when trade unions in the nineteenth century fought for 'fair wages', Marx thought this was absurd since the sale of labour for a wage was inherently 'unfair'. Within an appearance of 'free exchange of equals', the labour contract disguised 'exploitation', allowing surplus labour to be extracted without the need for the explicit 'theft' or forced extraction found in feudal or slave societies. The wage was thus the foundation of the exploitation of one class under 'capitalism'.

For a long time, Marx's account of the labour contract remained unexamined in left-wing circles. Then, in the 1970s and 1980s, a series of ethnographic texts – many of which became instant classics – took readers, for what seemed like the first time, into the 'dark' or 'hidden abode' of 'production' where the alchemical process of value creation 'really' took place. A series of stunningly readable studies of Leicestershire garment sweat-shops staffed by Asian women (Westwood 1984), of Ford's notoriously chaotic production line at Dagenham (Beynon 1973), of the life of pit-men (Dennis et al. 1969) and many others appeared, all of which demonstrated that the production line was always culturally constructed and its rhythms and speeds fought over (Burawoy 1985). Interestingly, very few of the workers observed complained of 'exploitation' per se, but all the authors argued in a functionalist fashion that *implicit* in struggles over the intensity and organization of labour, workers were battling to restrain 'exploitation' of their labour.

In one very telling later study, a Marxist historian did find a group of late nineteenth-century German textile workers insisting that they were being exploited. In a rich and dense text that contrasts understandings of the basic market contract in the textile industries of Britain and Germany, Richard Biernacki (1985) shows how culture is embedded in market economies, how it shapes the organization of a production line and how the norms that govern social relations in a textile factory arise out of local history and notions of person. He also shows that while British workers thought that they were selling 'the products of labour' (that it was the worked linen as a commodity that was exchanged for the wage), German workers' believed that it was their capacity for work or indeed their persons that were transacted. As Biernacki summarizes the position, German workers assumed that they 'put their person in the hand of their employer' when vending 'labour as a commodity' (1985: 271).

These varying, culturally constructed conceptions of the labour process underpinned different approaches to many aspects of the organization of production in Germany and Britain. So, while Biernacki's German textile workers were insistent that their employers paid them for time waiting for the right tools or materials to arrive (since in the textile industry almost all work was done 'to specific command' and the materials assembled afresh for each job), in Britain textile workers never considered being paid for unproductive time; instead, they insisted that the piece rate for their actual work be sufficient that they could live to a certain norm. So great was their attachment to the idea that it was the product of their craft that should be rewarded and nothing else that, in 1914, their representatives in Yorkshire ridiculed the idea of holiday pay, saying: 'I should be glad if workers were sufficiently well paid to be independent even of these [payments]' (Biernacki 1985: 368).

Even more relevant to our broader question, Biernacki shows, with evidence from autobiographies, pamphlet publications, accounts of workers' reading groups and a host of other data, that German workers made use of Marx's theory of labour exploitation in their negotiation with factory owners. Yet in Britain, even Marx's ardent admirers simply could not get their heads round his theory of exploitation and mistranslated his key popularizing texts, like *Wage Labour and Capital*, transforming 'the theory of exploitation into market cheating' (Biernacki 1985: 409).

In a concluding part of his historical detective work, Biernacki shows how these diverse conceptions of the exchange of labour as a commodity shaped the nature of 'class struggle' in Britain and Germany, respectively. In the latter, a stoppage of labour (a strike) involved workers downing tools at their bench and sitting there in silence, refusing to engage their 'labour power'. In Britain, workers talked of 'coming out' – pouring through the factory gates not to set foot again inside its bounds until the dispute was resolved. In Germany, ceasing to give one's labour power was a breach of that part of the contract that was in dispute (the level of fines, payment for time spent idle, and so on) but since the relationship between *Geselle* (the feudal term for journeyman was commonly in use in textile factories) and *Arbeitsgeber* involved their persons, the worker remained silently tied to the bench. In Britain, once the textile worker was not working, there was simply nothing left in the contract. From the British point of view, there was an agreement to deliver specific goods for particular pay and if that was no longer taking place, there was no point hanging around for charity. Thus, British workers 'came out', voluntarily renouncing their contractually defined and limited ties to their employers.

The lesson is surely the opposite of the one that Biernacki intended. If you look at wage labour in feudal terms, it can indeed seem exploitative, a denial of shared humanity, a reduction of a personal relationship to the exchange of wares. Then, every effort by the employer to behave as a 'rational innovator and entrepreneur' is an attack on your 'standing', your 'status', an abuse of your person – it is a denial of the unbreakable tie of 'protection' (*Schutz*) the lord owes his servants. It is remarkable that the very word *Arbeiter*, adopted in the nineteenth century to refer to 'worker' is derived from a German word for feudal serfs (Biernacki 1985: 259–312). But in the country most exposed to capitalist conditions, Marx's work fell on deaf ears. The very workers who ought to have had the rawest, most enduring and sophisticated experience of capitalist exploitation simply did not get the point.

Biernacki here is very close to Polanyi, who argued that while labour, land and money are organized on a market basis and are essential to a 'market economy', they are not in fact commodities because they were not 'produced for sale'. Labour for Polanyi refers to human life, which is not produced for sale, cannot be detached from the rest of existence and cannot be stored or mobilized like other resources. For Biernacki, as for Polanyi, 'the commodity description of labour is entirely fictitious' (Polanyi 1957: 72; Biernacki 1985: 384–85).[3] However, the British workers described by Biernacki saw their wages as more or less fair. As such, they engaged in frequent battles to set new 'norms' as to what was acceptable remuneration for their products. But since for them it was not the person who was commoditized – only the products of their labour were seen as wares for sale – there was no sense that some injustice has been committed if the worker voluntarily contracted, in the full knowledge of local market conditions, to sell their labour for a certain sum.

Another View of 'Usury'

I suggest that neither the Polanyist view of money as a fictitious commodity nor the dominant 'equilibrium theorists' model of the market reaching perfect clearance helps us to really understand the complex phenomena of money-lending in northern Hungary today. Instead, we should look at the actors of small villages in Hungary with an Austrian or Smithian eye.

In his two foundational texts, *A Theory of Moral Sentiments* and *The Wealth of Nations*, Smith authored a bottom-up, evolutionary-style account of how human individuals built up moral judgements by seeing action in its social context. For Smith, the market is social, geographical and political all at once (Norman 2018). Smith's awareness of the social context of action made him acutely sensitive to the partial knowledge that human actors have to operate with, the intuitions that they are forced to rely on, the improvisations they devise and the hedges they have to adopt to make their way in an ever-changing world. For Smith, economic actors are trying to make sense and act in an ever-uncertain present.

The price of money in north Hungary is a signal of relative scarcity that the Roma recognize – it is cheaper to borrow if you have standing or if you have collateral. Watching the behaviour of other market players, but making use of their own greatly enhanced local information – able to calculate the precise incomings and outgoings of their neighbours – these Romany entrepreneurs were able to carve out a new and viable niche for themselves. They acted on hunches and on their local knowledge, without the vast databases and computer-powered 'rational calculation' available to companies like Provident. They knew that they had to accept less than optimal outcomes and behaved exactly as 'Austrian economics' predicts an entrepreneur should, using 'rules of thumb' – everyday heuristics to work out what loans to make.

But neither were the Roma money-lenders or the borrowers of money in north Hungary abstract individuals, acting as atomized vehicles for preferences of classical economic theory. Rather, they were shape-shifters, dynamically engaged in social relations, 'constantly changing, being ordered and re-ordered and formed dynamically by the disposition to truck, barter and exchange with others' (Norman 2018: 192) and, in so doing, constantly trying to establish new norms and have those norms accepted. Durst (2016) tells the remarkable story of a Romany man who succeeded in getting himself elected as mayor of the village where she works, Lapos, on the basis of a promise to offer better life opportunities, creating a 'socially oriented' shop (*szocialis bolt*) with cheap loans. However, because this man miscalculated the scale of the demand for credit and failed to understand the rate and period of likely return, all his dreams for transforming Lapos fell into disrepair. With nearly €20,000 of credit out on loan within two months, he had to start refusing food to debtors at his innovative shop. An outraged villager – for whom the 'fair' old money-lenders may have charged 70 per cent interest but never cut her food off – reported him to the police for usury and he went to prison for his 'crimes'.

Romany understandings that 'the price of money' varies depending on who is asking, when and where points back to Smith's interest in the way humans arrive at moral judgements. For what is an accusation of 'exploitation' if not a moral judgement, an attempt to establish a 'norm'? For Adam Smith, the key stage in the formation of 'moral judgements' lies in the ability to see oneself, or others, from the point of view of an 'impartial spectator'. This move rests on a prior ability to see others with sympathy and empathy, that is, to understand the diverse contexts in which people act – to see human action in its social context. In making the distinction between 'vulturous' and 'normal' money-lending, this is just what the inhabitants of communities in Hungary do: they are assessing that some, who are 'a bit cleverer' and have invested what have often been windfall gains (redundancy pay or a successful Provident loan) in a business of lending money to their relatives are no worse persons than the owners of a bank like the Takarékszövetkezet. The Rom know that the local savings banks restructured their loan operations in the 1990s to enable unemployed Roma – their only clients – to go on borrowing money and they judge their 'cleverer' relatives no worse for this. For, as Philip Coggan (1998) has shown, the history of money is a struggle between debtors who want their burdens lightened and creditors who want their investments back.

Let me briefly broaden the frame again. Amongst the numerous anthropological studies of workers as economic actors, Rosemary Harris' 1987 study of an Imperial Chemical Industries (ICI) plant in Bristol stands out from the much more fashionable, but deeply functionalist, Marxist accounts of the way in which workers 'implicitly' struggle against exploitation as they negotiate what is fair or not in the workplace (see, among others, Beynon 1973; Burawoy 1985). What Harris showed is that the workers she studied were fully aware that their employer needed to be profitable and did their damnedest to ensure that this was the case, often in the face of totally irrational managerial actions that made their contributions as workers far more complex to deliver. They did not feel in the slightest bit exploited, nor did they have to be fooled to deliver 'surplus value' to the employer. Powerlessness to change the organization of work was 'at issue' in this factory, not exploitation (Strathern 1988).

Like the employees of ICI, the Roma of north Hungary today also know full well the contractual terms on which they enter business and they accept its terms and the norms which govern those. In the recent past, Roma from these villages have been taken as unskilled manual labourers to 'be sold' on the German labour market for a profit for those who organize the market, but, once again, those 'sold' express only pleasure that for the first time in their lives they have travelled abroad, have a real job and are no longer living on a 'Gypsy settlement'. They have no sense that they are 'enslaved' or need 'liberating'.

Labelling people who creatively find a way to lend money to (or find employment for) the 'unbankable' as 'usurers' does no better than the medieval scholastics who simultaneously denounced usurers for their sale of that which does not exist while praising merchants for bringing untold wealth and wellbeing to the world, in ignorance of the fact that these were, in so many cases, one and the same person (Le Goff 1988: 55). In the 1980s, the Romany people I knew were very keen on the idea that, contrary to official ideology, they could make something from nothing (sell something from other people's fictional 'nothing'). On the journey to the rubbish tip where we were forbidden to film, the women went through all kinds of hoops to refuse buying tickets for the train ride, negotiating in various ways with the conductor to avoid paying for the journey. They were, in a very small way, turning a fiction of the non-Gypsies (that the Gypsies are poor, have too many children to feed, are profligate and are to be tolerated like children themselves) into a reality that gave them power to shape the world in a way that suited them. Difficult as it is for us to accept, the self-insertion of Romany debtors-turned-creditors into the local money markets of rural Hungary may be just as promising an indicator of the belated rise of commercial society here as it was in thirteenth- and fourteenth-century Europe. For, as Chris Hann has shown us, through a lifetime of ethnographic enquiry, it is only in the concrete negotiations of 'everyday life' that we see how the fictions of one group of social actors can be made an empowering reality for another.

Michael Stewart is a social anthropologist who has worked in Hungary and Romania with Romany and other marginal populations. He is the author of *Time of the Gypsies* (1987) and edited *The Gypsy Menace: Populism and the New Anti-Gypsy Politics* (2012). He now heads the Public Anthropology section of UCL Anthropology, London, United Kingdom, where he leads a series of media and enterprise programmes aiming to open the university up to outside research and practice.

Notes

1. https://www.provident.hu (retrieved 12 December 2020).
2. As Chris Hann also acknowledges, for the awkward, that is to say the 'rural' classes, this language never made much sense (2019: 129–65).
3. See also Marx's description of 'credit' as 'fictitious capital' in volume 3 of *Capital* (cited in Peebles 2010). Credit is, of course, the basis of banking – it is the act that generates assets for banks that allows further lending – and the very motor of our entire prosperity in the modern world. That Marx thought it fictitious is both deeply revealing and frighteningly quaint.

References

Beynon, Huw. 1973. *Working for Ford*. Wakefield: E.P. Publishing.
Biernacki, Richard 1985. *The Fabrication of Labour, Germany and Britain, 1640–1914*. Berkeley: University of California Press.
Burawoy, Michael. 1985. *The Politics of Production: Factory Regimes under Capitalism and Socialism*. London: Verso.
Cannadine, David. 1998. *Class in Britain*. New Haven: Yale University Press.
Coggan, Philip. 1998. *Paper Promises: Debt, Money and the New World Order*. London: Allen Lane.
Dennis, Norman, Fernando Henriques and Clifford Slaughter. 1969. *Coal Is Our Life: An Analysis of a Yorkshire Mining Community*. London: Tavistock Publications.
Durst, Judit. 2015. 'Juggling with Debts, Moneylenders and Local Petty Monarchs: Banking the Unbanked in "Shanty-Villages" in Hungary', *Review of Sociology* 25(4): 30–57.
_____. 2016. 'New Redistributors in Times of Insecurity: Different Types of Informal Moneylending in Hungary', in Micol Brazzabeni, Manuela Ivone Cunha and Martin Fotta (eds), *Gypsy Economy: Romani Livelihoods and Notions of Worth in the 21st Century*. New York: Berghahn Books, pp. 49–67.
Hann, Chris. 2019. *Repatriating Polanyi: Market Society in the Visegrád States*. Budapest: Central European University Press.
Harris, Rosemary. 1987. *Power and Powerlessness in Industry: An Analysis of the Social Relations of Production*. London: Tavistock Publications.

Humphrey, Caroline. 1983. *Karl Marx Collective: Economy, Society and Religion in a Siberian Collective Farm*. Cambridge: Cambridge University Press.
Le Goff, Jacques. 1988. *Your Money or Your Life: Economy and Religion in the Middle Ages*. New York: Zone Books.
Marx, Karl. 1898 [1865]. *Value, Price and Profit*. New York: International Co.
Norman, Jesse. 2018. *Adam Smith: What He Thought, and Why It Matters*. London: Allen Lane.
Peebles, Gustav 2010. 'The Anthropology of Credit and Debt', *Annual Review of Anthropology* 39: 225–40.
Polanyi, Karl. 1957. *The Great Transformation: The Political and Economic Origins of Our Time*. Boston: Beacon Press.
Ritok, Nora L. 2011. Tanult tehetetlenség. HVG. Nyomorszéle blog, 9 November. Retrived 10 December 2020 from https://nyomorszeleblog.hvg.hu/2011/11/09/244-tanult-tehetetlenseg.
Strathern, Marilyn. 1988. *The Gender of the Gift: Problems with Women and Problems with Society in Melanesia*. Berkeley: University of California Press.
Szelényi, Iván, in collaboration with Robert Manchin, Pál Juhász, Bálint Magyar and Bill Martin. 1988. *Socialist Entrepreneurs: Embourgeoisement in Socialist Hungary*. Cambridge: Polity Press.
Varró, Szilvia. 2008. 'Uzsora Magyarországon – Fizetsz, Amíg Élsz', *Magyar Narancs*, 23 October. Retrieved 10 December 2020 from https://magyarnarancs.hu/belpol/uzsora_magyarorszagon_-_fizetsz_amig_elsz-69904.
Waters, Hedwig A. 2018. 'The Financialization of Help: Moneylenders as Economic Translators in the Debt-Based Economy', *Central Asian Survey* 37(3): 403–18.
Westwood, Sallie. 1984. *All Day, Every Day: Factory and Family in the Making of Women's Lives*. London: Pluto Press.

Chapter 7

Resilience and Surveillance in Hann's Eurasia

Steven Sampson

The Visegrád Fascination

Chris Hann's field research has centred largely on Hungary and Poland. His project for an anthropology of socialism and postsocialism, and what we can now call post-postsocialism (Sampson 2002a), is shaped by both his research and his personal experiences in these two countries, especially in Hungary. Chris has followed developments in Hungary continuously for forty years, with several periods of ethnographic research and vacation visits to 'his village' of Tázlár. When he returned home, there was no respite. He could continue testing his observations by discussing them, in fluent Hungarian, with his wife Ildiko Béller-Hann, a scholar of Turkic Asia. Chris truly never left the field. And the result is that no foreign anthropologist knows Hungary like Chris does. Period.

Chris' understanding of the anthropology of socialism takes its point of departure in Hungary and Poland. This deserves comment. For it was these two countries where the regimes were least repressive and where the rural populations tended to be more autonomous. Hungarian and Polish farmers could control their household resources for various reasons: they had remained private farmers, they could manipulate their obligations to the local collective farm, and/or they could maximize their private labour and informal networks to sell produce on the private market. If we measured the level of state control in socialist Eastern Europe during the 1980s, Hungary and Poland were definitely on the liberal end of the continuum (along with Yugoslavia). Hungary and Poland certainly suffered from the oft-cited weaknesses of stiff party autocracy and a perverted planned economy. However, the regimes in these two countries, certainly as a response to the popular revolts decades earlier, exercised less repression over people's everyday life. Their populations had more economic autonomy and more individual freedoms in terms of media access and travel. It was a form of social contract in which the population ceded political control to the Communist Party in exchange for economic and private autonomy. This social contract was encapsulated in the pre-1989 punchline, heard throughout Eastern Europe, of 'We pretend to work, they pretend to pay us a wage', and the dictum of Hungarian party chief Janos Kádár: 'He who is not against us is with us.'

The relative autonomy of these populations has been underscored by Chris Hann in several of his works, most recently in his *Repatriating Polanyi* (Hann 2019a). The Visegrád peasants made an accommodation with the socialist regimes of the time. This emphasis on accommodation is a kind of Visegrád fascination. In his work on socialist Hungary and Poland, Chris provides innumerable examples of how Visegrádians managed to cope successfully with regimes that were inefficient, paternalistic, corrupt but not necessarily brutal. Further south, however, things were different.

I did my original research down the road from Chris, in central Romania, and during the same decades of mid-1970s to mid-1980s – until being denied entry in 1985 (Sampson 2019a, 2020 and www.stevensampsontexts.com). The village where I carried out fieldwork was neither isolated nor desperately poor by Romanian standards. Nevertheless, I could readily observe how people tried to cope with the shortages and pressures of life under the brutal Ceausescu regime and the local party and security apparatus. It was a regime with 90 per cent collectivization of agriculture, restricted private markets and harsh requisitioning of domestic produce. Chris' depictions of life in Tázlár and Wisłok are relatively benign compared to the everyday struggles of Romanian villagers and urban dwellers. Villagers were not permitted to slaughter their own animals, were pressured by party activists to fulfil mandatory work quotas on their household plots, suffered horrific prohibitions on abortion and even birth control, were subject to rationed eggs, meat, milk, sugar, cooking oil, petrol and propane, were extorted for bribes by ruthless bureaucrats, doctors and police, and suffered innumerable other indignities and threats, including penalties for even speaking to a foreigner, much less having one stay overnight in their home without police permission. Urban dwellers in Romania saw entire neighbourhoods razed to build monuments to Ceausescu, had basically no possibility of travelling abroad or obtaining access to Western media, lived in ice-cold apartments during the winter months and were prohibited from using electric heaters or more than a single light bulb. Whatever progress had been made in the early 1970s in building an industrial urban Romania with basic state education and health services, Romanians had become so desperate by the mid-1980s that in 1989, they literally celebrated the brutal execution of their party leader and his wife by show trial and firing squad. I mention this in order to emphasize that the relationship between the Romanian socialist state and its rural or urban populations bore little resemblance to the kind of accommodation Chris describes for 'Visegrádia'. It was repression pure and simple. Romanians did not accommodate, they suffered. This repression was enabled by the constant continuing surveillance, control and intimidation by the state organs on society and by citizens on each other. The Romanian secret police kept an eye on all foreign researchers as well. They harassed and interrogated the people with whom we interacted, from peasants in the village to university professors in Bucharest. They made threats on our informants, bugged our phones, searched our rooms, opened our mail and filed hundreds of pages of reports about us. My own secret police file, which ended abruptly when I was declared *persona non grata* in 1985 (but re-activated when I applied for a tourist visa in early 1989), is 600 pages (far less than Katherine Verdery's 2,800 pages; see Verdery 2018). In sum, any description of life under Ceausescu's Romanian socialism in the 1980s would be far from the accommodation practices that Chris describes for Hungarian rural life. Basic shortages, brutal repression and ever-present surveillance were part of this difference. There was no kind of 'social contract' between society and the regime.

These remarks are not an accusation that Chris was using Hungary as an archetype socialist country. Rather, it is only to emphasize that the anthropology of socialism, and of the postsocialist era, requires emphasis on a wide range of social practices and life experiences that unfolded in these societies. This is why we need ethnography, and especially Chris Hann's ethnography.

In this context, I would like to propose that Chris' ethnographic career be viewed through two complementary lenses: that of resilience and that of surveillance. The resilience takes the form of how people accommodate changes in their lives, changes that may derive from local developments or from large-scale collapses, such as the 1989 collapse of socialism. The surveillance perspective, while not explicitly described in Hann's work, pervades it in the sense that state and market actors are constantly impinging on and controlling the villagers and citizens whom Hann observes. In the second half of this chapter, I will try to show how state authoritarian surveillance and the more recent, truly scary market-based surveillance are now creating a new kind of 'surveillance Eurasia'. Since surveillance is a form of intervention that causes people to cope with, adapt or transform their lifeways, I will propose that we view Chris Hann's work in this dual optic of resilience and surveillance.

Retooling after 1989

Like Chris, I also had to retool my research after 1989. From studying 'real socialism', we were now faced with the task of making sense of post-socialism and, later, what I called post-postsocialism (Sampson 2002a). Chris' interests turned in several directions: civil society, new kinds of property relations, the nature of religion, and the changing configuration of market, state and redistributive integration. He watched how the Visegrád states began to integrate with the European Union's political and economic regime and the global division of labour. His project here has been inspired by four eminent scholars: Ernest Gellner, Jack Goody, Keith Hart and Karl Polanyi. Each in their own way, these scholars provided signposts for Chris in his various works on civil society, property, economic anthropology, Eurasia, redistribution, exchange and integration. Two of these scholars, Gellner and Polanyi, have Central European roots, although their political sympathies clearly differed. Chris, despite – or perhaps because of – his upbringing in a peripheral area, has rooted himself in Central Europe as well. He has made continuing trips to Tázlár, has carried out twenty years of 'institution building' at the Max Planck Institute for Social Anthropology in (the formerly East German) Halle, and has spent nearly two decades recruiting, teaching and supervising a talented pool of doctoral students and young researchers. Many of these researchers, born in the ex-socialist countries, ended up focusing their research on the post-postsocialist world. Put this all together and you realize that Chris has been able to cobble together a unique combination of long-term empirical field research, continuing publication, field excursions from one end of Eurasia to another (Hungary, Poland, Turkey and all the way to Xinjiang, China, with Ildikó Bellér-Hann), all while organizing seminars, reading dissertations and editing books about postsocialist life. Go no further: Chris is your all-round Visegrád anthropologist.

'So how does he keep up?' you may ask. I think Chris has been able to do this by returning and 'mining' his intellectual inspirations – Gellner, Goody, Hart and Polanyi. His long-term project in promoting Karl Polanyi (Hann 1992a) is an example. We anthropologists have been obsessed with showing how our informants' economic and material lives are 'embedded' in social relations. How else could we differentiate ourselves from the economists? However, as Chris points out (most recently in *Repatriating Polanyi*), we also enjoy searching out those dramatic moments of disembedding. Since disembedding is always described as a bad thing, it becomes the point of departure for our 'critique'. Indeed, postsocialism has often been described as a massive disembedding project driven by the forces of a diabolical neoliberalism. The problem, however, is that such a critique of neoliberal-driven disembedding is often a cheap shot. What looks like 'disembedding' to us may actually be a new form of integration for the people we study. For example, Hungarians working in the United Kingdom may appear disembedded from their home communities and families, but a UK wage also gives them new income possibilities. Hence, it takes a bit more ethnographic nuance to determine whether what may on first sight look like disembedding – i.e. the loss of control, the insecurity, the uncertainty, the chaos – may in fact be a lead-up to a new kind of integration by the global market, in a mosaic of migrant labour, barter arrangements, import/export trade, cash remittances, loans, redistribution, reciprocity, plunder, theft and the creation of new fictitious commodities. Chris' fieldwork in the Visegrád zone shows us a postsocialist variant of what we in the West now call the 'gig economy'. Insofar as people exploited a range of material possibilities to subsist – wage labour, barter, self-exploitation, ripping off both materials and time from their state workplace – Eastern Europe was perhaps the original home of the gig economy. As Chris has never tired of pointing out (Hann 2019a, 2019b), there are innumerable continuities in social life from the socialist to the postsocialist era. Markets, for example, were not absent in socialism, they just operated differently in terms of what was sold and how prices were set. Similarly, state surveillance over people's everyday life did not disappear with the demise of socialism; it simply took on new forms, some more subtle, others more overt.

Postsocialism as Resilience

Anthropologists are often emotionally tied to their first fieldwork and their field settings. This is certainly true in my own case (Sampson 2020), and I suspect it is also the case with Chris. What happens, then, when the context of the fieldwork changes so abruptly, as happened in 1989? How does one become a 'scholar of postsocialism'? Do you insist on pointing out the many continuities between the two eras, as Chris has insisted on doing? Or do you emphasize the transformational nature of EU/neoliberal intervention into these societies as they integrated into the global market, as so many anthropologists have?

Chris' project has been more nuanced. He has shown us how historical practices continued to play a role, while showing us how people tried to accommodate themselves to the truly massive changes and uncertainties that took hold of their lives after 1989. I will use the rest of this chapter to show how he did this, because I think this strategy of exposing the path dependence without using path dependence tautologically is something we can learn from. The organizing concept I will use here is 'resilience'.

Now 'resilience' is definitely a hot word in several circles. Chris' own research department at the Max Planck Institute is called 'Resilience and Transformation in Eurasia', and Chris himself has a recent article that begins with the title 'Resilience and Transformation . . .' (2019b). So the term is there. But how precisely is it being used?

In trying to understand situations of rapid, unexpected change (which 1989 certainly was), anthropologists have often resorted to one of two strategies: either they identify stubborn continuities in practices, labelling them either 'tradition' or 'resistance'; or they emphasize the paralysis caused by all-encompassing changes and call it 'disembedding' or 'crisis'. During this postsocialist crisis period, 'social life had lost its mooring', 'once recognizable groupings and structural positions lost contour' and 'it is not yet clear . . . what structures will ground social action' (Verdery 1996: 135). It was a time of agency without structure.

Chris was less dramatic in his assessment. In trying to grapple with the contradictions of the postsocialist period, he returned to his intellectual mentors. Using Gellner, Goody, Hart and Polanyi, he has highlighted how agency and structure mingled and clashed in the postsocialist period. In this effort to figure out what the hell was going on, his years 'under the socialist yoke' served him well. Let me explain, using two examples from areas that have been a special focus of Chris' work, as well as my own; namely, 'civil society' and 'the second economy'.

The Rise and Fall of 'Civil Society'

Twenty-five years ago, Chris coedited a collection of papers on the anthropology of civil society (Hann and Dunn 1996). Chris had cultivated a rather sceptical view of civil society for some years (Hann 1992b, 2003, 2004, 2019a: 167–86). In the early 1990s, most social scientists, and especially those working on Eastern Europe (including myself), saw civil society in an unequivocally positive light. In a postsocialist conjuncture of corrupt states, distorted markets, nasty racism and rampant plunder disguised as privatization, we saw civil society activists and their non-governmental organizations (NGOs) as the vehicles for a successful transition, pushing the state to be honest, the people to be democratic, and ameliorating the gaps in the market by providing social services. Chris had little sympathy for 'democracy export' and 'civil society capacity building' (Hann 1992b, 2003, 2004, 2019a: 167–86), an enterprise in which I myself had participated, as I ran around the Balkans, counting up the number of NGOs, helping them write project applications and imploring government officials to see civil society as allies (Sampson 1996, 2002b, 2004, 2017). Earlier than most, Chris was able to observe that this assemblage of foreign consultants, donor funding, well-intended projects, local activists and empowerment rhetoric had some fundamental weaknesses: our aspirations were too grand, our local knowledge was too limited, and we failed to realize that even the most dedicated NGO activists and leaders had their own 'private projects' and career plans. Inspired by Gellner's views on civil society (Gellner 1994), Chris ended up describing a Polanyi-style 'double movement': for every civil society project or programme, there arises a resistance or even hostility toward what Chris called 'the church of civil society' (2004) or, as I often heard it called, the 'Soros mafia' who had appropriated the discourse of 'civil society' as theirs. Instead, Chris found other kinds of autonomous social action that lay far beyond, just beneath or right alongside the world of the donor-driven NGO capacity-building projects and training. Chris found civil society in the churches in Poland, in the cooperative arrangements in Hungary, and today, in the various populist 'uncivil' societies in Hungary as well (Hann 2019a: 167–86, 2019b). Hungarian and East European civil society did not need capacity building; it needed recognition. It did not need more training seminars or donor strategies or feasibility studies; it needed new theories of what civil society actually means in terms of everyday social life. Chris found this conceptual toolbox in Polanyi (Hann 2019a), in descriptions of what is today called 'sociality' and added to this Stephen Gudeman's (2008) concept of 'mutuality' (Hann 2019a: 18–20). It turns out, as the ethnography of Chris and others has shown, that there was plenty of civil society in Eastern Europe, including in the socialist era (Buchowski 1996). Civil society was all over the place in the everyday social interactions of ordinary people doing ordinary things – buying, selling, producing, cultivating land, networking, worshipping, accessing, complaining, bribing, migrating, reorganizing, reasserting old claims to former property and demanding rights to state services, in kinning and unkinning behaviour, in ripping off the state and, at times, ripping off each other. This kind of civil society existed in the socialist period in Poland (Buchowski 1996) and throughout Eastern Europe in different forms. And it continued and re-adapted in the postsocialist period. We might call this 'agency'. Or we might call it 'accommodation'. Today we have another name for this kind of social reorientation and adaptation: resilience.

In social science terms, resilience is minimally defined as a positive response by individuals or communities to adversity or disaster. The origins of resilience lie in the recovery of ecological habitats after a cyclone and from personal recovery following psychic trauma or abuse. When applied to social groups, the resilience concept is viewed differently. Some theorists understand resilience simply as a form of coping, a 'bouncing back' to a former state. Others focus on resilience as a mode of adapting to a new situation. Finally, a resilience response can generate a profound transformation of community life quite different from the popular understanding of 'bouncing back' (for further discussions, see, for example, Barrios 2016; Béné et al. 2012; Olsson et al. 2015; and Prosperi and Morgado 2011). The resilience concept is often invoked by anthropologists, but there are also doubts about whether it is useful. There are two reasons to be cautious about using the term; first, it is elastic in its definition, to the extent that any form of natural or social survival can be called 'resilience'; second, resilience seems always to be viewed in positive, desirable terms. Those who look for the neoliberal demon, for example, see neoliberalism deploying the resilience card as some kind of 'blaming the victim' tactic to hide structural violence. In this view, the real problem is not enhancing the resilience of a vulnerable group, but reducing the original structural vulnerability (Béné et al. 2012; Barrios 2016).

Is resilience a part of Chris' project? Not overtly. As mentioned, both Chris' MPI research group and his recent article (2019b) use the phrase 'Resilience and Transformation', as if they were opposites. But Chris does not theorize the word 'resilience' in his work. Certainly, he does not see today's postsocialist societies as recovering from some kind of earlier socialist catastrophe or collective trauma. In his optic, Visegrádian socialism was neither an unmitigated disaster nor a psychic trauma. Rather, his project has been to show how people manage to adapt to ever-changing conditions, some of which are as existentially dramatic as any kind of natural disaster. For some people, the period of postsocialism was indeed a situation where 'all that is solid melts into air', to invoke Marx. Socialism was a disaster for some, while for others it was postsocialism that was the disaster. But disaster research, including the disaster research by ethnographers, shows that people are resilient. They bounce back, they adapt and they transform their life conditions. Chris has in fact documented this resilience in his own studies and in his discussion of others' work. In line with recent trends in the resilience literature, where enhanced resilience is viewed as a developmental imperative (especially Béné et al. 2012), Chris shows that the postsocialist societies did more than bounce back from the 1989 confusion. They also adapted to new conditions and even transformed themselves. I would call this combination of coping, adapting and transforming a 'tripartite resilience'. Now Chris does not use this kind of terminology, but who cares! Instead, he uses his ethnography and invokes his conceptual inspirations in Gellner, Goody, Hart and Polanyi. He integrates them by describing how local groups accommodate to these ever-changing conditions. Without acknowledging it, Chris Hann is a scholar of resilience.

This emphasis on resilience has a strange side-effect: it makes the ethnographic conclusions rather undramatic. Indeed, throughout Chris' work, there is an emphasis on the accommodating, the compromising, the nuanced, the low-key, the subtle responses of the people whom he describes and the way they go about solving their material and social problems. Describing how people cope, how they adapt to new conditions and how they transform their life-worlds requires intense ethnographic observation; these kinds of processes certainly cannot be ascertained via surveys or questionnaires. Chris' descriptions of the Lemko, or those of Hungary from the decades of socialism to the decades after, are replete with descriptions of how his people accommodate, adapt, make do, manage, get by and in some cases prosper. The village houses have gotten a bit bigger, but everyone still congregates in the kitchen. There are supermarkets nearby, but people still keep their own chickens and slaughter a pig at home. It requires some ethnographic nuance to describe how this resilient life, this life of accommodation, manages to reproduce itself. But what we end up with is an anthropology of resilience.

Now I admit that having done research in Romania, I have found this kind of theme – accommodation and resilience – difficult to deal with. While Ceausescu's Romania certainly raised living standards for some groups, such as peasant-workers and heavy industry workers (at least for some years), the human costs were brutal, especially towards the end of his regime. Ceausescu's legacy revealed itself after 1989 in the mob violence, ethnic tensions, the horrific conditions in orphanages, the administrative corruption and the political incompetence of the new Romanian governments. It was hardly a sign of resilience that millions of disillusioned Romanians have emigrated to northern Europe with no intention of returning. These emigres are both the best and the brightest, but also the most marginalized (Roma). Calling the Romanian situation 'resilient' would be a misnomer, since adaptation without structural change can make people even more vulnerable and therefore less resilient (as we are now seeing in the economic aftermath of the COVID-19 pandemic). We can all 'cope' ... until we can't. Romanians living abroad, for example, must balance their marginal position in European labour markets with the obligations of having to support aging relatives, many of whom are caring for the émigrés' children back home. This is not resilience; it is balancing on a very thin wire.

It thus appears that in focusing on Hungary and the Lemko, Chris has managed to locate and describe particularly resilient societies or resilient forms of sociality. His description of how these people accommodate is not an ideological pronouncement or a celebration of their coping skills. It is the result of ethnographic fieldwork and observation, watching people adjust over decades of socialism and postsocialism, and incorporating studies by students and colleagues, including otherwise overlooked native ethnographers. While the 'resilience' concept has often been invoked to understand societies coping with disaster, Chris' work stimulates us to think of tripartite resilience – coping, adaptation, transformation – as an organizing concept in the early postsocialist and subsequent neoliberal contexts. Does this mean that all forms of coping can be classified as 'resilience'? I don't think so. No one looking at the populist movements in Eastern Europe or the desperation of communities in the Balkans or in the Romanian provinces would want to call them 'resilient' in this larger, tripartite sense. They are barely surviving. At best, they are Polanyi-style double movements of barely coping, alternating with syndromes of anomie and moments of spontaneous resistance.

The Second Economy as Resilience

My second example of Chris' work that can contribute to his 'anthropology of resilience' is another theme close to my own heart: the 'second economy'. Hungarian social scientists and journalists such as Elemér Hankiss (1990a, 1990b) and Janos Kenedi (1981) were crucial in developing concepts of 'second society' or 'second economy' during the socialist era. These terms became paradigms for explaining how socialist citizens coped with shortages by channelling their time and labour into personal projects that often ended up exploiting or undermining formal institutions. Almost every anthropologist working in the socialist world produced vivid descriptions of the effectiveness of these informal networks, which enabled people to obtain access to scarce material or social resources (see, for example, Wedel (1986) and additional summaries in Sampson (1986, 1987, 1988)). The 'second economy' approach fell out of fashion following the demise of the socialist planned economy and the increased role of market forces. However, it has been replaced by a larger emphasis on the informal sector, where 'informality' manifests itself as both quasi-market or illicit economic activities. Here Chris' work on property and new forms of exchange has added nuance to the informality approach launched five decades ago by Keith Hart's work on urban Ghana (1973) and now applied in the postsocialist world by scholars such as Ledeneva (2018), Polese (2016), Henig and Makovicky (2017), and many others. Chris demonstrates (1990, 2019a: 33–60) that all economies have their second economies and that the second economy is anything but secondary. In fact, in many ways, Hungarian households, and households elsewhere in the socialist and postsocialist world, have managed to get by as much from second economy transactions (domestic production, informal trade, barter and migrant remittances) as from the increasingly precarious forms of wage labour.

Here again, an approach that focuses not just on mere coping, survival and precarity, but also includes a tripartite resilience may be useful in showing us the variations in resilience. Polanyi's focus on integration may help us. For without using the term 'resilient', Polanyi's work, now re-actualized by Chris Hann, shows us that 'coping' may not be that resilient at all. Resilience has its price in that it prevents or precludes social change. It is through ethnography that we can really discover the tradeoffs that the different kinds of resilience entail. It is through ethnography that we can identify responses to adversity that go beyond mere coping and that might eventually strengthen people's ability to deal with their everyday challenges. Ethnography can show us that people's vulnerability (the opposite of resilience) can be diminished in certain areas of social life, under certain types of regimes and among certain social groups more than others. Deciphering what kinds of resilience appear when and where is precisely why we need the kind of ethnography that Chris pursues. For example, while 'civil society', formal associational life or NGO projects may be failing (or benefiting only the NGO project elites), other more viable forms of civil society resilience may be observed in the informal economy, in the way people reformulate their notions of property or in the way people reproduce what Polanyi called 'fictitious commodities': land, labour and money. When Chris discusses Polanyi, he often invokes new 'modes of integration'. Perhaps we could now speak of a 'resilient mode of integration'. Resilience as integration can perhaps be a useful anchor in reading Chris' work. A resilient mode of integration is not just tied to postsocialism, of course. It can extend further, to another one of Chris' obsessions: Eurasia.

Surveillance in Eurasia

Chris' work on Eurasia (2016), much inspired by Goody, has emphasized commonalities in forms of integration that encompass the Polanyi-style reciprocity, house-holding, redistribution and market. However, perhaps we need to identify another form of integration that spans the entire Eurasian continent: surveillance. Surveillance, as Bentham and Foucault remind us, has been with us for a very long time. The panopticon perspective has been most recently described in Shoshana Zuboff's monumental *The Age of Surveillance Capitalism*, which extends Polanyi's idea of fictitious commodities to the commodification of human experience itself (2019: 43–44). Zuboff's concept of 'surveillance capitalism' is centred on the role of high-tech firms such as Facebook and Google and the techniques and algorithms they use to turn the individual's life experiences into commodities. These technologies break down our tastes, our experiences and our very lives into bits and pieces that can be analysed, parsed and then sold.

What Chris' descriptions of state socialism, welfare capitalism, neoliberalism and Eastern authoritarianism have in common are the ever-more sophisticated mechanisms of social and political monitoring and control over populations. This is biopolitics with a vengeance. From China's facial recognition to the United Kingdom's CCTV, from Bluetooth links to our refrigerators and by simply clicking our phones, we are now constantly being watched, classified and monitored – by government institutions looking for subversion and by marketing firms predicting our latest consumer urge. In parts of Eurasia, the government's surveillance of the population, the monitoring and assessing of what we do, say, read or write, is heavy-handed and repressive, resembling the surveillance of the high Stalinist/Maoist periods (today they include the surveillance of the Uyghurs in China and of refugee-support activists in Hungary). Even before the COVID-19 disaster, more insidious algorithms and facial recognition measures were being used, either to directly reward or punish the population, as in China's 'point system', or merely to intimidate, as in 'illiberal' Hungary.

Viewed as a whole, we can conclude that the combination of surveillance capitalism and state digital surveillance techniques have merged into a comprehensive 'Eurasian' syndrome, a way of life. Were Jack Goody still with us, this scholar of technology and chronicler of the exchange between the eastern and western ends of Eurasia would be avidly describing Eurasian surveillance technologies in the way he described the spread of literacy or of plough agriculture. Indeed, Hungarian surveillance of

Roma minorities or refugee-support activists has a lot in common with Chinese surveillance of Uyghurs and of the Wuhan doctors who were trying to call our attention to the coronavirus.

These surveillance regimes are disembedding us from our most fundamental life experiences in horrific ways. The facial recognition software and the Chinese point system for good citizenship are just the beginning. Increasing powers are being given to (or usurped by) the state to first monitor and then control our every movement in the name of security or, now, to prevent coronavirus contagion. It portends a new kind of Eurasia, a Eurasia where different kinds of surveillance regimes converge: some market-based, others state-based, both meshing with the surveillance we carry out on each other, from snitching to whistleblowing (Sampson 2019b).

In his work, Chris has often compared different kinds of welfare regimes – more market-based in the West, more authoritarian in the East, stressing elements of convergence between them. Overlaying these welfare regimes are regimes of surveillance. We now see a Eurasia that oscillates between market-based surveillance in the West and more state-repressive surveillance in Hungary and in the east of Eurasia. In these various regimes of surveillance, we have nothing less than a 'Eurasia of surveillance'. Here we have the germ of future ethnographic projects that can identify the kinds of resilience this surveillance will generate. After all, like state regulations, state borders, state censorship and brutal neoliberal market forces, people also find ways to cope with, adapt and transform their lifeways.

Conclusion: Eurasia as Spheres of Resilience and Cultures of Surveillance

The surveillance technologies described above pose new challenges to how ordinary people will cope with states and markets trying to control the most intimate aspects of our lives. How will people accommodate to these changes? What patterns of resilience will emerge? What would Polanyi's 'double movement' be like under these circumstances? Understanding how resilience operates, how vulnerability is threatened and how surveillance affects us, and how these social transformations can enhance, alter or undermine our sociality – these form the very essence of Chris Hann's project. Without worrying about 'what resilience really means' (let the Cambridge people do that), Chris' work forces us to avoid drawing any final verdicts until we have the data. All of it. Hence, Chris advocates more ethnography, more nuance. He keeps us honest.

However, the question arises as to whether we can ever reach a point where we can come to a conclusion and say 'Now we know'. Can the call for more research ever be a refusal to actually draw a judgement – to call a spade a spade? For the resilience crowd, is there not a point where 'survival' or 'coping' become but euphemisms for misery or repression? In observing how people behave under the most adverse of circumstances, do we solve anything by calling it 'agency'? Is there a line in the sand to be drawn here?

Comparing Chris Hann's work in Hungary with my own experiences in Romania made me think again about this line. The various ways in which Hungarians and other Eurasian peoples have adjusted to the systems that affected their lives – brutal state repression, cumbersome bureaucracy, overt surveillance, brutal market swings, wage labour precarity and remaking of the self – all this is what makes resilience. And people's resilience, however we define it, is the stuff of anthropology. Yes, 'further research is needed'. However, what is also needed are some hypotheses and conclusions about possible 'spheres of resilience' and 'cultures of surveillance'.

In highlighting the need to research spheres of resilience and cultures of surveillance, we can perhaps follow Chris Hann's example and add him to the four inspiring anthropologists from whom he took inspiration. Resilience and surveillance are the new research frontiers, not just for the Visegrád states, but for all of Eurasia. Chris can't retire. He has work to do.

Steven Sampson is Professor (Emeritus) of Social Anthropology at Lund University and lives in Copenhagen, Denmark. He has researched state socialism in Romania, NGOs, corruption, conspiracy theory and business ethics.

References

Barrios, Roberto E. 2016. 'Resilience: A Commentary from the Vantage Point of Anthropology', *Annals of Anthropological Practice* 40(1): 28–38.

Béné, Christophe, Rachel Godfrey Wood, Andrew Newsham, and Mark Davies. 2012. 'Resilience: New Utopia or New Tyranny? Reflection about the Potentials and Limits of the Concept of Resilience in Relation to Vulnerability', Reduction Programmes, *IDS Working Paper*, no. 405. Retrieved 10 December 2020 from https://www.ids.ac.uk/publications/resilience-new-utopia-or-new-tyranny.

Buchowski, Michał. 1996. 'The Shifting Meanings of Civil and Civic Society in Poland', in Chris Hann and Elizabeth Dunn (eds), *Civil Society: Challenging Western Models*. London: Routledge, pp. 76–96.

Gellner, Ernest. 1994. *Conditions of Liberty: Civil Society and Its Rivals*. New York: Allen Lane.
Goody, Jack. 2010. *The Eurasian Miracle*. Cambridge: Polity Press.
Gudeman, Steven. 2008. *Economy's Tension: The Dialectics of Community and Market*. New York: Berghahn Books.
Hankiss, Elemer. 1990a. *East European Alternatives*. Oxford: Oxford University Press.
———. 1990b. 'Second Economy and Civil Society', *Journal of Communist Studies* 6(2): 21–44.
Hann, C.M.. 1992a. 'Radical Functionalism: The Life and Work of Karl Polanyi', *Dialectical Anthropology* 17(2): 141–66.
Hann, Chris. 1992b. 'Civil Society at the Grassroots: A Reactionary View', in Paul Lewis (ed.), *Democracy and Civil Society in Eastern Europe*. London: Macmillan, pp. 152–65.
———. 2003. 'Civil Society: The Sickness, Not the Cure?', *Social Evolution and History* 2(2): 34–54.
———. 2004. 'In the Church of Civil Society', in Marlies Glasius, David Lewis and Hakan Seckinelgin (eds), *Exploring Civil Society: Political and Cultural Contexts*. London: Routledge, pp. 44–50.
———. 2016. 'A Concept of Eurasia', *Current Anthropology* 57(1): 1–27.
———. 2019a. *Repatriating Polanyi: Market Society in the Visegrád States*. Budapest: Central European University Press.
———. 2019b. 'Resilience and Transformation in Provincial Political Economy: From Market Socialism to Market Populism in Hungary, 1970s–2010s', *Cargo* 1–2: 1–23.
Hann, Chris, and Elizabeth Dunn (eds). 1996. *Civil Society: Challenging Western Models*. London: Routledge.
Hart, Keith. 1973. 'Informal Income Opportunities and Urban Employment in Ghana', *Journal of Modern African Studies* 11(1): 61–89.
Henig, David, and Nicolette Makovicky. 2017. *Economies of Favour after Socialism*. Oxford: Oxford University Press.
Kenedi, Janos. 1981. *Do It Yourself: Hungary's Hidden Economy*. London: Pluto Press.
Ledeneva, Alena (ed.). 2018. *The Global Encyclopaedia of Informality*, vols I and II. London: UCL Press.
Olsson, Lennart, Anne Jerneck, Henri Thoren, Johannes Persson and David O'Byrne. 2015. 'Why Resilience Is Unappealing to Social Science: Theoretical and Empirical Investigations of the Scientific Use of Resilience', *Science Advances* 1(4) e1400217, 22 May. Retrieved 10 December 2020 from https://advances.sciencemag.org/content/1/4/e1400217.full.p819
Polese, Abel. 2016. *Limits of a Post-Soviet State: How Informality Replaces, Renegotiates, and Reshapes Governance in Contemporary Ukraine*. Stuttgart: ibidem-Verlag.
Prosperi, David C., and Sofia Morgado. 2011. 'Resilience and Transformation: Can We Have Both?', in Manfred Schrenk, V. Popovich and Peter Zeile (eds), *Proceedings REAL CORP 2011 Tagungsband 18–20 May 2011*, Essen. Retrieved 10 December 2020 from https://programm.corp.at/cdrom2011/papers2011/CORP2011_92.pdf.

Sampson, Steven. 1986. 'The Informal Sector in Eastern Europe', *Telos* 66: 44–66.
_____. 1987. 'The Second Economy in Eastern Europe and the USSR', *Annals American Academy of Political and Social Science* 493(1): 120–36.
_____. 1988. '"May You Live Only by Your Salary!": The Unplanned Economy of Eastern Europe', *Social Justice* 12: 145–67.
_____. 1996. 'The Social Life of Projects: Importing Civil Society to Albania', in Chris Hann and Elizabeth Dunn (eds), *Civil Society: Challenging Western Models*. London: Routledge, pp. 121–42.
_____. 2002a. 'Beyond Transition: Rethinking Elite Configurations in the Balkans', in Chris Hann (ed) *Postsocialism: Ideals, Ideologies and Practices in Eurasia*. London: Routledge, pp. 221–42.
_____. 2002b. 'Weak States, Uncivil Society and Thousands of NGOs: Benevolent Colonialism in the Balkans', in Sanimir Resic and Barbara Törnquist-Plewa (eds), *The Balkans in Focus: Cultural Boundaries in Europe*. Lund: Nordic Academic Press, pp. 27–44.
_____. 2004. 'Too Much Civil Society? Donor-Driven NGOs in the Balkans', in Lis Dhundale and Eric Andre Andersen (eds), *Revisiting the Role of Civil Society in the Promotion of Human Rights*. Copenhagen: Danish Institute for Human Rights, pp. 197–220.
_____. 2017. 'Introduction: Engagements and Entanglements in the Anthropology of NGOs', in Amanda Lashaw, Christian Vannier and Steven Sampson (eds), *Cultures of Doing Good: Anthropologists and NGOs*. Tuscaloosa: University of Alabama Press, pp. 1–18.
_____. 2019a. 'How I Became a "Romania Expert"'. *Studiu Sociologica Univ Babes Bolyai, Cluj* 2/2018: 13–28. https://www.ceeol.com/search/journal-detail?id=65 and https://stevensampsontexts.files.wordpress.com/2019/02/introplusromaniaexpertstudiosociologicacluj.pdf.
_____. 2019b. 'Citizen Duty or Stasi Society? Whistleblowing and Disclosure Regimes in Organizations and Communities', *Ephemera: Theory and Politics in Organization* 19(4): 777–806.
_____. 2020. 'Tattoos and Ankle Bracelets: Recalling Fieldwork in Romania', in Raluca Mateoc and François Ruegg (eds), *Recalling Fieldwork: People, Places and Encounters*. Berlin: Lit Verlag, pp. 119–42.
Verdery, Katherine. 1996. *What Was Socialism and What Comes Next?* Princeton: Princeton University Press.
_____. 2018. *My Life as a Spy: Investigations in a Secret Police File*. Durham, NC: Duke University Press.
Wedel, Janine. 1986. *The Private Poland*. New York: Facts on File, Inc.
Zuboff, Shoshana. 2019. *The Age of Surveillance Capitalism: The Fight for the Future at the New Frontier of Power*. London: Profile Books.

Part II

Economic Anthropology in a Changing World

Chapter 8

Hijra, Port and Market
Pre-Ottoman Economies in Southwest Arabia's Zaydi Realm

Andre Gingrich

The economic history of pre-Ottoman ('medieval') Southwest Arabia to some extent still remains unwritten. The present contribution[1] seeks to provide a few conceptual building blocks for filling existing gaps by focusing on developments and constellations in the Zaydi realms of the northern Yemeni highlands through the lens of economic anthropology, i.e. largely, though not exclusively, inspired by the work of Karl Polanyi.[2] Such an approach has been informed by the author's cooperation throughout more than two decades with Chris Hann, to whom this volume is dedicated and who has continuously demonstrated the relevance of Polanyi's oeuvre for economic anthropology.

For the present purposes, three of Polanyi's crucial orientations will be pursued. His most fundamental idea about any economy being *embedded* within wider social contexts and institutions is addressed by an outline of precisely that embeddedness in northern Yemen before the fifteenth century CE. This is then continued by discussing the *main systems of trade and exchange* in their institutional settings, as Polanyi's characteristic analytical perspectives on economic life. From this realm, the analysis then proceeds to a final consideration of Polanyi's enduring focus on *forms of integration* between the economy, society and religion for this northern Yemeni historical case study.

Notes for this chapter begin on page 131.

Temporal and Regional Contexts

Zaydism is understood as a specific orientation in Shiite Islam that has survived and flourished primarily in northern Yemen since the ninth century CE, when it was originally established there under the first Zaydi Imam, al-Hadi Yahya b. al-Husayn. The Zaydi presence in northern Yemen was established a couple of centuries after the main waves of migration out of Southwest Arabia during the first movements of Islam's expansion. Before and after the first Zaydi Imam's arrival, the Yemen remained somewhat peripheral to the main developments in the Muslim world. Like all major and minor orientations in Islam, Zaydism has always entailed not merely spiritual and ritual priorities, but also a number of legal, political and socioeconomic implications.

The Zaydi Imams originated in the Medina region in northwestern Arabia. Northern Yemeni emissaries invited the Imams to their own home regions near the towns of Sa'da and Najran[3] to settle protracted local intertribal conflicts (Heiss 2014). After al-Hadi had succeeded in this task, he settled down in the region and established the Zaydi Imamate with Sa'da as its enduring spiritual capital. From these beginnings, two basic sociopolitical features accompanied the rise of Zaydism in the northern Yemeni highlands.

First, Zaydism had its primary social recruitment base among the high status minority group of the Prophet Muhammad's descendants (*Ahl al-Bayt*) in the region. Their presence among the majority population depended upon that majority's hospitality and support. In turn, this was largely informed by the extent to which Zaydi rule was perceived as good governance, primarily in the field of just legal services with conflict resolutions as their core. Shari'a scriptural law in its Zaydi interpretation (Messick 2018) was thereby applied whenever the mechanisms of tribal customary law did not suffice. That majority population in these mountains and highland regions consisted of tribal sedentary groups based on mixed agricultural production. The tribal majority population largely identified with pre-Islamic ancestries of Ancient South Arabian background, while the Ahl al-Bayt were perceived as having a quite different (i.e. northwest Arabian) origin. Intermarriage between members of both groups was possible but rare. Succession to the Imam's office was determined by the interplay of meritocracy and loose inheritance: only adult male Ahl al-Bayt members were eligible to become a new Imam, but among that limited group of possible candidates, no directly inherited accession to office was accepted. Instead, the candidate who saw himself as best qualified and was accepted by others would become the new Imam. Therefore, transition periods between one Imam's death and the rise in office of a successor could often be characterized by competition, at times even between several rival self-declared Imams.

Second, Zaydism therefore represented a fairly fragile and unstable form of rule, particularly during the first three centuries of its Yemeni existence (i.e. the tenth to twelfth centuries CE). Aside from Sa'da, usually there were a few more permanent core areas as well as a number of peripheral areas under weaker Zaydi influence, ranging from southern Hijaz to the Sana'a basin. Moreover, which areas were peripheral and which were outside any direct Zaydi influence repeatedly changed according to the tides of military fortune or regional dissent. Sometimes Zaydi influence extended to Sana'a as the region's major city in the central highlands, while often it did not; by contrast, Aden in southern Yemen hardly ever came under any direct Zaydi influence except during rare and short interludes. Thus, Zaydi territories were constantly waxing and waning. The actual loci of Zaydi power were literally mobile: most of an Imam's year in office would be spent on the move, travelling from one arena of action to the next – for example, to engage with conflicts and their resolution in one or the other destination on an Imam's expeditions. In retrospect, it seems that this pattern of meritocratic and mobile Zaydi rule from the tenth century to the twelfth century had some, albeit limited, success. While Zaydism had lost out against most other rival orientations elsewhere in the Muslim world, it had established itself more or less permanently in this remote and inaccessible corner of the Arab peninsula by the early thirteenth century.

By the mid-thirteenth century, the Zaydi Imamate had solidified into somewhat more robust and stable forms in the tribal highlands north of Sana'a up to Asir (today in Saudi Arabia). The Zaydi orientation as led by the Ahl al-Bayt had succeeded in overcoming and absorbing a rival Zaydi movement led by local tribal members and Yemeni intellectuals (*Mutarrifiyya*), and had taken over some of its main institutional features. This had resulted in several innovations. Most important among them was the establishment (or the re-activation in new contexts) of sacred enclaves, or *Hijra*. Although the term is commonly used to designate the Prophet's 'flight' from Mecca to Medina (Yathrib), which marks the first year in the Islamic calendar, its basic meaning is not 'flight', but 'asylum'. This is the original and also its main Yemeni meaning. The Yemeni term 'Hijra' not only refers to 'asylum' but also, in a broader sense, to any other protected status that is set apart from the rest (Puin 1984).[4]

Within these sets of theological, legal and semantic meanings, the Ahl al-Bayt-led Zaydis had arranged with their tribal majority hosts that a pattern of dispersed Hijra settlements could be maintained all over the main highland regions under respective tribal legal and armed protection. Inside these Hijra settlements, Ahl al-Bayt families as well as Jewish and Muslim families of lower social status could live and professionally interact with each other as well as with their tribal environment. This primary social and legal innovation also marks the threshold time when the Yemeni Zaydi Ahl al-Bayt became referred to as Masters or Lords (Sada) in local and regional terminology. Public recognition by locals of the Ahl al-Bayt's superior social position and hegemony went hand in hand with a new terminology for tribal leaders, who previously had been addressed as 'Sada', but who now were increasingly referred to as Shaykh/Shuyukh, i.e. (tribal) headmen or chiefs (Heiss 2005). Since bride-giving designates a temporary or permanent position of social inferiority vis-à-vis bride-receivers all across South Arabia, these terminological transformations point at the beginnings of a new element in marriage patterns that has endured in Yemeni social history ever since. The old paramount chiefly tribal[5] families of the Yemeni highlands, as well as those of important subtribes, seem to have engaged since then in fairly recurrent patterns of hypergamous marriage with the Ahl al-Bayt. Therefore, by the mid-thirteenth century, Zaydi rule in Upper Yemen could rely on a more permanent network of marriage alliances between leading tribal families and the main Ahl al-Bayt families in the region, supported by a network of flourishing Hijra settlements (Gingrich and Kommer 2018; Hovden 2016; Madelung 1991).

The Zaydi Realm in Its Economic Contexts in the Thirteenth to Fifteenth Centuries

The social and institutional changes accomplished in the Yemen's Zaydi realms by the thirteenth century CE aimed at establishing more stability, not merely internally but also in view of developments in the immediate Yemeni vicinity and elsewhere. For several centuries, the southern parts of Yemen but equally, if not more importantly, large areas along the Southwest and South Arabian coastlines had become progressively engaged in maritime interactions across the Indian Ocean, especially with East Africa, South Asia and Southeast Asia. Together with the growth of Islamization in those regions, this had led to increasing flows of pilgrimage from there, via the Red Sea routes and coasts, to Mecca and back. Ever more new ideas, new technologies (e.g. in astronomy, geography, mathematics and medicine), imported goods and weapons, and slaves (Moorthy-Kloss 2019) had flowed into Southwest Arabia or were passing by its shores. Ever since the twelfth century, southern Yemen had been much more intensively integrated into these developments once the Ayyubid and Rasulid dynasties established themselves successively in the highlands and coastal areas. Well connected to their related dynasties in North Arabia and Egypt, they became active participants and crucial agents in these innovative cross-continental and intercontinental networks, in parallel to vibrant smaller entities along the western Red Sea coasts (e.g. Dahlak) and across many other East African islands and ports (Vallet 2011).

While these intercontinental and transmaritime developments were taking place in their immediate vicinity, it was much more difficult for leading figures in the Zaydi realm to actively participate in them. To an extent, this was related to the fact that the tribal and Ahl al-Bayt leaders in the Zaydi realm had very limited access to suitable nearby ports, let alone ones under their immediate control. While Aden was a well-protected volcanic rock harbour, the small ports along the eastern shores of the Red Sea south of Jidda were shallow and sandy. Moreover, they were controlled by coastal semi-tribal groups mostly beyond any immediate Zaydi influence. During the twelfth, thirteenth and fourteenth centuries, the Zaydi Imams therefore enhanced their efforts at gaining improved access to good ports and secure trading connections along the coast by means of diplomacy and warfare. This was one of the main background factors (apart from their denominational dissent) in the Zaydis' regular conflicts with the Rasulids in central Yemen until the latter dynasty died out in the mid-fifteenth century. At the same time, it seems that the Zaydi Imams, as well as tribal leaders from their realm, continued to entertain representatives of their own in several of those small Red Sea ports that they did not directly control, such as Aththar (a harbour that pre-dated the more recent port of Jazan and that subsequently silted-up) or Hali (further to the north, visited by Ibn Battuta (1958: 107) in around 1330). Similar practices of entertaining semi-permanent representatives or commercial delegates in distant but vital eastern Red Sea ports had already been known since the tenth century (Gingrich 2005, 2006).

The Zaydi realm was thus not entirely cut off from those commercial and technological innovations between the thirteenth and fifteenth centuries, but it took longer to actively participate in them, and the range of innovations that could potentially be absorbed was somewhat more limited. Still, the production of certain local commodities – such as honey, leather products and rare timber – seems to have increased for the purposes of growing long-distance export. At the same time, the cultivation and trading of two new cash crops also seem to have first entered the Zaydi realm during these three centuries. Coffee, imported from Ethiopia, was first mentioned as a luxury product for the post-Rasulid (Tahirid) elites (Varisco 2012). About the same time, Qat consumption emerged in a similar context, i.e. leaves imported from East Africa for south Yemeni elite consumption (Varisco 2012). Local (tribal) mountain farmers began to cultivate and grow coffee and Qat in the Zaydi realm during the late pre-Ottoman centuries if not earlier. Therefore, in several selected spheres, tribal agriculture and the raising of livestock became increasingly integrated into long-distance and intercontinental but perhaps also in regional market exchange. Together with these developments, an existing stratum of specialists in trade and commerce by necessity must have grown, partly as newcomers from the *nouveaux riches* and partly from established elite families among both Sada and tribes, but also including some from low-status groups.

Hijra, *Suq* and Port

The three institutions of Hijra, *suq* (market) and port may be identified as the central sites for the commercial exchange of goods and services in the northern Yemeni highlands between the thirteenth and the fifteenth centuries. Ritual exchange of gifts, endowments or voluntary taxes went through other channels, as we shall see.

Permanent markets seem to have been fairly rare during the centuries in question. Yet a few documents indicate that Aden, Sana'a and Sa'da hosted set (permanent) market areas in and between their main residential neighbourhoods. Otherwise, a number of unpublished tribal documents dating back to the fourteenth century indicate rotating weekly market days (*Suq al-usbu'*) in or near a particular rural settlement. If ethnographic evidence from the twentieth century is any indicator of the relevance of weekly markets during late pre-Ottoman centuries, then, in terms of product ranges, the markets certainly offered a partially different (e.g. pre-industrial) spectrum. Still, they would provide a combination of local and regional seasonal and nonseasonal products from agriculture, crafts and hunting to clients from the region as well as to traders. Some of the skills considered 'impure', such as slaughtering or tanning, would be carried out at a distance from the main market area, as would livestock sales. A specialized mediator (*dallal*) would facilitate the bargaining in all market transactions, which must usually have taken place as sales, i.e. using money rather than in kind. Barter in kind should not be excluded, but reliable sources for the tenth century already mention the existence of mints and of set rates of currency for certain measurement units for regular market commodities such as honey. Together with current numismatic research in Yemen's history (Smith 1990), this allows the provisional conclusion that money as the central means of standard exchange was already dominating the limited but existing sphere of non-ritual exchanges before the fifteenth century in the northern Yemeni highlands. In turn, this reveals the definite influence of the Imamic state on the monetary segment of the regional economy. While any direct supervision by state representatives would be quite unlikely for most weekly markets, those with high intertribal attendance would attain Hijra status on market day: most weapons would have to be left at the entrance and the tribal chief (or several of them) responsible for this particular territory would be in charge of resolving any legal conflict occurring during market day.

The situation in Red Sea ports would differ markedly. Here, the main agents would hardly be domestic consumers, but primarily regional and transregional traders in imports and exports, commercial representatives of dhows and other ships, semi-permanent delegates of tribal and Sada leaders, *dallal* facilitators and caravan entrepreneurs with their teams. Much larger sums would be in circulation and the question of currencies and of several exchange rates would be a ubiquitous topic of commercial conflict. Unfortunately, the available sources give us barely any hint as to how this very high level of pragmatic conflict potential might have been contained. In view of what was said above about semi-permanent resident delegates of Sada and tribal leaders, and about actual control over these small port sites by semi-tribal groups from the region, one hypothesis seems more plausible than others. In line with other conflict-limiting precautions in northern Yemen, it is probable that a composite group in charge of containing or solving serious conflicts integrated responsibilities in situ in these ports. This would have been a representative of the local semi-tribal group in question, as well as delegates from the Sada and from some of the highlands' tribal leaders. That group may or may not also have included an experienced *dallal*, at least as a witness skilled in how to facilitate the smooth running of big commercial transactions. Since this question also touches on Polanyi's concept of 'administered trade' (and various sub-versions of it), I shall continue working here with the hypothesis, as outlined above, of a 'composite port commission'.

Beyond its main spiritual and ritual features, often centring around a mosque, a Hijra settlement would also encompass a variety of more or less related services. This might include payments for legal services, such as negotiating and concluding a marriage contract or a religious endowment (*waqf*) (Hovden 2019), preparing a peace settlement in tribal conflict, legal assistance in sorting out inheritance questions and the like. It could also include handicrafts and services offered by resident members of Muslim groups of inferior status, such as those providing certain forms of attire, gravestones, scribes' work and so forth. Women from the same group would be engaged in weaving or textile activities, or in their fathers' or husbands' professions, and the respective products could also be acquired outside a weekly market by commission. In the event that a wealthy merchant from the same group or from the Sada was a Hijra resident, he could be a primary point of contact for a tribesman who wanted to commission the purchase of goods for sale elsewhere. In short, a Hijra could also be an important site for acquiring – mostly by commission – special services and goods, and it was an important place for experts from various status groups to be based. In many ways, a Hijra combined features of a small proto-city with aspects of a scriptural religious enclave.

Ritual Transactions, the Domestic Mode of Production and the Imamic State

As has been pointed out, the actual influence of Zaydi norms and values among the majority population solidified to an extent between the thirteenth and the fifteenth centuries; nevertheless, the spheres of Zaydi influence still included core regions, less reliable spheres and quite a few tribal zones at the periphery of any direct ideological or political state impact whatsoever. The extent to which these tribal majority populations practised the ritual transactions, as prescribed in Zaydi doctrine, differed according to their positioning. For some tribal groups near Sa'da, for instance, the regular payment of the alms tax (*zakat*) by those who have the means to support people in need is recorded throughout the centuries. For other large tribal groups living in remote areas, whose handwritten records I have examined back to the fourteenth century, not a single document or other testimony indicated any religious *waqf* endowment. Thus, it can be safely argued that the observance of Zaydi ritual transactions by members of tribal majorities was at best partial and inhomogeneous, while it had to be much more common among the Sada with their usually more affluent and pious social existence. One may also add that the abuse of *waqf* and *zakat*, which eventually contributed to the collapse of Imamic rule in the twentieth century, is likely to have had its historical precursors. Pious giving for the common good always represented a temptation to personal greed among those who supposedly administered it on behalf of the common good.

In my own analysis of the historical Yemeni highlands, I combine arguments made by Paul Dresch (1989) and Martha Mundy (1995) to characterize the majority agricultural population as being based in economic terms on a tribally organized domestic mode of production (Goody 1990; Sahlins 1972: 41–146). Inside tribal territories, whether or not they included a Hijra settlement, the economic emphasis had to be put on self-reliance and, for special occasions, on a reliable mutual cooperation between households. Such cooperation included repair works in irrigation and terrace construction, in building houses, in carrying out skirmishes, in mutual aid during agricultural bottleneck periods, and in jointly staging ceremonies and feasts, such as circumcision ceremonies or *istighatha* (a rain sacrifice). Only some areas of a household's economic activities were thus market-oriented (bee-keeping or cultivating coffee or Qat, for instance). Until late into the twentieth century, a main focus on self-sufficiency was maintained. Consequently, money must have existed in many of these local tribal households, but unless they were wealthy bee-keepers, for example, then money was usually scarce. Local and intertribal weekly markets were attended regularly, but on a weekly basis only if a household urgently wanted to sell available surplus or for other reasons. By far the most valuable transactions that occurred within a household's lifecycles were thus the passing on of property through inheritance and through marriage (Gingrich 2015b). As far as I have been able to examine family documents for the time periods under scrutiny here, these transactions usually involved minimal amounts of money.[6]

In short, from the perspective of an average tribal family household, a monetary economic sector was of only subordinate importance, while the main domestic economic activities were centred on self-sufficiency combined with pragmatic and ceremonial reciprocity between households. Within these households, a hierarchical division of labour between genders and generations prevailed, which included reciprocity as well as senior- and male-centred redistribution. Occasional skirmishes inside or across tribal borders are best described in Sahlins' (1972) terms as 'negative reciprocity'. Tribal and paramount chiefs benefited from their own efforts at maintaining local peace. At times, however, local and regional conflicts and skirmishes could indeed escalate towards a scale that made the intervention of skilled, neutral and superior mediators necessary, which fed into the original pragmatic raison d'être for the Ahl al-Bayt.

I have identified three sources of economically relevant income for the Zaydi Sada of Yemen in the period examined here: general legal services, participation in the pursuit of trade and commerce, and, finally, the administration of religiously legitimate taxation and endowment flows (including individual abuse of these flows). To the pursuit of trade and commerce as the peaceful acquisition of resources, we might also add direct and indirect services for the violent acquisition of other resources, i.e. by supporting relevant Imamic war efforts in the hope of benefiting from them. Sometimes, special war taxation was added to the burdens imposed on the common people. In sum, the Ahl al-Bayt's economic activities amounted to one part status-centred self-interest and one part common good.

A Polanyi-esque Visit to the Historical Highlands of Yemen

In this analysis, I have tried to demonstrate that a Polanyi-inspired approach in economic anthropology may be helpful to ask clear questions and scrutinize the relevant source materials. Chris Hann deserves credit indeed for consistently having pointed this out (Hann 2015, 2018). For Upper Yemen's history in late pre-Ottoman times, such an approach has at least facilitated and encouraged an investigation that otherwise could not easily have been initiated at all. For that region and time as much as for others, the economy cannot be understood without considering it as being *embedded* in religion, law, society and institutions. Moreover, in any precapitalist but increasingly commercially oriented formation such as this one, Polanyi's approaches to various *systems of exchange* remain fundamental. In the end, a focus on *forms of integration* between production, distribution and consumption, and, more importantly even, between religion and the socioeconomic realms continue to serve as a crucial guideline for economic anthropology in its historical dimension.

It may perhaps not come as a complete surprise that versions of reciprocity and redistribution could be identified as valid mechanisms both within and between households engaged in a tribal domestic mode of production. Moreover, it could be shown that money exchange informed some limited spheres of these households' activities, in addition to communal reciprocity and gift exchange. Further, these bottom-up perspectives could be integrated into wider regional and top-down perspectives. From those vantage points, it was possible to show how the ruling elite and their states influenced money exchange and, through 'composite port commissions', also some limited form of administered commerce via ports of trade. In the end, it could be clarified how Zaydi Imamic rule and their Ahl al-Bayt elites combined the pursuit of economic self-interest with redistributive services for the common good.

Andre Gingrich is a member of the Austrian and the Royal Swedish Academies of Sciences. He has conducted ethnographic fieldwork in Yemen, Saudi-Arabia and Syria. The results also inform his topical specialization in themes such as ethnicity, gender, concepts of identity, paradoxes of globalization, neo-nationalism, intercultural and comparative analysis and history of anthropological theory formation.

Notes

1. I thank this volume's editors, as well as Julene Knox (London) and Daniel M. Varisco (Princeton), for their helpful comments on first drafts of this chapter. At the Austrian Academy of Sciences (ÖAW) in Vienna, I am grateful for the draft text's discussion by Michael Alram and at the Academy's Institute for Social Anthropology (ISA) by Eva-Maria Knoll and ISA's Yemen Studies Group (Marieke Brandt, Johann Heiss, Odile Kommer, Lisa Lenz, Magdalena Moorthy-Kloss and Alexander Weissenburger). Some insights presented here result from a long-term research project (2011–19) supported by the ÖAW and ISA, but also by the University of Vienna and the Austrian Science Fund's (FWF's) SFB program (VISCOM – SFB F42-G18), which is duly acknowledged.
2. For the transliteration of Arabic terms, this text uses common Anglicized versions ('Yemeni', 'Zaydi') whenever available. Otherwise, a simplified form of IJMES transliteration rules is employed – with all appropriate apologies to the experts. Since the present analysis aims at a first conceptual overview, regional references are limited to a number of recent academic studies in which the main historical sources in Arabic are indicated.
3. Sa'da (today in Yemen's northernmost province) soon after the ninth century became a fortified ('mural') city, Najran (today in Saudi Arabia's neighbouring province to the northeast) has always remained an oasis settlement ('garden city'); on that distinction, see Gingrich (2016).
4. 'Asylum' in the historical Arabic sense thereby designates the legally successful accomplishment of 'flight', or any other movement beyond a person's previous residence, which affords the person a protected status comprising new residential and personal rights. Hijra therefore always implies a legal status with temporal (i.e. 'ending a previous movement away from home') and spatial dimensions (i.e. 'being protected in the territorial domain of the new sojourn').
5. The question of what 'tribe' and 'tribal' means in a Yemeni context, and in which sense this remains a valid emic and descriptive term for these and similar purposes, is discussed in Gingrich (2015a) and Varisco (2017).
6. On one occasion, it was specified for a seemingly 'big' marriage between the family members of two tribal subsections' chiefs that the 'bridewealth' would include silver jewellery worth 'two goats and a calf'. Zaydi coins existed, although the relevant mining sources usually were beyond Zaydi control.

References

Dresch, Paul. 1989. *Tribes, Government, and History in Yemen*. Oxford: Oxford University Press

Gingrich, Andre. 2005. 'Norm und Praxis: Zur Ordnung des Raumes am Beispiel der Siedlungsgeschichte von al- Qunfidha', in Johann Heiss (ed.), *Veränderung und Stabilität: Normen und Werte in Islamischen Gesellschaften*. Vienna: Verlag der ÖAW, pp. 91–119.

———. 2006. 'Wohnarchitektur im südwestlichen Saudi Arabien: Lokale Zeugnisse historischer Interaktionen mit Nachbarn, Herrschern und Fremden', in Walter Dostal (ed.), *Tribale Gesellschaften der südwestlichen Regionen des Königreiches Saudi Arabien. Sozialanthropologische Untersuchungen.* Vienna: Verlag der ÖAW, pp. 207–406, 576–613, 630–37, 676–82.

———. 2015a. 'Tribe', in James D. Wright (editor-in-chief), *International Encyclopedia of the Social & Behavioral Sciences*, 2nd edn, vol. 24. Oxford: Elsevier, pp. 645–47.

———. 2015b. 'Multiple Histories: Three Journeys through Academic Records, Medieval Yemen, and Current Anthropology's Encounters with the Past', *History and Anthropology* 26(1): 110–28.

———. 2016. 'Medieval Eurasian Communities by Comparison: Methods, Concepts, Insights', in Eirik Hovden, Christina Lutter and Walter Pohl (eds), *Meanings of Community across Eurasia: Comparative Approaches*. Leiden: Brill, pp. 468–97.

Gingrich, Andre, and Odile Kommer. 2018. 'Südwestarabien in islamisch-vorosmanischer Zeit: Ein Forschungsbericht zu Konflikt und Konsens aus der historischen Anthropologie', *Mitteilungen der Anthropologischen Gesellschaft in Wien* 148: 267–84.

Goody, Jack. 1990. *The Oriental, the Ancient, and the Primitive: Systems of Marriage and the Family in the Pre-industrial Societies of Eurasia.* Cambridge: Cambridge University Press.

Hann, Chris. 2015. 'Goody, Polanyi and Eurasia: An Unfinished Project in Comparative Historical Economic Anthropology', *History and Anthropology* 26(3): 308–20.

———. 2018. 'Economic Anthropology', in Hilary Callan (ed.), *The International Encyclopedia of Anthropology*, vol. 4. Chichester: Wiley Blackwell, pp. 1708–23.

Heiss, Johann. 2005. 'Ein šayh ist ein šayh, aber was für ein Ding ist ein sayyid? Zur Entwicklung einer Wortbedeutung', in Johann Heiss (ed.), *Veränderung und Stabilität: Normen und Werte in Islamischen Gesellschaften* (Veröffentlichungen zur Sozialanthropologie vol. 7). Vienna: Verlag der ÖAW, pp. 121–36.

———. 2014. 'Sa'da Revisited', in Andre Gingrich and Siegfried Haas (eds), *Southwest Arabia Across History: Essays to the Memory of Walter Dostal*. Vienna: Verlag der ÖAW, pp. 79–89.

Hovden, Eirik. 2016. 'Competing Visions of Welfare in the Zaydi Community of Medieval South Arabia', in Eirik Hovden, Christina Lutter and Walter Pohl (eds), *Meanings of Community Across Eurasia: Comparative Approaches*. Leiden: Brill, pp. 338–497.

———. 2019. *Waqf in Zaydī Islam: Legal Theory, Codification, and Local Practice.* Leiden: Brill.

Ibn Battuta. 1958. *Travels in Asia and Africa 1325–1354*, translated and selected by H.A.R. Gibb. London: Routledge & Kegan Paul.

Madelung, Wilferd. 1991. 'The Origins of the Yemenite Hijra', in Alan Jones (ed.), *Arabicus Felix. Luminosus Brittanicus: Essays in Honour of A.F.L. Beeston on His Eightieth Birthday*. Reading: Ithaca Press, pp. 25–44.

Messick, Brinckley. 2018. *Sharī'a Scripts: A Historical Anthropology*. New York: Columbia University Press.

Moorthy-Kloss, Magdalena. 2019. Slaves at the Najahid and Rasulid Courts of Yemen (412–553 AH / 1021–1158 CE and 626–858 AH / 1229–1454 CE), Ph.D. dissertation. Vienna: University of Vienna.

Mundy, Martha. 1995. *Domestic Government: Community and Polity in North Yemen*. New York: Tauris.

Puin, Gerd. 1984. 'The Yemeni Hijrah Concept of Tribal Protection', in Tarif Khalidi (ed.), *Land Tenure and Social Transformation in the Middle East*. Beirut: AUB Press, pp. 483–94.

Sahlins, Marshall. 1972. *Stone Age Economics*. Chicago: Aldine & Atherton.

Smith, G. Rex. 1990. 'Some Medieval Yemenite Numismatic Problems: Observations on Some Recently Sold Coins', *Arabian Archaeology and Epigraphy* 1(1): 29–37.

Vallet, Eric. 2011. *L'Arabie Marchande. Etat et Commerce sous les Sultans Rasûlides du Yémen (626–858/1229–1454)*. Paris: Publications de la Sorbonne.

Varisco, Daniel Martin. 2012. 'Qāt and Traditional Healing in Yemen', in Ingrid Hehmayer and Hanne Schönig (eds), *Herbal Medicine in Yemen: Traditional Knowledge and Practice, and Their Value for Today's World*. Leiden: Brill, pp. 69–102.

_____. 2017. 'Yemen's Tribal Idiom: An Ethno-historical Survey of Genealogical Models', *Journal of Semitic Studies* LXII(1): 217–41.

Chapter 9

From Social Norms to Legal Norms
Regulating Work in Postneoliberal Political Economies

Ruth Dukes and Wolfgang Streeck

Labour law scholarship is traditionally pluralist in its approach. Aiming to understand the regulation of work and working relations, scholars have recognized the importance of taking into account not only formal law – statutory and judge-made rules – but also the terms of collective agreements, norms originating from the 'custom and practice' of a particular trade, the rulebooks of factories and plants, and the constitutions of trade unions and employers' associations. Used descriptively in relation to labour law, the term 'pluralism' or 'industrial pluralism' has been intended to capture something of the 'complexity, heterogeneity and internal diversity', as Harry Arthurs put it, of the field. For him, pluralism meant:

> the inability of overarching normative regimes to penetrate and transform all contexts, such as places of work, and the persistent tendency of such contexts themselves to generate and enforce distinctive norms expressing values which are, at least in some respects, different from those of the encompassing society. (Arthurs 1985)

In industrial sociology, it has long been recognized that an important source of informal norms at work – shared beliefs about how the work ought to be done and by whom – are groups of workers at particular workplaces, with shared occupations: so-called 'occupational communities'. In the literature, occupational communities are defined as 'group[s] of people who consider themselves to be engaged in the same sort of

---

Notes for this chapter begin on page 142.

work; whose social and personal identity is drawn from such work; and who, to varying degrees, recognize and share with one another job specific (but, to various degrees, contentious) values, norms and perspectives that apply to but extend beyond work related matters' (van Maanen and Barley 1984). The *locus classicus* is a 1956 volume by Seymour Martin Lipset et al., *Union Democracy: The Internal Politics of the International Typographical Union* (Lipset et al. 1956). Undertaking to explain the unique structure and industrial power of the trade union in question, Lipset et al. pointed to the labour process in printing, which required printers to work at night. This isolated the workers from others with more conventional time schedules and made them dependent for their social life on each other. In turn, this made for a pattern of deep social integration in a collective culture formed around printing as an occupation. The degree of social integration sustained not only a powerful trade union but also book clubs, choirs and chess tournaments. Over time, it resulted in strong relations of solidarity and in the development of collective ideas of what the printers owed to their employer and what the employer owed them in return. In other words, it resulted in a sense of occupational or 'industrial justice', of a good day's wage for a good day's work, and of how work should be organized to respect a worker's dignity and his right to a life outside of work, together with friends and family (Selznick 1969).

The printers of the International Typographical Union were an extreme case, as Lipset et al. knew very well. However, like other extreme cases, their study threw into relief general phenomena present but less easily detectable elsewhere. In a 1967 study of compositors, for example, Isidore Cyril Cannon observed the creation and enforcement of rules and 'moral values' within communities of workers at workplaces and, more formally, within their 'chapels' – the compositors' works councils, or workplace organizations, which existed in parallel with the trade union, organizationally distinct from it (Cannon 1967). In the case of the compositors, the formation of occupational communities was again facilitated by the nature of the work, which allowed for easy contact between the workers and frequently required them to seek and provide each other with assistance. The compositors' rules regulated working practices within the firm, and relations between the workers, including especially relations of solidarity. If someone got married, or had a baby, or retired, for example, all co-workers were expected to contribute to a 'pass-round'. In addition to the trade union, workers were expected to join various friendly societies and to make periodic contributions to funds out of which pensions might eventually be paid, or assistance in case of injury or illness. Pensions for which eligibility was decided by popular vote provided a particularly strong incentive to win and maintain the approval of the community as a whole. As Cannon observed, transgressions from accepted behaviour were routinely discouraged informally by jokes, practical jokes or less gentle forms of group admonition or censure. Pressures to conform might extend to manners of dress and speaking, and even to leisure activities and choice of reading matter.

Today, in the aftermath of the decline of industrial work and the disappearance of male labour aristocracies, occupational communities might be expected to have disappeared. However, as even a cursory literature survey reveals, the concept of occupational community, referencing the moral embeddedness of work in life and life in work, remains very useful for the study of labour relations and the regulation of work. This is so even in the new service sector with its small firms, ostensibly low-skilled work, precarious and on-demand employment, and ambiguous work relations between contracting parties. The notion of the moral embeddedness of economic action is of course very usefully elaborated in Chris Hann's Polanyian economic anthropology.[1] Similarly framed ethnographic studies of the past twenty years indicate that even workers in low-status occupations tend to develop positive identifications with their work, typically based upon pride in the performance of work tasks perceived to be difficult.[2] Identification with work and occupation is reinforced and becomes collective identification through workers' interactions with fellow-workers (Adler and Adler 1999). As in the past, occupational communities straddle the boundary between work and non-work and seek a satisfactory balance between them (Sandiford and Seymour 2007). They perform important functions for the successful discharge of work duties and may, under favourable conditions, provide a social substructure for the formulation and articulation of the collective interests of workers (Adams et al. 2012). A fascinating recent example concerns app-based ride-hail drivers in Indonesia, a sizable proportion of whom have formed and joined community organizations that operate on a mutual aid logic, characterized by strong bonds of social commitment (Ford and Honan 2019). Like other gig workers, these drivers rely heavily on social media (in this case WhatsApp) to stay in touch while they perform their spatially isolated work tasks. Online communication facilitates mutual assistance and support 'on the job' and can lead to or supplement face-to-face contact at designated meeting places or social events.[3]

As Arthurs (1985) emphasized in his discussion of pluralism, informal norms of industrial justice are related to formal law in complex ways. In some cases, legal rules may have their origins in social norms or practices, for example, where elements of 'custom and practice' are held by the courts to be legally binding, or where the terms of collective agreements are accorded legal force by reason of a court ruling or statutory provision.

In other cases, however, legal rules and social norms may be at odds with each other, so that the former are perceived by those affected to be unfair or unrealistic. As a result, a breach of the law may go unchallenged in a manner that, over time, undermines its efficacy and legitimacy. It is also possible that the substance of applicable legal rules may shape workers' perceptions of what is fair in a given situation. The 'knowledgeability' of social and economic action is invested, we might say, with legal notions and concepts, even if these are apprehended by the actors themselves in the guise of practices, routines or shared understandings that are only dimly reminiscent of the legal rule from which they originally stem (Knegt 2018; Weber 1978).

How might the relation of informal norms to formal law at work (workplaces or occupations) be institutionalized to produce equitable and legitimate labour market regimes? For much of the twentieth century, collective bargaining – the setting of wages and conditions through collective negotiations between unions and employers, or associations of employers – performed this function. Of course, the concrete shape of collective bargaining differed between national 'labour constitutions' and over time, depending on the distribution of political and economic power, and the structure and fortunes of the national economy (Dukes 2014). Nonetheless, what its different incorporations had in common was that they instituted a chain from perceptions of industrial justice at the level of work groups and occupational communities to voluntary or semi-voluntary organizations – in particular, trade unions. These organizations then integrated the local sentiments into supralocal collective interests and represented them vis-à-vis employers and in national politics. At each stage, provided that union leaderships did not get too far divorced from their grassroots – provided, in other words, that unions remained democratic organizations – worker interests became more generally defined. Ultimately they were given expression as class interests for a national system of industrial relations, taking account of their prospect of realization and backed by increasingly broad collective solidarity.

In this manner, trade unions functioned as transmission belts between the life-world of workers in different workplaces and industries, and the general system of formal legal rules designed to provide for order and fairness in labour markets, by balancing the stark asymmetry inherent in 'contracting for work' among individuals rather than collectives. That is not to say, of course, that there was any kind of straightforward replication within collective agreements of the workers' notions of what was just. Periodically renegotiable, collective agreements are better understood as temporary compromises, signed by both sides in spite of unreconciled values and, often, irreconcilable interests. As such, collective bargaining was an essential part of postwar democracies. Postwar labour constitutions provided legitimacy and stability to parliamentary democracies by integrating the social classes within what was functionally a second tier of government – one that bore primary responsibility for effecting a redistribution of wealth and related elements of class compromise.

It is widely known that collective bargaining has been on the decline in recent decades, as have all institutions mediating between the market and the state, the local and the national (Streeck 2006). There were attacks on trade unions by governments, and employers cut workers off from upward chains of political integration and representation. Industrial and organizational change compounded the problem. For example, the emergence of smaller workplaces in the service sector with highly diverse employment systems made it more difficult to link local demands of workers for industrial justice to collective political projects and to support the local enforcement of general rights and regulation. A shift towards contract law pure and simple, private rather than public and individual instead of collective, cut workers and workplaces off from collective labour law, referring them to state-operated and typically overburdened institutions of ex post adjudication of grievances. As a result, in the regulation of work and working relations today, there is much greater variety – and inequality – between and within sectors, companies and workplaces. With the appearance of novel forms of contracting for work, such as zero-hours contracts and ostensibly self-employed 'gigging', large holes have opened up in national or sectoral floors of minimum standards, which unions appear powerless and governments disinclined to close up. Previously comprehensive systems of social welfare have in many countries been transformed into a combination of labour market activation devices and, increasingly, only the barest of provision for the otherwise destitute.

Against this background of the dismantling and fracturing of postwar labour constitutions, a stark comparison emerges between the industrial occupational communities of the past and their contemporary counterparts. The former, as we have seen, were often mainsprings of trade unionism. Especially where the nature of the labour process lent itself to frequent contact and relations of mutual assistance at work, and for socializing with co-workers at the end of the working day (or night), the workforce could become socially integrated with a collective culture that sustained relations of solidarity and effective trade unionism. Today, occupational communities continue to exist, performing important functions for the successful discharge of work duties. However, their capacity to form a social substructure for the formulation and articulation of workers' collective interests is hindered in a variety of ways, not least by a lack of contact and increased competition between workers, due either to the nature of the work or the way that it is organized by the employer.

A review of the literature on contemporary occupational communities suggests that service workers tend to have high levels of job satisfaction and deep commitment and involvement, even in low-wage, low-status jobs and precarious and casual employment (Korczynski 2003). A possible explanation is the presence of clients or customers in the work situation, taking the place of material objects in manufacturing and joining the employer as another patron demanding good work. Low morale – refusing to do one's best in protest at low wages and poor conditions – would in such circumstances hurt not just the employer but also real people asking for help face to face. As a result, solidarity among co-workers tends to centre first and foremost around mutual assistance with the job, as colleagues become an indispensable source of job-related knowledge (Adams et al. 2012). This seems to be especially true in occupations and sectors without codified training, where most learning is on the job, due to client needs being highly diverse so as to defy standardization, or because employers wish to save on investment in training programmes. This may make occupational communities above all communities of practice, which may or may not be conducive to their transformation into communities of adversarial interest formation. Where jobs with customers or clients are concerned, there also seems to be a high degree of self-selection by workers who are particularly eager to help others and who excel at it, even in adverse conditions (Korczynski 2003; Adams et al. 2012). One upshot might be that if something goes wrong, workers may tend to blame themselves rather than the demands of the job. Apparently, this adds to the tendency for workers to rely on occupational communities for mental and motivational 'repair work', even though this may be viewed with suspicion by employers because informal communication among workers is considered either a waste of time or as incipient insurrection. All of this may make it difficult to use the occupational communities of the new service sector as springboards of worker interest representation or trade unionism: the personal and social gratifications; the sense of duty that comes with working with people; the individualized nature of job tasks and performance; the experience of solidarity as task-centred support; and the mastery of difficult assignments.

Workers' understandings and beliefs no longer shape the rules governing the organization of work and the terms and conditions of employment as routinely and directly as they once did. Nonetheless, they remain highly relevant to the legitimacy of statutory and contractual rules, and of management policies, and to the efficacy and enforcement thereof. In new sectors and occupations in particular, legal rules made without the participation of workers on the ground may be rejected as impractical or useless, not just by employers bent on minimizing the influence and the range of worker-protective regulation, but also by the providers of labour power themselves. Focusing exclusively on formal legal norms (statutory rules, common law rules and contractual rules) and human resource management practices to the neglect of informal social norms cannot deliver a full understanding of the normativity of working life. Nothing less is required than in-depth empirical study of work and employment: a social anthropology of work that understands the embeddedness of occupational communities within the larger institutional contexts provided by the labour constitutions of the sectors and jurisdictions in question. As Chris Hann has untiringly pointed out, these in turn must be considered in their historical, political and cultural context, and in their complex relationship with the old and the new, and with traditional and capitalist ways of life.

If labour law aspires to be relevant, as originally intended, to the post-industrial workplaces of today – and, even more so, of the future – it must undergo a fundamental reconstruction. In particular, it must resist attempts to reduce it to a set of substantive legal rules designed to entitle individual workers or employers to bring individual grievances before the courts or tribunals. While such a reduction may lend itself to dogmatic consistency in the field of labour law, guaranteeing a dominant role for judges and jurists, it at the same time overlooks the collective nature of working life and of the interests arising in it: the ongoing everyday struggle between workers and employers over a proper balance between wage and effort, work and life. To create and preserve that balance, much more is needed than the possibility of raising a claim against an employer before the court. Rather than appeal to a third party, be it a judge or the legislature, workers should be empowered by a proper instructional framework to participate directly in both the setting of the rules applicable to their workplace and the enforcement of such rules. This is just another way of saying that labour law, in addition to state law, must also and again be *popular* law, law from below, created by workers and employers for workers and employers exercising a fundamental right to industrial self-government (Selznick 1969).

The task of reconstructing labour law so as to make it fit for a post-industrial, postneoliberal social order involves recourse to two logics of collective-political action: the logic of informal norm-setting and the logic of formal institution-building. Social anthropologists can help with the former, since they are well equipped to explore how different perceptions of work-in-life and life-in-work may turn into collective worldviews associated with distinct ideas of social justice. Sociologists and political scientists, in turn, can contribute insights into the channelling of collective action by formal institutions so as to make it compatible with the cultural values of an encompassing society, and thereby provide it with legitimacy. It is here that the notion of the *labour constitution* is central, not least because – analogous to the constitution of a state – it both guarantees and limits spheres of freedom to define, articulate and pursue collective interests. In this way, it on the one hand relieves the state of the need to get involved in the minute details of workplace governance – a need it cannot fill in any case – and on the other hand opens up a space for the democratic participation of the many and not just the few.

In the aftermath of the wave of neoliberal institutional destruction – or neoliberal statism, which is the same thing – the rebuilding of viable societies requires an effective norms-to-institutions-to-interests-to-politics-to-regulation chain that is responsive to the diversification of contemporary worlds of work. An institutional setting that satisfies the requirements of a legitimate translation of social norms into binding regulations must allow for discovery and expression of (potentially widely divergent) collective ideas of justice at the base of a society's political and economic system. Here a reconstructed labour law must see to it that there are spaces for free communication between workers who are protected from being narrowed or closed or penetrated, in whatever way, by the employers. Broader social institutions, in particular properly institutionalized trade unions, are then required to aggregate the specific concepts of justice forming among their constituents into a more general ideology; to transform them into 'realistic' collective interests, taking into account here not least the likelihood of their successful pursuit in the industrial and political arena.[4] In the political arena, the aggregated interests sustained by a variety of related concepts of justice enter into policy packages that reflect the intensity and the breadth of the support that can be mobilized on their behalf. In the administrative practice of government, they may then give rise to binding regulations enforceable before the courts, with the support of industrial citizens in the workplace. It is here that extant regulations have to prove their relevance to or *fit* with the social relations of production lest they are neglected or overturned in practice, restarting the process of involvement of local communities, occupational or otherwise, in the making and remaking of a society's labour law.

For labour law to recover its capacity to regulate working relations across the board, correcting the inherent asymmetries of contracting for work under contemporary, post-industrial conditions, it should take advantage of the insights that social anthropology can offer into the dynamics of norm formation within the small groups that make up a society. Similarly, the design of effective chains of communication and delegation between the different levels of a complex society could benefit from what sociologists and political scientists know about the interplay between the 'logic of membership' and the 'logic of influence' (Schmitter and Streeck 1999 [1982]). Social scientists in general – those concerned with the micromilieus of work communities as well as those exploring institution-building and institutional change at the level of entire societies – should recognize how much they can learn if they extend their perspective to include the legal system and, in particular, the extraordinary nature of labour law as, potentially, a participatory political regime. Exploring the peculiarities of small groups is exciting; the excitement can only be heightened if our gaze is widened to include the relationship of those groups to, and their interaction with, society at large and its political and legal institutions.

Ruth Dukes is Professor of Labour Law at the University of Glasgow, United Kingdom, and Principal Investigator on the European Research Council-funded project Work on Demand: Contracting for Work in a Changing Economy. She is a member of the Young Academy of the Royal Society of Edinburgh and the author of *The Labour Constitution: The Enduring Idea of Labour Law* (2014).

Wolfgang Streeck is a sociologist and Emeritus Director at the Max Planck Institute for the Study of Societies in Cologne, Germany. He is an Honorary Fellow of the Society for the Advancement of Socio-Economics, a member of the Berlin Brandenburg Academy of Sciences and the Academia Europaea, and a Corresponding Fellow of the British Academy. His books include *Buying Time: The Delayed Crisis of Democratic Capitalism* (2013) and *How Will Capitalism End? Essays on a Failing System* (2016).

Notes

1. See the introduction of the editors and the contributions to Hann and Parry (2018).
2. Cf. the hotel workers in Lee-Ross (2004), where a 'strong sense of worker identity with the job' is found, based on a perceived need for special 'skills and competences', in spite of transient employment. See also Sandiford and Seymour (2007: 217), who in their study of barmen find that jobs considered low status from the outside, because of no formal training and low pay, may be seen quite differently from inside the respective occupational community.
3. See also Rothstein (2019).
4. For a perceptive discussion of trade unionism in the service sector, see Cobble (1996).

References

Adams, May, Robert Glenn and Jill Maben. 2012. '"Catching up": The Significance of Occupational Communities for the Delivery of High Quality Home Care by Community Nurses', *Health* 14(4): 422–38.

Adler, Patricia A., and Peter Adler. 1999. 'Transience and the Postmodern Self: The Geographic Mobility of Resort Workers', *Sociological Quarterly* 40(1): 31–58.

Arthurs, Harry. 1985. 'Understanding Labour Law: The Debate over "Industrial Pluralism"', *Current Legal Problems* 38(1): 83–116.

Cannon, Isadore Cyril. 1967. 'Ideology and Occupational Community: A Study of Compositors', *Sociology* 1(2): 165–85.

Cobble, Dorothy Sue. 1996. 'The Prospects of Unionism in a Service Society', in Cameron Lynn Macdonald and Carmen Sirianni (eds), *Working in the Service Society*. Philadelphia: Temple University Press, pp. 333–58.

Dukes, Ruth. 2014 *The Labour Constitution: The Enduring Idea of Labour Law*. Oxford: Oxford University Press.

Ford, Michele, and Vivian Honan. 2019. 'The Limits of Mutual Aid: Emerging Forms of Collectivity among App-Based Transport Workers in Indonesia', *Journal of Industrial Relations* 61(4): 528–48.

Hann, Chris, and Jonathan Parry (eds). 2018 *Industrial Labor on the Margins of Capitalism: Precarity, Class, and the Neoliberal Subject*. Oxford: Berghahn Books.

Knegt, Robert. 2018. 'Labour Constitutions and Market Logics: A Socio-historical Approach', *Social & Legal Studies* 27(4): 512–28.

Korczynski, Marek. 2003. 'Communities of Coping: Collective Emotional Labour in Service Work', *Organization* 10(1): 55–79.

Lee-Ross, Darren. 2004. 'A Preliminary Cross-Cultural Study of Occupational Community Dimensions and Hotel Work', *Cross-Cultural Management* 11(4): 77–90.

Lipset, Seymour Martin, Martin Trow and James S. Coleman. 1956. *Union Democracy: The Internal Politics of the International Typographical Union*. New York: Free Press.

Rothstein, Sidney A. 2019. 'Unlikely Activists: Building Worker Power under Liberalization', *Socio-Economic Review* 17(3): 573–602.

Sandiford, Peter, and Diane Seymour. 2007. 'The Concept of Occupational Community Revisited: Analytical and Managerial Implications in Face-to-Face Service Occupations', *Work, Employment and Society* 21(2): 209–26.

Schmitter, Philippe C., and Wolfgang Streeck.1999 [1982]. 'The Organization of Business Interests: Studying the Associative Action of Business in Advanced Industrial Societies', *MPIfG Discussion Paper* 99/1. Max Planck Institute for the Study of Societies, Cologne.

Selznick, Philip. 1969. *Law, Society, and Industrial Justice*. New York: Russell Sage Foundation.

Streeck, Wolfgang. 2006. 'The Study of Organized Interests: Before "the Century" and after', in Colin Crouch and Wolfgang Streeck (eds), *The Diversity of*

Democracy: Corporatism, Social Order and Political Conflict. Cheltenham: Edward Elgar, pp. 3–45.

Van Maanen, John, and Stephen R. Barley. 1984. 'Occupational Communities: Culture and Control in Organisations', *Research in Organizational Behavior* 6: 287–365.

Weber, Max. 1978. *Economy and Society: An Outline of Interpretive Sociology*. Berkeley: University of California Press.

Chapter 10

The Moral Economy of Anthropological Scholarship

Monica Heintz

Anthropological scholarship is one of the first objects over which an anthropologist has a hold and can contemplate from a 'critical utopian' perspective – a view that Chris Hann desires for the discipline (Hann 2019a: 44). Indeed, behind the very existence of anthropological scholarship lurks the utopian view of humanity as equal and solidary. In a critical utopian mode, the anthropologist would address social realities critically while having such a utopian horizon as reference point. As Hann envisages it, in a critical utopian mode, 'the anthropologist engages with long-term history and is not afraid to theorize speculatively at very macro levels of human social organization' (2019a: 44). The macroscale being a scale with which anthropologists are shy to engage, in this chapter I only propose to exercise this critical eye at a much smaller scale – that of anthropological scholarship – as a first step. I shall refer here to anthropological scholarship as being the system of knowledge production recognized as legitimate by the anthropological community and shall not venture into the more complex recognition that other disciplines, state apparatus or the general public may additionally provide.

In order to critically evaluate the economy of anthropological scholarship, I propose looking at it in this chapter through the lens of open science. 'Open science', defined as 'the ongoing transition on how research is performed and knowledge shared',[1] is a concept that has received recent legal and institutional support due to the digitalization of data that enables the global circulation of ideas and information. Open science, as

---

Notes for this chapter begin on page 154.

an absolute positive ideal, is itself a universalist utopian stance, a dimension its proponents choose to neglect when they base the open science project more on normative philosophical positions and less on empirical sociological facts. Anthropology, with its focus on intercultural unequal encounters, is perhaps one of the best-placed disciplines to critically look at open science as utopia and reveal its empirical mechanisms through comparisons with other utopian projects. It can start doing this by looking into its own garden at anthropological scholarship.

Open science is certainly not a new concept. In the Western tradition, science started being universally shareable in the seventeenth century when the first academic journals appeared, thus allowing a quicker spread of innovations and resolving the question of precedence and the paternity of ideas (Nielsen 2012). In contrast to the esoteric knowledge of religious cults or the less perennial customs of particular places and times, science has been open and has had universal claims for more than three centuries. As such, is 'open science' a tautology? If yes, what are the political and economic stakes that resulted in its recent active endorsement by the European Commission in 2018[2] and by the United Nations Educational, Scientific and Cultural Organization (UNESCO) in 2019?[3] If 'open science' is not a tautology, then what prevents science from being open despite its universal credo: economic stakes such as private publishers' interests; technical issues such as language barriers or the inadequacies of digital support; ethical clashes with different views of knowledge; or authorship rights, risks and safety of data management?

When considering the issue of open science in anthropology, two separate contradictory positions stand out. On the one hand, anthropology is – in theory at least – concerned with openness and the sharing of data, mainly within the community in which data has been coproduced. Chris Hann has been involved in discussions and collaboration with local scholars, facilitating exchanges, publications and translations, and in the circulation of people, works and ideas. One would remember the vivid East-West debate with Michał Buchowski that highlights the engagement, despite criticisms received on the technicalities (Buchowski 2004; Hann 2005). Yet, as a fieldworker, Chris Hann has been involved in long-term relationships and knowledge exchanges outside the restricted circle of scholars, with local communities, where particular points of view on the postsocialist transformations were often silenced by the intellectuals' positions. Indeed, anthropology is about listening to, and protecting alternative views of, knowledge. These native views may contradict the scientist's own position towards the free circulation of knowledge. Collective intellectual property claims, accusations of knowledge appropriation (Young and Brunk 2009), reparatory or protective measures such as the Nagoya Protocol on access and benefit sharing derived from traditional knowledge on biodiversity[4] may sometimes enter in conflict with the credo of open science.

This chapter sets out to enrich the picture by looking at the ethical, technical, legal and economic facilities and hindrances encountered in the process of rendering anthropological data 'open'. It begins by asking whether open science could be a moral economic system that anthropologists should support. It then goes on to consider why anthropology is not yet an open science by looking at the scientific and institutional environment in which it is currently produced. Finally, it asks whether anthropology could be such an open science, given that its data has been coproduced in the ethnographic relation and its dissemination is thus bound to respect principles and views that do not come uniquely from the scientific community.

Is Open Science a Moral Economic System? The Utopian Project

Considering science from a moral economic point of view inevitably leads us to note, as Didier Fassin did in an article in 2009, that two directions of research using the term 'moral economy' have been developed in the social sciences. Both do not speak to each other (Fassin 2009: 1239). One was triggered by Lorraine Daston's 1995 article on the moral economy of science, upon which I will elaborate below. The second is the one with which anthropologists are most acquainted: the term 'moral economy', which appeared in an article by the Marxist historian E.P. Thompson (1971) and was taken over and popularized by James Scott in his book on Southeast Asian peasant economies (1976). In this understanding, 'moral economy' would differ from 'market economy' in the sense that goodness, justice and solidarity would be more important than rational market logic. The 'fair' price would then result from a moral evaluation of people's capacity to pay it and not from the rational but unmediated (Adam Smith's invisible hand) encounter between offer and demand (Thompson, 1971: 89). It is in this sense that Chris Hann's research has contributed, through his work that expands upon Polanyi's famous concept of the social embeddedness of economic life (Polanyi 1944 [1972]). Hann goes on to propose a human economy (Hann and Hart 2011) that answers twenty-first-century economic challenges, always based on thorough ethnographic analyses (Hann 2019b). He thus prefers to emphasize 'the moral dimension of economy' (Hann, 2018: 7) instead of using the term 'moral economy', which he views as too deeply enshrined in taken-for-granted unequal power relationships.[5]

But let us return to Lorraine Daston's reference to science as a moral economic system, as this should directly apply to the anthropological scholarship that is the subject of this chapter. At first sight, there is no link between her understanding of the workings of science and that of peasant markets, as Fassin has already noted (2009: 1251). What she understands by 'the moral economy of science' is 'a web of affect saturated-values that stand and function in well-defined relationship to one another' (Daston 1995: 4). She analyses in detail the quantification/estimation that needs precision, impartiality and a web of researchers that could contribute with their own findings to put together a complete picture of the truth. She also quotes empiricism, which rests on the scientist's witnessing of facts: a scientist who should be trusted. Objectivity is the effort to put one's own subjective self to one side in order to let truth emerge. All these moral principles for Daston have been integral to science since the seventeenth century. The production of anthropological knowledge, which rests on empiricist witnessing, has an open vow to objectivity that, at least since the 1980s, involves self-reflections on the anthropologist's persona and his or her ethnographic relation. In a situation where Frazer's or Levi-Strauss' ambitious projects of rendering the whole world's multicultural diversity based on separate scholars' tedious contribution through ethnographic accounts still receive the utmost esteem, one would surely confirm that anthropological scholarship is a moral economy in Daston's sense of the term.

The term 'moral economy' has expanded in different directions, either in the E.P. Thompson or Lorraine Daston sense; the term 'open science' has done the same. This could be explained by the fact that the concept has grown in the past thirty years to cover more and more aspects of scholarship, pressed on the one hand by the digital revolution and on the other hand by the increased monetization of scholarship by certain academic publishers. I follow here its most recent definition in the European context, where the elaboration of 'Plan S' in 2018 at the European level and its subsequent signature by a growing number of national research agencies has brought open science to the level of European legislation. Plan S is an initiative for open access publishing that was launched in September 2018. The European Commission and numerous European national research agencies initiated 'Coalition S' that promotes the so-called Plan S. On the Coalition S official website, the main reason given for the elaboration of Plan S is that: 'Universality is a fundamental principle of science (the term "science" as used here includes the humanities): only results that can be discussed, challenged, and, where appropriate, tested and reproduced by others qualify as scientific.' The statement goes on to condemn 'walls' built by the necessity to pay for access to scientific publications. These walls existed before, since books and academic journals were not free of charge, but they seem more obstructive since the digital environment has generated the birth of multiple 'intermediaries' – search platforms common archives with restricted (paid) access. Bacevic and Muellerleile note a similar criticism of intermediaries between open access tenants and the denunciation of intermediaries in the food revolts discussed by E.P. Thompson (2017: 181). The moral indignation behind the militancy for open science is clearly linked to the question of the open access of scientific publications. However, over time, the open science movement has slowly gone further and become more ambitious, replacing the first negative impulse ('open' as opposed to 'closed') with a more utopian view of the place of science in society.

Following an understanding of science as universal and freely accessible by professionals and amateurs alike, Coalition S advocates free access of the results (open access and open educational resources), as well as free access to the notebooks of scientists (open data) and to their tools (open source, open methodology and open peer review). This extended understanding of open science is a new version of science that reaches beyond academic scholarship and forces us to think beyond the economy of a small community of scientists. Open science became a utopian view of science that brings together scientists, private firms, nongovernmental organizations (NGOs) and the wider society in an unconditional pledge to knowledge. At this wider scale, the moral economic system of science is yet to be invented. Based on sharing and collaboration rather than on competition, open science would first need to find its economic equilibrium.

Is Anthropology an Open Science in the Sense of Open Access?

I shall now look at where anthropological scholarship stands in this picture. Chris Hann has been conducting research in Eastern Europe since the end of the 1970s and was involved in the debates of local researchers. He advocates that their scholarship is integrated into the wider web of science in order to bring its contribution to global science, but also so that it is taken into account.

In his reply to Michał Buchowski's complaint about the hierarchies of knowledge established between Anglo-Saxon scholars and Central and Eastern European (CEE) scholars (Buchowski 2004), Hann was quite outspoken about the efforts that local scholars should make in order to facilitate their integration in the web of science: they should write in English, language edit books and provide an index (Hann 2005: 194)! Indeed, a thorough review of different national anthropologies shows that the first barrier to the recognition of the contribution of countries such as those in Eastern Europe to anthropological knowledge is language (Barrera-Gonzales et al. 2017: 15). English has gradually become the language of science, but not without negative consequences for the production and circulation of scholarship in other native languages. German-language anthropologies lost the competition after the Second World War and switched to English, thus integrating within the wider web of anthropological science, but at the expense of cutting themselves off from their traditions and gradually neglecting previous scholarship that was written in German. French-language anthropologies resisted integration and have become marginalized in an increasingly English-speaking field. Language remains a barrier for the universality of science in disciplines where writing rather than simple communication of results is the norm (see Geertz (1989) and his analyses of the anthropologist as author).

Differences in the national legal and economic systems of scholarship production and evaluation systems appear more blatant as anthropology has become a global science. For instance, many CEE anthropologies had been forced into asocial and apolitical research during the communist period (Hann et al. 2005) and remained attached to folkloristic interests for at least another decade afterwards. Thus, apart from mainstream social anthropology, as Chris Hann already noted in his reply to Buchowski, CEE scholars were disengaged from the dialogue (2005). Applying the same scientific evaluation criteria internationally (for instance, evaluating the quality of scholarship through bibliometric indicators such as the author's impact factor that depends on the number of articles written in highly indexed English journals) has not only created hierarchies of knowledge internationally, but has also rendered more fragile small countries' anthropological scholarship within their national frame.[6] However, the same standards also meant inciting anthropologists and ethnologists to embark on the same common endeavours such as fieldwork, comparison and work outside one's own community, thus taking up criticisms that Chris Hann issued with regard to CEE anthropologies fifteen years ago (Hann 2005) and fully joining the anthropological community through common practices. The Max Planck Institute for Social Anthropology's recruitment, training and visiting scholarships opportunities, made possible to European anthropologists during Chris Hann's directorship of the Department of Resilience and Transformation in Eurasia at the Institute, have been crucial for the emergence of a pan-European community of anthropologists that share similar methodologies.[7]

However, there is one sense in which anthropological scholarship is already open. Prompted by the digitalization of anthropological writings, books and articles, such works have circulated freely in an anarchist contempt of copyrights and intellectual property rights. While the circulation of people has been linked to the precariousness of doctoral or postdoctoral positions that engage young scholars with nomadic lives across the world, this circulation has also entailed going beyond the national boundaries of science and bringing about a global economy of science. Preprints and prepublication versions of books and articles – supposedly available only to the authors – have been circulated by the writer, and independently by others, without concern for the ownership rights of the publisher. Initiatives such as the Open Anthropology Cooperative[8] created in 2009 have done much to spread information and encourage collaboration and exchange of knowledge at a large international scale. Numerous anthropological blogs and personal webpages have taken over and are shared freely in practice, undermining the wall of 'paid' access to information. More recently, social media or private platforms such as Academia.edu or ResearchGate offered at a large scale the possibility to disseminate articles, anarchically bypassing the barriers imposed by publishers' copyrights or simply playing with their rules. Reaching a climax, anthropological journals have appeared that were open access (HAU, the new Terrain) or have become open access (as I write, thirteen anthropological journals published by Berghahn Books have dropped their commercial walls and the number is increasing). Anthropological scholarship seems to have seized every opportunity to become more global in its scientific production.

Can Anthropology Be an Open Science in the Sense of Open Data?

Anthropological scholarship is looking forward to a new challenge. In 2018, two directions for the management of digital data appeared at the European level and are likely to influence the way in which anthropological scholarship will develop in the future. On the one hand, the General Data Protection Regulation that has been in effect from 25 May 2018 frames the treatment and use of personal data, completing the fundamental injunction in anthropology that obliges scientists to protect their data in order to protect their informants, an injunction that is translated into an almost systematic anonymization of ethnographic data. On the other hand, Plan S signed in November 2018 pushes for the opening of data research archives collected under public funding (which includes the great majority of Europe), thus accelerating the free circulation of information that has been prompted by digitalization in the past few years, beyond the scholarly perimeter.

Reconciling these two directions of data management is extremely sensitive in the intercultural context of production and management of data that characterizes anthropology. If the Nagoya Protocol refers to the intercultural treatment of protective legislation, it offers an ethical sensitivity but no concrete guidelines for dealing with the plurality of norms that frame the life of ethnographic data. One should remember that ethnographic data is collected (created) in the ethnographic relation between the anthropologist and the community studied. Data is then transcribed, transferred and filed, usually within the anthropologist's institution. How could this data be made available to the public? What are the categories of public that should be envisaged: the local population with which the data has been collected/created? The international scientific community? The anthropologist's 'near' public? If we look at the legal, ethical and practical complexity to which ethnographic museum collections (of physical objects) have already been confronted, we see that no long-lasting common solution has emerged. One should consider the mitigated response in France to the Savoy-Sarr report delivered at the end of 2018 that had a bearing on the restitution of controversial museum collections, many of which were gathered during ethnological missions by anthropologists. The requirement to return data, essentially coproduced with the communities, has future consequences for the dematerialized collections of photos, films, archives and sound collections, as well as all possible written data (including fieldnotes).[9] Thus, it is urgent to consider the new contours of the economy of anthropological scholarship and principles that should govern it. From the techniques of data archiving to the ethical dimensions of data sharing, the methodology of open tools for searching, scientific and ethical requirements meet and confront each other in the newly enlarged perimeter of anthropological scholarship.

In the last few years, critical heritage studies have prompted reflections concerning the restitution of data corpuses. As David Zeitlyn (2019) reminds us, archives are more than an obstacle to oblivion – they are also potential tools of power and subversion. Those who detain or manage archival data need to work in a well-delimited legal environment in order to make use of them or share this resource with the inheritors. Ethnographic collections (written, films, objects) have different legal statuses according to their origin, means of collection, and the political changes that occurred during and after the collection (Jamin and Zonabend 2002; Molinié and Mouton 2008; Rochette and Fau 2012). Sometimes confronted with accusations of cultural appropriation by the descendants of communities where ethnographic data have been collected (Young and Brunk 2009), the question of ownership of the ethnographic data collection is more and more acute, as is that of rights over museum collections or human remains. However, the use of new technologies radically differentiates the question of ownership of 'data' from the question of ownership of physical collections or human remains, because digital technologies facilitate sharing (a digital copy being as good as the original digital document, and the original paper document – if existent – being more often than not a technical embarrassment).[10] The open data policy that Plan S proposes should thus be salutary for the free dissemination of knowledge within local communities.

Notably, not all communities react positively to the perspective of having their data potentially 'exposed' internationally: objections to the principle of open science, claims of cultural ownership rights and ensuing cultural representation rights require personal or community data protection. In France, several new texts try to frame the systematic restitution of data towards the communities, which is increasingly seen as the new ethical norm in the discipline of social anthropology. In 2007, the Ethics Committee of the National Center for Scientific Research (CNRS) issued a policy paper on the need for equity between researchers and autochthonous populations[11] and later also provided a guide on digital information sharing (Ginouves and Gras 2018). In practice, some groups within communities object to past images being shared, while others do not. Consider communities such as the Syrian women, among which Bethany Honeysett (2014) worked, whose sense of the personal image evolved under religious influences and made them destroy their own past photographs. Would these women have approved of copies of the anthropologist's photographs, taken during the same period, to be shared via an open platform when they had already decided the photographs should forever disappear? Certainly not. Yet other generations in this community, opposed to the destruction, would have greatly appreciated the same photographs.

Conclusion

In this chapter, I set out to inquire into the economy of current anthropological scholarship by confronting it with the ideal(ogy) of open science. After considering whether open science in general could be considered to be a moral economic system, I have asked whether anthropology is, or could be, an open science in the sense of open access, as well as in the sense of open data.

With respect to the question of open access, it would be fair to say that anthropological scholarship functions as much as possible on principles such as reciprocity and justice that characterize a moral economy, due to the rather anarchic way in which its community bypasses copyrights and intellectual property rights in exchanging materials, the only true hindrance coming from language barriers. It would be equally fair to note that the globalization of anthropological scholarship, through the imposition of international standards of research that creates hierarchies of knowledge, has had a rather perverse effect on national anthropological scholarship. So, while technically anthropology could quickly become an open science in the sense of open access, one might wonder whether this would be enough for making it also a truly moral economic system.

With respect to the question of an open data policy in anthropology, this extends the perimeter of circulation of anthropological scholarship to include nonscholarly communities. Anthropologists are uniquely placed to allow the free circulation of data gathered, so that anthropological scholarship is returned to the communities researched, and also to fight for the limits of this circulation in order to protect the same communities. The challenge that confronts the discipline of anthropology under the new European regulations is bound to reshape the contours of the discipline with regard to its past and future archives. As a social anthropologist who has spent more than forty years collecting data and building scholarship within various local communities, I have no doubt that this question is one Chris Hann is likely to continue addressing in the future.

Monica Heintz is Professor of Social Anthropology at the University of Paris Nanterre and co-director of the Laboratoire d'Ethnologie et de Sociologie Comparative (UPN/CNRS). She has carried out research on the work ethic in Romanian enterprises, on moral education and civic initiatives in Moldova, on European East-to-West migration, and on the ethics of French organizations from the cultural and educational sphere.

Notes

1. The European Commission's definition. Retrieved 4 January 2021 from https://ec.europa.eu/research/openscience/index.cfm.
2. Retrieved 4 January 2021 from https://www.scienceeurope.org/our-priorities/open-access.
3. Retrieved 4 January 2021 from https://en.unesco.org/news/unesco-takes-lead-developing-new-global-standard-setting-instrument-open-science.
4. Retrieved 4 January 2021 from https://www.cbd.int/traditional/intro.shtml. The Nagoya Protocol of 2014 is an international agreement signed by ninety countries, which aims to share the benefits arising from the utilization of genetic resources in a fair and equitable way. It is the latest protocol stemming from the Convention on

Biological Diversity signed in 1992 in Rio and protecting collective property rights over traditional knowledge.
5. While I adhere to Hann's arguments, in this chapter I prefer to use the term 'moral economy' of scholarship in order to raise awareness of the unequal power relations that the injunctions to move towards open science reveal (in the relationship between governments and academia, or between academia and local communities), much in the spirit of what the term classically evokes.
6. The integration of natural sciences scholarship from small countries within the international arena was less arduous as language, topics and approaches had been international for much longer. This disadvantaged social sciences at the national level.
7. The European Association of Social Anthropologists hosted a panel dedicated to Chris Hann's work on the occasion of his retirement during its 2020 conference, in recognition of his role in the development of European anthropological scholarship. It should be noted that CEE scholars convened this panel.
8. Retrieved 4 January 2021 from http://openanthcoop.ning.com.
9. Following the implementation of Plan S in France, legal experts are considering the limits of openness of anthropological data according to the criterion 'as open as possible, as closed as necessary'. There is discussion as to whether an author's rights may apply to restrict access to fieldnotes when this is deemed necessary (personal communication with jurist Lionel Maurel from the National Institute of Social Sciences of the French National Center for Scientific Research).
10. The anecdotes on this topic are numerous in the Laboratory where I work and that retains distinct private collections of more than thirty anthropologists donated by them or their families. One of the most important collections, on the Dakar Djibouti mission headed by Marcel Griaule in the 1930s, is famously said to have started through rescuing documents from the bins and car park of the Musée de l'Homme.
11. Retrieved 4 January 2021 from http://www.cnrs.fr/comets/IMG/pdf/13-2007imperatif_equite-2.pdf.

References

Bacevic, Jana, and Chris Muellerleile. 2017. 'The Moral Economy of Open Access', *European Journal of Social Theory* 21(2): 169–88.
Barrera-Gonzales, Andrés, Monica Heintz and Anna Horolets. 2017. 'Introduction: Strength from the Margins. Restaging European Anthropologies', in Andrés Barrera-González, Monica Heintz and Anna Horolets (eds), *European Anthropologies*. Oxford: Berghahn Books, pp. 1–24.
Buchowski, Michał. 2004. 'Hierarchies of Knowledge in Central-Eastern European Anthropology', *Anthropology of East Europe Review* 22(2): 5–14.
Coalition S. 2020. 'Why Plan S'. Retrieved 4 January 2021 from https://www.coalition-s.org/why-plan-s.
Daston, Lorraine. 1995. 'The Moral Economy of Science', *Osiris* 10: 2–24.
Fassin, Didier. 2009. 'Les Economies Morales Revisitées', *Annales. Histoire, Sciences Sociales* 64(6): 1237–1266.
Geertz, Clifford. 1989. *Works and Lives: The Anthropologist as Author*. Stanford: Stanford University Press.
Ginouves, Véronique, and Isabelle Gras (eds). 2018. *La Diffusion Numérique des Données en SHS*. Aix-en-Provence: Presses Universitaires de Provence.

Hann, Chris. 2005. 'Correspondence: A Reply to Michal Buchowski.' *The Anthropology of East Europe Review* 23(1): 194-97.

_____. 2018. 'The Moral(ity and) Economy: Work, Workfare, and Fairness in Provincial Hungary', *European Journal of Sociology* 59(2): 225–54.

_____. 2019a. 'The Seductions of Europe and the Solidarities of Eurasia', *Lud* 103: 31–47.

_____. 2019b. *Repatriating Polanyi. Market Society in the Visegrád States*. Budapest: Central European University Press.

Hann, Chris, and Keith Hart. 2011. *Economic Anthropology*. Cambridge: Polity Press.

Hann, Chris, Mihaly Sarkany and Petr Skalnic (eds). 2005. *Studying Peoples in the People's Democracies: Socialist Era Anthropology in East-Central Europe*. Munich: LIT Verlag.

Honeysett, Bethany 2014. 'Kinship Discontinuities and the Construction of the Self in Damascus (Syria): What Family Photographs Reveal', *Ethnologie Française* 44(3): 439–47.

Jamin, Jean, and Françoise Zonabend (eds). 2002. 'Archives et Anthropologie', *Gradhiva* 30/31: 57–198.

Molinié, Antoinette, and Marie-Dominique Mouton (eds). 2008. 'L'Ethnologue aux Prises avec les Archives', *Ateliers du LESC* 32.

Nielsen, Michael. 2012. *Reinventing Discovery*. Princeton: Princeton University Press.

Polanyi, Karl. 1972 [1944]. *La Grande Transformation : Aux Origines Politiques et Economiques de Notre Temps*. Paris: Gallimard.

Rochette, Marc, and Guillaume Fau (eds). 2012. 'Ethnographiques : Présence et Questionnement des Collections D'Ethnographie', *Revue de la Bibliothèque nationale de France* 45.

Scott, James. 1976. *The Moral Economy of the Peasant: Rebellion and Subsistence in Southeast Asia*. New Haven: Yale University Press.

Thompson, Edward Palmer. 1971 'The Moral Economy of the English Crowd in the Eighteenth Century', *Past and Present* 50: 76–136.

Young, James, and Conrad Brunk. 2009. *The Ethics of Cultural Appropriation*. Oxford: Wiley Blackwell.

Zeitlyn, David. 2019. 'Des Archives pour L'Anthropologie : Futurs Possibles et Passés Contingents. L'Archive Comme Substitut Anthropologique', *Ateliers D'Anthropologie*. Retrieved 4 January 2021 from https://journals.openedition.org/ateliers/10817.

Chapter 11

Some Thoughts on Embeddedness, Value and the Moral Dimension in the Work of Chris Hann

Frances Pine

In the 1980s I wrote a review of Chris Hann's first English monograph (Hann 1980; Pine 1981).[1] One of the first ethnographies by a Western anthropologist about socialist Eastern Europe, *Tázlár* presented a vivid and compelling account of the mixed economy of a Hungarian pig-farming and wine-producing village. It was a critical analysis of a complicated political economy and I loved it. My one serious criticism in this review was that there was little attention paid to kinship. A few years later, Chris gave me a generally positive verbal review for a piece of work on rural Poland, but asked at the end, slightly incredulously, whether I really believed that kinship and gender were more important than economics. I think I responded that I couldn't separate kinship and economics; I saw them as inextricably linked. Looking back on these two exchanges, I suspect that Chris would have responded to my critique in the same spirit: kinship is part of, not separate from, political economy. It is certainly true that over the years, Chris has paid much more attention explicitly to kinship, including developing, with Ildiko Bellér-Hann, a major project on kinship and social support in China, and leading a Max Planck Institute (MPI) research group on the same theme in a wider geographical and ethnographic context. And of course, Chris has written a lot about Karl Polanyi and about the concept of embeddedness. It is the idea of the embedded nature of the economic sphere, or the mutual embeddedness of the social and the economic, and the ways in which discussion of this has developed in anthropology in relation to moral economy and

---

Notes for this chapter begin on page 166.

informal economy[2] that interest me here. In Chris' work on both economy and morality, the concept of embeddedness makes kinship a major underlying if not explicit theme.

In this chapter I consider two recent articles by Chris Hann about economy, morality, informality and embeddedness in Hungary (Hann 2018; 2019b). They interest me partly because in both, he is looking back at his early research and juxtaposing what he found then with what he is observing now. In both articles, it seems to me that he is widening a formal definition of economy and the economic to include a more substantive consideration of aspects of economic practices and processes that include morality, affective relations, kinship and friendship, and unregulated (informal) economic behaviours. Hann is critical of what he sees as the overuse, and I would add here misuse, of the concept of moral economy. As it moves further away from the original conceptualization of E.P. Thompson, moral economy has come to mean anything that has an element of the economic and an element of the emotional, affective or moral to it. Thus, we have moral economies not only of peasants or hunter-gatherers, but also of kinship, of neighbourhood, of gender, of the workplace and so on. Like the recent effervescence of 'ontologies', or earlier of 'modes of production', an overly broad use of the phrase threatens to obscure meaning.

In his work on Hungary in particular, but also in his Polish research and the research of the Postsocialist Property group (1999–2005) in his department at the MPI, Hann tends not to problematize the concept of moral economy, but to use it fairly consistently in the way that E.P. Thompson (1971) first proposed. In his recent work, he discusses the high moral value placed on labour in socialist ideology, linking it to financial or wider economic entitlements (Hann 2018; 2019a and b). He looks at the moral economy of the family, of the peasant household and of the collective (in the sense of both the collective farm – less relevant in the case of maverick Poland – and the collective community); he also discusses informal economy, and the various shades of grey area that surrounded this during socialism and continued through the decades following 1990 (Hann 2018; 2019a and b). Implicit in these discussions is a moral dimension to economic structure and institutions, which may either complement the official structure – of registered employment, tax systems and pensions, hierarchical work structures, and generally legal and formal regulation of economic practice – or subvert it. This is a dimension of economy and labour (production, consumption, reproduction) that is embedded in social relations and expectations about socially expected and proper behaviour, moral (rather than legal) rights and obligations, and entitlements. In this sense, the term broadly conforms to the ideas developed by Thompson, which were adopted and, in some ways, rendered more ethnographic by James Scott (1976, 1985). There is an unwritten understanding between those in power, who control production and the labour of others, and those others who perform the labour, that they have particular entitlements and expectations – perhaps best thought of as informal but established reciprocities – where the workers or the agricultural labourers or serfs work for low pay or remuneration, often in bad conditions, but can expect various perks, kinds of support and help. When this is withheld by the factory or landowners or indeed by the state, the 'crowd' feel entitled to claim for themselves, to protest, sabotage or steal.

Here a good example would be the Polish female textile workers in the city of Łódź. I interviewed many unemployed textile workers in the first half of the 1990s in Łódź, when the Balcerowicz Plan[3] was in full swing and most of the major factories had been closed or privatized. The women spoke movingly and proudly about their activism throughout the socialist period, describing how they occupied the factories or marched and protested, and went on strike, when the government raised the price of bread or rearranged the shift system to times that did not coincide with school hours. Their language was always telling; they would say things like 'we are the workers, but we are also the mothers of the nation. We work for the state, and the state has to allow us to feed and care for our children, who are the future' (see Pine 2002). On the whole, the women I spoke to had strongly supported the socialist state and continued to vote communist throughout the 1990s, but they also felt entitled to challenge and undermine work rhythms if they felt the state was failing to meet its moral obligations. The critiques these women had of the early postsocialist governments were severe – almost all those I spoke to felt that the new government had betrayed them in every way, by taking their work and forcing them into what they viewed as the amoral or even immoral informal sector.

Villagers in the Podhale, the region at the foothills of the Tatra Mountains in southwestern Poland, were more deeply critical of the socialist state than these factory workers, and told colourful stories of acts of violence or sabotage of agents of the state, including military police, factory managers and specialist cooperative officials. When they felt their entitlements were not being met, they said, they poured sugar in the Cooperative Director's carburettor and destroyed his engine, they pilfered materials and goods from the factory[4] and brought them home to use or sell, they watered the milk they delivered to the dairy cooperative in order to achieve what they felt to be the proper price. I think what is important here is that these and myriad other acts of secret aggression or independent economic activity were not viewed as wrong or considered as theft, but viewed as what people had to do to get by, and to claim what should have been given to them as workers, peasant farmers and so on. In the same vein, the Łódź textile workers felt morally entitled to chastise the state and to protest against it.

These standoffs between the state and its citizens in both urban and rural areas contrast sharply with the relative stability of what came to be called the moral economy of the rural/peasant house, the household or family/kinship, which I discuss below. The important point here is that within the peasant house economy, or the economic and social obligations, entitlements and reciprocities of kinship, there was also, as Hann discusses in relation to his own and to Thelen's work in Hungary (Hann 2019a: 110; Thelen 2004), a strict and at times quite brutal generation and gender hierarchy, and often a highly resilient patriarchal structure. People also felt, and demonstrated by their practice, a shared sense of belonging to the house and farm, of responsibility for the subsistence as well as the market-facing labour, and of obligations and entitlements that are morally binding. Thus, in the 1980s and the 1990s when I was doing this research, a division between a moral economy and a state economy for the textile workers (and I think also for other industrial workers such as miners, steel and shipyard workers) was one that primarily revolved around the perceived role and behaviour of the state itself on the one hand and of those who provided the labour – the factory workers and others – on the other. This is close to E.P. Thompson's (1971) original formulation. The workers have moral expectations of the state that transcend its political, economic and managerial rational structures, and occupy a less formal, more affective space. These two spaces, of the formal industrial structure and the informal, more personal or relational processes, both juxtapose the state and the workers, but in the former, the state plays a powerful and hierarchical role that allows for abuse and exploitation, while in the latter, the state colludes or compromises with the workers, through time-honoured moral relations and expectations, to support them.

The moral economy that was most apparent here was rooted in the relationship between those in power – state officials and factory management – and those with less or very little power: the workers. This does not mean that there were not spaces of kinship and gender solidarity and morality; there were (Pine 2002). However, I would argue that on the one hand, the dominant split in the industrial sector during socialism was between what was perceived and experienced as the bad, rational but duplicitous state, and the good, morally conscientious state, understood through its interactions with the workers, and how these maintained or damaged their relationships. On the other hand, in rural areas like the mixed economy production areas in Hungary that Hann wrote about and the small private family farms and state factories in the Polish mountains that I studied, perhaps the tension was between the state economy and the family or household economy, which were seen as being governed by different kinds of morality and rationality.

Hann's recent solution to the problem of the 'clumpish reification' (Hann 2018: 231) of the term 'moral economy' is to speak instead of moral dimensions, which is certainly one way of introducing the idea of morality, and concurrently dimensions other than rationality, without turning every practice or association into a distinct phenomenon: 'I prefer to recognise a moral dimension in the sense of a collective and systematic basis in long-term shared values' (Hann 2018: 231). It is helpful to consider exactly what he is referring to when he uses this term. It seems to me that he is trying to expand upon, and in so doing to dissolve, such divisive dyads as formal/informal, rational/irrational or subsistence/market production. This is of course not a new or revolutionary endeavour; rather, it is one that dates back at least to the substantivist position developed in the 1960s. However, if we follow what I understand is Hann's proposal and look not at different classifications or types of moral economy, but at moral dimensions of the economy generally, we automatically expand the economic field to include motives and emotions that act as norms in driving the social relations of production, consumption, circulation and exchange of goods, services and labour. As Hann points out, 'this approach, although it privileges individuals, still allows for recognition of resilient dominant values that facilitate social integration' (Hann 2018: 231). I think what might be lost here is the specific dimension of entitlements in relation to power that Thompson describes, but in Hann's own work, this is revealed in ethnographic detail and focus on both the individual and the wider field of social structures and values.

This explicit connection between domains or dimensions of economy makes visible the multiplex entanglements with (or embeddedness of) kinship and gender. These are often 'taken for granted' entanglements, which social actors themselves do not isolate or identify. Rather, they form part of the habitus or doxa of economy (Bourdieu 1977 [1972]) – that which is known, embodied and performed without question or conscious reflection. For instance, in the Polish mountains, labour was exchanged between circles of four or five houses, with each house in turn receiving help from all the others during planting, potato picking, hay making and harvest. This was represented as help freely offered and accepted, but a closer examination revealed a carefully balanced system, where each family sought to send exactly the same amount of labour that they received. If a house sent one adult man and one woman, and two teenagers, they would expect to receive the equivalent of that team when their turn came. If an adult man was not available, perhaps three women would be sent, or two women and three teenagers, or some other combination reflecting local ranking of relative values of labour by gender and age. The house where fields were being planted or harvested organized the labour team; the senior women of the house brought food out to the fields at lunchtime, and everyone sat on the ground or on the cart and ate together. Throughout the day, women and children would bring water or *kompot*[5] from the house for everyone to drink. At the end of the day, or sometimes the end of the work, a big meal would be provided in the house for everyone who had laboured, and food and vodka would be consumed long into the night.

One aspect of these kinds of reciprocal labour exchanges is that they rest more or less on assumptions of hierarchies within the house, and within the entire team, based on generation and gender, but there is a continual attempt to balance discrepancies in perceived labour value between houses. Thus, within each house, there is an assumption of both hierarchical inequality and shared moral value and commitment, but among all participating houses, as the circle of labour moves from one to the next, there is an assumption of and a visible effort to maintain equality. We see this in the idea of equal exchange of labour, of like for like, discussed earlier.

This becomes clearer when we look at houses and individuals who were excluded from the circles. One such category comprised the small handful of relatively large (12+ hectares) holdings at the very top and the landless houses at the very bottom (see Pine 2004). Those at the very top were unable to join a reciprocal circle because they had too much land. Their solution was usually a pragmatic combination of exchange with one or two other big farms, supplemented by paid day labour drawn from the landless houses. The former (labour exchange) was usually limited in scope because there was too much land to work in the time, and the latter (paid day labour) was somehow shameful because it implied that those at the top lacked the moral and social capital to mobilize the labour of their kin and neighbours. Those at the bottom were outside these exchanges because they had no land and had to rely on poor wages or payment in meals and in kind (Hann refers to similar descriptions by Yalçın-Heckmann for Azerbaijan (2019a: 137)). Finally, there were always a few people who were excluded. Occasionally these were women – in one case, for instance, an elderly widow with a middle-sized plot but no children or grandchildren to make a viable workforce. Usually it was men who were excluded, after being given several chances, because they were sloppy workers, heavy drinkers and considered not only unreliable but also a danger to the other workers and a successful harvest. However, when these men had families, the wife and children might still be included in the circle, but expected to work for longer hours on their neighbours' fields and to receive fewer hours of help on their own. In all of these cases, we can see the moral expectations of social relations and reciprocity being negotiated with the pragmatics of efficient and profitable production. In the case of families with unacceptably unreliable husbands but hardworking and impoverished wives and children, the other houses tended to maintain the moral expectations of kin and community by making sure they had enough food to get by and other things they might need, like children's clothes. In other words, the moral and economic dimensions coexist, but they shift in terms of relative importance.

It seems to me that in some ways the entanglement of economy and kinship, gender and generation, and the ways in which economy is simultaneously both relational and (impersonally) 'rational' were more obvious in rural areas under socialism than in urban, industrial contexts. There was an enormous difference between the socialist countries, and among different regions and populations within each country as well as between them. Hann suggests that in the postsocialist setting, in the more urban and industrialized areas anyway, there is a growth of individual interest or individualistic behaviour, and a decline in (at least some) of the moral underpinnings of economic obligations and reciprocities between generations within households and kin groups.[6] These ideas clearly link with others about movement and migration, globalization, and modernity (or more accurately social and cultural perceptions of modernity) itself. In the final section of this chapter, I try to historicize shifts in moral dimensions of the economic in terms of twenty-first-century capitalism.

If we move from a concept of moral economies encompassing rather too many possibilities and, following Hann, look instead at moral dimensions of economy and their entanglements with other domains such as politics, kinship and gender, we are perhaps better placed to understand how the postsocialist 'transition', and in several countries the EU accession that followed, reinforced some dominant ideas about the morality of social relations, and seriously challenged and unsettled others.

I have already referred briefly to the strong association in socialist ideology and practice between labour and a person's value. Value in terms of socialist ideology was conferred by labour; individuals realized their value through their labour and this in turn entitled them to recognition within the socialist system. There was also a strong correlation during the socialist period between value and types of labour. On the one hand, the 'lords of labour' (Parry 2018; Sanchez 2018) received the most state and public recognition (and probably the highest remuneration and best benefits in terms of plentiful food, access to consumer goods, etc.). On the other hand, labour, particularly in agricultural production, was also valued if it was seen as being for the common good – for 'the people'– and morally denigrated if it was seen as being only for personal gain, and outside the reciprocities and expectations of moral social relations. In my very brief account above of the collapse of the textile industry in Łódź, I referred to the pain and trauma the women experienced when their work, the source of their social and personal value, was taken away from them. In a very different context, Myriam Hivon (1997) wrote about the way in which collectivized agriculture in Russia was understood as production for the common good, and how in the 1990s the selling-off and allocation of land to new private farmers who used it for their own profit led to sabotage and acts of violence by the disinherited former workers on the collective farms. Here the morality of the economic structure as it was understood under socialism, and the collapse of this in the process of privatization, is made absolutely explicit. People labour on the land for their own subsistence, but also for the good of all. People who want to own land, and to hold on to it without producing for the people, or to turn it into individual profit-making schemes, are not entitled; they have moved outside the acceptable moral dimension of labour. Hann refers to something similar three decades later when he discusses the 'workfare' scheme in Hungary, a state-sponsored work programme. In the world of Viktor Orban, the moral implications here are perhaps a bit different from those that were current in the socialist regimes. According to Hann (2018: 238–47, 2019b: 17), the availability of low-paid but regular and visible community labour (clearing flowerbeds, planting, street cleaning, repairing ruined roads, etc.) instead of a 'welfare handout' has apparently pleased not only the state officials but also the programme participants (many of whom are Roma), and perhaps not surprisingly the local employed or otherwise self-sufficient ethnic Hungarians, who resented people who were seen as welfare-dependent scroungers undeserving of state support.

It is also possible to identify an anti-inclusive set of sentiments throughout the former Socialist Bloc, and indeed throughout most of Europe (definitely including the United Kingdom), since the refugee crisis of 2015, in which the postsocialist states, most (although differently) vocally Poland and Hungary, have been highly active. Like the ideas in the previous paragraph about labour, human value and moral social relations, this can be seen as a (new or modified) interpretation of the socialist equation between value and labour. In the postsocialist states, it could be argued that as the correlation between labour and entitlement and personal value grows in the context of capitalist individualism, moral consensus and a morally inclusive dimension to social relations appears to shrink or diminish.

Bridget Anderson (2013), in her incisive book *Us and Them*, has argued that in the context of the past two decades in the United Kingdom, it is too simplistic to focus on anti-migrant behaviour on its own. She shows that a strong division between 'us' and 'them' is developing in both formal state circles, and popular culture, in which 'failed citizens' (i.e. welfare dependants who are seen as scrounging and undeserving), and 'noncitizens' (i.e. migrants and refuges and hence unentitled) are part of 'them' and are subject to the same hostile scrutiny. Ultimately, both categories are excluded from 'the community of value', which is defined by visible and formal participation in the economy, adherence to a particular set of 'family values' and ways of living, and a lack of dependency on the state. What is absent in this discourse, which is of course also a highly moral although not liberal/left one, is recognition or acknowledgement of shared entitlements and areas of inclusion; in such evaluations of social, moral and economic worth, neither failed nor noncitizens qualify (see also Fassin 2011; Pine and Haukanes in press). It is interesting to note that Chris Hann (2019b) has also identified all of these phenomena, including migration and the refugee crisis, as playing a part in the current realignments of social and economic relations, and their moral dimensions, in the Hungarian countryside.

At the beginning of this chapter, I raised the question of the embedded nature of kinship and political economy. In thinking about some aspects of Hann's enormous range of research interests, theoretical engagements and writings over the years, it seems to me that what characterizes so much of his scholarship is a deep concern for these complexities of social relations, and a focus on the way that they play out historically, ethnographically and in different socioeconomic settings. The moral economy or the moral dimension of social life is neither an essential and unchanging human characteristic, nor always a reflection of a humane, equalitarian or inclusive social world. Side by side with this attention to history, and political economy and change, Chris Hann has maintained both a critical appreciation of the importance of including an understanding of the moral dimension and an intellectual scepticism that recognizes that ideas and politics of morality also change and vary.

Frances Pine is Emeritus Reader at the Department of Anthropology, Goldsmiths College, University of London. She has been conducting research in Eastern Europe for the past four decades. Her fieldwork has been located in the Polish Tatra Mountains, the countryside of eastern and central Poland, and the cities of Lublin and Łódź. She has worked on kinship and gender, place, history and memory, work, markets, informal economy, unemployment and restructuring, and migration and emerging inequalities.

Notes

1. I would like to thank the editors, and Victoria Goddard, for their careful and thoughtful readings of the first draft of the chapter, and for their clarity and very helpful comments.
2. It is interesting to note how often the ethnographic record shows that activities considered to be part of the 'grey' or 'informal' economy are seen by the people who practise them to be highly moral and often linked to the reciprocities of kinship and neighbourhood. This is particularly striking in the case of accounts from the socialist and postsocialist states (see, for instance, Firlit and Chlopecki 1992; Harboe Knudsen and Frederiksen 2015).
3. Leszek Balcerowicz was the Finance Minister in the first postsocialist government in Poland. He complied with the recommendations of the International Monetary Fund and the World Bank, and implemented the most extreme and draconian restructuring programme in the postsocialist bloc. Following his plan, many factories were sold off or closed down, health and social services were cut drastically and essentially privatized, and in some areas, including the Łódź region and the Podhale, unemployment reached 50 per cent in certain sectors in the early 1990s.
4. Poland, unlike the rest of the Comecon countries, did not collectivize land extensively in the postwar period. At most, only about 25 per cent of arable land was collectivized during the socialist period. Gomulka bowed to peasant resistance to collectivization in the 1950s and instead implemented a 'Polish road to socialism', which was based on machinery and distribution cooperatives rather than cooperative or collective land, and also on widespread industrialization of the countryside. In the region where I carried out fieldwork, there was a large shoe factory, a ski factory and a large dairy, as well as many other small industrial state-owned enterprises.
5. *Kompot* is a drink made from fruit such as plums, strawberries or mixed berries, sugar and water.
6. Hann (2019b: 16) discusses the absence of remittances and cash investment from migrant workers to family in the village. For Poland, see Pine (2017).

References

Anderson, Bridget. 2013. *Us and Them?: The Dangerous Politics of Immigration Controls*. Oxford: Oxford University Press.

Bourdieu, Pierre. 1977 [1972]. *Outline of a Theory of Practice*. Cambridge: Cambridge University Press.

Fassin, Didier. 2011. 'Policing Borders, Producing Boundaries: The Governmentality of Immigration in Dark Times', *Annual Review of Anthropology* 40: 213–26.

Firlit, Elżbieta, and Jerzy Chlopecki. 1992. 'When Theft Is Not Theft', in Janine R. Wedel (ed.), *The Unplanned Society: Poland during and after Communism*. New York: Columbia University Press, pp. 95–109.

Hann, C.M. 1980. *Tázlár: A Village in Hungary*. Cambridge: Cambridge University Press.

Hann, Chris. 2018. 'Moral(ity) and Economy: Work, Workfare and Fairness in Provincial Hungary', *European Journal of Sociology* 59(2): 225–54.

_____. 2019a. *Repatriating Polanyi: Market Society in the Visegrad States*. Budapest: Central European University Press.

_____. 2019b. 'Resilience and Transformation in Provincial Political Economy: From Market Socialism to Market Populism in Hungary, 1970s–2010s', *Cargo* 1–2: 1–23.

Hann, Chris, and Jonathan Parry (eds). 2018. *Industrial Labour on the Margins of Capitalism: Precarity, Class, and the Neoliberal Subject*. Oxford: Berghahn Books.

Harboe Knudsen, Ida, and Martin Demant Frederiksen (eds). 2015. *Ethnographies of Grey Zones in Eastern Europe: Relations, Borders and Invisibilities*. London: Anthem Press.

Hivon, Myriam. 1997. 'The Bullied Farmer: Social Pressure as a Survival Strategy?', in Sue Bridger and Frances Pine (eds), *Surviving Post-socialism: Local Strategies and Regional Responses in Eastern Europe and the Former Soviet Union*. London: Routledge, pp. 33–51.

Parry, Jonathan. 2018. 'Introduction: Precarity, Class and the Neoliberal Subject', in Chris Hann and Jonathan Parry (eds), *Industrial Labour on the Margins of Capitalism: Precarity, Class, and the Neoliberal Subject*. Oxford: Berghahn Books, pp. 1–38.

Pine, Frances. 1981. 'Review: *Tazlar: A Village in Hungary* by C.M. Hann', *Man* N.S. 16(1): 151–52.

_____. 2002. 'Retreat to the Household? Gendered Domains in Post-socialist Poland', in Chris Hann (ed.), *Postsocialism: Ideals, Ideologies and Practices in Eurasia*. London: Routledge, pp. 95–113.

_____. 2004. 'Reproducing the House: Kinship, Inheritance and Property Relations in Highland Poland', in Hannes Grandits and Patrick Heady (eds), *Distinct Inheritances: Property, Family and Community in a Changing Europe*. Münster: LIT Verlag, pp. 279–96.

_____. 2017. 'Lost Generations? Unemployment, Migration and New Knowledge Regimes in Post EU Poland', in Susana Narotzky and Victoria Goddard (eds), *Work and Livelihoods: History, Ethnography and Models in Times of Crisis*. London: Routledge, pp. 31–45.

Pine, Frances, and Haldis Haukanes. In press. 'Reconceptualising Borders and Boundaries: Gender, Movement, Reproduction, Regulation', in Haldis Haukanes and Frances Pine (eds), *Intimacy and Mobility in the Era of Hardening Borders: Gender, Reproduction, Regulation*. Manchester: Manchester University Press.

Sanchez, Andrew. 2018. 'Relative Precarity: Decline, Hope and the Politics of Work', in Chris Hann and Jonathan Parry (eds), *Industrial Labour on the Margins of Capitalism: Precarity, Class, and the Neoliberal Subject*. Oxford: Berghahn Books, pp. 218–40.

Scott, James C. 1976. *The Moral Economy of the Peasant*. New Haven: Yale University Press.
———. 1985. *Weapons of the Weak: Everyday Forms of Peasant Resistance*. New Haven: Yale University Press.
Thelen, Tatjana. 2004. 'Are the Kulaks Back? Inherited Capital and Social Continuity in Mesterszallas, Hungary', in Hannes Grandits and Patrick Heady (eds), *Distinct Inheritances: Property, Family and Community in a Changing Europe*. Münster: Lit Verlag, pp. 329–46.
Thelen, Tatjana, Stefan Dorondel, Alexandra Szoke and Larissa Vetters. 2011. '"The Sleep Has Been Rubbed from their Eyes": Social Citizenship and the Reproduction of Local Hierarchies in Rural Hungary and Romania', *Citizenship Studies* 15(3–4): 513–27.
Thompson, E.P. 1971. 'The Moral Economy of the English Crowd in the Eighteenth Century', *Past and Present*, 50: 76–136.

Chapter 12

Property, Resources and Gauging Social Change

Deema Kaneff

Chris Hann's call, in the late 1990s, for renewing the anthropological interest in property was both timely and pertinent (Hann 1998). The privatizing of land (and other properties) as a means for transforming East European political economies from socialist to capitalist represented a seismic shift in the world order in the late twentieth century, with long-term global consequences. As Chris Hann has noted, property arrangements are represented as central to understanding both socialist and capitalist paradigms (see especially Hann 1993: 100; 1998). In both forms of political economy, economic efficiency as well as social justice – be that 'equality' in the case of socialism or 'freedom' in the case of capitalism – is sought through different types of property relations, either collective or private ownership (respectively). Property ownership featured in the ideologies of both systems, as well as forming the basis of legal frameworks, and social and political institutions. In short, 'both paradigms elevate a property doctrine into a fundamental principle of social organisation' (Hann 1998: 45). The collapse of state socialism and the adoption of capitalist market principles necessitated a transformation of property arrangements. It was, as Hann realized, an ideal context within which to study property (1998: 18; 2000: 4).

In this chapter I begin by highlighting Chris Hann's contribution to the property topic. His approach gives primary focus to property relations at the time of social change. My own work 'inverts' this agenda: I analyse social change through a focus on 'property'. Bearing this in mind, after

---

Notes for this chapter begin on page 179.

an initial section – in which Hann's work on property is described – I take the discussion in the following two sections in a divergent direction: in terms of terminology (using 'resources' rather than 'property') and in terms of my primary theoretical interest in social change. Resource mobility, I suggest, provides a platform from which to explore processes of transformation.

Chris Hann on Property

Property was the main preoccupation of Chris Hann's research in the late 1990s and continued into the early to mid-2000s, following his appointment as a founding director of the newly established Max Planck Institute (MPI) for Social Anthropology in Germany. It also constituted the research agenda of the first group of scholars in his department (of which I was a part). Three contributions by Chris Hann stand out – to my mind – as significant in the development of the property theme during this period.

The first harks back to the dichotomy noted in the opening paragraph above. Hann emphasized that the 'socialist = collective: capitalist = private' (to put it in the crudest terms) dichotomy was a gross simplification that never comes close to the reality on the ground (2000: 5). His critique emphasized the importance of appreciating the complex mix of property forms in any political economy. This was a point he brought home through his own Hungarian material by focusing on 'specialist cooperatives' as institutions that promoted private ownership within a socialist framework, marrying individual with larger collective interests (Hann 1993). Economic reforms after 1989 were therefore carried out through a complex set of property rearrangements that were never a 'straightforward shift from collective to private' (Hann 1993: 99).

Second, such a stance relies on treating property as 'social relations between people and not ... as relations between people and the material things they own' (Hann 1993: 110; 1998: 4). The stance is built on a long anthropological tradition – going back to Gluckman's work carried out in the 1960s and even earlier – which takes a broad perspective on property (Hann 1993: 110; 1998: 26; Humphrey and Verdery 2004; Yalçın-Heckmann 2010: 9). In applying it to the East European context, Hann advocated pushing the definition of property much further, convincingly arguing that we need to broaden the concept beyond legal codes in order to consider a wide range of institutions and cultural contexts. He argued for the need to open up the study of property to include 'informal rules, community norms and citizenship entitlements' (Hann 2003: 36; see also

Hann 2000: 1, 5; 1993: 100; and 1998: 7). In this goal, he engaged with possibilities offered by Keebet and Franz von Benda-Beckmann, who similarly recognized the importance of taking into account a broader set of factors by proposing a multilayered approach to property (Hann 2000: 6; 2005: 4).

Third, and both following and pre-empting the previous two points, Hann emphasized the importance of the embeddedness of property in concrete local institutions and practices (1993: 112). Chris Hann has been a great advocate for promoting local understandings of property relations (2005: 2). This position informed the research interests of the first team of scholars at the MPI. The group covered a wide range of properties, including land, animals, forests, houses and culture (ownership of symbols, knowledge, etc.). They carried out their research across the Eurasia land mass, engaging with a variety of themes relating to property, including inequality, moral economy and nationalism, to name but a few (see Hann (2005) for more details concerning the projects). Despite this vast array of studies, a clear focus on the goal remained: a theorization of property relations along the broadly identified lines noted above. As Hann (1998: 7) states: 'If we adopt a broad analytic concept of property ... then it can be investigated anywhere in time and space.' The overall objective: to make property a key category in cross-cultural analysis (Hann 1998: 9).

Much progress was made along these lines during the project. Nor did the agenda conclude with the end of the founding group's tenure (for example, see the subsequent publications by Torsello (2003) and Ventsel (2005), amongst others). My own research trajectory, built on the foundations established during this early phase of research at the MPI, has taken a different direction in the course of the last two decades. In the rest of this chapter, I focus on my current work, which is still in progress: first, in terms of terminology; and second, in developing an analytical framework for the study of social change.

A Note on Terminology

If terminology is important, at least to the extent that it frames the way in which a problem is conceptualized or approached, then there is an argument for making greater use of the term 'resource', especially when the central interest is on social change.

Whether we speak of 'resource' or 'property', it seems important that the term can comfortably accommodate a wide range of phenomena, from material objects (such as land, oil and trees) to intangibles (such as authority, the past, knowledge and identities). Chris Hann was instrumental in extending the property definition beyond anthropological convention to include intangible forms. As he noted (1998: 5): 'The word "property" is best seen as directing attention to a vast field of cultural as well as social relations, to the symbolic as well as the material contexts within which things are recognized and personal as well as collective identities made ... the main advantage of approaching property relations in this way is that it carries minimal ethnocentric baggage.' I share this view. Much like property, 'resources' refers to a wide range of material and intangible phenomena. An apparently infinite range of phenomena can potentially be 'resources', although how they are distributed, managed and controlled is specific to time, place and available technologies that work within different political-economic milieus (Kaneff forthcoming).

Given both terms' ability to accommodate a wide range of phenomena, I offer two reasons why we might want to make better use of the term 'resource'. First, as Hann makes clear, 'property' is bound up with political ideologies, both Marxist-Leninist and capitalist ones. This highlights the importance of property in understanding these systems, but inevitably hinders the way in which we can discuss the topic. What is needed is a term that is less politicized or at least less closely affiliated in scholarly and lay writings with particular arrangements of political economy. Resource, I think, fits these criteria quite well. Unlike 'property' – a term that is the basis of legal/social/political infrastructures in both socialist and capitalist systems – 'resource' has not been instrumentalized to such an extent in the name of particular political ideologies.[1]

Second, at a time when we are increasingly recognizing that 'the world out there' is not a passive entity, but also actively influences and transforms our social world and relationships in a dynamic way, the traditional anthropological definition of property – with its focus on rights 'over' objects – conveys only part of the story. The definition of property as a 'relationship between people *about* things' is problematic because 'property' is separated out from 'relationships between people'. It indicates that social relationships have control over the 'thing', but provides less scope for how the 'thing' may determine social relations. The focus on social relationships (a feature of which we should not lose sight) assigns property a passive role in light of the social relatedness of the more active 'people'. It is also, at this point, that I find it hard to conceptualize 'intangible properties': how can they be separated off from the social relationships that create them in the first place? In short, the term establishes a problematic dichotomy.

Resources are no longer assumed to be givens in the 'natural' or 'social' world, out 'there' waiting to be exploited or colonized by humans. They are attributed a far less passive role, at least in the contemporary literature (see e.g. Franquesa 2019; Richardson and Weszkalnys 2014; Uchibori 2011): they are part and parcel of an interactive human environment. Resources transform and are transformed through human engagement (Kaneff 2018). Effort is always implicated in the making of resources (Ferry and Limbert 2008: 84); it is through human labour – defined in the broadest sense that includes both physical and mental activity – that resources are made, unmade and remade.

Thus, a framing of the 'property' question in terms of 'resource' has advantages. It liberates the topic from previous conceptual and ideological restrictions. It is also a way of highlighting that human involvement is always implicated in the re/production of resources, even if the mode of intervention varies. The transformative and dynamic qualities of resources, a result of their being created by human labour, is built into the very concept. This also hints at their potential suitability for a way of understanding social change, a topic to which I will now turn.

Analysing Social Change

My argument can be summarized as follows:[2] whether they are material (e.g. land, oil or trees) or intangible (e.g. identity or the past), resources are always created, as noted above, through human intervention – through labour defined in its widest sense. It is human effort that transforms sources into resources and gives them their value. Intrinsic to resources – through the labour by which they are created – is their perceived 'use' and also their capacity for 'exchange'. Use is a value obtained through the perceived ability of resources to satisfy needs; in the most general sense, they provision. Exchange value – a potential that is not always realized – is attributed to those resources that through socially mediated relations enable comparison and conversion. No doubt, there are other ways in which resources can be conceptualized to have value, but for my purposes, it is use and exchange that are of most significance.

Since value is defined in terms of use and exchange, the revaluation of resources occurs when a resource is attributed new forms of use and/or exchange, that is, when there is a shift in the way in which a resource is utilized or exchanged. This process often assumes new ownership arrangements or new forms of control and management. Social change occurs when resources are revalued: this might be a mobilization between different forms of use as resources gain new/additional uses and/or lose others, or it might be through a resource's movement through distinct circuits of exchange. In this latter case, the move might be from a nonmonetary form of exchange, such as barter, to a monetary circuit of exchange on the market as a commodity, or it might be a movement between different forms of nonmonetary exchange, such as barter to *blat*.[3] In all cases, social change happens when resources move within systems of use or within circuits of exchange. It is mobility within the same value category. Social change might also take place when resources 'jump' categories and gain exchange value when once they had only use value – or vice versa.

Thus, social change can be explored in terms of the shift of resources as they move *between* and *within* use and exchange systems, that is, as they are revalued (Kaneff 2018 and forthcoming). Otherwise phrased: resource mobility is an analytical tool for understanding processes of social change. The consequences of such shifts in resources include claims and counterclaims over the control, ownership of and access to (or exclusion from) resources. Such processes, in turn, create new community divisions and sometimes new solidarities. This seems like a particularly suitable way to discuss reforms of the magnitude witnessed following the collapse of state socialism after 1989/1991, when resources were made/remade/unmade – in short, when resources attained new values. However, such a framework could also be useful in any social situation where transformation is taking place.

I will now look at the case of a material resource (land) as a way to explore more practically the above points.[4]

Household Land

Household land in the village of Brega, Odessa oblast, Ukraine, has been dramatically revalued since 1991. Historically, this land[5] has not been used for production. From the village's first settlement in the early 1800s by Bulgarian migrants fleeing Ottoman rule,[6] household land was simply used to store grains/hay and provide shelter to the households' livestock. All crops – fruit, grapes, vegetables and grains – were produced in the privately owned lands outside the village's settled boundaries, and only after harvest were they brought back to the household. Thus, household land at this time was primarily used as a storage space. The situation did not change significantly after the region was incorporated into the USSR (in 1944). It is true that the vast agricultural lands outside the village were reformed into the *kolkhoz* and *sovkhoz* (agricultural collectives), but household land remained largely unproductive apart from the planting of some rows of grapevines for household wine once the private vineyards located outside the village had become collectivized in the mid-1950s. It was the collectives (for which the vast majority of villagers worked) that took over the production of fruit, vegetables and grains, as well as meat produce, all of which was made available at heavily subsidized rates to their employees. Household land continued to be untended, except for the rows of vines, a small number of livestock (usually limited to poultry) and a very small quantity of vegetables grown for immediate consumption during the warmer months. The vast quantities of fruit, vegetables and meat required for winter preserves were provided by the collectives.

It is only since 1991, with the collapse of the Soviet Union and the establishment of independent Ukraine, that for the first time in the village's 200 year history, household land has become central to the survival of families. Unemployed (as the privatized collectives laid off 90 per cent of their workers) and no longer being provisioned by the newly established agricultural enterprises, householders have turned to their plots, which have become a newly valued resource. Household land has shifted from having a supplementary role in the maintenance of the family to being central to its survival. In other words, there has been an intensification and expansion of the use of the land. Household land has also provided a basis for villagers' engagement in new forms of exchange, both nonmonetary and monetary.

Here I briefly highlight some of the use and exchange activities in which households are now involved and the associated changing social relations. I begin with the use value of household land.

No longer able to rely on subsidized foods from the agricultural enterprises, households have greatly expanded their production both in terms of the quantity and variety of crops grown: tomatoes, peppers, cucumbers, carrots, cabbages, beetroot, pumpkins, radishes, greens (beans, etc.), aubergines, potatoes, onions, garlic and all other vegetables that are consumed throughout the year are now produced at home. From previous socialist times, when houses usually only kept poultry, households have now also expanded their livestock: most have at least one pig and a few sheep, while a small number (about 10 per cent) keep a cow or two. One part of the household land – where the water supply does not usually reach – is allocated for growing corn for animal fodder. The grapevines continue to provide the domestic source of grapes for wine. As for the staple – bread – it is made at home from wheat received from the new agricultural enterprises that pay families an annual 'rent' (in lieu of cash) for the use of the lands surrounding the village now privatized and owned by the villagers.[7] This wheat is milled and used both for domestic bread and for feed for the household's livestock.

Changes in the use of the land have significant implications for relations between household members. Gone are the days of the entire adult household population being gainfully employed full time and thus being paid regular salaries (and other entitlements) as workers of the collectives. Soviet salaries somewhat levelled relations within the household in terms of gender and generation divisions.[8] Now, with full-time salaried work outside the household rare and survival dependent on the work carried out at home in the production of foods, many of the traditional hierarchies in terms of gender and age have renewed prominence. Thus, men have gained additional importance through their participation in maintaining the household, especially on the basis of their responsibilities for the care and slaughter of larger livestock (pigs and sheep) and the making of wine. Women's work has similarly gained significance. They care for the poultry and are responsible for the production of most of the vegetable and fruit conserves. These tasks, which in many cases have required villagers to develop new skills (forgotten from previous generations), have given both genders renewed importance in different realms of household maintenance. Apart from the strengthening of gender roles, hierarchies based on age have also become increasingly evident. At least in the case of women, it is the senior generation who have gained additional authority over younger women. The former, having married into the family and carried the responsibility of its biological reproduction, now also have the duty of making the household's staple food – the baking of bread. In this way, senior women are reasserting their responsibility for the reproduction of the household and in so doing also increasing their authority. Internal divisions, based on these (biological and social) forms of reproduction, are more prominent now, given that the levelling device of 'salaries' is no longer available. Newly relevant gender and age-specific activities have strengthened internal household hierarchies.

Only a small proportion of produce from household land is ever exchanged. The food produced remains primarily for the family's own consumption. Exchanges between households (either with neighbours or with kin from different houses) are rare. However, the produce does form the basis of food shared with guests invited for various important feasts – birthdays, name days, etc. – that dot the annual calendar. It is also used to feed close kin from other households who contribute their labour at times of household need.

Households with a large number of land titles from the privatized collective lands (often obtained through inheritance) – and therefore a surplus tonnage of wheat received as rent from the enterprises – may keep a number of extra pigs with the explicit aim of selling some of them for cash. Such 'extra' activities require that the households have sufficient family members to supply the additional necessary labour. Another source of cash, and one that is quite common, is the selling of the grapes from the household land. This only takes place if – as in the case of the household where I lived – there is no domestic need for the large quantities of grapes (the daughter has married out of the village and my host lives alone). There are also houses with young people who take on extra household land in the neighbourhood that is otherwise left untended due to migration or illness/death. In such cases, the household vines are harvested and sold to private sellers. Such cash crop activities remain important, especially at certain times of the household's lifecycle: when extra money is needed to send a child to university or for infrastructural projects such as connecting the house to the gas grid system.

The new forms of exchange in which households engage have transformed relations between households (rather than within). Productive activities that bring cash benefits to households can only be achieved through calling on additional assistance from outside the household. Caring for vines, for example, is labour-intensive, especially at harvest time when hundreds of kilograms need to be picked in the period of a couple of days. In such cases, households call on outside help. It is close kin – usually the husband and wife, their parents and their siblings with their partners – and *kum* (godparents) who are considered within this tight circle of 'helpers'. The assistance is never paid for with money (indeed, to raise the issue of payment in monetary terms would be considered highly offensive), but it is part of a labour exchange – help is always reciprocated. While earning money is a primary goal of such reciprocal labour exchanges and households cannot enter into a cash economy without help from outside the household, the labour exchanges remain quite separate from any monetary exchange system.[9] Thus, two exchange circuits are in play: connections between close kin and *kum* are maintained and strengthened through reciprocal labour exchange activities, and the crops harvested enable the household to engage in monetary cash exchanges (paying electricity bills, etc.). Families and kin who are not included in reciprocal labour exchanges become, at the same time, more socially distant.

In considering household land as a resource, we can see the significant ways in which its use and exchange capacities have changed over time, that is, the way in which the resource has been revalued. Such use and exchange activities articulate with each other in complicated webs (only briefly summarized here) and have important implications for changing relationships both within and between households. Both the use and the exchange value of household land (or more specifically its produce) has increased dramatically as a direct response to the establishment of new agricultural enterprises that have severely cut back on the workforce, while at the same time no longer provisioning households. The use value of household land has risen significantly through its more intensive working and the expanded range of crop production. Monetary exchange capacity has also transformed from being based on salaried employees of the collective to the new but limited possibilities presented by engagement in cash crops/livestock that can be produced only with the aid of nonmonetary exchanges of reciprocal labour arrangements between close kin.[10]

Such revaluations of household land (resulting, in part, from new production activities) have impacted on relations within and between households. New internal distinctions set gender and age in greater relief because of the expanded and more intensive farming activities on household land. At the same time, new alliances between close kin and a greater dependency (if not closeness) between particular households (that also implies a growing social distancing with other kin/households) arise from the household's need for cash.

Conclusion

In the course of the previous three decades since the implementation of reforms, life in rural Ukraine (and throughout the former socialist world) has undergone deep and dramatic changes. One source of these life-changing transformations is the revaluation of resources – their making/unmaking/remaking – that have been part and parcel of political-economic upheaval. What I have proposed in this chapter is a way to analyse such long-term changes and the inevitable tensions that accompany such change. I have argued that the conventional anthropological concepts of use and exchange can be usefully employed as an analytical tool in examining social change. The revaluation of resources – their mobilization between and within systems of use and circuits of exchange – provides a way of gauging transformation.

While postsocialist reforms across Eastern Europe present an ideal context for studying social change, transformation is by no means restricted to the dramatic events of 1989/1991, when an extensive overhaul of political, economic and social relations took place. Perhaps in a less dramatic and more banal, almost everyday way, transformation is an ongoing feature of all social life. The analytical framework suggested has wide applicability in the examination of social change in any situation where resources (that are always grounded in local cultural contexts) can be identified as having some form of 'use' and 'exchange' value.

The study of property against a backdrop of social change (Chris Hann's primary interest) and, conversely, my focus on social change through a study of resources, have been and continue to be engaging pursuits. The model suggested here fulfils the criteria Hann identified as fundamental to the study of property: to have cross-cultural applicability and be abstract enough to be applied widely, while at the same time remaining sensitive and true to local contexts. Hann's original work on property still stimulates and inspires – and no doubt will continue to do so in the future.

Deema Kaneff is Reader in Social Anthropology at the University of Birmingham in the United Kingdom and Research Partner at the Max Planck Institute for Social Anthropology in Halle, Germany. She has worked in Bulgaria and Ukraine, and her research interests and publications focus on property/resources and social change, global capitalism and inequalities, and the anthropology of postsocialism.

Notes

1. A more detailed comparative discussion of 'property' and 'resources' is called for; however, space constraints require me to put this challenge to one side for the present.
2. The summary of ideas presented here was first developed in a preliminary paper (Kaneff 2018) and is presented in far greater ethnographic and theoretical depth in Kaneff (forthcoming). I thank my coeditor Kirsten Endres, Rainer Hillebrand and Frances Pine for helpful comments to an earlier version of this chapter.
3. That is, personal connections used to attain goods, services and so on, often discussed as an 'economy of favours'; see for example, Henig and Makovicky (2017).
4. Unfortunately, space constraints do not allow me to discuss a second case of an intangible resource. However, see Kaneff (forthcoming) for a discussion of a range of different resources.
5. Varying in size from 0.18 to 0.50 hectares.
6. The migrants were granted status to remain in what was, at the time, at the frontiers of the Russian Empire. The region remained under Russian, and for a few brief periods Romanian, control until the territory's incorporation into the Soviet Union in 1944.
7. Since the end of Soviet times, villagers can no longer afford to buy bread at the bakery and en masse reverted to baking at home, as they had once done in pre-Soviet times. This situation continues today.
8. My research is based on long-term fieldwork conducted since 2000. I have not carried out fieldwork during Soviet times and this part of my analysis is based on villagers' memories of that time.
9. More often, labour exchanges are associated with production activities carried out on nonhousehold land. It is common for households with the means to take on a segment of vineyard land (that was formerly collectivized and is now under the control of the agricultural enterprises). The family keeps the profits after paying the enterprise a fee for services rendered – e.g. spraying or ploughing. Such arrangements originated in socialist times between households and collectives, and continue today with the new agricultural organizations.

10. The growing importance of household land does not mean that families are transformed into self-sufficient or autonomous economic units. Both in terms of use and exchange activities, reliance on the agricultural enterprises persists, although in a very different way from Soviet times. Dependency continues through the rent paid – wheat – that has use value. In addition, for those with sufficient land titles and a surplus 'rent' in the form of grain for animal feed, there are possible exchange benefits through the additional livestock that families can take on as a means to earn extra cash. Unlike Soviet times, when the relationship between households and collectives was based on the salaries workers received and was conducted largely as a monetary exchange, today most exchanges between households and enterprises are of a non-monetary form (e.g. the annual rent paid in kind to landowners).

References

Ferry, Elizabeth Emma, and Mandana E. Limbert. 2008. 'Introduction', in Elizabeth Emma Ferry and Mandana E. Limbert (eds), *Timely Assets: The Politics of Resources and Their Temporalities*. Santa Fe: School for Advanced Research Press, pp. 3–24.

Franquesa, Jaume. 2019. 'Resources: Nature, Value and Time', in James G. Carrier (ed.), *A Research Agenda for Economic Anthropology*. Cheltenham: Edward Elgar, pp. 74–89.

Hann, Christopher. 1993. 'Property Relations in the New Eastern Europe: The Case of Specialist Cooperatives in Hungary', in Hermine G. De Soto and David G. Anderson (eds), *The Curtain Rises: Rethinking Culture, Ideology, and the State in Eastern Europe*. Atlantic Highlands, NJ: Humanities Press, pp. 99–119.

Hann, C.M. (ed.). 1998. 'Introduction: The Embeddedness of Property', in C.M. Hann (ed.), *Property Relations: Renewing the Anthropological Tradition*. Cambridge: Cambridge University Press, pp. 1–47.

Hann, Chris. 2000. 'The Tragedy of the Privates? Postsocialist Property Relations in Anthropological Perspective', *Max Planck Institute for Social Anthropology Working Papers*. Halle/Saale: Max Planck Institute for Social Anthropology, Working Paper No. 2.

_____. (ed.). 2005, *Property Relations: The Halle Focus Group, 2000–2005*. Halle/Saale: Max Planck Institute for Social Anthropology.

Hann, Chris, and the 'Property Relations' Group. 2003, *The Postsocialist Agrarian Question: Property Relations and the Rural Condition*. Münster: LIT Verlag.

Henig, David, and Nicolette Makovicky (eds). 2017. *Economies of Favour after Socialism*. Oxford: Oxford University Press.

Humphrey, Caroline, and Katherine Verdery (eds). 2004. *Property in Question: Value Transformation in the Global Economy*. Oxford: Berg.

Kaneff, Deema. 2018, 'Resources and Their Re/Valuation in Times of Political-Economic Reform', *Max Planck Institute for Social Anthropology Working Papers*. Halle/Saale: Max Planck Institute for Social Anthropology, Working Paper No. 189.

_____. Forthcoming. *Resources and Reforms: Everyday Conflicts and Social Change in Rural Ukraine*. Manuscript currently under review for publication.

Richardson, Tanya, and Gisa Weszkalnys. 2014. 'Introduction. Resource Materialities', *Anthropological Quarterly* 87(1): 5–30.
Torsello, Davide. 2003. *Trust, Property and Social Change in a Southern Slovakian Village*. Münster: LIT Verlag.
Uchibori, Motomitsu. 2011, 'Theoretical Themes for an Anthropology of Resources', *Social Science Information* 50(1): 142–53.
Ventsel, Aimar. 2005. *Reindeer, Rodina and Reciprocity. Kinship and Property Relations in a Siberian Village*. Münster: LIT Verlag.
Yalçın-Heckmann, Lale. 2010. *The Return of Private Property: Rural Life after Agrarian Reform in the Republic of Azerbaijan*. Berlin: LIT Verlag.

Chapter 13

Birth, Property and the Male Descendant
Some Evidence from India

Chris Gregory

Introduction

The title of this chapter is an allusion to the work of Jack Goody, a man whose thoughts and advice have shaped Chris Hann's career. Goody was an anthropologist in the original sense of the term. His early ethnographic research on religion, kinship and property in West Africa was followed up with library-based research of a comparative and historical kind that eventually encompassed all of Africa and Eurasia. It was Goody who, as Hann's supervisor, encouraged Hann to undertake fieldwork in Eastern Europe rather than the South Pacific, advice that has enabled Hann to quite literally expand the field of economic anthropology. Hann has taken up Jack's interest in property transmission, the domestic sphere and the state, but developed them in his own way by integrating some of Polanyi's economic concepts into Goody's more sociological approach. The other defining characteristic of Hann's approach is his commitment to the fieldwork method, both his own – which now includes Poland, Turkey and western China in addition to his ongoing research in Hungary – and as team leader of large research projects. One of these was his large European Research Council project entitled 'Realising Eurasia: Civilisation and Moral Economy in the 21st Century', which compared civilizations across Eurasia by means of case studies, done by graduate students, on the moral economy of small businesses. I was privileged to follow the progress of this important study during short visits to Halle over the period 2014–019. In what follows, I offer some reflections on Hann's use of Goody and

Polanyi with some ethnographically informed comments on the intergenerational transmission of property in Indian families, contrasting the dilemmas faced by the very rich and the very poor.

Goody, Polanyi and the 'Special' Commodity

As Hann (2015: 309) has rightly noted, Goody's Marxian-cum-Weber-inspired materialist approach to the study of the relationship between religion, the domestic domain, and property transmission is somewhat paradoxical, in that it largely ignores the importance of the modern market economy. Enter Polanyi.

One of Polanyi's important contributions, as I see it, was to develop Marx's theory of the commodity both historically and conceptually. His *The Great Transformation* (1944) is not only a magisterial survey of the economic history of the market up to the 1940s, but also makes an important conceptual advance. Polanyi drew attention to the fact that Marx's distinction between exchange value and use value was cross-cut by another distinction which Polanyi made: between 'general commodities' and 'special commodities'. Most of the commodities we find in the market are of the 'general' kind. These include products like rice, wheat, steel and cattle that are produced by means of commodities in the primary and secondary sectors. Three commodities, land, labour and money, have distinctive properties that set them apart. Polanyi called these 'fictitious' commodities, an unhappy choice because it suggests that they are somehow not real. However, the fact is that these special commodities are very real and perhaps the most important of all. But what is it about them that makes them so special?

The first thing to note about special commodities is that their specificity is lexically marked (in English at least). The exchange value of a general commodity is called a 'price' in English, whereas the exchange values of special commodities have special words: 'wage', 'rent' and 'money' for labour, land and money, respectively. The specificity of special commodities lies in the fact that they are not produced for sale in the way that general commodities are (Polanyi 1944: 75–76). Labour is reproduced in the domestic domain, the world of kinship and marriage, not of capitalist commodity reproduction. Land, for its part, as earth is an elementary fact of nature alongside fire, air and water. Money, in the form of gold, is a general commodity like all others, but when it takes the form of state-issued notes and coins, special problems arise.

Land, labour and money then pose special problems for a theory of value, and the special words English has for the exchange value of these special commodities express this fact. Market values are, of course, only one form of value among many. The religious domain values land, labour and money in an altogether different way, and the domestic domain in yet another way. The very word 'labour' is an economic valuation of the generic category 'people', one that reduces our humanity to a use value in a production process; the development of the market system, as Polanyi notes, goes one step further and reduces our humanity to an exchange value, to a price we call 'wages'. But, at the end of the day, the worker goes home where he or she is valued as kin, be it son or daughter, brother or sister, or mother or father. For the landed elite, on the other hand, their income comes from property in the form of land, a very special non-commodity for the British aristocracy whose unique system of primogeniture and legal entailment ensured that property of this kind was transmitted from father to son or nearest male relatives in complicated ways that provided the storyline for many a Jane Austen novel.

Political economy has monopolized the value debate, but economic anthropology has challenged this drawing attention to the 'human economy', as Hann and Hart (2011: 6ff.) have called it. The human economy approach concedes that the market has created a globalized economy of great generality, but draws attention to the need to study the familial, political and cultural contexts in which people are embedded. Modern economics, for its part, reads this *generalized* spread of the market valuation system as a *universal* one. A critique of this dominant orthodoxy requires one that draws attention to the limits of the market by means of ethnographic studies grounded historically and geographically. Hann's project, 'Realising Eurasia: Civilisation and Moral Economy in the 21st Century', does precisely this. Polanyi's economic history is both dated and restricted in the main to England, a fact that poses two big questions among others: how has the global market system evolved since the 1940s? And what has happened in different parts of Eurasia and the world at large?

Answers to questions like this are beyond the scope of any one project, but by narrowing the focus to family firms in Eurasia, attention is directed to an approach that conceives of kinship, economy and religion as an integrated whole. The family firm is a generic form of economic organization found all across the Eurasian landmass (and beyond). The comparative question posed is how the different religions and different domestic domains found across Eurasia shape the sociocultural form of the economy found in different regions. In what follows, I offer a few ethnographic snippets for Hann to consider as he ponders the general significance of the rich collection of new data he and his doctoral students have assembled. My reflections are informed by fieldwork done in a small market town called Kondagaon in central India. I carried out thirteen months of fieldwork there in 1982–83 and have returned sixteen times over the past thirty-seven years. The focus of my research has been kinship, economy and religion in general, and the family firm in particular. In what follows, I ponder the question of the economic generality and sociocultural specificity of the Indian case with some comments on two of the three special commodities – land and labour – as I have dealt with the role of money as a special commodity in detail elsewhere (Gregory 1997: Chapter 7).

Land as a Special Commodity

When I arrived in Kondagaon in 1982 to commence fieldwork on the periodic marketing system, it was a small market town with a population of some 17,000 people, some 25 per cent of whom were relatively recent migrants. The administrative centre of a regional district of the same name, Kondagaon's Sunday market was the centre of a large network of periodic markets on the north Bastar plateau. My wife and I found a place to stay in Sargipalpara, a former village hamlet on the outskirts of town that had recently been reclassified as a ward of the expanding town. Our house, a new mudbrick, four-room house with a tiled roof, was one of the first to be built in the neighbourhood on land that a rich migrant had purchased a few years before from a poor local.

By 2019, the social and economic life of the inhabitants of Sargipalpara has been utterly transformed. The rapid commercial growth of Kondagaon has absorbed former small farming hamlets like Sargipalpara into its orbit and transformed them into city suburbs. The rapidly growing population of Kondagaon, fed by high local birth rates and rural–urban and interstate migration into Bastar, has sent urban land prices booming. Sargipalpara is now a desirable address for the emerging elite, whose new two- and three-storey mansions present a striking contrast to the mudbrick, thatched huts of the indigenous inhabitants.

The changes have also affected the relative prices of urban and agricultural land. Land in Sargipalpara is of two basic kinds: (a) productive, low-lying creek-bed land used mainly for growing rice; and (b) the relatively unproductive, higher land and the banks of the creek used for growing millet and housing. These two extremes define a continuum of productive values. The best low-lying land has seed-to-yield ratios in excess of 30:1. As one moves up the gentle slope from the creek, the yield ratio of the land declines to less than 10:1. However, the boom in residential land prices has turned these productive valuations upside down. In 2015 the best farmland sold for less that Rs100 per square foot, whereas residential land in Sargipalpara sold for over Rs700 (US$10) per square foot, a ratio of 1:7.

This phenomenon of booming urban land values can be found all over India and many parts of the world at large. Perhaps the world's most stunning example is to be found in Mumbai, where Mukesh Ambami, India's richest man and recent entrant into Forbes' list of top ten billionaires, built the world's most expensive house in the world after Buckingham Palace, a 27-storey skyscraper requiring 600 servants to maintain it. Sargipalpara is not Mumbai, but the changing skylines and recent history of both places have been shaped by the same dominant global values, the unequal economic consequences of which are quite literally there for all to see.

Thomas Piketty's (2014) bestseller gets to the heart of the matter from a global political economy perspective. He shows that the composition of wealth in market-value terms has changed dramatically over the past 300 years. Data on the metamorphosis of capital in France over the period 1700–2010, for example, shows that agricultural land constituted about 60 per cent of all wealth in 1700, but fell to less than 1 per cent by 1970. The share of capital wealth in the form of urban housing land, by contrast, maintained the same relative value (about 15 per cent) from 1700 to 1970, but then rose rapidly to account for some 60 per cent of all capital in 2010. In other words, France has been transformed from an agrarian capitalist economy to an industrial economy, and then to one where urban residential land is now the dominant form of wealth. Similar patterns are found in all rich countries.

This boom in land prices has created many problems, paradoxes and dilemmas for local people caught up in these global changes. In Sargipalpara, it has created the paradox of the poverty-stricken millionaire, the poor householders who now find that the residential land their houses stand on is worth a fortune. These land-rich, cash-poor householders are faced with a dilemma because if they sell up, their children will become both homeless and landless (Gregory 2018). This raises the general question of wealth and property transmission in Hindu India, an issue that is at the one time extremely simple, very complex and full of dilemmas.

The question 'What is wealth?' is a simple one for most Hindus; every time I asked someone this question in India, the instant answer I always get is the same: 'children'. That, at least, is the generic answer. Some, usually men, are quite specific and say 'sons'. Here is the paradox: if sons are the supreme form of wealth, then why is Lakshmi, the supreme Hindu deity of wealth, a daughter goddess? This question has no simple answer, but we can understand the question better after we have considered the cultural specificity of labour as a commodity in India.

Labour as a Special Commodity

Labour, notes Polanyi, is *not* a commodity in the sense that 'the postulate that anything that is bought and sold must have been produced for sale is emphatically untrue in regard to them ... Labour is only another name for a *human activity which goes with life itself,* which in its turn is not produced for sale but for entirely different reasons, nor can that activity be detached from the rest of life, be stored or mobilized' (1944: 75). Labour, then, is a special commodity because the 'factory' that produces it is the household, the domain of 'life itself' where economic values are encompassed by kinship values and religious values, and cannot be separated from them. One cannot talk about labour as a commodity, then, without reference to these non-economic values. This is especially so in the family firm where the employee–employer relationship is overdetermined by these relationships rendering notions like 'wage' problematic. The other special feature of labour as a commodity is that the 'supply' of labour is embedded in generational time rather than a moment in time. What is crucial here is the relative valuation parents place on sons and daughters, and on the relative valuation of an elder son over a younger. Such valuations effect inheritance patterns and the ultimate economic status of a son as employer or employee in the family firm. There are many ways in which heirs are selected, but all of them involve culturally specific ways of the relative valuation of kin. It is here that the matter becomes complicated in Hindu India because the ways in which this is done vary over time and region.

One measure of this variation is the child sex ratio (CSR), the ratio of girls per 1,000 boys in the age group 0–6. As nature favours boys, the normal ratio is around 950 girls born per 1,000 boys. The CSR in India, by contrast, has long been below this. It declined from 927 in the 2001 Census to 918 with a marked regional bias, being much lower in the millet/wheat-producing areas of western India and is less than 800 in some of the most prosperous areas of the country. Furthermore, the data reveal 'an almost universal pattern of decline' in the CSR across the country from 2001 to 2011 (UNFPA 2014: 8). In other words, the adverse CSR is correlated with growing prosperity rather than poverty. In Bastar District, where my fieldwork was carried out, the ratio was 1,009 in 2001, one of the highest in the country; this fell to 994 in 2011 along with the general historical trend, but is still above the 'natural' ratio of 950 girls per 1,000 boys. What makes this district in east-central India so special?

First, the region is a rice-growing region and Lakshmi, the goddess of wealth, is rice personified. Female priestesses, called *gurumai*, sing a 31,000-line oral epic about her life that is ritually enacted at rice harvest time. The story about Lakshmi the women sing is a recognizable variation on an all-India theme. Lakshmi, as good fortune personified, is attracted by virtuous behaviour, but is repelled by its opposite. Lakshmi's abode is the household rather than the market. The myths about her describe a domestic moral economy, one centred mainly on the behaviour of women. Lakshmi resides in those houses where good conduct and social harmony prevails; she leaves when she comes across bad conduct and social discord and her place is taken by Alakshmi, the goddess of misfortune and poverty. The association Lakshmi with rice, and Alakshmi with millet, is one found generally in the rice-growing regions of eastern India, but not, of course, in the hot dry areas of northwest India where wheat and millet are the staple. This is the homeland of the ancient Vedic hymns, hymns that are still chanted today. This religion centred around sacrificial offerings to Agni, the fire god who dwells in the household hearth and in the sky as the hot sun. Lakshmi is celebrated in these hymns, but in her primordial form of a lotus who dwells in a pond. The northwest of India is a riverine culture, one fed by the melting snows in the Himalayas. Bastar, by contrast, is part of monsoon Asia, a rice culture based on rainfed irrigation. Meng and Mengin, the god and goddess of the monsoon rains and parents of Lakshmi, are important deities here, much more important than Agni. Lakshmi, as rice, requires careful nurturing during her growth phase. Women spend long hours for weeks on end weeding the growing crop. Wheat, by contrast, is a more capital-intensive crop that does not have this demand for female labour.

Enough has been said to show that the culturally specific form of Hinduism and farming found in the rice-growing areas of eastern India must be part of any explanation of the regional variation in the CSR in India (Sopher 1980: 296–97) – but only part, because kinship is a second factor that defines the cultural specificity of Bastar, one that cross-cuts, as it were, the east/west axis defined by staple food and its deification. The kinship system of the Dravidian speakers in the south, as Trautmann (1981) has shown in his classic study of Indian kinship, is quite distinct from that of the Indo-Aryan speakers in the north, the presence of cross-cousin marriage in the south and its absence in the north being one distinguishing factor. He also shows that a third distinctive system is found in the 'transition zone' of central India that separates the north from the south. In other words, the cultural geography of Indian kinship defines three bands along a north/south axis that cross-cut the east/west, wet/dry staple food axis. Bastar District lies in the centre of the 'transition zone'.

Residents in Sargipalpara are very aware of the differences between their kinship system and those found in the north and south because their neighbourhood is now full of relatively wealthy migrants from the north and south who spend large amounts of money on showy weddings.

Hindu weddings in Bastar are similar to other parts of India, in that the bride is likened to Lakshmi and the groom to her husband Vishnu. They are dressed up like king and queen and are treated as such in the rituals, which effectively worship them as deities. But while the nouns used to refer to the bride as goddess (Lakshmi) or queen (rani) may be the same, the verbs used to describe the act of giving the bride away differ. For Brahmins, the language of *kanya dan* is used. *Kanya* translates as 'maiden' or 'young girl' and *dan* as 'religious gift of a non-reciprocal type to someone of higher status than the giver'. The classic form of *dan* is the one given to a Brahmin, which is to say that bride-takers are like Brahmins in north India. The Halbi speakers of Bastar are adamant that their wedding rituals do not involve the giving of *dan*. They describe the giving of the bride as *beti deto*, literally 'daughter-giving'. This is accompanied by rituals that celebrate the radical equality of bride-giver and bride-taker. For example, whereas a northerner bride-giver will touch the feet of the bride-taker, in Bastar the action is reciprocated in a greeting ritual that goes on for about 15 minutes involving mutual washing of feet, mutual feeding and other mutual acts. Halbi speakers give *dan*, but only at death ceremonies when the relatives of the deceased give *dan* to the deceased cross-nephew who is said to be 'just like a Brahmin' to his cross-uncle. They also say that northerner wife-takers have corrupted the *kanya dan* system by requesting that a 'dowry' (the English word is used) be given as well. This, they say, converts a wedding ritual into a commercial transaction: the bride-takers are demanding a price for their high-status groom. Thus, for Halbi-speakers, the English loanword 'dowry' means 'extortion' rather than premortem inheritance. The parents of the bride give some gifts that fall into this category, but these are motivated by love and concern for their daughter, who is the intended recipient, not the groom's parents.

The wedding industry in India is big business, if not one of the biggest, and one that grows bigger every year. The values driving this are very complex and vary greatly across the different regions of India. The commercialization of the *dan* system as a 'dowry' in the form of an extortionate groom price is doubtless one factor, but not the only one. The giving away of one's daughter as *dan* in the form of the goddess Lakshmi brings fame to the father and is something that obviously motivates many, especially the super-rich. For example, Lakshmi Mittal, named by *Forbes* magazine as one of the richest people in the world, reportedly paid US$80 million for his daughter's wedding, a six-day event for 1,500 guests in France's most sumptuous settings, including Versailles (Rai 2013). For those families not in the super-elite class, the double demand of the avaricious bride-taker and the social obligation to express one's fame with a lavish wedding and a well-endowed bride has no doubt led some to see sons as a financial benefit and daughters as a financial cost, and to resort to sex-selection strategies of the kind that the bring about an adverse child sex ratio.

It is possible to argue too that Hinduism has, from its very beginnings, valued sons over daughters. The desire for sons as an ideology is a very ancient one. It can be found, for example, in the Vedic hymns, the earliest religious poetry of India that date back to 1400–1000 BCE. The hymns are songs sung in praise of the god to whom they address. 'Worshipers', as the translators of a recent English edition of these hymns note, 'are not shy about specifying what they want in exchange: the good things of this world – wealth, especially in livestock and gold, *sons*, and a long lifespan – and divine aid in defeating opponents, be they enemies in battle or rival sacrificers' (Jamison and Brereton 2014: 7, emphasis added). Having a son enables a man to pay back one of the 'three debts' that he acquires at birth: his debt to the gods, his teachers and his ancestors. His debt to his gods is discharged by the regular performance of household rituals and sacrifices, his debt to his teachers is discharged by teaching his wife, and children, and his debt to his ancestors is discharged by marrying and having a son (Dumont 1983).

This bring us back to the paradox mentioned above: if sons are the supreme form of wealth, why is wealth personified as a daughter goddess called Lakshmi? The paradox dissolves when one realizes that the debt to the ancestors cannot be discharged without the help of another man's sister or daughter who will become one's wife and mother to one's son. Daughters, then, are highly valued in India. What appears in the statistics of the demographer as a preference for sons is in fact the sociocultural product of the battle between the values of man-as-husband and the values of man-as-brother to the same women. This is the principal contradiction in Indian kinship, one that has resolved itself in different ways in the three different kinship regions of India. The differences in marriage rules define these regions in broad terms, but these can only be understood by exploring the lower-level complexities in the rituals that accompany births, weddings and deaths.

This complex cultural geography of kinship, religion and food crops is further complicated by recent economic history. While a booming Indian economy has widened the gap between rich and poor, it has also raised the general level of health, education and wellbeing. One marker of this is declining fertility rates: women are having fewer children. For the super-rich, this is a particular problem because the absence of a son means the absence of an heir to inherit the familial property. This is a problem all the elite family businesses in India are facing. Take the Birla family, for example, one of the richest families in India. This was founded five generations ago at the end of the nineteenth century. These four brothers had six sons and since then, the male reproduction rate has shown a progressive decline: four sons in the third generation, three sons in the fourth generation and only two sons in the fifth generation. Like all family firms, the divisions have emerged over the generation, but the problem of property transmission has been a constant one for all. It is one thing to endow a daughter with gold and silver at her wedding, but quite another to give her a share in the trading capital of the brotherhood because it allows outsider males in the form of sons-in-law to gain control over the family business.

For the not so wealthy small family, the desire is not a preference for boys, but for a boy and a girl (and in that order). Recent research has shown that 'what most families are particularly averse to is the real possibility of being a daughter-only family (John 2018: 4). It is not a husband that parents most desire for their daughter, but a brother. The research finds that 'it is the proportion of girl only families in a given population in contemporary contexts of fertility decline that is the most robust indicator of the extent and nature of the problem of a gender imbalance' (John 2018: 4).

Goody, Polanyi and Eurasia: An Unfinished Project in Comparative Historical Economic Anthropology

I take the title of my conclusion from a recent article by Hann (2015), which, for me, captures the essence of the method needed to deal with the problem of special commodities. The market economy is based on an elementary principle of great generality, 'the truth that, under whatever skies, men prefer to buy cheap and sell dear' (Geertz 1978: 29). This has enabled political economy to develop theories of great generality and political significance insofar as it relates to the values of general commodities. The special commodity, by contrast, requires an analysis of the special conditions that give rise to them in different places and times. This not only includes a study of economic history, as my case of the poverty-stricken millionaire landowner of Sargipalpara reveals, but also to the specific sociocultural geography of the case in question. India is divided roughly east/west in terms of staple food and roughly north/south in terms of kinship and marriage. While these divisions may not explain the reasons for the adverse sex ratios in the relatively wealthy wheat-growing areas of northwest India where large dowries are given, it does help to pose the question, as I hope my ethnographic snippet from a relatively poor rice-growing area of east-central India illustrates. History, of course, is a curse because it renders even the best analysis outdated as soon as it is published. The project will always be unfinished. This, for me, is the central message of Goody's and Polanyi's contribution. Understanding the human condition is a never-ending task.

Chris Gregory is Emeritus Professor of Anthropology at the Australian National University. He has been engaged in ongoing fieldwork in central India since 1982 and lived and worked for seven years in Papua New Guinea and Fiji. His research interests include the political economy and culture of rice growing in central India, kinship, gift exchange, money, the value question and morality.

References

Dumont, Louis. 1983. 'The Debt to Ancestors and the Category of *Sapinda*', in Charles Malmaoud (ed.), *Debts and Debtors*. New Delhi: Vikas, pp. 14–15.

Geertz, Clifford. 1978. 'The Bazaar Economy: Information and Search in Peasant Marketing', *American Economic Review* 68(2): 28–32.

Gregory, Chris A. 1997. *Savage Money: The Anthropology and Politics of Commodity Exchange*. London: Harwood.

_____. 2018. 'The Rise of the Poverty Stricken Millionaire: The Quest for the Good Life in Sargipalpara', in Chris A. Gregory and Jon Altman (eds), *The Quest for the Good Life in Precarious Times: Ethnographic Perspectives on the Domestic Moral Economy*. Canberra: ANU Press, pp. 197–223.

Hann, Chris. 2015. 'Goody, Polanyi and Eurasia: An Unfinished Project in Comparative Historical Economic Anthropology', *History and Anthropology* 26(3): 308–20.

Hann, Chris, and Keith Hart. 2011. *Economic Anthropology: History, Ethnography, Critique*. Cambridge: Polity.

Jamison, Stephanie W., and Joel P. Brereton (eds). 2014. *The Rigveda: The Earliest Religious Poetry of India*. New York: Oxford University Press.

John, Mary E. 2018. *The Political and Social Economy of Sex Selection: Exploring Family Development Linkages*. New York: UNFPA.

Piketty, Thomas. 2014. *Capital in the Twenty-First Century*, A. Goldhammer (trans.). Cambridge, MA: Harvard University Press.

Polanyi, Karl. 1944. *The Great Transformation: The Political and Economic Origins of Our Time*. New York: Rinehart.

Rai, Saritha. 2013. 'Steel Tycoon Mittal's Niece Has Big Fat Indian Wedding in Spain', *Forbes*, 17 December. Retrived 5 January 2021 from https://www.forbes.com/sites/saritharai/2013/12/17/steel-tycoon-mittals-niece-weds-in-big-fat-indian-wedding-in-spain/#1746cfe01780.
Sopher, David E. 1980. 'The Geographical Patterning of Culture in India', in David E. Sopher (ed.), *An Exploration of India: Geographical Perspectives on Society and Culture*. London: Longmans, pp. 289–326.
Trautmann, Thomas R. 1981. *Dravidian Kinship*. Cambridge: Cambridge University Press.
UNFPA. 2014. *Missing: Mapping the Adverse Child Sex Ratio in India*. New Delhi: The United Nations Population Fund.

Chapter 14

What Has Happened to Turkish Tea?
Thoughts on a Cash Crop, the Turkish State and Society in This Millennium

Lale Yalçın-Heckmann

In the 1990s, public images of Mustafa Kemal Atatürk, the founder of the Turkish Republic, were fundamentally changing. Based on her observations in this decade, Esra Özyürek (2006) argues that the representations of Atatürk were becoming varied in size and style, showing him as more humane, carrying out sportive, teaching or informal activities, or simply relaxing and having a cup of Turkish coffee. These were dramatically different images from those of the earlier period of the 1930s to the 1960s, which depicted Atatürk as unapproachable and iconic. Özyürek links these changes – in the way in which Atatürk is represented – to the emerging neoliberalism in Turkey after the 1980s and the accompanying political changes to public life. Democratization was accompanied by market-oriented consumerism and with the strengthening of civil society; 're-claiming the republic' with individually internalized democratic values that were primary messages to both national and international publics. Chris Hann had been observing the political economy of Turkey a decade earlier in the 1980s and during this period had made another product of leisurely consumption the focus of his attention – Turkish black tea. Contrasting Özyürek's interpretation that the image of Atatürk drinking Turkish coffee should be read as a step for democratizing Turkey, with Hann's analysis of the political economy of tea (1990a), one could say that democratization was accompanied by a change in consumer preference for Turkish tea instead of coffee. Coffee had been a luxurious consumer good (Çaksu 2018; Erdoğdu 2015), especially during the

---
Notes for this chapter begin on page 203.

Ottoman era as it was consumed by the Ottoman elites and later by the political elites of the Turkish Republic. In contrast, Turkish tea (*çay*) as the main and most widespread beverage for leisurely sociality came much later; Hann demonstrates that this was possible after Turkey had started cultivating tea in the Black Sea region with state support, subsidies and infrastructure, expanding the area of cultivation, allowing the smallholding cultivators to earn a decent living, protecting the tea market from foreign competition and making Turkish tea a major consumer product in Turkey.

In this chapter I outline Chris Hann's work and his main theses on Turkish tea as an example of the relations between state and economy in Turkey. I also describe and comment on some of the developments since Hann's research and writing in the late 1990s. My aim is to underline the relevance of his findings and trajectories concerning state and economy relations in contemporary Turkey.

Turkish Tea and the Region of Rize in the 1980s

Hann's focus, study and arguments at the time were highly original. Turkish social and economic scientists were debating the transformation of Turkish agriculture and the emergence of petty commodity production (cf. Keyder 1983; Margulies and Yıldızoğlu 1983 (cited in Hann 1985b)) – many were broadly referring to Marxist models of capitalist economy – but not necessarily examining the variation and different outcomes of state support in agriculture as in the case of Turkish tea.[1] The attention among these social scientists was to the peripheral economic position of the Turkish economy and peasantry, and to the emergence of petty commodity production, which – so the argument went – led to its entrenchment and to the lack of class struggle. Hann did not hesitate to challenge these dominant paradigms of agricultural transformation amongst Turkish social scientists (see Hann 1985b and 1990b). Using an anthropological perspective based on fieldwork and observations in Rize, he pointed out a continuity in the role of the state in supporting agriculture in a protectionist way – despite the formal end of étatism in 1980s – and that sharecropping as well as regional specificities were leading to new cleavages within the rural sector (Hann 1985b, 1990b; Bellér-Hann and Hann 2001a and 2001b).

Let us first consider how and why Hann came to study Turkish tea at this juncture. Hann states that he was interested in investigating smallholders in a country outside the socialist world as he had become familiar by then with the Hungarian and Polish cases. The aim was to comparatively discuss the relevance of state agricultural policies (see e.g. Hann 1995). Hann had already published his Hungarian and Polish village monographs (Hann 1980 and 1985a, respectively). The other strand of comparisons he had in mind was the global economy of tea, an agricultural produce that had become a global consumption product and was already studied at the time (see Harler 1964; Sarkar 1972 (cited in Hann 1990a)). His first research – supported by the British ESRC (Economic and Social Research Council) – was in 1982–83, followed by further research, together with Ildikó Bellér-Hann, between 1983 and 1988. The research area was in the province of Rize, primarily in the districts of Pazar and Fındıklı, and in the village of Sümer.

The Tea Industry and State Policies: Hann's Main Findings and Arguments

In the first part of his 1990a monograph,[2] Hann examines the physical, regional, economic and political specificity of the Turkish tea industry. Accordingly, even if tea was introduced in the 1920s and 1930s, successful cultivation was not established until the 1950s in a comparatively small area on the East Black Sea coast of Turkey, in a hilly and very humid geography. Tea came to replace maize and hazelnut cultivation fairly quickly and following the physical, cultural and human landscape of the region, the organization of its cultivation primarily took the form of smallholdings. The social structure prior to tea cultivation was marked by a dependency on circular migration (mostly young men), on households' multiple economic activities for livelihood and 'serious economic inequalities in rural districts' (p. 8). The young Turkish state introduced a protected agricultural system of encouraging tea cultivation. The passing of a law in 1940 provided the tea industry with state support, the area to be cultivated was placed under state control, and the state had a monopoly in the import and distribution of tea (and coffee). Cultivators were encouraged by free supplies of tea bushes, state experts provided guidance and the state agricultural bank offered cheap credits.

Hann follows up this initial period with discussions of three further stages: (1) consolidation (1950–73); (2) a first crisis and its resolution (1973–83); and (3) a liberal revolution (1983–90). The first period covers the era of establishing and consolidating tea as a major product in the region. The consolidation comes with the change to the multiparty system and in 1950 the election of the first liberal party, the Democratic Party. With the expansion of infrastructure and development policies, production areas were enlarged and '[b]y 1955 Rize was able to supply about one third of the domestic market for tea' (p. 13). After the military coup in 1960, which banned the Democratic Party, new and old parties continued supporting the local tea industry and did not allow cheap international tea to be imported into Turkey. The new industry in the Black Sea region also created employment opportunities for the local population, where even a half-hectare tea garden could sustain an average family throughout the year (p. 14). Hann points out the specificity of tea as an agricultural product; even if the Democratic Party has been often associated with introducing commercial incentives for large landowners, especially in East Anatolia, this did not happen in the Black Sea region. With tea as a cash crop, high income could be generated even on small plots of land, hence 'in the Rize region the egalitarian rhetoric of the Democratic Party *was* translated into practice' (p. 15, emphasis in original). However, the Democratic Party followed the strong state policies of protecting producers as well as consumers and there was no privatization (pp. 16–17). Turkish consumers were not allowed to have cheap and better-quality tea and even with the Democratic Party's offered incentives to develop the periphery through extending the capitalist market, the state remained as the main agent for development. Hann suggested that the new wealth through tea had an equalizing effect and broke the power monopoly of former local big wealthy families.[3]

The second phase depicts the 'first crisis and its resolution', the decade of 1973–83 (pp. 23–34). In this period, direct control of the tea industry was passed from the State Ministry of Customs and Monopolies to Çaykur, the Tea Corporation that was established in 1971. Soon after it became one of the State Economic Enterprises, 'not subjected to effective market constraints' (p. 23). The point was to control and guide tea cultivators and buy their product: 'permission to establish a tea garden had to be granted by officials' (p. 24). Nevertheless, strict controls did not work for long; smallholders continued following their own interests rather than obeying the rules concerning the quantity and quality of tea production. As tea continued to be a source of cash, the area of cultivation expanded and tea collectors started using shears to increase the amount produced and to speed up cultivation. This contributed to lowering the quality of tea. The political instability of the 1970s aggravated the situation, in that political parties tried to appeal to the cultivators as voters, offering them generous price increases for buying their tea.

After the 1980 military coup, state controls became tighter again. Shears were banned, a quota system for the daily purchase of a certain amount of tea per a certain garden size was introduced, and staff controlled and prevented overpicking tea leaves to improve the quality. However, after a few years, the 'expansionary process was resumed again' (p. 31). Hann argues that although the local producers had been aware of the problems of overproduction and low tea quality, they nevertheless resented the administrative measures taken by the state (p. 33). Turgut Özal's Motherland Party with its new liberal policies had an easy win and received the majority of votes in Rize in the 1983 elections.

Hann depicts the last era of the tea industry (1983–90) as 'a liberal revolution'. In the early 1980s, Özal had to follow the International Monetary Fund's recommendations and end import-substitution industrialization, as well as abandoning many of the inefficient national industries, in order to open up the country to further Western loans. This would have implied the end of subsidies for the tea industry, as well as a relaxation of controls. Controls over methods of cultivation (e.g. using shears) were indeed relaxed and quotas were increased, yet Çaykur was not privatized and the price support policy was retained. Instead, with a reform law in 1984, the state's monopoly over tea was ended and private factories were allowed (p. 36). Hann defends Çaykur's status as having 'ensured that the market remained stable, and had offered to consumers a product which satisfied them, even if it did not satisfy those who control the international tea economy. In doing so, it [i.e. Çaykur] had also transformed a hitherto backward region into one of the most prosperous in the country' (p. 37). Foreign teas could also be imported, yet their high price (due to the depreciation of the Turkish lira) meant that they could still not compete with Turkish tea (p. 37). Hann notes in his 1990 book that he could not accurately estimate the outcome of the new competition between the private sector and Çaykur, as he could not stay in the region long enough. The tendencies were nevertheless clear: one needed to differentiate between small-scale private operators who supplied tea cheaper than Çaykur. Then there came a multinational firm that produced a tea that did not quite conform to Turkish tastes, but nor was the tea suitable for the world market (p. 38).[4] This firm, according to Hann, was interested in having a share of the Turkish market. Locals were critical of the new private operators (p. 41), while at the same time acknowledged that they provided another opportunity for selling the produce. The quality remained a secondary issue to receiving a good price for tea. Hann concludes that the locals, with no alternative, were both profiting from the liberalization as well as being critical of it. They supported state control in terms of quality and quantity, hence they managed to 'tame the centre' through protest (withdrawing their votes) and subversion (expanding the methods of cultivation and area) in tea cultivation. This demonstrated, as Hann argues, 'the triumph of the periphery' (p. 43).

In the following section, I will look at some of the developments in the region: changes in the tea industry and in its organization in the period after Hann's study. I will also revisit Hann's assessment of the place of Turkish tea in the world. Recent literature and publications suggest some continuities as well as new developments.

The Afterlife of Turkish Tea

Rize's Demography and the Tea Industry in This Millennium

Turkey's population, as well as urbanization, has been increasing steadily in the last several decades. This is a factor that had an impact on the organization of the tea industry in Rize, as Hann (1990a) indicated in his monograph. The population in the region of Rize has been consistently showing negative rates of migration between 1975 and 2017,[5] even if this negative rate has been declining (calculated from the data source of the Turkish State Statistical Office (TÜIK); see also Sümer 2014: 172, Table 4). Gülizar Çakır Sümer in her study of urbanization in Rize notes that until about 2000, the rural population constituted a majority, and between 2000 and 2010, Rize's population declined (Sümer 2014: 169–70). In 2012 the urban population for Rize was 64 per cent and the rural population was 36 per cent.[6] Furthermore, the average median age for Rize in 2018 was thirty-seven, higher than Turkey's average median age of thirty-two, which could be interpreted as young people moving out of Rize.

Hann argued that tea cultivation had an effect on migration patterns. In the consolidation era between 1950–1973, tea offered the possibility of an improved livelihood and led to a decline of outmigration from the region: 'At least some of those who had previously been compelled to migrate in search of wage labour opportunities could now raise equivalent incomes by staying at home and cultivating tea' (1990a: 15). However, in a footnote, Hann adds that the migration pattern is complex and that tea incomes have helped some families to send their children to be educated or for new jobs in the cities (1990a: 15, note 35). This trend seems to have become dominant in this millennium.[7] Sümer (2014: 174) mentions a further factor influencing the families' migration behaviour: changes in the compulsory education system and the closing down of many village schools have led village populations in Rize (in a similar fashion to the situation in Turkey more generally) to move to urban centres in order to enable children to go to school. Accordingly, these villagers return to their villages only at the time of tea harvesting.

Again, in line with Hann's arguments, tea cultivation and the tea industry in Rize continue to illustrate an interdependency between the agricultural sector and the industry around tea production. Sümer (2014: 176, Table 7) shows that in 2011, 26 per cent of the working population in Rize was employed in agriculture, 36.3 per cent in industry and 39.9 per cent in the services sector (the 2011 Turkey total figures were 22.7 per cent in agriculture, 27.2 per cent in industry and 50.1 per cent in the services sector). That the rates of employment in agriculture and industry were higher than Turkey averages is remarkable and can be seen as a consequence of the continuing centrality of both tea cultivation and the industry in the region.

Nevertheless, outmigration and urbanization challenge the availability of rural workers. Hann (1990a: 41) mentions that already in the late 1980s, locals had difficulty in finding reliable workers. Georgian migrant labourers seem to have filled this gap. Sümer (2014: 175) suggests that Georgian seasonal pickers have become indispensable, although they are often paid less than the local resident or migrant pickers.[8]

The contemporary situation of the tea industry and its employment structure in Rize is described by Sümer as follows:

> Industry in Rize, which is dominated by tea, has some 205 large and small industrial units, 170 of them are tea factories and processing units. Of the tea factories 34 of them belong to the state owned Çaykur and the rest are privately owned.[9] In these tea processing units 15 thousand persons are employed, according to the 2013 figures of the provincial government (*valilik*) of Rize. During the tea campaign, villages become lively again and the urban population is drawn to rural areas. Rize receives seasonal labour migration for tea, workers arriving from Georgia, as well as urban returnees for the same period. (Sümer 2014: 175, my translation)

Tea Consumption and Production in Turkey

Tea consumption in Turkey is steadily increasing. Turkey led the world by a comfortable margin in 2016, consuming 7 pounds (c. 3.5 kg) of tea per capita during the year.[10] In 2019, newspapers reported that in Turkey, 260,000 tons of tea have been consumed. The demand for tea was primarily met by production in the East Black Sea region (including Rize, Trabzon, Giresun and Artvin), where some 83,000 hectares of land was being cultivated by nearly a million farmers.[11]

The Turkish State Statistical Office (TÜIK) notes that tea production (calculated as unfermented green tea) has increased between 2001 and 2019 from 825,000 tons to 1,408,000 tons.[12]

Competition between Private Firms and Çaykur

Since Hann's research, the number of private firms has increased considerably. Sezai Ercişli reports that between 1985 and 2009, the share of

Çaykur's overall dry tea production has declined from some 96 per cent in 1985 to 54 per cent in 2009; this was the case even if the amount of dry tea being produced annually had increased from 138,000 tons in 1985 to 209,000 tons in 2009, hence an increase of nearly 50 per cent (2012: 313, Table 11.1).

Which sector is able to buy the best quality tea? A relatively recent report by the Rize Commodity Exchange (Rize Ticaret Borsası) shows that in 2018, of the green tea (i.e. the best quality of first flush, *ilk sürgün*) bought from tea producers in Rize, 45 per cent of the total was bought by Çaykur and 55 per cent by private firms. From the second flush, the share of Çaykur and private firms changed to 52 per cent and 48 per cent, respectively.[13] This means that the higher-quality tea was being sold more to private firms than to Çaykur and that the latter was buying more of the second and further quality teas from the cultivators. (With the purchase of third flush tea, Çaykur's share in 2018 went up to 56 per cent.)

Tea Cultivators and Subsidies

A total of 80 per cent of the tea plantations had a size of 0.05–0.5 ha, where Erci̇şli concludes that 97 per cent of tea plantations in Turkey (of which the Rize region covers 65 per cent of the total tea cultivation area) would be family businesses (Erci̇şli 2012: 312).

As the report of the Chamber of Agricultural Engineers (ZMO) cited above indicates, the outmigration from rural areas of the East Black Sea coast remains a problem for the sustainability of the tea industry. Sharecropping, already mentioned by Hann in the late 1980s, seems to have become more widespread.

What does state support look like today? According to a tea report that appeared in 2015, tea cultivation supports one million people's livelihoods. The state subsidizes the price each year, after Çaykur publicizes each year its own price for buying unfermented green tea.[14] The subsidies are in two main areas: the first is to support the loss from productivity when tea shrubs are cut for regeneration (*budama desteği*), while the second applies to the difference paid per kilogram of green tea (*yaş çay fark ödemesi desteği*) bought by Çaykur. The latter payment of difference was reintroduced in 2003.

What Has Happened to Çaykur?

Hann pointed out that Çaykur was continuing to be a main source of stability for the tea industry. This statement still holds. However, the status of Çaykur has changed since 2017, when all stakes in Çaykur were handed over to the Turkey Wealth Fund. The Turkey Wealth Fund (Türkiye Varlık Fonu) is a sovereign wealth fund founded in August 2016 that is owned by the Turkish government.[15] This is a joint stock company closely managed by the government, with President Recep Tayyib Erdoğan presiding and his son-in-law Berat Albayrak, the Minister of Treasury and Finance (until 9 November 2020), as his deputy on the board. It governs various former state-owned industries, including the national postal and telecommunication services, mining and the former national state oil company, and it owns half of the shares of Turkish Airlines. Çaykur is the only food industry in this fund and it is not difficult to guess the reason for this: as Hann has suggested, it supports a vital industry for the economic livelihood of the region.

There are some critical concerns expressed relating to the incorporation of Çaykur into the state fund. Umut Oran, a Member of Parliament belonging to CHP (the Republican People's Party), writes critically about what the consequences of this takeover might mean. He claims that the local tea producers are complaining and predicts that Çaykur will no longer be subject to public control or accountability and can be privatized at the will of the president.[16] On the government's side, ministers often reiterate the president's close attention to the interests of tea cultivators.[17] In 2019, when the Minister of Agriculture and Forestry visited Rize and declared the official price of buying tea, he explicitly cited the president as having encouraged a higher price than what was suggested by the ministry.[18]

Some Conclusions

Turkey's and, more specifically, Rize's tea industry, although producing high amounts of tea (fifth or sixth in the world market as producer, depending on the source), nevertheless shows low levels of tea export. This is a concern for the tea industrialists, the state-supported Çaykur as well as many agricultural experts, ministries and politicians. The reports give various reasons for this. First, Turkish tea shows a very high level of internal consumption (first in the world market for consuming at c. 3 kg per capita per year). Second, Turkish tea is not considered to be of high quality worldwide, even if it has improved its quality substantially in the last few decades. The experts note that Turkish state support for the tea industry forces the continuation of stable tea-buying prices, independent of its quality, in order to support the tea farmers. Third, the high export taxes on tea discourages exports and stabilizes Turkey's internal market and prices independent of world price fluctuations.[19]

Even if many of Hann's observations and predictions still hold, and the private and state sectors in the Turkish tea industry still coexist, a more recent agricultural policy seems to threaten this coexistence. The Turkish government has been seeking to stop the decline of the rural sector and the dwindling of the rural population in general through preventing the further fractioning of agrarian lands through inheritance. One of the measures against the reduction of land holdings through inheritance was to introduce a change in the inheritance laws of agricultural land. The other and related measure was to increase the number of contractual agricultural producers (*sözleşmeli çiftçilik*). This allows the producer to have state support in agricultural costs and guarantees some subsidies, as in the case of tea. In a newspaper report in 2018, the Minister of Agriculture and Forestry was cited as announcing the introduction of contractual producers in tea cultivation. This would require tea cultivation areas to have a minimum size of 10 hectares (100 *dönüm*) in order to qualify for state support and for access to a subsidy system.[20]

Would this be the end of smallholders in the Turkish tea industry and the Rize region? This is a topic for further research. Whether domesticating tea is still enough to democratize the state is even harder to ascertain; the region seems to be overdependent on state backing and continued support for the present presidential and authoritarian regime. Taking a critical stance with respect to governmental policies – for instance, being against the construction of ecologically controversial water power stations – is harshly suppressed, and this includes the protesting voices of many rural people. One might conclude then that what is regionally equalizing is not necessarily equalizing for the whole country.

Lale Yalçın-Heckmann is a senior researcher and coordinator at the Max Planck Institute for Social Anthropology in Halle/Saale, Germany, and docent at the University of Pardubice, Czech Republic. Her research areas include Kurds in Turkey and the Caucasus, migrants and Islam in Europe, gender and kinship, property and the rural economy in Azerbaijan, citizenship, migration, ethnicity, informal economy, and economic and political anthropology, especially in relation to the Caucasus and Turkey.

Notes

1. There were a few anthropological exceptions looking at specific commodities, such as cotton and the organization of labour in an Aegean village (Sirman 1988 and 1990), on sugar beet and household reproduction in Eastern Anatolia (Morvaridi 1987) and on

sugar, the Turkish Sugar Corporation and the state (Alexander 2002). For a good overview of the social scientific discussions on Turkish rural transformation in the period 1950–90, see Akşit (1993).
2. All the references with page numbers in this section refer to Hann (1990a).
3. These had been studied in the 1960s by the American anthropologist Michael Meeker, who focused more on local social, historical and cultural organization in the province of Trabzon, west of Rize (see Meeker 1972 and 2001).
4. This company introduced the most common technology of the international market of manufacturing tea – CTC (Crush, Tear, Curl) – and Hann says that in those years, Turkish consumers did not favour this tea. However, over time, the method has become better established, as making tea with tea bags has become very widespread in Turkey and Turkish consumers increasingly value quality and variation, as in the introduction of green tea, organic tea, iced tea and the like.
5. This means there were more people leaving Rize than moving in.
6. Sümer 2014, 169 and 171, Table 2.
7. The Turkish Chamber of Agricultural Engineers' report on tea from 2015 states that: '95 per cent of tea cultivators have an additional income from outside the tea industry. Tea is no longer the sole source of livelihood. Outmigration is continuing in the region.' Retrieved 5 January 2021 from http://www.zmo.org.tr/genel/bizden_detay.php?kod=25738&tipi=38&sube=0.
8. See also the newspaper article on the tea economy and the need for cheap Georgian tea pickers in *Hürriyet*, 30 July 2009; Retrieved 5 January 2021 from http://www.hurriyet.com.tr/ekonomi/cayin-tadi-kaciyor-toplamayi-ucuz-gurcu-isciler-yapiyor-12175371.
9. Hann cites the figures of 64 private operators and 45 tea factories belonging to Çaykur in 1988 (1990a: 40). In a report from 2017, the Rize Commodity Exchange (Rize Ticaret Odası) mentions 197 firms in the tea sector, 46 of them belonging to Çaykur and 151 being privately owned. A total of 154 of the overall 197 were in Rize province. See *Pazar Araştırması raporu*, Ekim 2017 (market research report from October 2017), of the Turkish Ministry for Science, Industry and Technology together with the Rize Commodity Exchange.
10. Retrieved 5 January 2021 from https://www.statista.com/statistics/264189/main-export-countries-for-tea-worldwide.
11. Retrieved 5 January 2021 from https://www.haberturk.com/turkiye-de-cay-tuketimi-artti-2498337-ekonomi (published on 25 June 2019). This sounds like an exaggerated figure. In a state-led research report published in 2017, it says that some 76,000 hectares of land were allocated to tea cultivation and cultivators amounted to some 205,000 persons (*üretici* in Turkish, i.e. producer in the report). The number of farmers might be an estimate of how many people are directly or indirectly dependent on tea cultivation as members of producer household/families, if one takes a producer having a family of four. The figure of one million people is often repeated in media reports.
12. For tea production see TÜİK. Retrieved 31 January 2021 from https://data.tuik.gov.tr/Kategori/GetKategori?p=tarim-111&dil=1.
13. Retrieved 5 January 2021 from https://www.rtb.org.tr/uploads/files/253-2014-2018_ya%C5%9F%C3%A7ay.pdf.
14. *Ziraat Mühendisleri Odası Bülteni* (News bulletin of the Chamber of Agricultural Engineers), http://www.zmo.org.tr/genel/bizden_detay.php?kod=25738&tipi=38&sube=0 (retrieved 5 January 2021).
15. See https://en.wikipedia.org/wiki/%C3%87aykur (retrieved 5 January 2021).
16. See https://umutoran.com/2018/12/05/umut-orandan-rize-raporu, published on 5 December 2018 (retrieved 5 January 2021).
17. The president's father was originally from Rize, something of which the president is immensely proud.

18. See the report of the regional section of the Ministry of Agriculture and Forestry, *Rize Tarım Gündemi*, (Agricultural Agenda of Rize) 2019 (16): 'Cumhurbaşkanımız bizim düşündüğümüzün de biraz daha ötesinde bir çay fiyatı açıklamamızı istedi' ('Our president wanted us to declare a price that is higher than what we have been thinking of'). https://rize.tarimorman.gov.tr/Belgeler/Yayinlar/rize_tarim/say%C4%B1%20 16%20dergisi.pdf (retrieved 31 January 2021).
19. See https://www.rtb.org.tr/uploads/files/791-46)_S%C3%BCrd%C3%BCr%C3%BClebil ir_%C3%87ay_%C3%9Cretimi.pdf (retrieved 5 January 2021).
20. See https://www.yeniakit.com.tr/haber/cayda-sozlesmeli-aile-isletmeleri-geliyor-4579 75.html, published on 2 May 2018 (retrieved 5 January 2021).

References

Akşit, Bahattin. 1993. 'Studies in Rural Transformation in Turkey 1950–1990', in Paul Stirling (ed.), *Culture and Economy: Changes in Turkish Villages*. Huntingdon: Eothen Press, pp. 187–200.
Alexander, Catherine. 2002. *Personal States: Making Connections between People and Bureaucracy in Turkey*. Oxford: Oxford University Press.
Bellér-Hann, Ildikó, and Chris Hann. 2001a. *Turkish Region: State, Market and Social Identities on the East Black Sea Coast*. Oxford: James Currey (published in Turkish: *İki Buçuk Yaprak Çay: Doğu Karadeniz'de devlet, piyasa, kimlik*. Istanbul: İletişim Yayınları, 2003).
_____. 2001b. 'Mazlum olan kim? Rize'de çay üreticileri örneği' ['Are Peasants Always the Underdogs? The Case of Tea Producers in Rize'], *Toplum ve Bilim* 88: 55–68.
Çaksu, Ali. 2018. 'Turkish Coffee as a Political Drink from the Early Modern Period to Today', in Akadiusz Blaszczyk and Stefan Rohdewald (eds), *From Kebab to Cevabcici: Foodways in (Post-)Ottoman Europe*. Wiesbaden: Harrassowitz, pp. 124–43.
Ercişli, Sezai. 2012. 'The Tea Industry and Improvements in Turkey', in Liang Chen, Zeno Apostolides and Zong-Mao Chen (eds), *Global Tea Breeding: Achievements, Challenges and Perspectives*. Heidelberg: Springer, pp. 309–21.
Erdoğdu, Ayşe. (ed.) 2015. *Türk Kahvesinin 500 Yıllık Öyküsü* [*The 500 Year Story of Turkish Coffee*]. Istanbul: Topkapı Sarayı Müzesi and Türk Kahvesi Kültürü ve Araştırmaları Derneği.
Hann, Chris. 1980. *Tázlár: A Village in Hungary*. Cambridge: Cambridge University Press.
_____. 1985a. *A Village without Solidarity: Polish Peasants in Years of Crisis*. New Haven: Yale University Press.
_____. 1985b. 'Rural Transformation on the East Black Sea Coast of Turkey', *Journal of Peasant Studies* 12(4): 101–10.
_____. 1990a. *Tea and the Domestication of the Turkish State*. Huntingdon: Eothen Press.
_____. 1990b. 'Second Thoughts on Smallholders: Tea Production, the State and Social Differentiation in the Rize Region', *New Perspectives on Turkey* 4: 57–79.

_____. 1995. 'Subverting Strong States: The Dialectics of Social Engineering in Hungary and Turkey', *Daedalus* 124(2): 133–53.
Harler, Campbell R. 1964. *The Culture and Marketing of Tea*. (3rd edition). London: Oxford University Press.
Keyder, Çağlar. 1983. 'Paths of Rural Transformation in Turkey', *Journal of Peasant Studies* 11(1): 34–49.
Margulies, Roni, and Ergin Yıldızoğlu. 1983. 'Agrarian Change in Republican Turkey: Evidence and Interpretation, 1923–1970'. School of Development Studies, University of East Anglia, Norwich, Discussion Paper No. 141.
Meeker, Michael E. 1972. 'The Great Family *Agha*s of Turkey: A Study of a Changing Political Culture', in Richard Antoun and Iliya Harik (eds), *Rural Politics of Social Change in the Middle East*. Bloomington: Indiana University Press, pp. 237–66.
_____. 2001. *A Nation of Empire: The Ottoman Legacy of Turkish Modernity*. Berkeley: University of California Press.
Morvaridi, Behrooz. 1987. 'The Process of Agrarian Transition: Household Production and Reproduction in a Sugar Beet Growing Region of Turkey'. Ph.D. thesis. Canterbury: University of Kent at Canterbury.
Özyürek, Esra. 2006. *Nostalgia for the Modern: State Secularism and Everyday Politics in Turkey*. Durham, NC: Duke University Press.
Rize Tarım Gündemi. 2019. 'Bakanımız Bekir Pakdemirli 2019 Yılı Yaş Çay Alım Fiyatını Açıkladı', Sayı 16, Yıl 2019, Tarım ve Orman Bakanlığı Rize İl Müdürlüğü Yayın Organı. (State Ministry of Agriculture and Forestry, Rize Branch Publication, News about the Minister Pakdemirli Declaring 2019 Tea Price).
Sarkar, Goutam K. 1972. *The World Tea Economy*. Bombay: Oxford University Press.
Sirman, Nükhet. 1988. 'Pamuk Üretiminde Aile İşletmeleri', in Şevket Pamuk and Zafer Toprak (eds), *Türkiye'de Tarımsal Yapılar*. Ankara: Yurt Yayınları, pp. 209–31.
_____. 1990. 'State, Village, and Gender in Western Turkey', in Andrew Finkel and Nükhet Sirman (eds), *Turkish State, Turkish Society*. London: Routledge, pp. 21–52.
Sümer, Gülizar Çakır. 2014. 'Rize'de Kentleşme Süreci' ['Urbanization Period in Rize'], *Ekonomik ve Sosyal Araştırmalar Dergisi* (*International Journal of Social and Economic Research*), 10(1): 163–84.

Part III

Economies of the Sacred and Secular

Chapter 15

Economy Is a Ritual

Stephen Gudeman

From 2008 to 2012, Chris Hann and I oversaw two research projects at the Max Planck Institute entitled 'Economy and Ritual' and 'Oikos and Market'. Consisting of six comparative studies in Eastern Europe and Asia, they were undertaken by accomplished anthropologists whose results were published in two books (Gudeman and Hann 2015a, 2015b).[1]

Focused on the unsettled time after the fall of socialism, the projects showed that as market institutions slowly expanded in the six areas, they were supplemented by increased reliance on the house economy for provisioning. This transition was accompanied by the growth of communal rituals that helped make local connections, which were no longer supported by socialist organizations.

From the outset of our work, I harboured the desire to replace one of our project titles, 'Economy and Ritual', with 'Economy is a Ritual', because the alternative label turns accepted thought on its head and asserts that ritual is economy's foundation and not a mystification of the productive forces as suggested in Marxism or a separate realm of belief as presumed in capitalism. The Polanyi-imbued critic may consider the argument to be a variation of his notion of the embedded and disembedded economy. I am suggesting that all economies should be seen as rituals saturated by revered beliefs about how humans must and do fashion their livelihood. Before turning to brief examples of this inverted perspective, I offer my everyday views of both ritual and economy.

Notes for this chapter begin on page 218.

Rituals, anthropologists have told us, create solidarity, soothe people, stifle rebellions, represent the proper social order, present social dramas and cleavages, bring models of behaviour together with models for behaviour, and can be deciphered like a language or code. These interpretations of rituals show how they function for individuals or a society, provide a structure or anti-structure within a group, operate in a quasi-legal way or offer symbolic statements about how the world is composed (Geertz 1973; Gluckman 2004 [1963]; Leach 1954, 1961, 1976; Turner 1969).

I start with an everyday understanding of ritual. It is customary, learned behaviour. Ritual consists of routine, expected practices. Table manners at home, in a restaurant, at high table and other places are a ritual. Praying alone or with others is a ritual. Patterns of dress, modes of greeting and parting, as well as holiday celebrations are rituals, as are many classroom procedures. Just as bad table manners offend us because they controvert the accepted way of eating, deviating from other rituals may draw comments or raise eyebrows, although rituals do change over time.

The definitions of economy are fewer and some overlap. Economy is often seen as the production, distribution and consumption of material things and services. It can be defined in terms of labour following Marx, or the use of labour and land after Polanyi. Economy can be seen as achieving efficiency in markets and practices outside them (Marx 2010 [1867]; Polanyi 1957 [1944], 1978). This definition overlaps the idea of rational choice as the key element in economy. Being called 'irrational' is shaming just as poorly functioning markets are said to be 'inefficient' and should be improved.

By my everyday definition, economy refers to the usual practices of a people involving the making or growing, the transmission or provision, and the use (by the self, in the family or in a community) of things and assistances. This specification worked well when I conducted fieldwork in Panama, Colombia, Guatemala and Cuba.

These ways of seeing ritual and economy suggest they often intertwine. Assisting others can take a ritual turn as in religious rites. Conversely, when a man in Panama bends over, digs a shallow hole and plants rice, he utters the short supplication: 'May it grow up well.' Brushing one's teeth is an everyday ritual and a way of maximizing not going to the dentist, which itself can be seen as a way to avoid pain and save money. Eating the same breakfast every day can be a customary practice or ritual, and a way to economize the effort of choosing from among different foods. We thus separate economy and ritual in ordinary language, but intertwine them in practice. Yet are they different and related by more than everyday entanglements?

Consider creativity. In economy, creativity is known as innovation, which is the engine of growth. Most businesses today try to create conditions that enhance multiple innovations, whether on the shop floor or on the computer. Amazon, Facebook, Apple and others exemplify this creativity today, but the Jacquard loom, the steam engine, the light bulb and just-in-time production are earlier, more singular examples. Joseph Schumpeter (1983) through his notion of 'creative destruction' highlighted the role of innovation in business and enhancing profit, but one of the better definitions of innovation comes from the Bible and admonitions of Christ, according to St Matthew, who repeatedly declared: 'It was said, but I tell you' (Matthew 5:17–48).

The successful innovator in religion and ritual has charismatic qualities that draws followers – Christ, Moses with Aron, Buddha, Muhammed – and is recalled through rituals, just as the successful innovator in business – Ford, Jobs, Edison – is embodied in his or her charismatic products that draw purchasers. Today, even the titans of finance, business and software are termed 'gurus', a word taken from Sanskrit that is used for teachers or guides in Eastern religions.

Both ritual and economy are explained and justified by beliefs that concern what the human is and should strive to be. Both offer 'models of' and 'models for' behaviour to be brought together *in* behaviour, as Geertz (1973) once described for ritual. In economy, we have the model of the rational 'man' or *homo economicus*, which putatively describes both what we do and should do.

The beliefs that justify or legitimate religion and economy separate people into groupings – Christianity, Islam, Judaism – each of which has denominations (such as Orthodox, Conservative and Reform Judaism), and often there are sects within these. Capitalism has its competing followers who believe in unfettered capitalism, capitalism mixed with socialism or a degree of central planning. There are sects in economic theory as well. One sect proclaims that we 'satisfice' in economy, another says we maximize and some talk about bounded rationality. Other sects are devoted to different tax systems designed to mitigate inequality, reward profit or provision public services and goods. Capitalism even has its atheists, exemplified by communism, central planning and anarchism.

I am speaking to more than the idea that economy is embedded or disembedded in society, and I am speaking to more than the idea that ritual can be distinguished as we usually do from other social formulations, such as kinship or politics. I am denying a sharp conceptual division between economy and ritual. We use words to suggest they are different, but they look much the same in form, practices and beliefs, even if some of their contents or material touchstones differ. Let us consider three varying examples in which economy is a ritual.

The Gogo of Tanzania were studied by Peter Rigby (1969) over half a century ago. Females controlled agriculture, and men cleared the bush and threshed the sorghum and millet they raised. No one had permanent rights to the earth and access was free as cultivable land was plentiful. Farming was regulated, however, since Gogo country was divided into ritual domains, each of which was managed by a local ritual leader. Agriculturalists in the domain of each respective ritual leader had to follow the leader's instructions.

The ritual leader, known as 'the owner of the essence of the land', belonged to the patriclan with precedence in the area. Considered to be the living embodiment of his ancestors, whose dispositions made the land productive he was responsible for the flourishing of the crops. Through ancestral rainstones that he held, the ritual leader communicated and offered pleas to the ancestors, which was his primary responsibility. He also conducted annual fertility ceremonies and kept crop diseases and pests away through ritual transactions with the ancestors.

The leader could not set foot outside his domain because that would sever his ritual relation to the land, and even in his domain he observed precautions when outsiders entered, because physical contact with strangers could endanger his ritual area. Despite the ritual leader's importance, he had few economic privileges. The ritual leader collected the tusks of an elephant and the scales of a pangolin killed in his domain, but did not receive a regular flow of tribute or other recompense.

The leader's powers were not a mystifying ritual that justified extraction of a material surplus, and they were not a rational economic choice that aligned resources with optimal outcomes in the area. Material life and ritual acts were not separate domains in Gogo life. The cultivation of millet and sorghum was a ritual performance from the moment rights were granted to till a land area in a ritual domain, to farming with success, to the ingestion of food that expressed and signified the dispositions of the ancestors who controlled the land's productivity. Provisioning life was the culmination of a successful ritual performance.

In Panama and Colombia, I found a ritual economy based on the circulation of strength (*la fuerza*) or vital energy (Gudeman 1978; Gudeman and Rivera 1990). People said they needed strength to live, which I initially understood to mean physical strength. Men would point to a bicep, bend it and say 'oomph, strength'. Eventually I understood that this action with its word has a physical sense and signifies man's place on the earth. Human actions, based on the use of strength, are a ritual about God's power over the world.

Strength in the crops they eat, people said, comes from the trees, the sun, the wind and the earth. Work in the fields only 'composes' these elements to make food that provides strength. Humans arrange the components, but do not create strength. Like a barber, people plant, trim and 'cut' (harvest) what grows. Agricultural workers are artisans or craftsmen who fashion what is before them.

Strength, the energy of life, is a current that comes from the environment and is accumulated in harvests and consumed by people who turn it into a flow of vital energy to secure more. Crops in the field are part of a cycle made up of seeding, raising, harvesting and eating, or a flow of strength running from its material components through humans who use it to secure more.

This current of life connects people to the environment and to others through sharing food and work. In the house, one person's expenditure of strength becomes part of another's through the food they share that one or the other has helped to raise. A house is composed of people related by kinship and conjugality, and by the flow of shared vital energy.

Strength moves among houses as well, because it is transferred when one person works for another so that his strength helps compose their vital energy through the food he helps to produce for them, and their strength becomes part of his through the work or food they offer in return. A house gives and receives vital energy through work that goes back and forth, and by complex patterns of exchange, it circulates in a community and outside it.

The everyday economy in these cultures is based on the flow of strength from the earth that comes together through human effort, but its components have a larger founding. People distinguish the power or might (*el poder*) of God from the strength that enables them to live, for life's strength comes from the ultimate power. I once asked a group of people: 'If it takes strength to make strength from where did strength first come?' Eventually, a quiet voice in the back of the silent group answered 'the Garden of Eden', which was a fitting response for it was the original source of strength. As they also explained, six days of the week are devoted to securing strength. The seventh is kept in respect of the enabling power.

When I understood that this ritual economy of vital energy is anchored by God, I finally grasped a ritual that takes place on the final night of a wake when the people, who had gathered in the deceased's house and uttered prayers through the night, walked out the door of the stick and thatch house, extinguished with a puff of breath their candles that had been kept lighted through the night, and reshaped the house to exclude the bed of the deceased. Their ritual practice said that the deceased was no longer part of the flow of vital energy in the house. Both his spirit and strength had left, and so his bed was placed outside their current of vital energy.

Six years after my fieldwork in Panama, when I returned for a visit and showed the villagers a picture of our first daughter, Rebecca, many said: 'She looks Panamanian.' I thought they were teasing me, because my wife, Roxane, had stayed a few weeks in the village – after I left – to complete her studies, and a single woman was always suspected of having lovers. Then, I realized they were connecting our daughter to them, which was kind, but eventually I understood their idea that the earth and other elements provide the strength of life through food, and because Roxane and I were eating food from the village's soil shortly before Rebecca's conception, she embodied some of their vital energy and was connected to them.

The distinction between godly power that enables life and earthly strength that supports it is replicated in the difference between godparents and earthly parents. Godparents are linked to their godchild and his parents by spiritual ties that are formed at baptism. In Panama, godparents were rarely asked for material help or money to support their godchildren. The spiritual parent represents a higher status and is due greater respect than the parent just as spiritual power makes material strength possible. Borrowing money and reneging on the loan would disrupt this relationship.

This encompassment of strength by power means that economy in Panama and Colombia represents more than working the earth to support ordinary life. Economic practices enact a belief in God's supreme power that provides life and enables the securing of earthly strength or the current by which people live. The routine, everyday practices of securing, exchanging and consuming vital energy that maintains humans are an economic ritual that makes the power of God immanent in all individuals.

The market economy in the United States (and some other places) is a ritual of living as a rational person. We embody, engage and try to live this ideal, assuming that everyone else is doing so, because if others do, then we must as well or fail in the competitive economy. The rational person is the model of and the model for the economy, and we are taught to believe in this icon. When we do not embody this ideal in behaviour, we are disparaged and told 'that's irrational' or 'inefficient', which are shaming words that produce feelings of inadequacy in us. The rational person is the godhead, the economic saint, who guides our action.

According to Max Weber, the rise of the Protestant Ethic, which expressed the belief that earthly success is a sign of eternal salvation, led to a greater degree of rational action, unremitting work and the rise of capitalism. This commitment to work, taken as a mark of faith in the hope of receiving the sign of one's destiny, eventually was loosened from its religious significance and became an autonomous action and an 'iron cage'. I think it has become a sacred part of identity in a different way, for when we do not adhere to its rationale of rationality and fall out of the market economy, we become destitute and impoverished, which is our version of hell on earth.

The rational person, we are told, chooses the outcome that offers the highest personal utility. The anthropologist observes that utility is an abstract word that overlaps other intangibles, such as value, worth, satisfaction and pleasure. When the rational person chooses according to her private taste – minimizing her cost or maximizing her return for the cost – the market achieves the golden end of efficiency, meaning that no one could have a better position through trading without someone else being worse off, but this divine end is achieved only when competitive conditions are perfect, and few if any people have experienced this finality.

I am using the ritual language of the expert practitioners who have served an apprenticeship before being allowed to become priests of the economy who write and speak to others – they have gone through a rite of passage – changing them from novices to authorities, and have learned this formal language. The ritual words, it might be said, started with Aristotle, but probably the chief saint is Adam Smith, although there are others, such as Ricardo, Mill, Marx, Pareto, Schumpeter, Keynes, Friedman, Samuelson, Arrow and many more. A few of these are Nob(e)ly enshrined, but others are venerated as well. All, according to Keynes, one of the chief saints, have heard 'voices in the air' that they 'madly scribble' to spread their influence (Keynes 1964: 383).

The collection of rituals and beliefs associated with economy's clerics constantly proliferates into sects, just as Christ's death is differently re-enacted on Sundays and at Easter by different religious groups. These economic cults, from laissez-faire capitalism to rational expectations, to monetarism, to social capitalism and to institutionalism – stemming from one or another economic saint (few of these saints are women) – rise and fall in size, depending in part on the charisma of the leader and his embodiment in others.

This overlapping, spreading and spoken set of rituals is designed to influence or be embodied in ordinary people so that their actions conform to its strictures. It has never been completely clear, however, whether the rituals, written in words or as formulae, graphs and tables, are prescriptive or descriptive. Sometimes they are a conflation of 'models of' and 'models for' behaviour.

As in the cases from Africa and Latin America, this ritual economy is learned, passed along and expressed by knowledgeable elders, but its impact derives from its influence on everyday behaviour, which happens in numerous ways.

Some priests of the economy serve in the polity, such as the head of the US Treasury that issues the tokens (rather than seashells), which people use in exchange, and has a voice about the timing of their issuance in relation to expenditures in the economy. The Treasury charges for use of this token in the economy and in other economies. The most sacred position in this ritual economy is the central bank that controls the level of the charge for use of the chits, and putatively makes certain that everyone is employed, although the connection of the two is slightly circuitous. As with most ritual counsellors, this small group that controls the shared national bank meets in secret and then, like a divine king, emerges only periodically to let the awaiting populace know how much will be charged for use of the national chits.

If the oracular utterances from these high priests can sometimes be predicted, there is another unpredictable and disruptive but charismatic leader, known as the entrepreneur or undertaker, who sees not to the dead, but to the creation of a money-making enterprise. This newbie is the agent of 'creative destruction', according to the oxymoron of one priest of the profession. He often becomes the leader of a new assemblage of followers who produce as he proclaims, while others offer chits for the products they introduce. Such leaders, it is claimed, make the economy grow for everyone, although their receipt of chits often far outbalances the returns that others receive for their efforts.

Even without innovation, this ritual economy never stays on the same course, because like the others, it is susceptible to changes in its physical and human surroundings, and it produces its own contradictions. Sometimes this ritual economy is 'depressed', like humans are said to be, while in other cases 'it' indulges and becomes 'bubbly' as if on champagne or fermented wine. In these 'up' and 'down' instances, the priestly managers of the chits may 'intervene' to restore order. But the priests can see only into the near future, and sometimes they change their foresight and the number of available chits every three months. Over the longer run, this ritual economy can produce its hell, its day of reckoning, its catastrophe, for the never-sated monsters it creates, trains, fosters and feeds seem to be blindly destroying the materials and life forms which they consume. This ritual economy, with its elaborated beliefs, practitioners and believers, which is more complex than the prior two, may create an apocalypse that destroys the people who participate in it, others who do not and the planet on which all of them depend.

We have, then, examples of three ritual economies, each of which is distinct. In the first, ancestral dispositions through lineage land influence the prosperity of the crops on which people feed. These lineal ancestors are separate from the crops that their human descendants grow, but their intentions are revealed through the plenitude or scarcity of the food provided. In the second example, God's might or power enables the vital energy that brings crops to fruition and whose consumption provides life in humans. This second ritual economy promises a continuous and immanent flow of strength in which humans are embedded and participate until they die – or, better said, die when the flow no longer courses through their bodies and binds together the economy. In the third case, the human is born as, lives, increasingly becomes and is a ritualistic representation of rational choice that enables material life. This third economy seems designed to destroy the material foundations on which it is built and the lives of its participants. These inhabitants, some of whom recognize their possible end, often invoke the undertaker of innovation as their salvation. However, earthly creativity cannot be planned, just as this undertaking redeemer does not fit the presumption by which the rest live, that they embody rational choice, unless they also calculate that it is rational to destroy human and animal life.

The anthropologist encounters many different economies. Some are practised, some are observed, some are historical and some are prescriptive. Some are spread through writing, while others are orally transmitted. All are based on assumptions about power in the world, such as the sway of ancestors, the influence of a god or the calculated wisdom of humans. Today, most of the economies once known have disappeared and almost all now presume the existence of rugged individuals, who live with few obligations to society and have differently valued preferences that they act to maximize, as do the producing firms that surround them. Because it is said that their resources are limited and their wants continually expand, and they are so trained to feel that way by advertising and competition, choice among their desires must be continually exercised. These presumptions and observations fit a form of ritual economy known as capitalism that is revered by many of its high priests as well as its human participants, although there are dissenters.

Stephen Gudeman is Research Partner of the Max Planck Institute for Social Anthropology and a Board Member of the Max-Cam Centre. He co-directed with Chris Hann two Max Planck projects in Eastern Europe and Asia during the period 2009–12. Previously, he carried out research in four countries of Latin America. The author or editor of twelve books, he is also Emeritus Professor of Anthropology at the University of Minnesota.

Note

1. Our project team included Jennifer Cash (Moldova), Nathan Light (Kyrgyzstan), Miladina Monova (Macedonia), Detelina Tocheva (Bulgaria), Monica Vasile (Romania) and Bea Vidacs (Hungary) who published in *Economy and Ritual* and *Oikos and Market*.

References

Geertz, Clifford. 1973. *The Interpretation of Cultures*. New York: Basic Books.
Gluckman, Max. 2004 [1963]. *Order and Rebellion in Tribal Africa*. Abingdon: Routledge.
Gudeman, Stephen. 1978. *The Demise of a Rural Economy*. London: Routledge & Kegan Paul.
Gudeman, Stephen, and Chris Hann (eds). 2015a. *Economy and Ritual: Studies of Postsocialist Transformations*. New York: Berghahn Books.
Gudeman, Stephen, and Chris Hann (eds). 2015b. *Oikos and Market: Explorations in Self-Sufficiency after Socialism*. New York: Berghahn Books.
Gudeman, Stephen, and Alberto Rivera. 1990. *Conversations in Colombia*. Cambridge: Cambridge University Press.
Keynes, John Maynard. 1964 [1936]. *The General Theory of Employment, Interest, and Money*. New York: Harcourt, Brace & World.
Leach, Edmund. 1954. *Political Systems of Highland Burma*. London: G. Bell and Sons.
_____. 1961. *Rethinking Anthropology*. London: Berg.
_____. 1976. *Culture and Communication*. Cambridge: Cambridge University Press.
Marx, Karl. 2010 [1867]. *Capital, Vol. 1*. London: Electric Book Company.
Polanyi, Karl. 1957 [1944]. *The Great Transformation*. Boston, MA: Beacon Press.
_____. 1978. *Primitive, Archaic, and Modern Economies*. Boston, MA: Beacon Press.
Rigby, Peter. 1969. *Cattle and Kinship Among the Gogo*. Ithaca, NY: Cornell University Press.
Schumpeter, Joseph. 1983 [1934]. *The Theory of Economic Development. An Inquiry into Profits, Capital, Credit, Interest, and the Business Cycle*. New Brunswick, NJ: Transaction Publishers.
Turner, Victor. 1969. *The Ritual Process*. New York: Cornell University Press.
Weber, Max. 1958. *The Protestant Ethic and the Spirit of Capitalism*. New York: Charles Scribner's Sons.

Chapter 16

The Rice, the Rice Goddess and the Sickle
An Agricultural 'Revolution' among the Bru of Khe Sanh, 1989

Gábor Vargyas

'For centuries, swidden cultivation has been one of the most important land use systems in the tropics, including Southeast Asia. Numerous studies, including those of Conklin ... showed that in many situations it is in fact a rational economic and environmental choice for farmers in the humid tropical uplands' (Mertz et al. 2009: 259). Since the 1950s, when swiddening emerged as an important theme of scientific interest, sociocultural anthropologists, human ecologists, sociologists, agricultural specialists and rural development experts have convincingly argued that, given the fulfilment of certain conditions, swiddening is not harmful for the natural environment (Conklin 1957, 1963; Condominas 1983; Spencer 1966; Mertz 2002). Nevertheless, an almost general set of negative stereotypes (see Condominas 2009; Fox 2000) coupled with pressures from governmental and international agencies (FAO Staff 1957; Circular of the Ministry of Forestry 1992) demanded swiddeners abandon their 'harmful' methods. As a consequence, a rapid change is taking place in areas formerly dominated by swidden cultivation across Southeast Asia, the old system being replaced by or transformed into other land uses. A vast body of literature deals with the technological, developmental, ecological and sociopolitical aspects of this change, as a transition from one sort of ecosystem (swiddening) to another, centred mostly on wet-rice agriculture (Burling 1965; Cramb et al. 2009; Geertz 1972; Mertz et al. 2009; Padoch et al. 2007).

Notes for this chapter begin on page 228.

Interestingly, in this bewilderingly rich literature, one rarely finds a study on how religious representations and rituals associated with agriculture act upon, influence, hinder or foster the above-mentioned process (Low and Pugh-Kitingan 2015). Gudeman and Hann rightly formulate the problem in a more general way, 'for most economists, ritual and economy have little to do with one another in the contemporary world. Economy is treated ... as a realm ... of material production on which ritual actions are ... a cultural barrier to efficiency' (2015: 2). Thus, a discourse on 'development' means that the interrelatedness of economy and ritual are downplayed. However, as O'Connor states, 'in Southeast Asia agriculture is a locus of meaning, not just a means to subsist. As these societies arise performatively ... farming's technical practices easily become ritual acts ... that constitute a moral stance ... and define ethnic identity' (1995: 969). As is well known, agriculture and rituals go hand in hand among the hill populations of Southeast Asia in general and in Vietnam specifically (Boulbet 1966; Condominas 1972 and 1983; Izikowitz 1951; Maurice 1993; Maurice and Roux 1954, etc.), hence Condominas' apt expression of 'ritual technologies' (1986). Theoretically, any change on the technological-social level may predestine a similar change in the religious-ritual field or vice versa.

In what follows, I shall describe an agricultural 'revolution' both from technological and religious points of views that occurred among the Bru in the Khe Sanh area, Quảng Trị Province, in 1989.[1] Because I have been unable to return since the completion of my fieldwork, what I present here is necessarily a snapshot from a longer process and I leave the dénouement partially unfinished. The present tense used throughout this chapter is the 'ethnographic present' (1985–89). The chapter consists of two parts: first, I introduce the Bru agricultural system, the history of wet-rice cultivation in the area, and some technological, ecological and economic problems associated with moving from one ecosystem to the other; second, I describe and analyse the adoption of new harvesting and threshing methods – a 'revolutionary' change not only from a technical but also from a religious point of view.

Swiddens (*Saráí*) and Wet-Rice Fields (*Nia*): History of the Wet-Rice Cultivation in the Area of Khe Sanh

The Bru are subsistence farmers practicing swidden agriculture; their staple crop is dry rice (*saro*), supplemented by maize, manioc, millet, sesame, tobacco and vegetables. However, from three generations ago, dry rice cultivation has been complemented by wet-rice cultivation.

According to the oldest informants, the generation of their grandfathers had hired Vietnamese peasants for the construction of rice-fields near the current location of the Cóc and Dông Cho villages. If we assume twenty-five years as a generation, the rice-fields were constructed around 1914. At that time, the two villages did not even exist: the population of Cóc lived in Hoong, which was still the religious and political centre of the area in 1989, while Dông Cho was located some miles further to the east. The reason for the foundation of Cóc village was that the newly constructed wet-rice-fields were too far from Hoong village and part of the population preferred to move nearer to the fields, thus provoking the segmentation of the original land-owning lineage.

The original motifs for constructing these wet-rice fields remain unclear. One would naturally be inclined to think of an external pressure. As a matter of fact, the Bru told me in 1987–88 that swidden cultivation was officially forbidden,[2] but during my fieldwork, this interdiction was not observed in the Khe Sanh area. With no other means of subsistence, the Bru had not ceased to cultivate swiddens. However, a unique military document from 1947 may provide a clue here (see Vargyas 2000: 257–297). The author of the report, Lieutenant Barthélémy, mentions a severe degradation of the original forest cover on the Vietnamese side of the Annamese Cordilleras and the rapid spread of the 'elephant-grass' or savannah. Whatever the reasons for it, the Bru (Kha Leu for Barthélémy) were said to migrate in great number to the Laotian side of the mountains, thus causing 'border problems' from the early 1910s onwards. The general migration of the Bru following the degradation of the forest cover in Vietnam since the 1910s seems to concord well with my field data concerning the date of the construction of the first rice-fields.

Wet-rice-fields were thus a relatively new phenomenon, a cultural borrowing initiated by the Bru without any detectable pressure from the French or Vietnamese. The whole vocabulary of cultivation testifies to this foreign origin. Most of the words are obvious Vietnamese (but also Thai/Lao and perhaps French) loanwords,[3] just as the technology itself is borrowed entirely from the Vietnamese.

The data thus suggest an intrinsic change from swiddening to wet-rice cultivation. One would be inclined to say the Bru had recognized the advantages of wet-rice and opted for what is generally considered the 'more developed' method. However, why did they not stop swiddening altogether? What is the explanation for the merely additional, supplementary role of wet rice against dry rice?

First of all, there are a number of limiting natural factors. In the hilly region of the Cóc/Dông Cho villages, there are only a few areas suitable for rice-fields (disregarding terrace-making, a method that requires an enormous surplus in manpower investment). According to my informants, even these 'plain' areas had to be levelled in the past with painstaking labour, requiring manpower and animal power beyond that available for the Bru. In addition, one should not forget the labour involved in building the dikes, and clearing the area of the trees and their roots in order to make the land suitable for ploughing. All this demanded not only enormous investment in man power but also knowhow.[4] This is why the swidden-cultivator Bru, defying any stereotype about 'poor' and 'subaltern' hill people, *hired Vietnamese peasants* for payment in buffaloes. Today such an investment would be impossible for both economic and social reasons. Since the Vietnam War, the Bru have been impoverished, their herds (buffalo, cattle, elephants) decimated, their property (silver money, bronze utensils, earthenware vessels, gongs) destroyed, while their social position has declined markedly since the end of the Vietnam War. Today, they live as a relatively marginalized minority somewhere halfway between 'cultural and economical-social marginalisation' (Goudineau 2003: xii). What was possible three generations ago is unimaginable today.

Another factor is water supply. A constant problem even with the existing wet-rice-fields is that there is not enough water that can be channelled towards them. Although in reality there are as many, or more, creeks than hills in the area (this is why in toponyms '*kóh* = hill' is synonymous with '*hoq* = creek or source'), many of the creeks are irregular, too small or too far from the fields to provide a constant supply of water for irrigation. Moreover, there are two wet-rice cycles in an agricultural year as against one dry-rice cycle. The first cycle starts somewhere around May (the other in November/December), right in the middle of the dry season. Therefore, the creeks are often dry or shallow in the moment when, after ploughing and harrowing, the fields have to be flooded. As a consequence, each year a part of the existing fields remains unused due to lack of water. In short, the few suitable areas have been turned into wet-rice-fields long ago, the remaining areas are either unsuitable or would demand an enormous investment in manpower. Until there is enough forest in the neighbourhood to sustain shifting cultivation, i.e. until the circumstances do not constrain a radical change in the subsistence pattern, nobody will accept the tremendous amount of surplus work needed to create new wet-rice-fields.

Let me quote a concrete case here. In January 1988, I witnessed a pig sacrifice in the fields of Cóc village in connection with a plot of land that had just been transformed from swidden to wet-rice cultivation. As one might suppose, several weeks if not months of hard work were put into this enterprise by three families belonging to the same lineage. They had constructed a wooden and earthen dam lined with woven mats and vegetable materials at the nearby stream that had to be diverted into a new artificial bed for at least one kilometre to reach the fields. After several weeks of unsuccessful attempts, the construction was abandoned: they were unable to retain and properly channel the water and, besides, the fields were not properly levelled and the small amount of arriving water escaped in every direction. The project thus failed due to a lack of know-how. A year later, I learned that the plot of land had been converted back into swidden.

Rice from a Religious Point of View: Ritual Technologies of the Agricultural Cycle

From a religious point of view, the Bru agricultural cycle is an intricate complex where each technological phase is preceded or accompanied by an appropriate 'ritual technology' in Condominas' sense. Its essence is that rice is not simply a plant or food, but is more than that: a living being whose 'soul' or divinity, yīang[5] Abon, imagined as an old lady (ayoaq = grandmother or old lady, a term that is often used interchangeably with yīang), lives in the plant. During the agricultural year, yīang Abon is thought to leave the house and to establish herself in the swidden, from where she only returns after harvest, when the last panicles are collected. Most of the agricultural ceremonies re-create this symbolic cycle: first the seeds are 'awakened', then yīang Abon departs to the swidden, where a miniature hut is built for her. She spends the whole season there and manifests herself in each rice plant and stalk; hence the numerous prescriptions and taboos surrounding the whole cycle that define not only the appropriate rituals but also the proper technologies from sowing to harvesting. For instance, from sowing until the last panicle is taken home, it is forbidden to walk through the rice, to pollute it by urinating or defecating on it, to make noise at the swidden or even to name the rice in order not to frighten yīang Abon – and, from a technological point of view, most importantly, it is forbidden to hurt yīang Abon in any way: by cutting the rice with a sickle, which would cause her to bleed, or by 'hitting her' while threshing. This is an eloquent example of how religious ideology may influence seemingly simple technological questions and how the two are bound together in an inseparable whole. It also explains why the Bru have a unique form of harvesting: collecting rice with their bare hands, manually stripping each panicle.[6] The cycle ends when, after harvest, the 'soul' of yīang Abon is ritually taken home and the last panicles are placed into the rice divinity's altar where *yĭang* Abon, i.e. the rice, will 'sleep' until awakened again at the beginning of the new cycle.

As we have seen, the religious ideology prescribes and defines not only the appropriate rituals but also the proper technologies. Nevertheless, the Bru were able to introduce new harvesting and threshing methods in their rice-fields and adapt them to their traditional world view. How was this possible? The solution is very simple: since the varieties of rice grown in the wet-rice-fields had also been taken over from the Vietnamese, they are not considered to be 'true' or 'autochthonous' rice. They are named by a generic Vietnamese name (*mạ* > *maq*) and the whole related technology is regarded as 'foreign'. Thus, since this rice is not equated with the rice divinity *yĭang* Abon, nothing hinders treating it with the new method: cutting it with a sickle and threshing it. And this is precisely what the Bru do. In their permanent wet-rice-fields, they cut and thresh the rice without bothering at all about *ayɔaq* Abon and her religious taboos. There is only one stipulation as a consequence: it is forbidden to use this rice in religious rituals for religious purposes (such as sacrifice). It is used 'only' for eating, and even then it is considered to be an almost 'tasteless' rice that one eats only in the absence of anything better. 'Vietnamese rice' (*dỗi Yuan*) is thus relegated, both ideologically and from the point of view of the value system, to a secondary position.

However simple this solution, one would expect it to still exclude the introduction of new methods into the swiddens. In them, 'true Bru rice' is grown in which *ayɔaq Abon* dwells and it would be unthinkable to treat her in an improper way. However, the creativity of the Bru religious system is able to overcome even this difficulty, as I will demonstrate using a concrete case study proving that the Bru are able to cope with any new situation or technological innovation.

An Agricultural 'Revolution' in the Area of Khe Sanh, 1989

Let us turn now to this case: the introduction of new harvesting and threshing methods into the swiddens. My first data concerning this go back to 1 October 1989, when I witnessed a man aged about thirty, *mpoaq*[7] Ayưn, announce with a formal apology to his lineage elders his intention to cut the rice in his swidden at the coming harvest with a sickle: 'I am sinning against you', he said, 'I want to *cut* the rice' (tantamount to threshing it as well: the rice is being *hit* against something).

Surprised as I was to learn about this 'revolutionary' innovation, I subsequently learned that the issue had been raised repeatedly in the past. There had been several failed attempts in the past. I was given two main reasons for the spread of this new method of harvesting with a sickle. First, harvesting with bare hands is a painful, slow process, 'ruining their hands', i.e. this method is not only tiresome but trying: the sharp stalks of rice cut the harvesters' palms, causing severe sores. Second, in the nearby district of Hướng Hiệp, and 'downwards the Vietnamese plain', 'everybody' had taken up this new method. With a surprising ease of innovation and improvisation, they explained that they had made a sacrifice (with two chickens) in which they 'requested yĩang Abon to let them cut the rice with a sickle' and that 'now they are authorized to do this'.[8] Their only remaining extra duty was to make the usual sacrifice (arô achu Abon, 'to call Abon to come home') at the end of the agricultural cycle with one pig and *seven* chickens instead of one pig and *four* chickens.

When I pushed the question as to whether they were absolutely sure of what they were doing and whether they were not afraid of yĩang Abon, who, being displeased, could strike them down with some misfortune, their answer was: 'If Abon is discontent with us, she will let us know through some ailments or divinations. Then we shall make some more sacrifices and during them, we shall request cutting the rice with a sickle once again. If she gives us her consent [through divinations], then everything will be in order!' – meaning, of course, that if they would not receive permission, they would not dare to act against her. In this regard, they quoted the case of one family in the village who started cutting the rice with a sickle a year earlier. Soon after, one of their family members suddenly died in an accident. They organized a shamanic séance during which they asked yĩang Abon whether she would still let them continue cutting the rice. The answer being negative (a very rare occurrence in divination!), they gave it up immediately and changed back to their traditional method.

However, the procedure is still not as simple as it might seem. We have seen that *mpoaq* Ayưn had to inform his lineage and also gain their permission. This is because the lineage acts as a corporate unit and in the case of misfortune, the whole community bears the consequences of its members' deeds Thus, the individual is not as free to innovate as he or she would like. He is under the control not only of the supernatural world but also of his society. A year earlier, *mpoaq* Ayưn had cut the rice with a sickle without asking the approval of his lineage elders. This provoked a general uproar: 'How is it possible that we share the same divinities [i.e. our lineage-ancestors are common, and we belong to the same lineage], and you still do not consult us and ask for our authorisation?' As a consequence, in 1989 he informed them formally (as I witnessed) and requested their permission. However, in that year, he was thought to be the only one from his whole lineage wanting to proceed in this way, so he was warned: in the event of an illness of any of the lineage's members,[9] he could be blamed (through divination) and consequently obliged to pay for all the necessary sacrifices – a fact that points to the conservatively retractive nature of the community.

It is clear from the above that in such circumstances, there are only two positive solutions: either the individual is confident enough to take the risk of defying the community or the community joins him in his undertaking. In this latter case, they would face the consequences together, i.e. share the costs of the necessary sacrifice ('we share the sin, we share the sacrifice'). This is precisely what happened in the end.

Let us return to the story. When *mpoaq* Ayưn assumed his personal responsibility, he made the necessary sacrifice with two chickens to inform *yĩang* Abon about his intention. As one would imagine, he proceeded with much caution: he asked permission only for one year, not forever, and only for the 'small varieties of rice', not for the 'great ones'. This is again a detail that merits our attention. The Bru make a distinction between 'small or quick' and 'big or slow' varieties of rice depending on the length of their ripening period. The former bear fruit in four months, the latter in six. According to the local value system, the varieties of 'great' rice are much more important than the 'quick' ones. Thus, *mpoaq* Ayưn made one more concession, not wanting to overly abuse the tolerance of the divinity and of his own society. All this supports the point that technological changes, especially such 'revolutionary' ones, have to take place gradually and slowly, with necessary caution even when initiated by the interested parties without being forced by an outside agency.

A few weeks later, *mpoaq* Ayưn started a real revolution. Perhaps it would be more precise to say that he was the catalyst of a process that has been going on for some time by then. As the responsibility of the first, decisive step had been taken, nobody wanted to miss out on the opportunity. The whole village was busy in discussing the matter. On 6 November 1989 before harvesting, my host, *mpoaq* Toan, also decided to cut the rice with a sickle and performed the necessary sacrifice with two chickens. He too took some extra precautions: besides cutting only the 'small' varieties, he added in his prayer that his family did not want to 'hit' (i.e. thresh) the rice, but to tread it out with their feet – a less harmful method to *ayoaq* Abon (but a very slow and painful one). A day later, he performed the same ritual on behalf of a close relative. The 'new mood' swept the village. According to my field notes, by 10 November (i.e. three days later), of the twenty-one houses of the village, twenty performed the sacrifice and thus adopted the new system.

Epilogue

Ten years after the events, in 1997, I ventured to predict the future:

> Until there is enough forest, and no outside pressure or effective forest control, the Bru will continue swidden cultivation with some technological innovations such as described above. If an unpredictable misfortune will happen that could be explained as a retaliation of the supernatural world, they will fall back temporarily on their old system. However, gradually and slowly new techniques will surely supersede the old ones. The lesson of this story is that the Bru, when given enough time and the necessary understanding, are able to manage their changing microcosm and to give adequate responses to the challenges of the outside world invading their traditional world with a threatening speed. (Vargyas 1997)

Unfortunately, history did not give the Bru the time and the chance to adapt themselves according to their own pace. Vietnam's turbulent economic development and tremendous demographic growth in the past two to three decades completely subverted their world. The snapshot necessarily ends here. For lack of new data, I leave the dénouement partially unfinished. However, my transient experiences in 2018–19 in Khe Sanh, thirty years after the events discussed above, remind me of the resigned and nostalgic words of Condominas, who raised his voice in 2009 in Hanoi, at what was his last public lecture, in favour of the autochthonous populations and their swiddens: 'They cannot be eliminated in a systematic, authoritarian way because their many and varied models are a testimony to the creative richness of humans as social beings' (2009: 267). 'Cannot be' or could not have been eliminated? I am afraid the sentence is more correct in the past conditional.

Gábor Vargyas is a scientific counsellor at the Institute of Ethnology of the Research Center for the Humanities, Eötvös Lóránd Research Network (formerly Hungarian Academy of Sciences), Budapest, and Professor at the Department of European Ethnology and Cultural Anthropology, University of Pécs, Hungary. He was the first foreign anthropologist to study the Bru Vân Kiều people in the Central Vietnamese Highlands in depth.

Notes

1. The Bru (Vân Kiều in the Vietnamese literature) – *not to be* mistaken for the Bru/Brao/Lave/Loven of Cambodia (see Matras-Troubetzkoy 1983) – are one of the fifty-four officially recognized and named ethnic groups (*dân tộc*) in the Vietnamese Socialist Republic. They live in the Central Vietnamese Highlands, mostly in Quảng Trị and the neighbouring provinces, around the seventeenth parallel (the former Vietnamese Demilitarized Zone), on both sides of the Laotian-Vietnamese border. I conducted eighteen months of fieldwork between 1985 and 1989 in the villages of Cóc and Dông Cho (Hướng Linh sub-district, Hướng Hoá [Khe Sanh] district). In 2007, I carried out an additional six months of fieldwork among a resettled Bru community in Đắc Lắc Province (Krông Pắc district, Ea Hiu commune) in the framework of the Max Planck Institute for Social Anthropology's Research Group 'Social Support and Kinship in China and Vietnam'.
2. At that time, the Ordinance on the Protection of Forests (Pháp lệnh quy định việc bảo vệ rừng), promulgated in 1972, was officially in force. The law reiterated the ownership of forests by the state and Article 6 expressly forbade swiddening: 'Cấm phát rừng, đốt rừng để làm nương rẫy' ('Forest clearing and firing for swiddening is forbidden'). See https://vanbanphapluat.co/phap-lenh-bao-ve-rung-1972-147-lct (retrieved 17 March 2020). For the negative assessment of, and measures against, swidden cultivation by the French and Vietnamese, see McElwee (2016).
3. E.g. rice-field = *nia* in Bru comes from Thai/Lao *naa*; dikes = *yương* in Bru originates probably from Vietnamese *đường* = path, road (the đ > y change being a typical feature in the southern Vietnamese dialect) owing to the fact that the dikes are used for traffic; the rice plant = *maq* in Bru comes from the Vietnamese *mạ* as opposed to the rice of the swiddens (*saro*); all the implements used are loanwords: the hoe = *kuôk* from Vietnamese *cuốc*, the plough = *kái* from Vietnamese *cái cày*, the harrow = *bươ* from Vietnamese *cái bừa*, the yoke = *yu* probably from French *joug*, the sickle = *liem* from Vietnamese *cái liêm*.
4. For a similar situation in Laos, see Halpern (1961: 179).
5. *Yĩang* = generic denomination in Bru language for divinities, supernatural beings.
6. This seemingly very archaic method is not as bad as it might seem. What is lost on the swings is made up on the roundabouts: harvesting and grain-producing ('threshing') are done at the same time, with one action instead of two (cutting and threshing). In addition, there is no loss of grain through this method. However, a major shortcoming in harvesting with bare hands is that it is very slow and tiring and that it ruins the palms, causing severe sores. It should be noted that according to FAO enquiries (Appiah et al. 2011), harvesting losses are higher (2.93 per cent) in sickle harvesting than in panicle harvesting (1.39 per cent). In Vietnam, a large amount of the total grain production is lost because of inappropriate threshing and drying methods. According to Nguyen (n.d), in the Mekong River Delta, the most important and technologically most developed rice-producing region in Vietnam, the losses due to cutting are on average between 2.1 and 3.3 per cent according to the seasons. Losses due to threshing are in general lower than cutting, varying between 2.1 and 2.7 per cent.
7. *Mpơaq* = father. According to the Bru custom of teknonymy, a person is named after his son, later his grandson, etc. *Mpơaq* Ayưn = Ayưn's father.
8. Due to space constraints, I cannot elaborate here on the flexibility of the Bru religious system and the many ways of introducing new elements. It is enough to state that one of the most conspicuous features of the Bru religion is constant negotiation with the divinities. Sacrifices are literally 'bargains' in which a return is expected for the sacrificial 'investment'. The very common divination procedures in Bru shamanism are also

in essence a way of negotiating with the divinities (see Vargyas 1993, 1998 and 2001). In this way, many changes may be initiated.
9. This lineage consisted of twelve houses.

References

Appiah, Francis, Ramatoulaye Guisse and Paul K.A. Dartey. 2011. 'Post-harvest Losses of Rice from Harvesting to Milling in Ghana', *Journal of Stored Products and Postharvest Research* 2(4): 64–71.

Barthélemy, Lieutenant. 1947. *Rapport du Lieutenant Barthélemy, Délégué administratif de Tchépone, concernant les problèmes que pose l'actuelle frontière séparant les provinces, laotienne de Savannakhet, et vietnamienne de Quangtri.* Tchépone, le 31 Décembre 1947 (typewritten document, 40 pages, published integrally in Vargyas 2000: 257–97)

Boulbet, Jean. 1966. 'Le *Miir*, culture itinérante avec jachère forestière en pays maa: Région de Blao – Bassin du fleuve Daa'Dööng (Dông Nai)', *Bulletin de l'École Française d'Extrême Orient* 53(1): 77–98.

Burling, Robin. 1965. *Hill Farms and Padi Fields*. Englewood Cliffs, NJ: Prentice Hall.

Central Population and Housing Census, Steering Committee/Ban Chỉ đạo, Tổng điều tra Dân số và Nhà ở Trung ương. 2010. *The 2009 Vietnam Population and Housing Census: Completed Results./Tổng điều tra Dân số và Nhà ở, Việt Nam Năm 2009: Kết quả Toàn Bộ.* Hà Nội: Statistical Publishing House. Retrieved 7 January 2021 from https://www.gso.gov.vn/default_en.aspx?tabid=515&idmid=5&ItemID=10799.

Circular of the Ministry of Forestry. 1992. *Decree 14/CP of the Government issued on Dec.5th, 1992 about Punishment on Infringement of Public Administration Relating to the Management and Safekeeping of Forests* [Thông tư của Bộ Lâm Nghiệp. Hướng dẫn thực hiện Nghị định 14/CP của Chính phủ ban hành quy định xử phạt vi phạm hành chính trong lĩnh vực quản lý và bảo vệ rừng].

Conklin, Harold C. 1954. 'An Ethnoecological Approach to Shifting Agriculture', *Transactions of the New York Academy of Sciences* 17(2, Series II): 133–42.

_____. 1957. *Hanunóo Agriculture in the Philippines*. Rome: Food and Agricultural Organization of the United Nations.

_____. 1963. *The Study of Shifting Cultivation*. London: Routledge & Kegan Paul.

_____. 1980. *Ethnographic Atlas of Ifugao: A Study of Environment, Culture, and Society in Northern Luzon*. New Haven: Yale University Press.

Condominas, Georges. 1972. 'From the Rice-Field to the *Miir*', *Social Science Information* 11(2): 41–62.

_____. 1983. 'Aspect Ecologiques d'un Espace Social Restreint en Asie du Sud-Est', *Études Rurales* 89–91: 11–76.

_____. 1986. 'Ritual Technology in Mnong Gar Swidden Agriculture', in Irene Nørlund, Sven Cederroth and Ingela Gerdin (eds), *Rice Societies: Asian Problems and Prospect*. London: Curzon Press/The Riverdale Company, pp. 28–46.

———. 2009. 'Anthropological Reflections on Swidden Change in Southeast Asia', *Human Ecology* 37: 265–67.
Cramb, Rob A., Carol J.P. Colfer, Wolfram Dressler, Pinkaew Laungaramsri, Quang Trang Le, Elok Mulyoutami, Nancy L. Peluso and Reed L. Wadley. 2009. 'Swidden Transformations and Rural Livelihoods in Southeast Asia', *Human Ecology* 37(3): 323–46.
FAO Staff. 1957. 'Shifting Cultivation', *Unasylva* 11(1). Retrieved 7 January 2021 from http://www.fao.org/3/x5382e/x5382e03.htm.
Fox, Jefferson. 2000. 'How Blaming "Slash and Burn" Farmers Is Deforesting Mainland Southeast Asia', *Asia Pacific Issues* 47: 1–8.
Geertz, Clifford. 1963. *Agricultural Involution: The Process of Ecological Change in Indonesia*. Berkeley: University of California Press.
———. 1972. 'Two Types of Ecosystems', in Paul W. English and Robert C. Mayfield (eds), *Man, Space, and Environment. Concepts in Contemporary Human Geography*. New York: Oxford University Press, pp. 165–180.
Goudineau, Yves. 2003. 'Préface', in Mathieu Guérin, Andrew Hardy, Nguyễn Văn Chính and Stan Tan Boon Hwee, *Des Montagnards aux Minorités Ethniques. Quelle Intégration National Pour les Habitants des Hautes Terres du Viet Nam et du Cambodge?* Paris: L'Harmattan; Bangkok: IRASEC, pp. xiii–xxv.
Gudeman, Stephen, and Chris Hann. 2015. 'Introduction. Ritual, Economy, and the Institutions of the Base', in Stephen Gudeman and Chris Hann (eds), *Economy and Ritual: Studies of Postsocialist Transformations*. New York: Berghahn Books, pp. 1–30.
Halpern, Joel. 1961. 'The Economies of Lao and Serb Peasants: A Contrast in Cultural Values', *Southwestern Journal of Anthropology* 17: 165–77.
Izikowitz, Karl Gustav. 1951. *Lamet: Hill Peasants in French Indochina*. Gotherberg: Ethnografiska Museet.
Josselin de Jong, Patrick Edward. 1965. 'An Interpretation of Agricultural Rites in Southeast Asia, with a Demonstration of Use of Data from Both Continental and Insular Areas', *Journal of Asian Studies* 24(2): 283–98.
Low, Kok On, and Jacqueline Pugh-Kitingan. 2015. 'Field Note. The Impact of Christianity on Traditional Agricultural Practices and Beliefs among the Kimaragang of Sabah: A Preliminary Study', *Asian Ethnology* 74(2): 401–24.
Matras-Troubetzkoy, Jacqueline. 1983. *Un Village en Forêt. L'Essartage Chez les Brou du Cambodge*. Paris: SELAF.
Maurice, Albert-Marie. 1993. *Les Mnong des Hauts Plataux (Centre-Vietnam)*. 2 Vols. Paris: Harmattan.
Maurice, Albert-Marie, and George-Marie Proux. 1954. 'L'Ame du Riz', *Bulletin de la Société d'Études Indochinois* 29(1–2): 123–259.
McElwee, Pamela D. 2016. *Forest Are Gold: Trees, People, and Environmental Rule in Vietnam*. Seattle: University of Washington Press.
Mertz, Ole. 2002. 'The Relationship between Fallow Length and Crop Yields in Shifting Cultivation: A Rethinking', *Agroforestry Systems* 55: 149–59.
Mertz, Ole, Christine Padoch, Jefferson Fox, Rob A. Cramb, Stephen J. Leisz, Nguyen Thanh Lam and Tran Duc Vien. 2009. 'Swidden Change in Southeast Asia: Understanding Causes and Consequences', *Human Ecology* 37(3): 259–64.

Nguyen Duy Lam. n.d. 'Post-harvest Research and Development in Vietnam'. Retrieved 7 January 2021 from http://unapcaem.org/Activities%20Files/A20/12%20Vietnam.pdf.

O'Connor, Richard A. 1995. 'Agricultural Change and Ethnic Succession in Southeast Asian States: A Case for Regional Anthropology', *Journal of Asian Studies* 54(4): 968–96.

Padoch, Christine, Kevine Coffey, Ole Mertz, Stephen J. Leisz, Jefferson Fox and Reed L Wadley. 2007. 'The Demise of Swidden in Southeast Asia? Local Realities and Regional Ambiguities', *Geografisk Tidsskrift-Danish Journal of Geography* 107: 29–41.

Spencer, Joseph E. 1966. *Shifting Cultivation in Southeastern Asia.* Berkeley: University of California Press.

Vargyas, Gábor. 1993. 'The Structure of Bru Shamanic Ceremonies', in Mihaly Hoppál and Keith D. Howard (eds), *Shamans and Cultures.* Budapest: Akadémiai Kiadó – International Society for Trans-oceanic Research, pp. 120–27.

———. 1996. 'Les Ancêtres et la Forêt Chez les Brou du Vietnam', *Diogène* 174: 101–10.

———. 1997. 'Continuity and Change amongst the Bru'. Unpublished paper read at the Third International EUROVIET Conference, Amsterdam, the Netherlands.

———. 1998. 'Conjurer L'Inéluctable', *Péninsule. Etudes Interdisciplinaires Sur l'Asie du Sud-Est Péninsulaire* 37: 99–156.

———. 2000. *A la Recherche des Brou Perdus, Population Montagnarde du Centre Indochinois.* (Les Cahiers de PENINSULE No. 5) Etudes Orientales, Olizane.

———. 2001. 'Divináció a Vietnami Brúknál [Divination among the Bru]', in Éva Pócs (ed.), *Sors, Áldozat, Divináció.* Budapest: Janus/Osiris, pp. 85–102.

Chapter 17

The Dharma and the Dime
Money and Buddhist Morality

Christoph Brumann

Kyoto in August 2016: on a roadside open space in a central city neighbourhood, the ritual propitiating the *bodhisattva* Jizō (Skt. Kṣitigarbha), the guardian of children, whose image is housed in a small shrine, has just ended. Before the children's games and entertainments central to the Jizōbon summer festival begin, the Buddhist priest in charge of conducting the rite turns to the assembled neighbours for a short sermon. He refers to a lacquer tray between him and the audience, where around half-a-dozen envelopes containing banknotes are piling up. As his key point, the priest posits a fundamental difference between *o-fuse* (donations to Buddhist priests) and everyday payments. He says he has no idea what the envelopes contain and the donor's economic position is not always an indication. The feelings (*kimochi*) behind the donation are key, he argues, and it is futile to fix monetary sums and attach price tags to everything. When he is finished, he pockets the unopened envelopes and is seen off, mounting his scooter in his priestly robes to drive to his next appointment on this busy day. The neighbours, however, are unimpressed – the amounts they give, they tell me, are set by custom, not by feelings, and if anyone is unsure, more experienced people can tell them what is appropriate. In an interview conducted three years later, the priest insists to me that *o-fuse* should be 'one's best effort', which defies standardization – 'I cannot know what's your best effort' (*anata no seiippai o shiranai*), he says. He claims to no longer worry the way he used to about being able to sustain a temple whose parishioner (*danka* or *monto*) base has been rather narrow to begin with, even before the current trend of simplifying Buddhist rituals and correspondingly reducing donations to priests set in. Indeed, he spends a good deal of his energy on non-traditional and unpaid activities to spread the Buddhist message. He therefore appears sincere in emphasizing voluntary giving. However, he too is aware of custom, suggesting specific amounts when uncertain clients ask him, and the income so derived sustains not only him but also his wife and children.

So is *o-fuse* talk merely a decorative veneer painted over what are at heart market transactions, with the recipients of the service remunerating the provider with a fee according to the Kyoto going rate? Building on the results of the Max Planck research group 'Buddhist Temple Economies in Urban Asia' within Chris Hann's department and the debates with its other members (Saskia Abrahms-Kavunenko, Kristina Jonutytė, Hannah Klepeis and Beata Świtek), I will demonstrate in this chapter that this is not the case. While Buddhist aloofness from money has on the whole diminished, both clergy and laity took care to distinguish Buddhist transactions from ordinary market exchanges in every Buddhist society we studied. I will show that, rather than being the 'radical leveller' (Marx 1889: 108), money is symbolically productive here, motivating boundary work. According to Gudeman and Hann, many theorists of modernity treat the spheres of the economy and of ritual as separate: the former is the domain of the rational and of self-interested maximization of utility, while the latter is the realm of the 'cultural' that is at best a drain on resources (2015: 2). They contest this position and insist on the intertwinement of the two spheres and I have no intention of arguing against what economic anthropologists, particularly from the substantivist camp, have been emphasizing all along. However, even if the separation does not do much for describing actual practice, it can nonetheless work as a powerful religious ideal, as I will show below.

The Challenge of Money

Money becomes an issue in Buddhism since the ideal practitioner is a world renouncer: living the life of a monk or (more rarely) a nun, he or she foregoes family life, sexual relations, intoxicants, meat and many physical comforts, all of which are a hindrance to the pursuit of enlightenment and salvation through rituals, meditation, ascetic practices or textual study. Ordinary householders are held to support such a lifestyle through donations of food, clothes, money and other resources. For this, they do not expect specified returns from the recipients, but rather karmic merit, which improves their chances of a favourable rebirth and of becoming world-renouncers themselves in a future life. Making themselves available to the lay spiritual need of giving has been seen as a major motive for the original communities of Buddhist mendicants to settle down permanently and found monasteries (Strenski 1983). Yet still, there is no contractual relationship of support in this scheme, and what the renunciates receive is conceived of as leftovers rather than scarce resources for which they actively compete. More than in other world religions, the renunciation of or, rather, aloofness from material resources is being emphasized for the clergy, with the monastic rules (*vinaya*) not only narrowly circumscribing the scope of licit possessions, but also prohibiting the handling of money. At least this is the ideal. In actual fact, Buddhist monasteries became prosperous from an early age, accumulating what could be huge amounts of agricultural land, livestock and corvée labour. The proceeds sustained what were often feudal institutions: lay tributes and rents, rather than voluntary prestations, allowed the specialists to focus on their otherworldly pursuits and, where discipline lagged, on a lavish lifestyle that provoked criticism and sometimes even persecution. Also, from very early on, individual Buddhist monks violated the taboo on money, all the way to lending it with interest, an activity that was sometimes even expected by their monasteries, which would share in the profits (Benavides 2005: 85–86; Ch'en 1956; Gernet 1995; King 2016; Ornatowski 1996; Schopen 2004; Walsh 2009). Obviously, this was responding to the opportunities and needs of the surrounding societies, and in time, fairly complex property and financial arrangements developed. The monasteries of Tibetan Buddhism, for example, usually have a general account, but the college-like subunits (*khamtsen*) do have their own separate accounts. Still other property is that of a specific *tulku* or reincarnate with whom it stays through what is conceived of as successive lifetimes, and alongside this, dedicated accounts exist for the conduct of specific periodic rituals. Flows of money go back and forth between all these budgetary units and the individual monks and nuns, and outside lay households are involved as well through owning the residential buildings in monastic precincts that their monastic descendants use (Gutschow 2004: 77–122; Mills 2001: 53–81). In Japan, Buddhist temples usually register as religious corporations (*shûkyô hôjin*), which has the advantage of making *o-fuse* and contributions received in connection with religious activities tax-exempt. But the resident priest (*jûshoku*) of such a temple and occasionally also his wife and successor child – celibacy is rare these days – receive an income from the corporation to cover their living expenses, and this salary must be taxed (cf. also Covell 2005: 140–64, Świtek 2021: 24–27).

Contemporary Buddhism does not take living off lay contributions lightly. For the resumption of monasticism in China, economic independence was a major condition posed by the socialist state that condemned the former feudal arrangements. A younger generation of monastics has largely internalized this demand, supporting the production of revenue through shops, tourism and the like (Caple 2010, 2021) or – in the case of an abbot in the border region of Sipsong Panna – running a craft business as a sideline in order not to be a burden on temple parishioners (Casas 2021: 135–38). In other contexts, Buddhist institutions feel driven to prove their worth to society by returning money and other benefits to the laity rather than remaining on the receiving end. This holds for the Traditional Sangha of Buryatia's 'Social Flock' project in which poor laypeople in this Siberian republic receive sheep in order to start their own herds (Jonutytė 2021: 99–101), for the hospitals and schools that the *khruba* (charismatic Buddhist saints) of the upper Mekong region fund from the lavish donations they receive from wealthy sponsors (Horstmann 2021), or for the many projects of 'Socially Engaged Buddhism' run by prominent and internationally connected lamas in Ladakh, India (Williams-Oerberg 2017). Even the forest monks of Sri Lanka who, in their dedicated pursuit of Buddhist fundamentals, strictly observe the injunctions against money and have lay supporters handle their finances do not let the donations that their admirers shower on them go to waste. While redistributing donations to the laity would violate the rules, they are aware that the ordinary temples to which they instead pass the excess are less exacting in this regard (Sirisena 2021: 155). There are thus multiple legal, social and moral pressures on contemporary Buddhist clergy to not be indifferent to what the laity bestows upon them, but rather put it to licit, economically prudent, charitable and morally defendable uses.

In many Buddhist societies, what is acceptable in money matters has shifted. Whereas in the Thailand of the 1970s, the use of lay stewards for the finances of temples and monk was still widespread (Bunnag 1973), monks in Bangkok have individual bank accounts nowadays, even when they still go to ATMs outside their neighbourhood in order not be seen by their lay supporters (Borchert 2021: 44–46, 48–49). Also, the *khruba* do not refrain from handing out money bills in person to the crowds assembling for their rituals, making for a potlatch-style display of generosity (Horstmann 2021: 204). A popular temple in Ulaanbaatar, Mongolia keeps price lists for rituals and a cash register to pay them right inside the main hall (cf. also Abrahms-Kavunenko 2021: 188), and those who prefer a one-off, fixed-price relationship with priests to the customary multigenerational attachment can buy Buddhist funeral and memorial rites on Amazon Japan (Świtek 2021: 23–24). We have found no society where Buddhist specialists' engagement with money has become more constrained during the past few decades, whereas the opposite is fairly widespread, both in formerly socialist countries and those that have only known capitalism. Given also that contributions in kind are increasingly substituted by cash gifts in many places such as Tibet (Sihlé 2021: 69–70) or Ladakh (Mills 2021: 115–18), the average Buddhist religious specialist has never been closer to money.

Drawing the Line

The closeness to money is an uneasy one, however, and a line is being drawn between proper and improper uses in all cases. This may be through symbolic means marking off Buddhist prestations as distinct from ordinary market transactions, such as with the unopened *o-fuse* envelopes in Kyoto. Similarly, when remunerating the *ngakpa* Tantric practitioners who they call to conduct house rituals, Tibetan patrons use crisp money bills and hold them with a ceremonial scarf rather than with their bare hands (Sihlé 2021: 63), and Buryats who consult lamas about their concerns will also present the remuneration either with a bow or just leave it on the table, instead of handing it over as if to a shop clerk (Jonutytė 2018: 26-27, 183-184). While what Buryat Buddhists pay to see the miraculously preserved body of Lama Dashi-Dorzho Itigelov in a temple outside Ulan-Ude is in fact a set fee, it is still styled as a donation for worshipping purposes (Jonutytė 2018: 54), and Kyoto temples too – even the ones most given to tourism – invariably charge a 'worshipping' (*sanpairyô*), rather than entrance, fee.

Where the line is not defined by explicit etiquette, it can move to the forefront through perceived breaches: Borchert is astonished about a Bangkok monk who not only asks for a donation but also specifies the amount, in stark contrast to expected behaviour (Borchert 2021: 37–38). A friend in Kyoto was shocked when following the death of his father, the family priest calling him lost no time on condolences but instead demanded what the friend considered a hefty sum for the funeral. Klepeis' informant who facilitates a large donation to the Sumtsenling monastery in Shangrila (the former Zhongdian in Yunnan province, China) is alarmed by the receiving monk's initial reluctance to issue a receipt, as this must indicate plans to embezzle the money (Klepeis 2021: 84–86). A visitor to the likewise Tibetan monastery studied by Caple is shocked to see lay clerks working in the monastery shop, as this converts it into an ordinary business in her eyes, devoid of the trustworthiness that monastic personnel inspires (Caple 2021: 167). In all these cases, the line setting off acceptable Buddhist transactions rises to consciousness once it is crossed.

Concern over spillover is widespread beyond such single incidents: in a large number of Buddhist societies, lay worries about monks, priests and other specialists becoming corrupt and obsessed with money fuel constant debate and gossip, be it in the Tibetan areas of China (Caple 2021: 164–66; Klepeis 2021: 84–86; Sihlé 2021: 70–71), Mongolia (Abrahms-Kavunenko 2021: 188–89), Thailand (Borchert 2021; Horstmann 2021: 201) or Japan (Świtek 2021: 22, 27–28). Clerics, on their part, are worried that ordinary businesses drag them away from their true purposes (Casas 2021: 137–38) and into a market mentality, which they associate with deception (Caple 2021: 186–87) or more generally towards a capitalist mindset, as several Kyoto priests told me. Finally, there is concern that even when the transaction as such is appropriate, money might still carry the moral contamination acquired on its previous trajectory, making some monks in Shangrila reject donations from disreputable Han Chinese businessmen who seek their blessing (Klepeis 2021: 86).

Dilemmas can result: among the tantrists of the Repkong area in Tibetan China, too much engagement in remunerated house rituals for the benefit of clients is frowned upon, but requests for funeral rituals cannot be rejected (Sihlé 2021: 70). Monks are concerned about shopkeeper duties rubbing off on their morality, but feel pressure to make a profit since the monastery depends on this income (Caple 2021: 166–67). Debate is never laid to rest: Shangrila Buddhist laypeople perennially discuss what makes a good monk in monetary terms, but never agree. Acceptable transactions respond to traditional relations and obligations, observing the taboo on monks giving to their natal household rather than receiving from it. However, how to assess individual cases and whether responding to potentially fake monks' requests for donations is seen as acceptable or not is unclear (Klepeis 2021). The resolution of such debates is also hindered by the hesitation in quite a few Buddhist societies to openly criticize clergy so that confronting them about lackadaisical performance is unthinkable. Doing so would not just be disrespectful, but would also amount to a lack of faith that is detrimental to ritual outcomes (Klepeis 2021: 79; Sihlé 2021: 71). This means that doubts and open questions linger.

Grey areas can be the result: while temples in Japan must register as religious corporations to benefit from tax exemption, thus subjecting themselves to state regulation, they must only report the balance of land and financial holdings to state authorities once a year. No detailed accounting of *o-fuse* revenues and temple expenditures is required and unless the parishioners – at least one of whom joins the priest on the corporation's board of directors – request it, no balance sheet must be prepared. Thus, what exactly the temple corporation pays as a priestly salary may be known to the taxman, but not to parishioners. I spoke to one priest whose temple had returned to this loose practice from earlier, more detailed accounting, as it also saves work time. He thinks that parishioners see enough of his family's lifestyle to know that they do not revel in luxury, something that his predecessor impressed on him as inappropriate for a priest. Other observers report a studied ignorance of monetary details on the clergy's side, such as among the Thai monks who shared their financial practices with Borchert (Borchert 2021: 44–45) or a Tokyo priest's refusal to monitor whether all participants to a temple event actually paid the requested fee (Świtek 2021: 28–31). Obliviousness is seen as bespeaking a lack of attachment, a virtue in Buddhist doctrine – rather than money as such, being obsessed with it is condemnable.

In many cases, it appears that participants are able to employ two different perspectives alternatively, shifting back and forth between them, with neither of the two being dominant. Anthropological work concerning the gift has observed similar phenomena, with Pierre Bourdieu characterizing it as Janus-faced: gifts must be presented as one-off, altruistic prestations in order to be acceptable, but conversely, they are often carefully calibrated to the relationship between giver and recipient and what the two have exchanged on previous occasions (Bourdieu 1977: 194). Bourdieu appears to take the calculating side as the true face (Smart 1993: 395), but others such as Smart on Chinese gifts and favours (1993) or I myself on Japanese cash gifts at lifecycle celebrations (Brumann 2000) have stressed the copresence of both views in the protagonists' minds. Very much the same holds when, as noted in the opening vignette, both priests and laity, while very much aware of market prices, stick to an *o-fuse* framework. The copresence of the pious view appears to be a constant in Buddhist monetary transactions, however much they are also remunerations for services rendered on demand (Sihlé 2015).

Occasionally, the pious and the rational views coexist within the temple itself. In Sirisena's forest monastery in Sri Lanka, monetary decisions are the abbot's prerogative; this allows all other monks to remain blissfully unaware of them (Sirisena 2021: 149–52). Two Kyoto temple priests told me that they do not open the *o-fuse* envelopes themselves, but hand them to their wives who do the finances, with one of them not even being a proper temple wife (*bōmori*), but holding an outside job instead. By doing so, these priests say, amounts received do not influence their treatment of parishioners, which should be the same for everyone, whatever the sums involved. One of them recalls his resentment when at the time his mother was still handling temple finances, she would occasionally complain about a stingy contribution. Much better not to learn these details, he says, and until a recent tax review required his involvement, he claims to have had no idea of the financial state of the religious corporation he himself officially heads.

Conclusion

The priest in question follows *vinaya* prescriptions by shaving his head, unlike quite a few colleagues in his denomination. However, he is married, has children, eats meat, practises sport and often wears everyday gear outside rituals. What is more, although he himself does not drink, he occasionally runs a bar in a refashioned storehouse on temple precincts, serving cocktails he learned to prepare in a past job as a bartender. To Southeast Asian Buddhists, as well as the Sri Lankan forest monks, all this would be anathema: they are vegetarians, wear robes all the time and do not just practise strict celibacy, but also would not even stay in the same room with an unaccompanied woman. Interpretations of proper clerical discipline vary widely across the Buddhist world.

However, a concern with money and its proper religious and moral treatment appears to be a constant, even where actual practices diverge significantly from the initial monastic code. Buddhist clerics are ritual service providers in many societies, either as a sideline or, in such places as Mongolia or Japan, as their main occupation. What they receive in return, as Sihlé (2015) has outlined, must be seen as remunerations in many cases, with the laity rewarding the service rendered with a monetary sum proportional to the invested effort. Yet, pains are taken to distinguish these transactions from ordinary market exchanges and to generally set limits to the kind of exchanges in which proper Buddhist specialists and laity may engage. This may involve a special etiquette or just the perennial reassessment in everyday discourse of the tacit and explicit rules and their application by actual practitioners. I propose seeing *o-fuse* style social customs and the moral comment that Buddhist clergy and laity make on their monetary affairs as an essential part of contemporary Buddhist experience, crucially relevant for both clergy and laity. More so than in the other major 'world' religions of the Eurasian landmass, money is a touchstone of Buddhist morality, and the work of reining it in never quite ends, not even where market forces and neoliberalist policies are turning contemporary societies upside down.

A clean separation of ritual and economy is as elusive in contemporary Buddhism as in other walks of life – the examples I have presented show much uncertainty, improvisation and muddling through. But as an emic model and guide for action and reflection, the separation is ubiquitous: Buddhists are gratified when religion and economy keep a certain distance, and when religious and nonreligious transactions of goods and services retain distinct features. Using a Polanyian term that has been key to Chris Hann's economic anthropological thinking (e.g. Hann 2009), money and its uses must remain morally and symbolically embedded in order to be acceptable. There must be envelopes, be they made from paper, words or practices.

Christoph Brumann is Head of Research Group at the Max Planck Institute for Social Anthropology in Halle, Germany, and Honorary Professor of Anthropology at Martin Luther University Halle-Wittenberg. In addition to Buddhist temples, he has also worked on the social life of cultural heritage and urban development in Kyoto, the UNESCO World Heritage arena, the concept of culture in anthropology, utopian communes and Japanese gift-giving.

References

Abrahms-Kavunenko, Saskia. 2021. 'Regeneration and the Age of Decline: Purification and Rebirth in Mongolian Buddhist Economies', in Christoph Brumann, Saskia Abrahms-Kavunenko and Beata Świtek (eds), *Monks, Money, and Morality: The Balancing Act of Contemporary Buddhism*. London: Bloomsbury Academic, pp. 179–94.

Benavides, Gustavo. 2005. 'Economy', in Donald S. Lopez (ed.), *Critical Terms for the Study of Buddhism*. Chicago: University of Chicago Press, pp. 77–102.

Borchert, Thomas. 2021. 'Merit, "Corruption", and Economy in the Contemporary Thai Sangha', in Christoph Brumann, Saskia Abrahms-Kavunenko and Beata Świtek (eds), *Monks, Money, and Morality: The Balancing Act of Contemporary Buddhism*. London: Bloomsbury Academic, pp. 37–50.

Bourdieu, Pierre. 1977. *Outline of a Theory of Practice*. Cambridge: Cambridge University Press.

Brumann, Christoph. 2000. 'Materialistic Culture: The Uses of Money in Tokyo Gift Exchanges', in John Clammer and Michael Ashkenazi (eds), *Consumption and Material Culture in Contemporary Japan*. London: Kegan Paul International, pp. 224–48.

Bunnag, Jane. 1973. *Buddhist Monk, Buddhist Layman: A Study of Urban Monastic Organization in Central Thailand*. Cambridge: Cambridge University Press.

Caple, Jane. 2010. 'Monastic Economic Reform at Rong-Bo Monastery: Towards an Understanding of Contemporary Tibetan Monastic Revival and Development in a-Mdo', *Buddhist Studies Review* 27(2): 197–219.

———. 2021. 'Monastic Business Expansion in Post-Mao Tibet: Risk, Trust and Perception', in Christoph Brumann, Saskia Abrahms-Kavunenko and Beata Świtek (eds), *Monks, Money, and Morality: The Balancing Act of Contemporary Buddhism*. London: Bloomsbury Academic, pp. 159–76.

Casas, Roger. 2021. 'Monks and the Morality of Exchange: Reflections on a Village Temple Case in Southwest China', in Christoph Brumann, Saskia Abrahms-Kavunenko and Beata Świtek (eds), *Monks, Money, and Morality: The Balancing Act of Contemporary Buddhism*. London: Bloomsbury Academic, pp. 127–40.
Ch'en, Kenneth. 1956. 'The Economic Background of the Hui-Ch'ang Suppression of Buddhism', *Harvard Journal of Asiatic Studies* 19(1/2): 67–105.
Covell, Stephen G. 2005. *Japanese Temple Buddhism: Worldliness in a Religion of Renunciation*. Honolulu: University of Hawaii Press.
Gernet, Jacques. 1995. *Buddhism in Chinese Society: An Economic History from the Fifth to the Tenth Centuries*. New York: Columbia University Press.
Gudeman, Stephen, and Chris Hann. 2015. 'Introduction: Ritual, Economy, and the Institutions of the Base', in Stephen Gudeman and Chris Hann (eds), *Economy and Ritual: Studies of Postsocialist Transformations*. New York: Berghahn Books, pp. 1–30.
Gutschow, Kim. 2004. *Being a Buddhist Nun: The Struggle for Enlightenment in the Himalayas*. Cambridge, MA: Harvard University Press.
Hann, Chris. 2009. 'Embedded Socialism? Land, Labor, and Money in Eastern Xinjiang', in Chris Hann and Keith Hart (eds), *Market and Society: The Great Transformation Today*. Cambridge: Cambridge University Press, pp. 256–71.
Horstmann, Alexander. 2021. 'Saintly Entrepreneurialism and Political Aspirations of Theravadin Saints in Mainland Southeast Asia', in Christoph Brumann, Saskia Abrahms-Kavunenko and Beata Świtek (eds), *Monks, Money, and Morality: The Balancing Act of Contemporary Buddhism*. London: Bloomsbury Academic, pp. 195–208.
Jonutytė, Kristina. 2018. 'Beyond Reciprocity: Giving and Belonging in the Post-Soviet Buddhist Revival in Ulan-Ude (Buryatia)'. Doctoral thesis. Halle/Wittenberg: University of Halle-Wittenberg.
———. 2021. 'Donations Inversed: Material Flows from Sangha to Laity in Post-Soviet Buryatia', in Christoph Brumann, Saskia Abrahms-Kavunenko and Beata Świtek (eds), *Monks, Money, and Morality: The Balancing Act of Contemporary Buddhism*. London: Bloomsbury Academic, pp. 93–108.
King, Matthew. 2016. 'Buddhist Economics: Scales of Value in Global Exchange', in Oxford University Press (ed.), *Oxford Handbooks Online*. Oxford University Press. Retrieved 8 January 2021 from https://www.oxfordhandbooks.com/view/10.1093/oxfordhb/9780199935420.001.0001/oxfordhb-9780199935420-e-64.
Klepeis, Hannah. 2021. '"Bad" Monks and Unworthy Donors: Money, (Mis)Trust and the Disruption of Sangha-Laity Relations in Shangrila', in Christoph Brumann, Saskia Abrahms-Kavunenko and Beata Świtek (eds), *Monks, Money, and Morality: The Balancing Act of Contemporary Buddhism*. London: Bloomsbury Academic, pp. 75–90.
Marx, Karl. 1889. *Capital: A Critical Analysis of Capitalist Production*. New York: Appleton.
Mills, Martin A. 2001. *Identity, Ritual and State in Tibetan Buddhism: The Foundations of Authority in Gelukpa Monasticism*. Richmond: Curzon.
———. 2021. 'Exorcising Mauss' Ghost in the Western Himalayas: Buddhist Giving as Collective Work', in Christoph Brumann, Saskia Abrahms-

Kavunenko and Beata Świtek (eds), *Monks, Money, and Morality: The Balancing Act of Contemporary Buddhism*. London: Bloomsbury Academic, pp. 109–24.

Ornatowski, Gregory K. 1996. 'Continuity and Change in the Economic Ethics of Buddhism: Evidence from the History of Buddhism in India, China and Japan', *Journal of Buddhist Ethics* 3: 187–229.

Schopen, Gregory. 2004. *Buddhist Monks and Business Matters: Still More Papers on Monastic Buddhism in India*. Honolulu: University of Hawaii Press.

Sihlé, Nicolas. 2015. 'Towards a Comparative Anthropology of the Buddhist Gift (and Other Transfers)', *Religion Compass* 9(11): 352–85.

———. 2021. 'Ritual Virtuosity, Large-Scale Priest-Patron Networks and the Ethics of Remunerated Ritual Services', in Christoph Brumann, Saskia Abrahms-Kavunenko and Beata Świtek (eds), *Monks, Money, and Morality: The Balancing Act of Contemporary Buddhism*. London: Bloomsbury Academic, pp. 51–74.

Sirisena, Prabath. 2021. 'Wealthy Mendicants: The Balancing Act of Sri Lankan Forest Monks', in Christoph Brumann, Saskia Abrahms-Kavunenko and Beata Świtek (eds), *Monks, Money, and Morality: The Balancing Act of Contemporary Buddhism*. London: Bloomsbury Academic, pp. 141–58.

Smart, Alan. 1993. 'Gifts, Bribes, and Guanxi: A Reconsideration of Bourdieu's Social Capital', *Cultural Anthropology* 8(3): 388–408.

Strenski, Ivan. 1983. 'On Generalized Exchange and the Domestication of the Sangha', *Man* 18(3): 463–77.

Świtek, Beata. 2021. 'Economic Exchanges and the Spirit of Donation: The Commercialization of Buddhist Services in Japan', in Christoph Brumann, Saskia Abrahms-Kavunenko and Beata Świtek (eds), *Monks, Money, and Morality: The Balancing Act of Contemporary Buddhism*. London: Bloomsbury Academic, pp. 19–36.

Walsh, Michael J. 2009. *Sacred Economies: Buddhist Monasticism and Territoriality in Medieval China*. New York: Columbia University Press.

Williams-Oerberg, Elizabeth. 2017. Socially Engaged Sangha Economies in Ladakh, India. Paper presented at the conference 'Sangha Economies: Temple Organisation and Exchanges in Contemporary Buddhism', Max Planck Institute for Social Anthropology, Halle, 21 September.

Chapter 18

Stealing Goddesses
The Political Economy of Kingship in Premodern India

Burkhard Schnepel

The Problem

In his introduction to *The Social Life of Things,* Appadurai (1986) does not really discuss 'things', but focuses on 'commodities' instead. Appadurai makes this small but in many respects decisive step from things to commodities on the basis of four premises. First, he defines commodities as anything that has commodity *potential*; things need not be commodities in the here and now in order to be classified as commodities, but it is enough for them to be capable of becoming such. Second, for Appadurai, a given 'commodity potential' and value are realized in the realm of exchange and not (as for Marx) in the domain of production. Third, commodities are not just found under the capitalist mode of production, but all over the world whenever things are exchanged for other things or money, and even where they are bartered or gifted. Fourth, Appadurai's focus is not really on the *social* or *cultural* life of commodities, but on their *political* life and, more precisely, on the *politics* of value and the political economy of commodities.[1]

Against the background of these premises, what is especially important for Appadurai are the 'paths and diversions' of things in and out of the commodity phase.[2] Some such processes of commoditization and de-commoditization are of similar significance in Kopytoff's contribution to the same volume (Kopytoff 1986). For Kopytoff, in order to become a

---

Notes for this chapter begin on page 252.

commodity a thing has to be exchanged, and in order to have the capacity to be exchanged, it needs to have something in common with some other thing. For him, commoditization, if the pun may be allowed, is the 'common-ditization' of the singular.[3] Like Appadurai's 'paths and diversions', Kopytoff's focus is on the life histories or, as he calls them, the 'cultural biographies of things'. Significantly, he argues that not only humans but also things can have biographies. In this context, he identifies processes of commoditization in both noncapitalist or precapitalist societies and in the present-day monetarized commercialized world in which certain objects are '*re*-singularized' by being withdrawn from sphere(s) of exchange. Kopytoff also identifies things that were never commodities in their life histories, but that were singular(ized) from the start. For Kopytoff, these are things that were never meant to be commoditized or commercialized and are often imbued with sacrality.

This is where the present chapter enters the debate. It is concerned with sacred things, in particular idols (*murti*s) of goddesses within the politico-economic context of kingship in Orissa (Odisha since 2011), East India. These idols never enter, leave or re-enter a commodity phase, but are singularized and sacred per se, and are enlivened.[4] One could pinpoint their existential mode by saying that they do not even have commodity *potential*. Nevertheless, these bronze or copper *murti*s (often called 'kanaka' or 'golden') may circulate or even be 'exchanged', if this term can be applied at all to an act of theft. For in Orissa's history, there are many instances in which the mobile statues of goddesses were stolen from their royal patrons by other kings.[5] Contrary to how theft is judged in our modern capitalist society, these 'thefts' of divine statues are not considered to be illegitimate or even crimes; rather, the power to steal a goddess from another king is considered legitimate. Or, to phrase it in Weberian terms, the successful theft of a goddess adds authority and legitimacy to one's power. These goddesses (or their statues) become trophies, while their theft or the prevention thereof constitute, in Appadurai's words, 'tournaments of value' (1986: 21).

In the following ethnohistorical sections of this chapter, it will be shown that the political economy of kingship in Orissa was mainly acted out and decided in what we would consider a ritual domain. Ritual enactments were seen by the actors as being more effective than fights over material goods, which were admittedly also going on all the time. All in all, then, this chapter seeks to contribute to the intellectual issues that Chris Hann (in close cooperation with Stephen Gudeman) tackled in the 'Economy and Ritual' Research Project conducted during the period 2009–12 at the Max Planck Institute for Social Anthropology in Halle.[6] It proposes an additional, and in some respects alternative, look at the complex relationship between economy and ritual, focusing especially on the interface of ritual and *political* economy as two analytically distinct but not separate domains. In line with one of the aims of this group, my main attention is less on production than on exchange, barter, gift-giving and, significantly, the moral economy of theft, an issue that Chris Hann also addressed so pertinently in his Huxley Memorial Lecture entitled 'Economy and Ethics in the Cosmic Process' in London in December 2019.[7]

The Political and Ritual Landscape of Premodern Odisha

The cases of stolen goddesses to be discussed here occurred at a time when the Indian subcontinent was scattered with innumerable kingdoms of the Hindu type, more than 5,000 of all sizes, even in late colonial British times. It is important to understand that these kingdoms were not mono-archies but units in a poly-archic system of ritually linked, but structurally opposed and hierarchically ordered kingdoms. As integral units of these multicentred systems, these kingdoms are best labelled 'little' and 'great' (rather than 'small' and 'large') so as to make it clear that the relationship and the hierarchical status of a king and kingdom vis-à-vis others is first of all a ritual matter. Size, economic power and military force do of course play important roles as to where in the hierarchically ordered politico-ritual system a king finds himself. But success or failure in this 'game of thrones' is mainly contested, made palpable and symbolically effective in the realm of ritual, and not in the realm of size and military might.[8]

One important element in the ritual policy of Indian kings is their becoming and remaining the patrons of powerful deities who in turn become their tutelary deities, supporting them in everyday matters, but also in cases of natural disaster or war. In this context, it is important to realize the extent to which Odisha's ritual landscape has been dominated by mother and earth goddesses, who are worshipped in the form of stones, trees, wooden posts, earthen mounds and other non-iconic symbols. Characteristically, these goddesses possess a strong territorial rootedness, their fields of influence fading out at the borders of their own villages or clan localities. However, within their sacred domains (*ksetra*s), they are immensely powerful and feared, more so than any other deity who might also be worshipped there. As embodiments of *shakti*, a dynamic force associated with life, fertility, growth, sexuality and abundance, these goddesses have an ambivalent character that can either grant and sustain life or else threaten and even destroy it. Several of these originally tribal deities have undergone various processes of Hinduization, leading to the anthropomorphization of their originally non-iconic symbols. Minimal additions in this process of making a *murti*-like image out of their stones, trees or other natural embodiments consist in painting or plastering eyes and a large protruding tongue upon the natural symbol. The priests of these goddesses, though not themselves belonging to the Brahman caste, have adapted the Hindu form of worship called *puja* as their role model, offering vegetarian gifts and other 'services' (*upacaras*) to the human-like idols.[9]

In the following, I discuss six cases of stealing goddesses from Orissan history. These cases are not ordered chronologically, but, as far as the first three are concerned, according to the status of the 'thieves' and their victims: (1) great king from great king; (2) little king from great king; and (3) little little king from little king. Cases 4 and 5 specify the special relation of kings to their tutelary goddesses, while case 6 discusses the theft and demolition of the tutelary deity of the Orissan Gajapati, or great king, through Muslim invaders.

Stealing and Patronizing Goddesses: Six Cases

Case 1

Time: the end of the fifteenth century. Place: the temple town of Puri in central Orissa. This is the sacred abode of Jagannath ('Lord of the World'), the undisputed 'state deity' of Orissa. Here also lives the 'king of kings' of the Orissan empire, namely the Gajapati ('Lord of the Elephants') in his palace.

During the annual Car Festival (*ratha yatra*) in July in honour of Jagannath, Gajapati Purushottama Deo (1467–97), one of the most powerful Hindu kings on the subcontinent at that time, climbed on to the wooden car of Jagannath, sprinkled the platform in front of the deity with water and then swept the floor, using a broom with a golden handle. This ritual act resulted in war. According to a popular Orissan legend, Purushottama had intended to marry the beautiful Princess Padmabati, the daughter of the king of Kanchipuram in south India. However, the prospective father-in-law withdrew his consent when it was reported to him that Purushottama had done the work of a sweeper. Purushottama considered this withdrawal an affront not only to himself but also to Jagannath. Hence, he determined to seize the princess by force, marched south with his warriors, defeated Kanchipuram, captured Padmabati and, after some hesitation, took her as his wife. The war between Puri and Kanchipuram was thus induced by the so-called *chera pahamra* ritual, which is still conducted by the Gajapati in Puri in front of tens of thousands of exultant pilgrims. Through this act of ritually humbling himself, the 'Lord of the Elephants' publicly expresses his great devotion to the 'Lord of the World', though by doing so he also emphasizes his privileged position in the cult of Jagannath.[10] In Purushottama's case, this splendid ritual performance led to a ritual of a quite different kind, namely to Purushottama's war expedition against Kanchipuram. The ritual of devotion resulted in a ritual of violence and an exhibition of power. However, it did not end tragically, but in marriage.

Case 2

Time: again, the end of the fifteenth century. Place: a jungle path bordering the little kingdom of Jeypore, one of the largest, most powerful and superior jungle kingdoms in south Orissa.[11]

When Purushottama returned from his campaign against Kanchipuram, he was attacked by Vijaya Chandra (1467–1510), the second king of the dynasty of Jeypore, while traversing a jungle path on his estate. Following a brief fight, the jungle king and his indigenous warriors managed to take hold of one of the Gajapati's elephants and flee with it into the bush. This animal was carrying part of the war booty taken by Purushottama from Kanchipuram, most prominently a golden statue of the Hindu goddess Durga. The family chronicle of the Jeypore royal dynasty also reports that this *murti* was installed in Jeypore's royal capital with great ceremony. Durga was then proclaimed the tutelary deity of the kingdom. The annual celebration of Durga *puja* in Jeypore in October is said to have been performed so splendidly that it brought 'good name and fame all over India' to the kingdom.[12] The family chronicle of the Gajapatis of Orissa, on the other hand, does not even mention what to them was a very humiliating theft.

Case 3

Time: the middle of the nineteenth century. Place: Bissamcuttack, the realm of a semi-independent 'thatraja' on the eastern border of the jungle kingdom of Jeypore.

According to one legend told to me at the temple of Markama, the tutelary deity of the Bissamcuttack 'little little kings', the king of Jeypore once attacked his Bissamcuttack feudal retainer because allegedly he had not paid tribute for several years. In the middle of the fight, when many local soldiers were losing their lives, Markama joined in. She disguised herself as a milkmaid and sold poisoned curd to the soldiers of the Jeypore overlord, whereupon they died and the fortunes of the battle turned. One of the king's generals then inquired about the temple of this goddess, went there and shot her head off using a gun. But Markama took revenge by letting the general die soon afterwards. At this, the king of Jeypore considered it best to settle his disagreement with the *thatraja* amicably, demanding no further payments of tribute. This story is not narrated in the family chronicles of the Jeypore kings. In Orissa we thus encounter not only the theft of mobile *murti*s of goddesses; persons fighting for power and territorial sovereignty also attempted to obtain access to the temples of powerful local goddesses and to establish themselves as patrons of their cults. In this way, they often managed to forge meaningful bonds with the earth and its inhabitants over whom they ruled or were asked to rule. Alternatively, as in this case, they tried to destroy the tutelary deity of an enemy, thus hoping to destroy a major source of his power.

Case 4

Time: the mythical past, but also the time of the celebration of Durga *puja*, a festival held annually in October at the end of the rainy season.

The demon king Mahisha succeeded in appropriating Indra's place as supreme god for himself and in ruling the world in his stead. As the other gods were worried about this state of affairs, particularly about their share in the sacrifices, they called on Durga for help. In order to assist the goddess in restoring the cosmic order, they gave her several weapons, such as Shiva's trident, Vishnu's disc, Indra's thunderbolt and Varuna's snare. Accordingly, apart from this, the goddess holds in her twelve hands a bow and arrow, and, most significantly, the sword that she uses to cut off the demon's head when he tries to flee from his buffalo form.[13] This killing of the buffalo demon, which is reported in classical writings as well as in innumerable folk stories, is ritually re-enacted during the eighth night of Durga *puja*. As far as Jeypore is concerned, many of the buffaloes sacrificed each year were sponsored by the king, one or two of which he killed himself. The king also established himself during the Durga *puja* celebrations as Durga's husband through a series of symbolic and ritual acts. In the myth and ritual of the destruction of demonic rule by Durga and her close (marital and sexual) association with a king, we encounter a social, political and also cosmic drama during which an endangered world is saved and imbued with new order and power.[14]

Case 5

Time: October 1941. Place: Jeypore.

Sahu (1942: 33–36) describes the *dasara* feast in Jeypore, which is celebrated immediately after the nine nights of Durga *puja* and closely linked to it in ritual and mythical terms in the following words:

> The Dussara at Jeypore is a sight not only for me but for gods ... What a sight! People have thronged in their thousands ... They have come with their banners, their drums and flutes and various other musical instruments. Hundreds of ceremonies have gone on for the past seven days and ceremony after ceremony is going on. The Maharajah has been fasting in the midst of it; for religious ceremony requires it. And though he has been going through such purificatory penance, so to say, he bears it calmly without any show of it on his face. The procession begins. (Sahu 1942: 33–36)

As this eyewitness report makes clear, the king was the central actor in this cultural performance of *dasara*, functioning as Durga's chief devotee and as patron of the ritual proceedings. In order to participate in the *dasara* festivities, thousands of individuals headed for the politico-ritual centre of the kingdom, namely the royal palace, with its ceremonial hall and the temple of Durga attached to it. Within the ceremonial hall, the king was sitting on the throne together with Durga, whose *murti* was placed on a cushion next to him. After an audience in the ceremonial hall for the most important functionaries and estate holders, who offered gifts and in return received the king's blessings and a *sari* symbolizing their legitimacy as office holders, the procession started from the palace led by the king and Durga riding on an elephant, as if they were leading an army into war. They were followed by the holders of the various military fiefs and estates of the kingdom and by the foot soldiers of these estates, who held flags symbolizing their territorial segments of the kingdom and its respective local tutelary deities.[15]

Case 6

Time: 1568. Place: Cuttack and Puri in central Orissa.

In 1568, the army of the Kararani Sultanate of Bengal defeated the army of the Gajapatis of Orissa in a decisive battle. Following his victory, the Afghan general immediately marched towards Cuttack, the then royal capital of the Lord of the Elephants, and killed Gajapati Mukunda Deo. He then turned towards the pilgrimage centre of Puri, where he stormed the temple of Jagannath and stole the god's wooden effigy. This was taken north to the banks of the Ganges, where it was burnt. However, the temple chronicles of Puri report that an Oriya man succeeded in saving the inner essence of the god from the smouldering effigy. He buried this vital part of the god – the so-called *brahmapadartha* substance, which is stored in a cavity in the wooden god's belly – in a hole next to the village of Kujang in central Orissa. Thirty years later, when Orissa was still without a Gajapati and the Puri temple was still closed, Jagannath appeared to the little king of Khurda in a dream, revealing the hidden whereabouts of his *brahmapadartha*. Subsequently, this king, Ramachandra Deo, with the help of the priests of Puri, 'found' this live substance and had a new wooden effigy of Jagannath built that was re-installed in Puri. Ramachandra thus managed to get himself acknowledged as the new Gajapati of Orissa – a step from 'little' to 'great'. Even after these events, during the period from the early seventeenth to the middle of the eighteenth centuries, Puri and the temple of Jagannath were repeatedly attacked and sometimes plundered by Muslim forces. However, the priests of the temple and the various Gajapatis always succeeded in fleeing with the effigy in time.

Conclusions

All these cases have in common the fact that in them, individuals or groups give spectacular expressions to their claims to power, authority and territorial sovereignty by getting close to a deity or stealing it, and sometimes even by attempting to destroy it. In this context, we find two different kinds or manifestations of the Great Goddess (*Mahadevi*): one possesses a strong local rootedness and is represented by an originally aniconic idol, while the other has her *shakti* emanate from a mobile *murti* identified with the great Hindu goddess Durga. One of the major differences between the *murti*s of the goddess Durga and tribal goddesses, then, consists in their territoriality. The former are not indissolubly bound to a certain locality. Their force or *shakti* radiates from their statues and not, as is the case with most tribal deities, from the earth or locality they are standing on.

While the territorialized deities can be approached and their patronage contested, only the mobile statues can be stolen and exchanged. Only they can become 'common' and commodities. The tribal goddesses can also become sources of power and legitimacy for royal patrons, these being territorially bounded and 'singularized'. In the two manifestations of the goddess as static and mobile, as well as in their respective cults, we thereby encounter different concepts of royal authority. These are pinpointed by Stein when he writes about Indian ritual politics (referring to the mediaeval Chola empire): 'On the one hand, there was a form of kingship which was universalistic, absolutistic, fiscally and extractively oriented; on the other hand, there was a form of lordship, very like kingship, but localistic, relativistic, or collegeal, and redistributivist' (Stein 1985: 408). However, as the Orissan cases show, we are not dealing with two strictly opposed concepts or, territorially speaking, with two different spheres of the expansion of royal and divine authority. The various territorial levels overlapped, from the local estate of the Bissamcuttack *tharaja* via the little kingdom of Jeypore to the regional empire of the Gajapatis. The corresponding realms are thus best understood not with reference to some ill-conceived notion of borders, but when seen as fields of energy and power that are open at the peripheries. These circles at places overlap with other circles of the same kind or are encompassed by circles of higher orders. In the various centres of these circles, we find deities who radiate energy and give force to their patrons and closest devotees. These deities were approached by the bearers of royal authority or by those who were striving to obtain it in two essentially different ways: either they tried to establish themselves as the patron of a deity patron and thus attempted to link their secular realm (*ksatra*) with that deity's sacred realm (*ksetra*), or else they tried to destroy the existing *ksatra/ksetra* symbiosis of an enemy by destroying or stealing the *murti* of his tutelary deity.

Why, then, did these persons steal or even try to destroy the material representations of deities in their capacity as stores of power? Why did they try to make symbolic conquests? Why was it their main aim to achieve prestige or to humiliate an enemy in the realm of ritual rather than to conquer his land, subdue him militarily and even kill him? By stealing a *murti*, becoming the patron of a goddess or destroying the material representation of an enemy's tutelary deity, it was possible to conquer, subdue and dominate an enemy in a symbolic way. These conquests, then, were not 'merely symbolic', but actual conquests by means of symbolic and ritual acts. In a sense, these ritual enactments of power and authority were more than 'merely factual' because they occurred in a realm of values that possessed higher, timeless sanctions and validity. The sacred and the secular were distinct, but not separate spheres, the sacred being superior.

Burkhard Schnepel is Professor of Social Anthropology at the Institute for Social Anthropology at the Martin Luther University in Halle, Germany. Between 2013 and 2020, he was also Head of the Max Planck Fellow Group entitled 'Connectivity in Motion – Port Cities of the Indian Ocean'. Among his main theoretical and thematic interests are ritual and politics in India, as well as 'World History', especially the ethnohistory of the Indian Ocean world.

Notes

1. See Appadurai (1986). See also my more detailed discussion in Schnepel (2021).
2. See especially Appadurai (1986: 16–29).
3. As elaborated in a section entitled 'The Singular and the Common' (Kopytoff 1986: 68–70).
4. On the bringing to life of 'idols' in the Hindu religious context, see Schnepel (2013).
5. I have dealt with the 'theft' of goddesses in greater detail elsewhere (Schnepel 2004), though my interpretative focus there was on the performative dimension of stealing, while here it is on the political economy dimension. Terms like 'stealing' or 'theft' are used here not to imply judgements about the illegal nature of these actions, but to denote a specific form of appropriation and encompassment in the political economy and ritual life of premodern India.
6. See especially Gudeman and Hann (2015).
7. See https://www.therai.org.uk/events-calendar/eventdetail/634/-/huxley-lecture-chris-hann (retrieved 10 January 2021).
8. As I have discussed elsewhere at length (Schnepel 2002: Chapter 1), the description of a king as 'little' (or 'great') acquires heuristic value only when it is used in understanding the dynamic network of relationships between kings of different ranks. The identification of a kingdom or king as 'little' (or 'great') is therefore based not on absolute, clearly measurable criteria, but rather on relational, abstract, politico-ritual criteria, which can change rapidly historically and are often subject to contradictory interpretations by those involved. In brief, a king is 'little' (or 'great') only in terms of a changeable, tense relationship with another king, who, in this very same relationship, counts as 'great', but may count as 'little' in another relationship.
9. On the cult of tribal goddesses in Orissa, see Eschmann (1978); Kulke (1993); and Schnepel (1993 and 2002: Chapter V).
10. On the 'Cult of Jagannath', see especially Eschmann, Kulke and Tripathi (1978); and Kulke (1979).
11. In my *The Jungle Kings* (Schnepel 2002), I identified a special type of the little kingdom, namely the jungle kingdom, that needs to be distinguished from the many coastal little kingdoms by the fact that geopolitically their hilly and forested realms are withdrawn from direct interference by great kings and that the inhabitants of these kingdoms – as well as their rituals and ideas of political legitimacy – were mainly of the Adivasi or tribal type.
12. See Sarma (1938: Verses 147–55).
13. On the battle between Durga and Mahisha, see Berkson (1995); and Erndl (1993).
14. On 'Durga and the King', see also Schnepel (1995).
15. A more detailed discussion of the *dasara* festival in Jeypore can be found in Schnepel (2000).

References

Appadurai, Arjun. 1986. 'Introduction: Commodities and the Politics of Value', in Arjun Appadurai (ed.), *The Social Life of Things: Commodities in Cultural Perspective*. Cambridge: Cambridge University Press, pp. 3–63.

_____. (ed.). 1986. *The Social Life of Things: Commodities in Cultural Perspective*. Cambridge: Cambridge University Press.
Assmann, Jan, and Harald Strohm (eds). 2013. *Orakel und Offenbarung. Formen göttlicher Willensbekundung*. Munich: Wilhelm Fink.
Berkemer, Georg, and Margret Frenz (eds). 2004. *Sharing Sovereignty: The Little Kingdom in South Asia*. Berlin: Klaus Schwarz Verlag.
Berkson, Carmel. 1995. *The Divine and Demoniac: Mahisa's Heroic Struggle with Durga*. New Delhi: Oxford University Press.
Erndl, Kathleen M. 1993. *Victory to the Mother: The Hindu Goddess of Northwest India in Myth, Ritual and Symbol*. Oxford: Oxford University Press.
Eschmann, Anncharlott. 1978. 'Hinduization of Tribal Deities in Orissa: The Sakta and Saiva Typology', in Anncharlott Eschmann, Hermann Kulke and Gaya C. Tripathi (eds), *The Cult of Jagannath and the Regional Tradition of Orissa*. New Delhi: Manohar, pp. 79–97.
Eschmann, Ancharlott, Hermann Kulke and Gaya C. Tripathi (eds). 1978. *The Cult of Jagannath and the Regional Tradition of Orissa*. New Delhi: Manohar Publishers.
Gudeman, Stephen, and Chris Hann (eds). 2015. *Economy and Ritual: Studies of Postsocialist Transformations*. Oxford: Berghahn Books.
Kopytoff, Igor. 1986. 'The Cultural Biography of Things: Commoditization as Process', in Arjun Appadurai (ed.), *The Social Life of Things: Commodities in Cultural Perspective*. Cambridge: Cambridge University Press, pp. 64–94.
Kulke, Hermann. 1979. *Jagannatha-Kult und Gajapati-Königtum: Ein Beitrag zur Geschichte religiöser Legitimation hinduistischer Herrscher*. Wiesbaden: Franz Steiner Verlag.
_____. 1993. *Kings and Cults: State Formation and Legitimation in India and Southeast Asia*. New Delhi: Manohar.
Kulke, Hermann, and Burkhard Schnepel (eds). 2000. *Jagannath Revisited: Studying Society, Religion and the State in Orissa*. New Delhi: Manohar.
Sahu, Lakshmi N. 1942. *The Hill Tribes of Jeypore*. Cuttack: Orissa Mission Press.
Sarma, Ramanatha N. 1938. *Jayapura Raja Vamsyavali: A History of the Solar Dynasty of Jeypore-Orissa*. Madras: Vavilla Press.
Schnepel, Burkhard. 1993. 'Die Schutzgöttinnen: Tribale Gottheiten in Südorissa (Indien) und ihre Patronage durch hinduistische Kleinkönige', *Anthropos* 88: 337–50.
_____. 1995. 'Durga and the King: Ethnohistorical Aspects of the Politico-ritual Life in a South Orissan Jungle Kingdom', *Journal of the Royal Anthropological Institute* 1: 145–66.
_____. 2000. 'Kings and Rebel Kings: Rituals of Incorporation and Dissent in South Orissa', in Hermann Kulke and Burkhard Schnepel (eds), *Jagannath Revisited: Studying Society, Religion and the State in Orissa*. New Delhi: Manohar, pp. 271–96.
_____. 2002. *The Jungle Kings: Ethnohistorical Aspects of Politics and Ritual in Orissa*. New Delhi: Manohar.
_____. 2004. 'The Stolen Goddess: Ritual Enactments of Power and Authority in Orissa', in Georg Berkemer and Margret Frenz (eds), *Sharing Sovereignty: The Little Kingdom in South Asia*. Berlin: Klaus Schwarz Verlag, pp. 165–80.

_____. 2013. 'Zur Stofflichkeit religiöser Erfahrungen: "Idolatrie" in Ostindien', in Jan Assman and Harald Strohm (eds), *Orakel und Offenbarung. Formen göttlicher Willensbekundung*. Munich: Wilhelm Fink, pp. 77–98.

_____. 2021. 'Cargoes: A Thematic and Methodological Introduction', in Burkhard Schnepel and Julia Verne (eds), *Cargoes in Motion: Materiality and Connectivity in the Indian Ocean*. Athens, OH: Ohio University Press, pp. 1–28.

Schnepel, Burkhard, and Julia Verne (eds). 2021. *Cargoes in Motion: Materiality and Connectivity in the Indian Ocean*. Athens, OH: Ohio University Press.

Stein, Burton. 1985. 'State Formation and Economy Reconsidered I', *Modern Asian Studies* 19: 387–413.

Chapter 19

Dalits and the Market
Liberation or Oppression?

David N. Gellner

> [T]he material and the moral are equally fundamental. Understanding the moral dimension ... involves tracking dominant values through history ... and their concrete reconfigurations and enactment through social relations.
> —Chris Hann, 'Moral(ity and) Economy'

Introduction: The Self-Sufficient South Asian Village

There is a romantic vision of the South Asian village as having once upon a time been self-sufficient, a little republic unto itself, a haven of community, mutual support and embedded exchange unsullied (at least relatively so) by markets, capitalism, modernity or colonialism.[1] Mahatma Gandhi was a keen advocate of this view. Its roots can be traced back to the publications of James Mill and Charles Metcalfe in the early years of British rule over India; it was subsequently adopted by both Maine and Marx (Srinivas 1987 [1975]; Jodhka 1998). Such a moral vision, insofar as it is shared by villagers themselves, may have considerable power, but, as Chris Hann points out in the quotation above, it is how those moral ideas are embodied in particular institutions and social relations that is crucial. In the present case, ideas of solidarity come so bound up with ideas of hierarchy that it is the supposedly free market, and not traditional inter-caste relationships, that is viewed as liberating and given moral value. Individualism and competition are seen as morally better than mutual

---

Notes for this chapter begin on page 263.

solidarity and hierarchy. I will show how this is so through an analysis of *jajmani* relations (ritual and economic ties between different castes) in the anthropology of South Asia and through some ethnographic material from Nepal.

In the years following Indian independence, the romantic image of the Indian village as a little republic came under fierce attack from a variety of very different theoretical perspectives (Kosambi 1970: 16–17; Srinivas 1987 [1975]; Inden 1990).[2] Dumont and Pocock (1957: 26) went so far as to say that fieldworking anthropologists had conferred on the village 'a kind of sociological reality which in fact it does not possess' – a position that was itself a consequence of Dumont's determination to make caste and kinship, understood as structured relationships, the sole sociologically real entities. It was left to Ambedkar, with his personal experience of growing up as an Untouchable in an Indian village and living outside the village boundaries subject to numerous exclusions, to provide the most radical denunciation of the 'village republic' simile:

> In this Republic, there is no place for democracy. There is no room for equality. There is no room for liberty and there is no room for fraternity. The Indian village is a very negation of Republic ... The republic is an Empire of the Hindus over the Untouchables. It is a kind of colonialism of the Hindus designed to exploit the Untouchables. The Untouchables have no rights ... They have no rights because they are outside the village republic and because they are outside the so-called village republic, they are outside the Hindu fold. (Ambedkar 1989b: 3970, cited in Jodhka 2002: 3351)

In his more considered analysis of caste, Ambedkar wrote:

> [The] Caste System is not merely a division of labourers ... it is an hierarchy in which the divisions of labourers are graded one above the other. In no other country is the division of labour accompanied by this gradation of labourers ... Each caste takes its pride and its consolation in the fact that in the scale of castes it is above some other caste. As an outward mark of this gradation, there is also a gradation of social and religious rights ... The higher the grade of a caste, the greater the number of these rights and the lower the grade, the lesser their number. (Ambedkar 1989a [1936]: 94, 120–1)

Ambedkar's onslaught was largely ignored (with the exception of Dalit circles) for several decades. The romantic view of villages survived well into the first twenty or thirty years of India's independence. In more scholarly accounts, a key pillar supporting the picture of village autarchy was provided by W.H. Wiser's little book (1936), building on his and his wife's earlier monograph (Wiser and Wiser 1932), describing the *jajmani* system as it functioned in a village near Delhi. He saw it as the ancient and traditionally sanctified way of organizing the division of labour within a caste system and claimed that it was 'somewhat like the old feudal system, yet unlike it' (1936: 2), because 'Each in turn is master. Each in turn is servant' (1936: 10). Blacksmiths, barbers, watercarriers, carpenters, washermen, tailors and other skilled service providers give their services in return for gifts in kind that are not conceived of as one-off payments.

The key point about these *jajmani* relationships was that they were hereditary and obligatory, linking households across generations. Thus, they were socially embedded moral relationships, quite consciously opposed – at least in the way they were supposed to operate – to the meretricious, self-interested, negative reciprocity of the market. In a *jajmani* relationship, each side had duties and expectations of the other that were a commitment for life and beyond. And yet, though opposed to the market, the relationship could be treated like property. Thus, a *jajmani* specialist could sell or mortgage their rights to serve a particular patron, and the patron would have no say in this.

Jajmani relations were opposed to market relations in at least seven different ways, as shown in Table 19.1 below. The religious nature of the relationship was indicated by the very terminology: *jajman*, the word for patron, came from the Sanskrit *yajamana*, 'he who orders a ritual sacrifice', and receives the benefits of it, as opposed to the ritual specialists who enable him (and it was usually him) to carry it out.

Following Wiser, many ethnographies of South Asia referred to the *jajmani* system (Kumar 2016). *Jajmani* relationships exist in Nepal too (Gaborieau 1977; Gellner and Quigley 1995; Adhikari and Gellner 2019) and similar relations between patrons and specialists, with different terminologies, exist in Pakistan, Bangladesh and Sri Lanka. The *jajmani* system became a model applied to the whole of South Asia (Beidelman 1959; Dumont 1980: Ch. 4). A simplified version of the model, positing

Table 19.1. Contrasting characteristics of *jajmani* and market relationships.

Jajmani	Market
Annual retainer and benefits in kind	Payment in cash
Multistranded relationship	One-off relationship
Security in hard times	No insurance against hard times
Affective link	Impersonal
Patron has no choice of specialist	Buyer has ability to shop around
Client inherits right to provide service	Seller must compete with other sellers
Client can sell, lease or mortgage rights	Seller has no control over buyers

embedded intercaste economic relationships that (a) integrated people at the level of the village in a nonmarket way, but that (b) were breaking down in the face of modernization, migration, marketization and urbanization entered the textbooks (see e.g. Eriksen 2015: 178–79).

In the vast majority of places in South Asia, *jajmani* relations have been in decline for a long time, as service castes either refused to provide the service or migrated out of the village for work elsewhere, or patrons stopped calling their clients and sought cheaper or more easily available market alternatives. We are fortunate to have a fine and detailed ethnographic re-study of Wiser's own village, done on the basis of over twenty years' work, by Susan Wadley (1994). Wadley found that only three out of 327 households relied on *jajmani* relations for income, a massive decline compared to twenty years earlier in the 1960s, which itself was a decline on the figure from Wiser's day (the 1920s). As specialists abandoned their caste-specific professions, people talked nostalgically about the old days when patrons really looked after their *kamins* (Wadley 1994: 82f).

Just at the point when discussion of the '*jajmani* system' was itself in severe decline and scholars were openly doubting if it had in fact ever existed, Gloria Goodwin Raheja (1988a) wrote a powerful, highly detailed ethnography focused on prestations between different castes in a village in western Uttar Pradesh, northern India. Through careful attention to local terminology and practice, Raheja demonstrated that *jajmani* relations consisted of multiple and complex exchanges. In particular, she showed that there were two contrasting types of prestation: those classified as religiously sanctioned 'gifts' (*dan*) and those classified as equivalent to payments. The two types had radically different moral loads, as gifts and market exchanges respectively. But the gifts had all the ambiguous qualities (the 'poison' of her book's title) that made them hard to digest.

Clients had a duty to accept those prestations that I label 'G-type' (see Table 19.2) and they incurred 'inauspiciousness' in so doing. This kind of prestation must never be returned (cf. Parry 1986). The ethnography of north India had long established that the most prestigious and meritorious prestation of this sort is the 'gift of a virgin' (*kanyadan*) in which one gives one's daughter in marriage, and it has long been known that the father (and other collateral relatives) of the bride must never accept even so much as a glass of water from the house to which the bride is given. The religious merit of the gift depends on there *not* being any kind of exchange relationship; *all* prestations must flow from wife-givers to the wife-receivers (Parry 1986; Gellner 1991).[3] By contrast, the other kind of prestation, which I label 'E-type' (see Table 19.2), *is* explicitly and

Table 19.2. Two opposed kinds of prestation (derived from Raheja 1988a).

G-type	E-type
Typical form: *dan*	Typical form: *phaslana*
Patron's right to give	Specialist's right to receive
Specialist's duty to receive	Patron's duty to give
No return must ever be accepted	Given as a return (for work or ritual service)
Amount at giver's discretion	Amount specified by tradition
Acceptance involves the acceptance of inauspiciousness	No stigma attached to acceptance
Specialists dislike receiving and abandon if they can	Specialists like this kind of prestation since it is in kind, which is not subject to the vagaries of inflation

consciously analogous to a payment. With G-type prestations, precisely because material goods only flow in one direction, the recipient must also accept, along with the material goods, some 'spiritual' evil or nongood along with it. With E-type prestations, there is no question of this arising. This contrast captures a pan-South Asian structural logic of exchange and may be illustrated by the Nepali proverb 'What is given freely as a gift cannot, in anger, be converted into a loan' (*khushiko dan risko rin huna sakdaina*).[4]

Raheja's rich monograph was a major challenge to Dumont's structuralist, Brahmin-focused theory of caste. She provided serious ethnographic support for the Hocartian King- or Kshatriya-focused alternative view, in which the Brahmin was just one of a number of ritual specialists serving the royal/dominant caste sacrificial division of labour (Hocart 1950; Raheja 1998b; Quigley 1993; Parry 1986, 1998). Raheja's ethnography also showed that Wiser had been naïve in thinking that everyone was alternately master and servant. In fact, the dominant caste in Raheja's case is proud that it stands at the centre and its members are always givers, never receivers, of *dan*. One consequence of this is that there are different kinds of persons, though some will find themselves in both categories, acting, at different times, both as givers and as receivers of *dan*. It was left to Chris Gregory (1992) to point out that in her descriptions of the working of the system, Raheja tended to adopt the position of her dominant-caste Gujar informants and failed to investigate how the system of exchanges looked from the point of view of lower-status service providers or to ask whether they fully shared the understandings of the dominant-caste participants.

Questions remain: how generalizable are Raheja's conclusions? Does her village Pahansu represent a late flowering and exceptional case of thoroughgoing *jajmani* relations? Is it really the case that *dan* (nonreciprocal gifts) always carry inauspiciousness with them (Parry 1991)? Is it not necessary to grade inauspiciousness hierarchically, i.e. the inauspiciousness of death is far greater than that of other prestations? As mentioned above, by the 1980s scholars of South Asia began to doubt whether there ever was a *jajmani* system as such and whether it was found in all parts of India (Fuller 1989). Not only was the system itself rapidly in decline by the mid-twentieth century, but historical work suggested that the classic form of the system, with household-to-household links inherited as property from generation to generation, actually came into existence only in the last quarter of the nineteenth century, replacing a system where artisans were beholden to the village as a whole rather than to specific households (Mayer 1993). If this conclusion is correct, one must conclude that under the conditions of traditionalization that characterized the British Raj, some artisan specialists succeeded in modelling their links to specific households on those of Brahmin priests and collectively brought into being a system of hereditary links and rights to support across north India and beyond, a system that colonial administrators and anthropologists subsequently took, quite wrongly, to be as ancient as Hindu civilization itself. However, it is striking that this kind of hereditary household-to-household link *also* emerged in Nepal, which was not directly under the Raj at all. The relative newness of such links may explain the very patchiness of the system, with some parts of the Nepalese middle hills viewing the links between priest and patron and tailor and patron as unbreakable and hereditary, whereas elsewhere, in culturally very similar and not so distant parts of the middle hills, these same relationships need to be renewed each year by a ritual gift and are therefore viewed as more like a contract.

Dalits and *Jajmani* Relations in Nepal

Research in a cluster of connected villages in Kaski district, Nepal, not far from the regional centre of Pokhara, demonstrates that *jajmani* relations (locally called *balighare*) are definitely in severe decline.[5] We surveyed 540 households, plus a further survey of 1,203 individuals drawn from 326 of the households. There are four major caste groups: Bahun (Brahmin), Chhetri (Kshatriya), Gurung and Dalit. The Bahuns are divided into two subcastes – priestly and nonpriestly – and the Dalits consist of three distinct castes: Vishwakarma (Blacksmiths), Mijar (Cobblers) and Pariyar (Tailor-Musicians). Thus, there are seven major groupings overall and we attempted to include roughly equal numbers of each in our samples.

Nepal has an extremely high rate of international labour migration. Where previously people (mainly men) migrated to India, since 1990 they have gone to the Gulf, to Malaysia and (if lucky) to South Korea, Japan or Hong Kong. In the area studied, 78 per cent of households have at least one member who has gone abroad for work and half of all households have someone abroad currently. Many other household members are away from home working elsewhere in Nepal. All groups migrate frequently, but there is a marked difference by caste: priestly Bahuns migrate the least, with only 50 per cent having a member who has worked abroad. The highest rates of foreign migration are among the Dalits. Among Vishwakarmas, 90 per cent of households have at least one person who has worked abroad either recently or in the past. Many households have several sons abroad at once. But though they may be able to raise the money (by mortgaging land and/or taking loans) to go to work as a labourer in the Gulf states, Dalits are less able than other castes to afford to move to towns and cities within Nepal, and, lacking education and other forms of cultural and social capital, they are much less able to migrate for work and/or settlement to 'advanced' countries such as the United Kingdom or Australia.

One factor that may make work in Gulf countries attractive to Dalits, despite the well-known disadvantages of working there, is that there is effectively no caste prejudice. All Nepalis are treated equally by the employers and all Nepalis suffer equally from the same discriminatory labour relations: Indians are routinely paid more than Nepalis for doing the same job. Furthermore, in this context other Nepalis do not discriminate against Dalits either; they are happy to share food and living quarters without any hesitation. This is the almost universal report of those who have worked there, both Dalits and non-Dalits. However, about 50 per cent of respondents state, often with considerable regret, that they cannot maintain the same easy and nondiscriminatory relations once they are back in Nepal.

In our sample, when asked whether they could carry on their parents' profession, overall most respondents indicated that they would prefer not to. Clearly, the idea of avoiding the hard work of being a peasant and moving to the city is attractive across the board. Yet, compared to others, Dalits are slightly more open to the possibility of carrying on their caste profession, though few in fact do so. Most of the Pariyars who continue to work as tailors do so in the modern style and have their own shops either locally or in Pokhara (i.e. they no longer visit and sew clothes for their patrons in their homes). Almost no one now gives annual grain payments to Dalits, though the village watchman and some Pariyars who perform special rituals at the annual Dasain festival do still circulate at harvest time and collect a small portion of paddy from each household.

Younger, more educated Dalits are less attached to tradition. For example, they resent it if some 'high-caste' person reminds them that their grandfather used to be the ploughman of their household; the young Dalit is likely to see this as an attempt to remind them of inferiority, even to humiliate them, rather than (as some 'high' castes may interpret it) as an attempt to establish intimacy. Dalits also resent the fact that even though they too are now sending their children to school, all the office jobs 'from the peon up to the boss (*hakim*)' seem to go to Bahuns. The introduction of reservations (quotas) for Dalits in recruitment to the bureaucracy is too recent for perceptions on this score to have been changed, while it has already generated resentment on the part of 'high' castes.[6]

Conclusion: The Rejection of *Jajmani* Relationships

Some of the early scholars who worked on the *jajmani* system did acknowledge the importance of power relations in maintaining the system, as well as the potential and tendency for conflict (Beidelman 1959). Others, such as Wiser, overemphasized what Raheja calls mutuality at the expense of the exclusions. What is perhaps not recognized by either is the degree to which contempt and distrust were built into the relationship. It is not that everyone is equally master and servant, as Wiser thought. Some are definitely not servants at all (usually members of the dominant caste), and even for those who occupy both roles, there are degrees and gradations. Those at the bottom are expected to act out their servility. Cameron (1998: 5, 79; 2007), writing on Far West Nepal, describes how Dalit service providers, in order to obtain ongoing material support from their patron, have to act out their moral inferiority – to wheedle, coax and even curse the patron as stingy – as prescribed by local custom. Thus, it is not enough to say – true though it may be – that everyone is subject to exclusions in a caste society, that communities do not have to be egalitarian and that 'the exclusion of Harijans from certain important activities, areas, and facilities cannot therefore be interpreted as evidence of their not being part of the village community' (Srinivas 1987 [1975]: 57). The exclusions of Dalits are more extreme and more absolute than any of those faced by other 'higher' castes.

Given the choice, then, it is not surprising that younger Dalits are keen to give up servile ties to their *jajman* and to seek independence through the market. This is a pattern that has been repeated throughout the subcontinent. They have also rejected ritual roles that define them as low, often to the outrage of higher castes. Yet, competing in the market does not always work out as well as might be expected. Opening hotels or restaurants is deeply challenging for Dalits, as customers may simply avoid them. When they follow their traditional caste occupations – such as tailoring, butchering, cobbling and selling shoes, ironwork, and musicianship – they continue to be stigmatized for doing so, whereas 'high' castes who take up these professions are not stigmatized and are often more successful in the market. Therefore, in many small and often invisible ways, exclusions continue.

Shah and her colleagues in *Ground Down by Growth* (2018) suggest that the biggest victims of development in India are Dalits (ex-Untouchables) and Adivasis (tribals). It says something about the level of psychic humiliation involved in the ongoing relations of the *jajmani* system that Dalits would nonetheless prefer to take their chances in the market, harsh and insecure though it is, and despite the manifold obstacles that remain in their path there (Mosse 2018). The fact that Dalits choose the market is a reminder that embedded forms of economy – preferred and held up as a model by opponents of market relations – are often so inescapably tied up with value-laden hierarchies of prestige and contempt, not to mention lack of freedom, that they are simply not viable as an option in a modern world that places the highest value on equality and liberty.[7] Not only are the moral and the material equally important, as Chris Hann says in my epigraph; sometimes the moral overpowers the material, as when Dalits refuse to practise their hereditary profession or role, even when it would be materially advantageous to do so.

David N. Gellner is Professor of Social Anthropology and a Fellow of All Souls, University of Oxford. Since 1980, he has been researching religion, ritual, politics, ethnicity, borderlands, activism, class and related topics in Nepal and South Asia. Among his many books are *The Anthropology of Buddhism and Hinduism: Weberian Themes* (2001), *Borderland Lives in Northern South Asia* (ed., 2013) and *Religion, Secularism, and Ethnicity in Contemporary Nepal* (ed., 2016).

Notes

1. This chapter draws on forty years of field research in South Asia. The material from Kaski district, Nepal derives from the UK-ESRC-funded project 'Caste, Class, and Culture: Changing Bahun and Dalit Identity in Nepal' [ES/L00240X/1], jointly carried out with Krishna Adhikari and Arjun B.K. (see Adhikari and Gellner 2016; Gellner and

Adhikari 2019; Adhikari and Gellner 2019; Gellner, Adhikari and B.K. 2020). I thank K.P. Adhikari, D.P. Martinez and J. Pfaff-Czarnecka for their helpful suggestions on an earlier draft.
2. For a more recent collection that no longer deems it necessary to contest the autarchy theory, see Mines and Yazgi (2010).
3. This was the model. In practice, many did not follow the model fully; there might be counterprestations, etc.
4. I owe this point to Krishna Adhikari.
5. For further details on the material presented in this section, see Adhikari and Gellner (2019). For simplicity and comparability, I have retained the terminology of *jajmani*, even though the term *jajman* is used in Nepal only to refer to the patron's relationship to a priest, not for other specialists. On Dalits in Nepal, see Caplan (1972); Cameron (1998, 2007); and Gellner and Adhikari (2019) and the references given therein.
6. See Thorat et al. (2016) and Sunam and Shrestha (2019) for arguments attempting to refute the usual objections to reservations. For Nepali Dalits' disadvantaged position in the new marketplaces of knowledge, see Pfaff-Czarnecka (2018, 2019).
7. Hierarchy continues to exist of course, even if transformed or only semi-legitimately. Piliavsky's edited volume (2014) provides plenty of evidence of the continuing importance of patronage within South Asia, which, to use a Dumontian term that the collection's contributors would probably not appreciate, arguably 'encompasses' the *jajmani* system. On the suppressed forms that hierarchy takes within modern Nepal, see Gellner (2016, n.d.); and Adhikari and Gellner (2016).

References

Adhikari, Krishna P., and David N. Gellner 2016. 'New Identity Politics and the 2012 Collapse of Nepal's Constituent Assembly: When the Dominant Becomes "Other"', *Modern Asian Studies* 50(6): 2009–40.
_____. 2019. 'International Labour Migration from Nepal and Changing Caste-Based Institutions and Inter-caste Relations' *Contributions to Nepalese Studies* 46(1): 167–91.
Ambedkar, Bhimrao R. 1989a [1936]. 'The Annihilation of Caste' in V. Moon (ed.), *Dr Babasaheb Ambedkar's Writings and Speeches*, vol. 1. Bombay: Government of Maharashtra, pp. 71–146.
_____. 1989b. 'Untouchables or the Children of India's Ghetto', in V. Moon (ed.), *Dr Babasaheb Ambedkar's Writings and Speeches*, vol. 5. Bombay: Government of Maharashtra, pp. 3947–4071.
Beidelman, Thomas O. 1959. *A Comparative Analysis of the Jajmani System*. Locust Valley, NY: J.J. Augustin.
Cameron, Mary M. 1998. *On the Edge of the Auspicious: Gender and Caste in Nepal*. Champaign: University of Illinois Press.
_____. 2007. 'Considering Dalits and Political Identity in Imagining a New Nepal', *Himalaya* 27(1–2): 13–26. Reissued in Arjun Guneratne. 2010. *Dalits of Nepal: Towards Dignity, Citizenship and Justice*. Kathmandu: ANHS, Social Science Baha and Himal Books.
Caplan, A. Patricia. 1972. *Priests and Cobblers: A Study of Social Change in a Hindu Village in West Nepal*. London: Intertext.

Dumont, Louis. 1970 [1957]. 'For a Sociology of India', in *Religion, Politics, and History in India: Collected Papers in Indian Sociology*. Paris: Mouton, pp. 2–18.
Dumont, Louis. 1980. *Homo Hierarchicus: The Caste System and its Implications*, tr. M. Sainsbury. Chicago: The University of Chicago Press.
Dumont, Louis, and David Pocock. 1957. 'Village Studies', *Contributions to Indian Sociology* 1(1): 23–41.
Eriksen, Thomas Hylland. 2015. *Small Places, Large Issues: An Introduction to Social and Cultural Anthropology*, 4th edn. London: Pluto.
Fuller, Christopher J. 1989. 'Misconceiving the Grain Heap: A Critique of the Concept of the Indian Jajmani System', in J. Parry and M. Bloch (eds), *Money and the Morality of Exchange*. Cambridge: Cambridge University Press, pp. 33–63.
Gaborieau, Marc. 1977. 'Systèmes traditionelles des échanges de services spécialisés contre remuneration dans une localité du Népal Central', *Purusartha* 3: 1–70.
Gellner, David N. 1991. 'Hinduism, Tribalism, and the Position of Women: The Problem of Newar Identity' *Man* (N.S.) 26(1): 105–25.
_____. 2016. 'The Idea of Nepal', M.C. Regmi Lecture 2016. (soscbaha.org/wp-content/uploads/2019/11/mcrl2016.pdf).
_____. n.d. 'Ghosts of Hierarchies Past: Disasters, Responsibilities, and Blame in Nepal'.
Gellner, David N. and Declan Quigley (eds). 1995. *Contested Hierarchies: A Collaborative Ethnography of Caste among the Newars of the Kathmandu Valley, Nepal*. Oxford: Clarendon.
Gellner, David N., and Krishna P. Adhikari (eds). 2019. *Nepali Dalits in Transition*, special issue of *Contributions to Nepalese Studies* 46(1).
Gellner, David N., Krishna P. Adhikari and Arjun Bahadur B.K. 2020. 'Dalits in Search of Inclusion: Comparing Nepal with India', in Aakash Singh Rathore (ed.), *B.R. Ambedkar: The Quest for Social Justice, Vol. 2: Social Justice*. Delhi: Oxford University Press, pp. 91–115.
Gregory, Chris A. 1992. 'The Poison in Raheja's Gift: A Review Article', *Social Analysis* 32: 95–110.
Hann, Chris. 2018. 'Moral(ity and) Economy: Work, Workfare, and Fairness in Provincial Hungary', *European Journal of Sociology* 59(2): 225–54.
Hocart, Arthur M. 1950. *Caste: A Comparative Study*. London: Methuen.
Inden, Ronald. 1990. *Imagining India*. Oxford: Blackwell.
Jodhka, Surinder S. 1998. 'From "Book View" to "Field View": Social Anthropological Constructions of the Indian Village', *Oxford Development Studies* 26(3): 311–31.
_____. 2002. 'Nation and Village: Images of Rural India in Gandhi, Nehru and Ambedkar', *Economic and Political Weekly* (Aug): 3343–53.
Kosambi, D.D. 1970. *The Culture and Civilisation of Ancient India in Historical Outline*. Delhi: Vikas.
Kumar, Mukul. 2016. 'Contemporary Relevance of *Jajmani* Relations in Rural India', *Journal of Rural Studies* 48: 1–10.
Mayer, Peter. 1993. 'Inventing Village Tradition: The Late 19th Century Origins of the North Indian "Jajmani System"', *Modern Asian Studies* 27(2): 357–95.

Mines, Diane P., and Nicolas Yazgi (eds). 2010. *Village Matters: Relocating Villages in the Contemporary Anthropology of India*. Delhi: Oxford University Press.

Mosse, David. 2018. 'Caste and Development: Contemporary Perspectives on a Structure of Discrimination and Advantage', *World Development* 110: 422–36.

Parry, Jonathan P. 1986. '*The Gift*, the Indian Gift and the "Indian Gift"', *Man* 21(3): 453–73.

_____. 1991. 'The Hindu Lexicographer? A Note on Auspiciousness and Purity', *Contributions to Indian Sociology* (n.s.) 25(2): 267–85.

_____. 1998. 'Mauss, Dumont and the Distinction between Status and Power', in W. James and N.J. Allen (eds), *Marcel Mauss: A Centenary Tribute*. Oxford: Berghahn Books, pp. 151–72.

Pfaff-Czarnecka, Joanna. 2018. 'Nepal and the Wealth of Knowledge: Inequality, Aspiration, Competition and Belonging', M.C. Regmi Lecture. Kathmandu: Social Science Baha.

_____. 2019. 'Burdened Futures: Educated Dalits' Quandaries in Contemporary Nepal', *Contributions to Nepalese Studies* 46(1): 55–87.

Piliavsky, Anastasia (ed.). 2014. *Patronage as Politics in India*. Cambridge: Cambridge University Press.

Quigley, Declan. 1993. *The Interpretation of Caste*. Oxford: Clarendon.

Raheja, Gloria G. 1988a. *The Poison in the Gift: Ritual, Prestation, and the Dominant Caste in a North Indian Village*. Chicago: University of Chicago Press.

_____. 1988b. 'India: Caste, Kingship, and Dominance Reconsidered', *Annual Review of Anthropology* 17: 497–522.

Shah, Alpa, Jens Lerche, Richard Axelby, Dalel Benbabaali, Brendan Donegan, Jayaseelan Raj and Vikramaditya Thakur. 2018. *Ground Down by Growth: Tribe, Caste, Class and Inequality in Twenty-First-Century India*. London: Pluto Press.

Srinivas, M.N. 1987 [1975]. 'The Indian Village: Myth and Reality', in *The Dominant Caste and Other Essays*. Delhi: Oxford University Press, pp. 20–59.

Sunam, Ramesh, and Krishna Shrestha 2019. 'Failing the Most Excluded: A Critical Analysis of Nepal's Affirmative Action Policy', *Contributions to Nepalese Studies* 46(1): 143–65.

Thorat, Sukhadeo, Nitin Tagade and Ajaya K. Naik. 2016. 'Prejudice against Reservation Policies: How and Why?', *Economic and Political Weekly* 51(6): 61–69.

Wadley, Susan. 1994. *Struggling With Destiny in Karimpur, 1925–1984*. Berkeley: University of California Press.

Wiser, Charlotte V., and William H. Wiser 1932. *Behind Mud Walls*. London: G. Allen & Unwin.

Wiser, William H. 1936. *The Hindu Jajmani System: A Socio-economic System Interrelating Members of a Hindu Village Community in Services*. Lucknow: Lucknow Publishing House.

Chapter 20

Polanyi Goes to Mauritius
Economy and Society in the Postcolony

Thomas Hylland Eriksen

Shortly after arriving in Mauritius in early 1986, I was struck by the different ways in which people marked the boundaries of their real estate. Most Mauritians lived in single-family houses, from the very modest (a few still had roofs made of straw, and many lacked piped water and electricity) to the extravagantly opulent. Some Mauritians had high fences and iron gates surrounding their house and garden; others made do with low fences in bricks and mortar; yet others had nothing at all with which to mark the physical boundaries of their property, their yards segueing into those of their neighbours, dogs, chickens and children freely roaming across invisible boundaries with no sanctions imposed.

These differences may be said to be all about class. The more you own, the more jealously you protect it. Ethnographic fieldwork among the poor tends to be easy, at least in terms of access, since they have nothing to lose and everything to gain by allowing a stranger into their lives; by the same token, elite studies raise particular methodological problems regarding regular access. However, in polyethnic Mauritius, class cannot be understood without taking ethnicity into account. The two markers of ethnic difference and social inequality are not entirely congruent, but overlap. Briefly, then, the houses hemmed in by high fences would typically belong to the Franco-Mauritian elite, descendants of the plantocracy that settled in the island with their slaves in the eighteenth century. Those with lower fences that you could easily peer or climb over would often be Hindus, descendants mainly of the indentured labourers recruited from British India to replace the emancipated slaves, arriving in the island from 1840 until the First World War. And the third category, those whose territorial boundaries mattered least, if at all, would tend to be Creoles, descendants of the aforementioned slaves.

Chris Hann's important and highly influential work in economic anthropology has a consistent empirical basis in his long-term and ongoing fieldwork in Eastern and Central Europe. On one of my first visits to the then recently established Max Planck Institute in Halle, he casually remarked that in his department, the ethnographic focus was on 'anywhere east of Halle'. At the same time, Hann's comparativist approach implies significant theoretical ambitions, as witnessed in his theorizing, inspired by Jack Goody's wide-ranging comparative research, about Eurasia as a region as opposed to (Sub-Saharan) Africa or the societies of the New World. Moreover, Hann has engaged increasingly with questions of values and religion as they articulate with the economy (which, in a market society, emphasizes value rather than values), a perspective which is expressed strongly in his recent REALEURASIA project, which draws equally on Polanyi's economic history and Weber's sociology of religion as sources of inspiration (Hann 2016).

In this contribution, I draw inspiration from Hann's recent publications, including his important new monograph about markets in the postsocialist Visegrád states of Central Europe (Hann 2019), in a reflection on economy and society in the post-slavery plantation and industrial society of Mauritius, discussing to what extent his Eurasian perspectives can shed light on a main social, economic and cultural faultline in the island, namely that which can be drawn between Hindus and Creoles.

The Plural Economy of Mauritius

It is not obvious that Polanyi has any business going to Mauritius. It is in many ways a New World society, uninhabited upon colonization in the early 18th century. Yet some of its dominant demographic groups, notably the Chinese, the Hindus and the Europeans, arguably carry with them a heavy baggage from the Old World where economy was not yet disembedded from society. Franco-Mauritians, whose ancestors might have arrived on the island before the 1789 revolution, may routinely assume a semi-feudal relationship with their maids and gardeners, which entails moral obligations and responsibilities towards them beyond that of paying salaries. For example, if a housemaid falls ill, her employer would typically take pains to ensure proper medical treatment, and should a gardener's son be a drug addict, the employer would be likely to look for ways to help. Regarding the Chinese, or more accurately Sino-Mauritians (most arrived at the outset of the 20th century and cannot be considered simply Chinese), their economic organization is based on kinship, more accurately the hierarchical patrilineal clan. The Muslims, whose Indian ancestors arrived as indentured labourers on the same ships as the Hindus, share many practices with the Hindus in their local organization. In this short analysis, I limit myself to a comparison between Creole and Hindu economic practices.

Social life in Mauritius is all about striking a balance between difference and similarity, unity and diversity. Seen by many if not most Mauritians as a 'rainbow society' managing its cultural and ethnic diversity in peaceful ways, the island, independent since 1968, is a functioning parliamentary democracy with the rudiments of a welfare state. At the same time, there are strong correlations between class and ethnicity, the causes of which are complex, while the effects are highly visible in Mauritian society.

The traditional upper class (historically slaveowners, currently large landowners) is made up exclusively of Franco-Mauritians, *les quinze familles* of estate owners. There are nevertheless economic elites in every ethnic group except the Creoles, and the Sino-Mauritian minority in particular have been active forging and renewing ties with Hong Kong, China and Singapore since the industrialization of Mauritius and the surging forward of the Chinese economy. The large landowners remain Franco-Mauritian, but others also own land, usually for growing sugarcane or raising livestock.

Le petit morcellement, 'the small subdivision [of land]', took place between the end of slavery in 1839 and 1851. As shown by Richard Allen (1999), a large number of ex-slaves purchased land in this process and took up farming. As further emphasized by Peerthum (2016), there was in Mauritius a great deal of arable land available at the end of slavery, unlike in some Caribbean islands. The ex-slaves, or Creoles, who set up shop as independent farmers, grew a variety of crops for their own consumption as well as the market. Other ex-apprentices became agricultural labourers on one of the large plantations, smallplanters or *métayers* (sharecroppers). However, already by 1851, the proportion of Creoles who engaged in agriculture had dropped significantly (Peerthum 2016). Peerthum proposes several explanations for this shift, including demographic change (Indian immigration mainly) and high mortality, but the most important single factor was arguably the lack of credit. Setting up a small (or indeed large) agricultural enterprise in a remote colony involves many uncertainties and depends on the availability of credit. This was generally not available through the banks, which de facto forced the Creole farmers to relinquish their enterprises.

This historical detail deserves some attention because it later became a stereotype, still alive today, to assume that Creoles have an aversion to agricultural work. By the late twentieth and early twenty-first centuries, few Creoles are involved in either livestock or sugarcane, except as employees, and in the latter case, they tend to work at the mill and not in the field.

Le grand morcellement from the 1860s to the early 1900s had more enduring consequences and offers an important contrast to the immediate postslavery situation. It was aimed to enable Indian migrant workers to contribute more effectively to the economy after the end of their indentureship. As many as 400,000 Indians arrived as indentured labourers to boost production and replace the slaves, changing the demographic composition of the island completely. When slavery ended in 1839, Mauritians of African origin constituted the majority of the population; since the end of Indian indentureship, they have made up less than 30 per cent. When the indentureship contracts of the Indians expired, the colonial authorities saw it as useful to encourage them to stay, which the vast majority did, most as plantation workers, but many eventually as independent small planters. They purchased land and paid their debts while mainly producing sugar and keeping livestock, usually cattle (Benedict 1961).

By the time Mauritius became independent in 1968, an ethnic division of labour was well established (see Eriksen 1988; Selvon 2001). The Franco-Mauritians (≈2 per cent) were landowners and professionals; the majority of the Hindus (52 per cent) were small planters and plantation labourers; the Creoles (28 per cent, of African and Malagasy origin) were fishermen, craftsmen and factory workers at the plantations; the *gens de couleur* (≈3 per cent, of mixed European-African origin) were professionals such as lawyers, teachers and journalists, the Chinese (3 per cent) were shopkeepers and the Muslims (16 per cent) were mainly field labourers, but were also represented in many other professions. Naturally, there were many exceptions to these crude generalizations, which nevertheless continued, and continue even today, to serve as a cognitive map designating the groups that made up the 'plural society' (Furnivall 1948) of Mauritius and their place in the economy of the island-state.

The late colonial division of the population into four large statistical categories was inconsistent and inaccurate; the four 'communities' were Hindus, Muslims, Chinese and the 'General Population'. The latter includes Creoles, people of mixed origin and Franco-Mauritians, presumably on the basis of their shared Catholic religion, but they have no common identity that can be mobilized economically or politically. Sino-Mauritians speak different dialects (Hakka and Cantonese), and although most are Buddhists, many are Catholics. They are divided by clan membership, origins and religion. The approximate half of the population who are Hindus do not share a strong corporate identity either. Although the largest segments are of North Indian origin, Tamils, Telugus and Marathis are also present in numbers that are not negligible and consider themselves – and are considered by others – as forming separate groups. Caste is important in politics, marriage practices and informal networking, although it is undercommunicated publicly. The Muslims, who are of Indian origin, are not typically described as Indians (*lendyen* in Kreol), but are defined on the basis of religion (see Eriksen (1988, 1998) for more details).

The Significance of Ethnicity

Overt racism or 'communalism' is frowned upon and sanctioned morally. Yet at the same time, there is no public encouragement for the 'communities' to mix through intermarriage, even if this is not uncommon and exists across Mauritian society (Eriksen 1998). In fact, in the early 1990s, the Catholic Archbishop of the Mascareignes, Mgr. Jean Margéot, echoed a widely shared sentiment when he said that the colours of the rainbow (society) should be kept distinct in order for it to remain beautiful (Eriksen 1997). With the exception of certain milieus, informal networks are usually monoethnic and people primarily tend to rely on their ethnic, religious and kinship networks for support. Mauritius is a liberal multiparty democracy, and thus the ethnic organization of society, especially in the realms of politics and the economy, is regularly criticized and challenged. Yet, ethnicity remains very resilient. The Franco-Mauritian elite has largely retained its control over the national economy despite fifty years of independence (Salverda 2015), and Creoles are seriously overrepresented among the deprived and impoverished segments of society (Boswell 2006).

The downside of the officially recognized multiculturalism of Mauritian society is evident in the persistence of ethnic stereotyping and uneven development. Although racism is strongly disapproved of in public settings, ethnic stereotypes are routinely drawn upon in informal social life in order to account for political and economic events. While Hindus may speak of Creoles as lazy and undisciplined, the corresponding Creole stereotype may depict Hindus as stingy and 'clannish'. These stereotypes build on real existing differences in social and economic organization.

Economic changes in Mauritius since the mid-1980s have all but eradicated unemployment, improved the material standard of living considerably and led to massive infrastructural development, from highways and shopping centres to a light railway currently being built to connect the main urban centres, from Curepipe in central Mauritius to Port Louis, the capital, in the northwest. At the same time, not all have benefited equally from the economic boom, a result of deregulation leading to fast growth in the manufacturing sector and a consolidation of tourism and sugar as important earners of foreign currency. Many villages and suburbs (*cités ouvrières*) primarily inhabited by Creoles have changed, or developed, far less than the majority of the country. In the 1990s, concerned clergymen from the Catholic Church began to speak about *le malaise créole* (the Creole ailment) as a social ill, the symptoms of which were underemployment and an overrepresentation in unskilled, badly paid work, substance abuse and teenage pregnancies, a lack of strong organizations and interest groups, and low social mobility compared to the rest of the population (Boswell 2006).

Polanyi, Creoles and Hindus

I will now consider the Creole–Hindu contrast roughly through the same Polanyian lens as that employed by Hann in his recent work (especially Hann 2019). Obviously, the differences are substantial. In Hann's work, the state is a central actor as a legislative and redistributive force, while markets were less dominant during the socialist years. Although Mauritius has the rudiments of a welfare state, the formal economic system is emphatically capitalist and market-oriented. At a first glance, Mauritius is thus a poor candidate for a study of the double movement and the possible embeddedness of the economy in social institutions. The fictitious commodities (Polanyi 1944) of land, labour and money were always taken for granted in the colony and are no less so in independent Mauritius, which remains a small cog in the global capitalist economy. Settled in the eighteenth century as a trading port and, increasingly throughout the nineteenth century, a sugar colony, the proto-factory of the plantation (Mintz 1974) and the warehouse by the port were the templates of the Mauritian economy from the first day. As noted by Benedict (1964), the cash economy was part of the Indian indentured workers' lives from the very beginning, and the liberated slaves also immediately incorporated cash into their economy, often using it, as noted above, to buy land.

In other words, there were no traditional forms of land tenure or a premonetized economy in Mauritius, and labour was also commoditized from the beginning – indeed, in the most brutal and demeaning ways. Would it still make sense to look for a double movement? Of the four

Polanyian forms of integration – redistribution, reciprocity, householding and market exchange – it may seem obvious that the latter dominates in Mauritius. However, as emphasized by Polanyi himself and demonstrated by Hann on numerous occasions, not least in his long-term research in Tázlár, Hungary, the fact that one form of (economic) integration is dominant does not mean that it is the only one. Moreover, identifying the dominant form of integration is not always easy and straightforward.

In the Creole village most familiar to me in the 1980s and 1990s, paid work tended to be irregular, temporary and uncertain. Many families had their main source of income through fishing, itself an unpredictable endeavour, and supplemented this through road maintenance work for the government, secretarial jobs in local administration and odd day jobs, while some had regular wagework outside the village. About half a dozen of the women worked in the salt pans at Tamarin a short bus ride away, while others were employed in one of the luxury hotels at Le Morne, also just a few kilometres away. There are no major sugar plantations in the area, which is the driest in Mauritius. Moreover, there was a substantial informal sector involving fowls and pigs, marijuana and miscellaneous services.

Although the village is massively dominated by Creoles numerically, other communities are also represented, and the division of labour is strikingly ethnic in character. The village grocery is run by a Sino-Mauritian family, like many similar shops on the island. The only Muslim family in the village is responsible for the dispensary and complains of being socially isolated. A handful of Hindu families also live in the village, which is located in a part of the island that is strongly associated with the Creoles, although the large village La Gaulette nearby is mainly Hindu. Some of the Hindus were small planters selling their produce to factories further north, one joint family consisted of a schoolteacher and a small businessman, and at least two families ran small shops selling sweets, cigarettes and other inexpensive items. The village economy also encompassed the services of itinerant hawkers on motorcycles, who passed through once or twice a week selling items of clothing, household utensils, pickled mangoes and miscellaneous small goods. The hawkers were all Hindu (including Tamil). Another itinerant trader of more substantial influence was the *banyan* or middleman, also a Hindu, who was a wholesale buyer of fish from the local fishermen.

Market exchange has been the main form of economic integration in Mauritius since its foundation as a colony, but it was never the only one, and I should argue that it is not even the dominant form at the level of local integration.

Hindu and Creole forms of social organization are in some respects strikingly different from one another. Hindus have deep genealogies, patrilineal kinship systems supplemented by caste and strong moral injunctions to take responsibility for relatives. Drawing on village fieldwork in the late 1950s, Benedict (1964) showed the ways in which Hindus were able to pool money for major investments, offer interest-free loans to each other within the extended kin group and make collective plans for their economic improvement. Strategic alliances between kin groups were forged through arranged marriages (and still are).

The Creole moral economy is based on a different set of values and, one might say, a different concept of personhood. Individual freedom is valued highly among Creoles. Possibly a legacy from slavery (Eriksen 1986), this value encourages creativity in music and the arts – many of the most popular musicians and poets are Creoles – while at the same time militating against collective organization. Creole genealogies are shallow, no strict principle of endogamy is practised, and rules of inheritance are flexible. While social mobility in other ethnic groups in Mauritius often relies on connections and networks established within the group, this is not possible to the same extent among Creoles. Partly owing to the weak kinship organization, upwardly mobile Creoles have no culturally sanctioned obligation to help less resourceful Creoles to improve their lot. Among Hindus, by contrast, it is a paramount kinship obligation to assist family members if one has the opportunity to do so.

It might seem, at first glance, as if the Creole ethos – individualist, presentist – is perfectly compatible with, and indeed encompassed by, the logic of market exchange, while the Hindu ethos remains staunchly Eurasian (in Hann's sense; Hann 2015, 2016) in incorporating the economy seamlessly into social life, where reciprocity and redistribution are necessary elements in the reproduction of the community. However, the reality is more complicated.

Sharing is a moral obligation in the Creole community. Fishermen whiling away the day after returning from sea may congregate in the shade of a clump of large trees near the village shop, where they play dominoes and share whatever snacks, drinks and cigarettes they have. When I first arrived in the village, I knew nobody and asked the first person I met if he knew a family that might be able to rent out a room. He consulted his friends and they agreed that I should approach a particular family because they were struggling and needed the money. Like the Caribbean island Providencia described in Peter J. Wilson's *Crab Antics* (Wilson 1978), persons who have received a windfall without sharing with their neighbours and friends are frowned upon and avoided. Economic resources are perceived not as an end in themselves, but as a means to strengthen friendship, social capital, moral standing and a host of other qualities reminiscent not only of Polanyi's descriptions but also of Mauss' exploration of reciprocity (Mauss 1954 [1925]).

Among Hindus, accounts are kept, debts of gratitude are quantified, often in pecuniary ways, and the 'fictitious commodities' of land and labour are taken seriously. At the same time, their economy and society, at the local and domestic levels, are thoroughly 'Eurasian' in the sense that they are seamlessly integrated, often through the principles and practices of kinship (cf. Hann (2019: 163) on classes and clans). The disembedding presumably wrought by the monetization of the economy has not taken place either with the Hindus or with the Creoles, although their historical trajectories were very different: with the Hindus, there was a deep continuity with India and they were able to re-create their Hindu villages after arrival in Mauritius (Eisenlohr 2001). The ancestors of Creoles were uprooted and severed from their social and political life in Africa, and were thrown into the cruel, dehumanizing world of slavery. The fact that something resembling a human economy (Hann and Hart 2009) has grown out of the legacy of slavery may suggest that the opening lines of Polanyi's *The Great Transformation*, where the author argues that laissez-faire economics have proved their limitations once and for all, still hold true. Market exchange is necessary for the supply–demand mechanism to function, but it is totally inadequate as an organizing principle for society.

Human Economy in the Disembedded Society

Redistribution, reciprocity and householding are fundamental to the economic lives of both Hindus and Creoles in village Mauritius, although in different forms and based on different histories, kinship systems, moral principles and notions of personhood. In this brief chapter, I have exaggerated the contrast, and the usual caveats apply. Of course, there are hybrid forms, individual exceptions, historical changes and various idiosyncrasies. However, since the moral obligations founded in kinship differ between Creoles and Hindus, and since their economic situation differs owing to the different outcomes of the *morcellements* of the nineteenth century, the structural difference between the groups is there, notwithstanding individual variations. Moreover, just as the double movement witnessed by Hann in postsocialist Central Europe produces tensions between a moral economy and a pecuniary economy, so are comparable tensions visible in Mauritius, between 'redistribution and exchange as the dominant forms of integration' (Hann 2019: 326), although the former takes place at the community level and involves the state to a lesser degree than in Hann's material. This observation nevertheless suggests that Hann's ambitious comparative work across Eurasian societies may fruitfully include some of their diasporic offspring as well, and that the state may not necessarily be the main or even most efficient source of redistributive practices.

Thomas Hylland Eriksen is Professor of Social Anthropology at the University of Oslo and former President of the European Association of Social Anthropologists. His research has mainly focused on the cultural implications of globalization, identity politics and creolization. Recently, he has directed research on 'overheating', accelerated global change and its local implications.

References

Allen, Richard. 1999. *Slaves, Freedmen, and Indentured Labourers in Colonial Mauritius*. Cambridge: Cambridge University Press.
Benedict, Burton. 1961. *Indians in a Plural Society: A Report on Mauritius*. London: Her Majesty's Stationery Office.
_____. 1964. 'Capital, Saving and Credit among Mauritian Indians', in Raymond Firth and B. S. Yamey (eds), *Capital, Saving and Credit in Peasant Societies*. London: Allen & Unwin, pp. 330–46.
Boswell, Rosabelle. 2006. *Le Malaise Créole: Ethnic Identity in Mauritius*. Oxford: Berghahn Books.
Eisenlohr, Patrick. 2001. *Little India: Diaspora, Time and Ethnolinguistic Belonging in Hindu Mauritius*. Berkeley: University of California Press.
Eriksen, Thomas Hylland. 1986. 'Creole Culture and Social Change', *Journal of Mauritian Studies* 1(2): 59–72.
_____. 1988. 'Communicating Cultural Difference and Identity: Ethnicity and Nationalism in Mauritius', Oslo: Department of Social Anthropology, Occasional Papers, No. 16.
_____. 1997. 'Multiculturalism, Individualism and Human Rights', in Richard A. Wilson (ed.), *Human Rights, Culture and Context*. London: Pluto Press, pp. 49–69.
_____. 1998. *Common Denominators: Ethnicity, Nation-Building and Compromise in Mauritius*. Oxford: Berg.
Furnivall, J.S. 1948. *Colonial Policy and Practice: A Comparative Study of Burma and Netherlands India*. Cambridge: Cambridge University Press.
Hann, Chris. 2015. 'Goody, Polanyi and Eurasia: An Unfinished Project in Comparative Historical Economic Anthropology', *History and Anthropology*, 26(3): 308–20.
_____. 2016. 'A Concept of Eurasia', *Current Anthropology* 57(1): 1–27.
_____. 2019. *Repatriating Polanyi: Market Society in the Visegrád States*. Budapest: Central European University Press.

Hann, Chris, and Keith Hart (eds). 2009. *Market and Society: The Great Transformation Today*. Cambridge: Cambridge University Press.
Mauss, Marcel. 1954 [1925]. *The Gift*, trans. Ian Cunnison. Glencoe, IL: Free Press.
Mintz, Sidney. 1974. *Caribbean Transformations*. Chicago: Aldine.
Peerthum, Satyendra. 2016. '"Making a Life of Their Own": Ex-apprentices in Early Post-emancipation Period, 1839–1872', in Abdul Sheriff, Vijayalakshmi Teelock, Saada Omar Wahab and Satyendra Peerthum, *Transition from Slavery in Zanzibar and Mauritius: A Comparative History*. Dakar: CODESRIA, pp. 109–48.
Polanyi, Karl. 1944. *The Great Transformation: The Political and Economic Origins of Our Time*. New York: Rinehart.
Salverda, Tijo. 2015. *The Franco-Mauritian Elite: Power and Anxiety in the Face of Change*. Oxford: Berghahn Books.
Selvon, Sydney. 2001. *A Comprehensive History of Mauritius*. Port Louis: Mauritius Press.
Wilson, Peter J. 1978. *Crab Antics*, 2nd edn. New Haven: Yale University Press.

Publications by Chris Hann

Note: Reports, reviews, translated books and articles, newspaper articles, commentaries and blog entries are not included.

Books

2021

ed., *Work, Society, and the Ethical Self: Chimeras of Freedom in the Neoliberal Era.* New York: Berghahn Books.

2020

ed., with Don Kalb. *Financialization: Relational Approaches.* New York: Berghahn Books.

2019

Repatriating Polanyi: Market Society in the Visegrád States. Budapest: Central European University Press.

2018

ed., with Johann P. Arnason. *Anthropology and Civilizational Analysis: Eurasian Explorations.* Albany: SUNY Press.

ed., with Jonathan Parry. *Industrial Labor on the Margins of Capitalism: Precarity, Class, and the Neoliberal Subject.* New York: Berghahn Books.

2015

ed., with Stephen Gudeman. *Economy and Ritual: Studies of Postsocialist Transformations*. New York: Berghahn Books.
ed., with Stephen Gudeman. *Oikos and Market: Explorations in Self-Sufficiency after Socialism*. New York: Berghahn Books.

2013

ed., with Aleksandar Bošković. *The Anthropological Field on the Margins of Europe, 1945–1991*. Berlin: LIT Verlag.

2011

with Keith Hart. *Economic Anthropology: History, Ethnography, Critique*. Cambridge: Polity Press.

2010

ed., with Hermann Goltz. *Eastern Christians in Anthropological Perspective*. Berkeley: University of California Press.

2009

ed., with Keith Hart. *Market and Society: The Great Transformation Today*. Cambridge: Cambridge University Press.
ed., *The Postsocialist Religious Question: Faith and Power in Central Asia and East-Central Europe*. Münster: LIT Verlag.

2008

Antropologia Społeczna. Kraków: Wydawnictwo Uniwersytetu Jagiellońskiego.

2006

'Not the Horse We Wanted!' Postsocialism, Neoliberalism, and Eurasia. Münster: LIT Verlag.

2005

ed., with Paul R. Magocsi. *Galicia: A Multicultured Land*. Toronto: University of Toronto Press.
ed., with Mihály Sárkány and Peter Skalník. *Studying Peoples in the People's Democracies: Socialist Era Anthropology in East-Central Europe*. Münster: LIT Verlag.

2003

with Ildikó Bellér-Hann. *Iki Buçuk Yaprak Çay: Dogu Karadeniz'de; Devlet, Piyasa, Kimlik*. Istanbul: İletişim Yayınları.

ed., with the 'Property Relations' Group. *The Postsocialist Agrarian Question: Property Relations and the Rural Condition*. Münster: LIT Verlag.

2002

ed., *Postsocialism: Ideals, Ideologies and Practices in Eurasia*. London: Routledge.

2000

Social Anthropology. Teach Yourself Books. Lincolnwood: NTC Publishing Group.

with Ildikó Bellér-Hann. 2000. *Turkish Region: State, Market & Social Identities on the East Black Sea Coast*. Oxford: Currey.

ed., with Stanisław Stępień. *Tradycja a tożsamość: Wywiady wśród mniejszości ukraińskiej w Przemyślu* [*Tradition and Identity: Interviews among the Ukrainian Minority in Przemyśl*]. Przemyśl: Południowo-Wschodni Instytut Naukowy w Przemyślu.

1998

ed., *Property Relations: Renewing the Anthropological Tradition*. Cambridge: Cambridge University Press.

1996

ed., with Elizabeth Dunn. *Civil Society: Challenging Western Models*. European Association of Social Anthropologists. London: Routledge.

1994

The Skeleton at the Feast: Contributions to East European Anthropology. Canterbury: University of Kent.

ed., *When History Accelerates: Essays on Rapid Social Change, Complexity and Creativity*. London: Athlone.

1993

ed., *Socialism: Ideals, Ideologies, and Local Practice*. London: Routledge.

1990

ed., *Market Economy and Civil Society in Hungary*. London: Frank Cass.
Tea and the Domestication of the Turkish State. Huntingdon: Eothen Press.

1985

A Village without Solidarity: Polish Peasants in Years of Crisis. New Haven: Yale University Press.

1980

Tázlár: A Village in Hungary. Cambridge: Cambridge University Press.

Articles and Book Chapters

2021

'Introduction: Work and Ethics in Anthropology', in Chris Hann ed., *Work, Society and the Ethical Self: Chimeras of Freedom in the Neoliberal Era*. New York: Berghahn Books.

2020

'In Search of Civil Society: From Peasant Populism to Postpeasant Illiberalism in Provincial Hungary', *Social Science Information* 59(3): 459–83.
'Marketization and Development on a European Periphery: From Peasant Oikos to Socialism and Neoliberal Capitalism on the Danube-Tisza Interfluve', *Environment and Planning A* 52(1): 200–15.
'Preface', in Chris Hann and Don Kalb (eds.). *Financialization: Relational Approaches*. New York: Berghahn Books, pp. ix-xii.

2019

'Anthropology and Populism', *Anthropology Today* 35(1): 1–2.
'Azok a 90-es évek, Kiskunhalason: külföldi szemmel', in József Kovácz and Aurél Szakál (eds), *Kiskunhalas Története: Tanulmányok Kiskunhalasról a 20. század második feléből* 4. Kiskunhalas: Kiskunhalas Város Önkormányzata; Halasi Múzeum Alapítvány; Thorma János Múzeum, pp. 551–65.
'Multiple Pasts for a Troubled Present: The Case of Hungary', *ISRF Bulletin* (XVIII): 31–36.
'Resilience and Transformation in Provincial Political Economy: From Market Socialism to Market Populism in Hungary, 1970s–2010s', *Cargo* (1–2): 1–23.
'The Road to Populism', *Global Dialogue* 9(3): 21–22.
'The Seductions of Europe and the Solidarities of Eurasia', *Lud* 103: 31–47.

'Socialism: Ethics, Ideologies, and Outcomes', in Jeremy MacClancy (ed.), *Exotic No More: Anthropology for the Contemporary World*. Chicago: University of Chicago Press, pp. 121–36.
'Threats to Regional Identity: From Atheist Communists to the Virgin Mary', *Nationalities Papers* 47(3): 526–29.
'Zsákutcából zsákutcába? A rendszerváltás Kiskunhalason; Polányi szemével', *Eszmélet* 123: 55–65.

2018

'Afterword: Anthropology, Eurasia and Global History', in Johann P. Arnason and Chris Hann (eds), *Anthropology and Civilizational Analysis: Eurasian Explorations*. Albany: SUNY Press, pp. 339–353.
'Countryside – Soul of the Nation: Ideals and Realities in Contemporary Hungary', in Magdalena Marszałek, Werner Nell and Marc Weiland (eds), *Über Land: Aktuelle literatur- und kulturwissenschaftliche Perspektiven auf Dorf und Ländlichkeit*. Bielefeld: Transcript, pp. 187–200.
'Economic Anthropology', in Hilary Callan (ed.), *The International Encyclopedia of Anthropology* Vol. 4. Hoboken; Chichester: Wiley Blackwell, pp. 1708–1723.
'Eurasian Dynamics: From Agrarian Axiality to the Connectivities of the Capitalocene', *Comparativ* 28(4): 14–27.
'John Rankine Goody, 1919-2015', *Biographical Memoirs of Fellows of the British Academy* XVI: 456–481.
'Marketization and Development on a European Periphery: From Peasant Oikos to Socialism and Neoliberal Capitalism on the Danube-Tisza Interfluve', *Environment and Planning A*: 1–24.
'Morality and Economy: Work, Workfare, and Fairness in Provincial Hungary', *Archives Européennes de Sociologie* 59(2): 225–54.
'Preface', in Chris Hann and Jonathan Parry (eds), *Industrial Labor on the Margins of Capitalism: Precarity, Class, and the Neoliberal Subject*. New York: Berghahn Books, pp. ix–xi.
'Preface: Recognizing Eurasia', *Comparativ* 28(4): 7–13.
'Ritual and Economy: From Mutual Embedding to Non-profit Festivalisation in Provincial Hungary', *Lietuvos Etnologija* 18(27): 9–34.

2017

'Embeddedness and Effervescence: Political Economy and Community Sociality through a Century of Transformations in Rural Hungary', *Ethnologie Française* 3(167): 543–53.
'Eurázsia ma: Kínai biciklik, német autók és vidéki magyar közösségek', *Eszmélet* 116: 151–66.
'The Human Economy of Pálinka in Hungary: A Case Study in Longue Durée Lubrication', in David Henig and Nicolette Makovicky (eds), *Economies of Favour after Socialism*. Oxford: Oxford University Press, pp. 117–39.

'Long Live Eurasian Civ! Towards a New Confluence of Anthropology and World History', *Zeitschrift für Ethnologie* 142(2): 225–44.
with Ildikó Bellér-Hann. 'Magic, Science, and Religion in Eastern Xinjiang', in Ildikó Bellér-Hann, Birgit N. Schlyter and Jun Sugawara (eds), *Kashgar Revisited: Uyghur Studies in Memory of Ambassador Gunnar Jarring*. Leiden: Brill, pp. 256–75.
'Making Sense of Eurasia: Reflections on Max Weber and Jack Goody', *New Literary History* 48(4): 685–99.
'Migration und Integration aus der Perspektive der Visegrád-Staaten und -Gesellschaften', in Berlin-Brandenburgische Akademie der Wissenschaften (ed.), *Migration – Integration: Streitgespräche in den Wissenschaftlichen Sitzungen der Versammlung der Berlin-Brandenburgischen Akademie der Wissenschaften am 10. Juni 2016 und am 9. Juni 2017*. Berlin: Berlin-Brandenburgische Akademie der Wissenschaften, pp. 59–66.
'Multiscalar Narrative Identities: Individual and Nation, Europe and Eurasia', *Politeja* 49: 15–36.
'Reflections on an Anglophone Academic Sect', *Australian Journal of Anthropology* 28(2): 242–47.

2016

'The Anthropocene and Anthropology: Micro and Macro Perspectives', *European Journal of Social Theory* 20(1): 183–96.
'A Concept of Eurasia', *Current Anthropology* 57(1): 1–10.
'Cucumbers and Courgettes: Rural Workfare and the New Double Movement in Hungary', *Intersections* 2(2): 38–56.
'Eurovision Identities: Or, How Many Collective Identities Can One Anthropologist Possess?', in Thomas Hylland Eriksen and Elisabeth Schober (eds), *Identity Destabilised: Living in an Overheated World*. London: Pluto Press, pp. 240–49.
'Jack Goody (1919–2015) Obituary', *American Anthropologist* 118(1): 226–29.
'Overheated Underdogs: Civilizational Analysis and Migration on the Danube-Tisza Interfluve', *History and Anthropology* 27(5): 602–16.
'Postcard: Actually Exiting Socialism? Could Cuba Pioneer Forms of Syncretism in the Field of Political Economy?', *Arena* 142: 42–45.
'Postsocialist Populist Malaise: The Elections of 2014 and the Return to Political Monopoly in Rural Hungary', in Elena Soler and Luis Calvo (eds), *Transiciones Culturales: Perspectivas desde Europa Central y del Este*. Madrid: Consejo Superior de Investigaciones Científicas, pp. 25–45.
'The Wisłok Project, 1978–1985', *Lud* 100: 83–92.

2015

with László Kürti. 'Agrarian Ideology and Local Governance: Continuities in Postsocialist Hungary', in Adam Bedřich and Tomáš Retka (eds), *Knight*

from Komárov: To Petr Skalník for His 70th Birthday. Prague: AntropoWeb, pp. 93–115.
'After Ideocracy and Civil Society: Gellner, Polanyi and the New Peripheralization of Central Europe', *Thesis Eleven* 128(1): 41–55.
'Backwardness Revisited: Time, Space, and Civilization in Rural Eastern Europe', *Comparative Studies in Society and History* 57(4): 881–911.
'Carpathian Rusyns: An Unresolved Problem for Eurasia in the Heart of the European Macro-region', in Valerii Padiak and Patricia A. Krafcik (eds), *A Jubilee Collection: Essays in Honor of Paul Robert Magocsi on His 70th Birthday*. New York: Valerii Padiak Publishers, pp. 247–57.
'Declining Europe: A Reply to Alessandro Testa', *Anthropology of East Europe Review* 33(2): 89–93.
'The Fragility of Europe's Willkommenskultur', *Anthropology Today* 31(6): 1–2.
'Goody, Polanyi and Eurasia: An Unfinished Project in Comparative Historical Economic Anthropology', *History and Anthropology* 26(3): 308–20.
with Stephen Gudeman. 'Introduction: Ritual, Economy, and the Institutions of the Base', in Stephen Gudeman (ed.), *Economy and Ritual: Studies of Postsocialist Transformations*. New York: Berghahn Books, pp. 1–30.
with Stephen Gudeman. 'Introduction: Self-Sufficiency as Reality and as Myth, in Stephen Gudeman (ed.), *Oikos and Market: Explorations in Self-Sufficiency after Socialism*. New York: Berghahn Books, pp. 1–23.
'(Kultur-)Kämpfe der Gegenwart: Deutschland, Ukraine, Europa, Eurasien', in Ingo Schneider and Martin Sexl (eds), *Das Unbehagen an der Kultur*. Hamburg: Argument Verlag, pp. 157–79.
'Minderheiten, Mehrsprachigkeit und Kofferpacken im 20. Jahrhundert: in Osteuropa und anderswo', in Dietmar Müller and Adamantios Skordos (eds), *Leipziger Zugänge zur rechtlichen, politischen und kulturellen Verflechtungsgeschichte Ostmitteleuropas*. Leipzig: Leipziger Universitätsverlag, pp. 279–90.
'Obštirnata gradina na Antropologijata i nejnite bezkrajno plodonosni poleta', *Bălgarska Etnologija* XLI(3): 361–73.
'Property: Anthropological Aspects', in James D. Wright (ed.), *International Encyclopedia of the Social & Behavioral Sciences 19*. Amsterdam: Elsevier, pp. 153–59.
'Ungarn: ein Land Mitteleuropas oder Mitteleurasiens?', in Johann P. Arnason, Petr Hlaváček and Stefan Troebst (eds), *Mitteleuropa? Zwischen Realität, Chimäre und Konzept*. Prague: Univerzita Karlova v Praze, Filozofická Fakulta: Filosofia, pp. 115–31.
'Why Postimperial Trumps Postsocialist: Crying Back the National Past in Hungary', in Olivia Angé and David Berliner (eds), *Anthropology and Nostalgia*. New York: Berghahn Books, pp. 96–122.
'Wo und wann war Eurasien? Kontrastierende Geschichtskonstruktionen auf kontinentaler Ebene', in Jürgen Heyde et al. (eds), *Dekonstruieren und doch erzählen: Polnische und andere Geschichten*. Göttingen: Wallstein, pp. 285–92.

2014

'After the Euro', *Soundings* 56: 123–36.
'Beyond Cold War, Beyond Otherness: Some Implications of Socialism and Postsocialism for Anthropology', in Christian Giordano, François Ruegg and Andrea Boscoboinik (eds), *Does East Go West? Anthropological Pathways through Postsocialism*. Münster: LIT Verlag, pp. 35–56.
'Birds, Crowns and Christian Europe: The Ritual Symbolism of the Postsocialist Hungarian Nation-State', in Dariusza Niedźwiedzkiego (ed.), *Kultura, Tożsamość, Integracja Europejska*. Kraków: Nomos, pp. 71–84.
'The Economistic Fallacy and Forms of Integration under and after Socialism', *Economy and Society* 43(4): 626–49.
'Evolution, Institutions, and Human Well-Being: Perspectives from a Critical Social Anthropology', *Journal of Bioeconomics* 16(1): 61–69.
'Harmonious or Homogenous? Language, Education and Social Mobility in Rural Uyghur Society', in Trine Brox and Ildikó Bellér-Hann (eds), *On the Fringes of the Harmonious Society: Tibetans and Uyghurs in Socialist China*. Copenhagen: NIAS, pp. 183–208.
'The Heart of the Matter: Christianity, Materiality, and Modernity', *Current Anthropology* 55(S10): S182–S192.
'Imperative Eurasia', *Anthropology Today* 30(4): 1–2.
'Varieties of Capitalism and Varieties of Economic Anthropology', in Vassilis Nitsiakos et al. (eds), *Balkan Border Crossings: Third Annual of the Konitsa Summer School*. Berlin: LIT Verlag, pp. 9–30.

2013

'Introduction: Nations and Nationalism, Societies and Socialism, Fields and Wars', in Aleksandar Bošković and Chris Hann (eds), *The Anthropological Field on the Margins of Europe, 1945–1991*. Berlin: LIT Verlag, pp. 1–28.
'Levels of Parochialism: Welsh-Eurasian Perspectives on a German-European Debate', *Comparativ* 23(4–5): 122–35.
'Merre Forog Az Idő Kereke Tázláron (És A Társadalomnéprajzban)?!', *Eszmélet* 25(4): 167–85.
'Sad Socialisms – and Even Sadder Postsocialisms?', *Androgógia és Művelődéselmélet* 1(1): 11–18.
'Still an Awkward Class: Central European Post-peasants at Home and Abroad in the Era of Neoliberalism', *Praktyka Teoretyczna* 3(9): 176–98.
'The Uncertain Consequences of the Socialist Pursuit of Certainty: The Case of Uyghur Villagers in Eastern Xinjiang, China', *Antípoda* 17: 79–105.
'The Universal and the Particular in Rural Xinjiang: Ritual Commensality and the Mosque Community', in Magnus Marsden and Konstantinos Retsikas (eds), *Articulating Islam: Anthropological Approaches to Muslim Worlds*. Dordrecht: Springer, pp. 171–91.

2012

'Big Revolutions, Two Small Disciplines, and Socialism', in David Shankland (ed.), *Archaeology and Anthropology: Past, Present and Future*. Oxford: Berg, pp. 19–39.

'Civilizational Analysis for Beginners', *Focaal* 62: 113–21.

'Europe in Eurasia', in Ullrich Kockel, Máiréad Nic Craith and Jonas Frykman (eds), *A Companion to the Anthropology of Europe*. Chichester: Wiley Blackwell, pp. 88–102.

'The Europe Trap', *Lud* XCVI: 31–49.

'Faltering Dialogue: For a Doubly Rooted Cosmopolitan Anthropology', *Focaal* (63): 39–50.

'Humans and Their Hierarchies: Cosmological and Sociological', *Archives Européennes de Sociologie* 53(3): 315–22.

'Laiklik and Legitimation in Rural Eastern Xinjiang', in Nils Bubandt and Martijn van Beek (eds), *Varieties of Secularism in Asia: Anthropological Explorations of Religion, Politics and the Spiritual*. London: Routledge, pp. 121–41.

with Ildikó Bellér-Hann. 2012. 'Mágia és vallás a politika árnyékában Kelet-Xinjiangban', in Ildikó Landgraf and Zoltán Nagy (eds), *Az elkerülhetetlen: Vallásantropológiai tanulmányok, Vargyas Gábor tiszteletére*. Budapest: L'Harmattan, pp. 151–70.

'Personhood, Christianity, Modernity', *Anthropology of this Century* 3(January). Retrieved 11 January 2021 from http://aotcpress.com/articles/personhood-christianity-modernity.

'Transition, Tradition, and Nostalgia: Postsocialist Transformations in a Comparative Framework', *Collegium Antropologicum* 36(4): 1119–28.

'Universalismus hinterfragen, Eigentumsbegriffe hinterfragen: Ursprünge der Wirtschaftsethnologie im Leipziger Raum', *Comparativ* 22(2): 126–36.

2011

'Auf der Suche nach Europa: Zwei Beispiele aus der Peripherie einer peripheren Halbinsel', in Reinhard Johler (ed.), *Where Is Europe?/ Wo ist Europa?/ Où est l'Europe?: Dimensionen und Erfahrungen des neuen Europa*. Tübingen: Institut für empirische Sozialforschung, pp. 221–40.

'Back to Civilization', *Anthropology Today* 27(6): 1–2.

'Foreword', in Veronica Strang and Mark Busse (eds), *Ownership and Appropriation*. Oxford: Berg, pp. xv–xvii.

'Moral Dispossession', *InterDisciplines* 2(2): 11–37.

'Ostchristentum und westliche Sozialtheorie', in Anna Briskina-Müller (ed.), *Logos im Dialogos: Auf der Suche nach der Orthodoxie; Gedenkschrift für Hermann Goltz (1946–2010)*. Münster: LIT Verlag, pp. 583–93.

'Predely Konstruktivizma V Teorii Etničnosti: Razdum'ja po povodu "četvertoj Rusi" i "vtoroj Germanii"', in El'za-Bair Gučinova and Galina Komarova (eds), *Antropologija Social'nych Peremen: Sbornik Statej; K 70-Letiju Valerija Aleksandroviča Tiškova*. Moscow: ROSSPĖN, pp. 115–28.

'Smith in Beijing, Stalin in Urumchi: Ethnicity, Political Economy and Violence in Xinjiang, 1759–2009', *Focaal* 60: 108–123.
'Zivilgesellschaft', in Fernand Kreff, Eva-Maria Knoll and Andre Gingrich (eds), *Lexikon der Globalisierung*. Bielefeld: Transcript, pp. 447–50.

2010

'Civil Society', in Alan Barnard and Jonathan Spencer (eds), *The Routledge Encyclopedia of Social and Cultural Anthropology*. London: Routledge, pp. 122–23.
'Class, Clans and Moral Economy in Rural Eurasia', in François Ruegg and Andrea Boscoboinik (eds), *From Palermo to Penang: A Journey into Political Anthropology – De Palerme à Penang: Un Itinéraire En Anthropologie Politique*. Berlin: LIT Verlag, pp. 195–204.
'"Die Sváben und die Tóten sind ausgestorben!" Über Stereotypen und "Kulturen" im ländlichen Ungarn', in Josef Wolf (ed.), *Historische Regionen und ethnisches Gruppenbewusstsein in Ostmittel- und Südosteuropa: Grenzregionen – Kolonisationsräume – Identitätsbildung*. Munich: Oldenbourg, pp. 471–97.
with Hermann Goltz. 'Introduction: The Other Christianity?' in Chris Hann and Hermann Goltz (eds), *Eastern Christians in Anthropological Perspective*. Berkeley: University of California Press, pp. 1–29.
'Moral Economy', in Keith Hart, Jean-Louis Laville and Antonio David Cattani (eds), *The Human Economy: A Citizen's Guide*. Cambridge: Polity Press, pp. 187–98.
'Problems with the (De)Privatization of Religion', in Bryan S. Turner (ed.), *Secularization. Vol.4: The Comparative Sociology of De-Secularization*. Los Angeles: Sage, pp. 137–48.
'Tattered Canopies across Eurasia: New Combinations of the Religious, the Secular, and the (Ethno-)National after Socialism', *Cargo* 1–2: 4–26.

2009

'Does Ethnic Cleansing Work? The Case of Twentieth Century Poland', *Cambridge Anthropology* 29(1): 1–25.
'Embedded Socialism? Land, Labour, and Money in Eastern Xinjiang', in Chris Hann and Keith Hart (eds), *Market and Society: The Great Transformation Today*. Cambridge: Cambridge University Press, pp. 256–71.
'From Ethnographic Group to Sub-sub-ethnicity: Lemko-Rusyn-Ukrainians in Postsocialist Poland', in Elaine Rusinko (ed.), *Committing Community: Carpatho-Rusyn Studies as an Emerging Scholarly Discipline*. New York: Columbia University Press, pp. 175–88.
with Keith Hart. 'Introduction: Learning from Polanyi 1', in Chris Hann and Keith Hart (eds), *Market and Society: The Great Transformation Today*. Cambridge: Cambridge University Press, pp. 1–16.
'Miestne poznanie? Dunajské vízie kapitalizmu od Polanyiho po Kornaia', *Občianska Spoločnost* 3: 98–108.

'Of Conferences and Conflicts: 16th Congress of the IUAES, China, Summer 2009', *Anthropology Today* 25(6): 20–23.
'Poznań Manifesto: For a Public Anthropology in the European Public Sphere', *EASA Newsletter* 50(December 2009): 6–9.
with Mathijs Pelkmans. 'Realigning Religion and Power in Central Asia: Islam, Nation-State and (Post)Socialism', *Europe Asia Studies* 61(9): 1517–41.
'The Rooted Anthropologies of East-Central Europe', in Harry G. West and Parvathi Raman (eds), *Enduring Socialism: Explorations of Revolution and Transformation, Restoration and Continuation*. New York: Berghahn Books, pp. 214–30.
'The Theft of Anthropology', *Theory, Culture & Society* 26(7–8): 126–47.

2008

'Fieldwork in Bulgaria: An Interview with Carol Silverman' in Vintilă Mihăilescu, Ilia Iliev and Slobodan Naumović (eds), *Studying Peoples in the People's Democracies II: Socialist Era Anthropology in South-East Europe*. Münster: LIT Verlag, pp. 397–404.
'Interethnisches Vertrauen im Postkommunistischen Polen: Eine Fallstudie aus Social Anthropological Sicht', in John Eidson (ed.), *Das anthropologische Projekt: Perspektiven aus der Forschungslandschaft Halle/Leipzig*. Leipzig: Leipziger Universitätsverlag, pp. 171–97.
'Preface', in Stéphanie Mahieu and Vlad Naumescu (eds), *Churches In-between: Greek Catholic Churches in Postsocialist Europe*. Berlin: LIT Verlag, pp. vii–xi.
'Reproduction and Inheritance: Goody Revisited', *Annual Review of Anthropology* 37: 145–58.
'Towards a Rooted Anthropology: Malinowski, Gellner and Herderian Cosmopolitanism', in Pnina Werbner (ed.), *Anthropology and the New Cosmopolitanism: Rooted, Feminist and Vernacular Perspectives*. Oxford: Berg, pp. 69–86.

2007

'The Anthropology of Christianity per se', *Archives Européennes de Sociologie* 48(3): 391–418.
'Chronologičeskite orientacii na antropologijata i nejnoto bădešte v Iztočna i Centralna Evropa', *Balgarska Etnologija* 33(2–3): 96–112.
'Comparative Social Structure or Local Folk Culture? Towards a Unified Anthropological Tradition in Eurasia', *Lietuvos Etnologija* 6(1): 11–30.
'Die Griechisch-Katholischen heute: Eine ethnologische Perspektive', in Hans-Christian Maner and Norbert Spannenberger (eds), *Konfessionelle Identität und Nationsbildung: die griechisch-katholischen Kirchen in Ostmittel- und Südosteuropa im 19. und 20. Jahrhundert*. Stuttgart: Franz Steiner, pp. 79–101.
'A New Double Movement? Anthropological Perspectives on Property in the Age of Neoliberalism', *Socio-Economic Review* 5(2): 287–318.

'Odpověď: Nikoli nevýrazný hybrid, ale partnerství, které má říz', *Sociologický Časopis* 43(1): 209–20.
'Otnosenija sobstvennosti v postsocialisticeskich obscestvach', *Zhurnal issledovanii social'noj politiki* 5(2): 151–78.
'Propertization und ihre Gegentendenzen: Beispiele aus ländlichen Gebieten Europas', in Hannes Siegrist (ed.), *Entgrenzung des Eigentums in modernen Gesellschaften und Rechtskulturen*. Leipzig: Leipziger Universitätsverlag, pp. 84–98.
'Reconciling Anthropologies: Reflections on an Unremarked Centenary', *Anthropology Today* 23(6): 17–19.
'Rozmanité časové rámce antropologie a její budoucnost ve střední a východní Evropě / Anthropology's Multiple Temporalities and its Future in East-Central Europe', *Sociologický Časopis / Czech Sociological Review* 43(1): 15–30.
'Weder nach dem Revolver noch dem Scheckbuch, sondern nach dem Rotstift greifen: Plädoyer eines Ethnologen für die Abschaffung des Kulturbegriffs', *Zeitschrift für Kulturwissenschaften* 1: 125–34.

2006

'Between East and West: Greek Catholic Icons and Cultural Boundaries', in David R. Olson and Michael Cole (eds), *Technology, Literacy, and the Evolution of Society: Implications of the Work of Jack Goody*. Mahwah, NJ: Lawrence Erlbaum, pp. 73–100.
'The Gift and Reciprocity: Perspectives from Economic Anthropology', in Serge-Christophe Kolm and J. Mercier Ytier (eds), *Handbook of the Economics of Giving, Altruism and Reciprocity: Vol. 1; Foundations*. Amsterdam: Elsevier, pp. 207–23.
'Introduction: Faith, Power, and Civility after Socialism', in Chris Hann and the 'Civil Religion' Group, *The Postsocialist Religious Question: Faith and Power in Central Asia and East-Central Europe*. Münster: LIT Verlag, pp. 1–26.
'Nation and Nationalism in Central and Eastern Europe', in Gerard Delanty and K. Kumar (eds), *The Sage Handbook of Nations and Nationalism*. London: Sage, pp. 399–409.
'Peripheral Populations and the Dilemmas of Multiculturalism: The Lemkos and the Lazi Revisited', in Bogdan Horbal, P. Krafcik and E. Rusinko (eds), *Carpatho-Rusyns and Their Neighbors: Essays in Honor of Paul Robert Magocsi*. Fairfax: Eastern Christian Publications, pp. 185–202.
'Social Anthropological Reflections on Citizenship', in Francois Rüegg, Rudolf Poledna and Calin Rus (eds), *Interculturalism and Discrimination in Romania: Policies, Practices, Identities and Representations*. Berlin: LIT Verlag, pp. 29–43.

2005

'The Anthropology of Eurasia in Eurasia', in Peter Skalník (ed.), *Anthropology of Europe: Teaching and Research*. Prague: Set Out, pp. 51–66.

'Correspondence: Reply to Michał Buchowski', *Anthropology of East Europe Review* 23(1): 194–97.
'Eurázsia antropológiája Eurázsiában', *Korunk* 16(8): 20–33.
with Mihály Sárkány and Peter Skalník. 'Introduction: Continuities and Contrasts in an Essentially Contested Field', in Chris Hann, Mihály Sárkány and Peter Skalník (eds), *Studying Peoples in the People's Democracies: Socialist Era Anthropology in East-Central Europe*. Münster: LIT Verlag, pp. 1–20.
'The Limits of Galician Syncretism: Pluralism, Multiculturalism and the Two Catholicisms', in Chris Hann and Paul R. Magosci (eds), *Galicia: A Multicultured Land*. Toronto: University of Toronto Press, pp. 210–37.
'Memory Tracks: State, Nation and Everyday Life in 1970s Budapest', *Berliner Osteuropa-Info* 23: 17–23.
'Postsocialist Societies', in James G. Carrier (ed.), *A Handbook of Economic Anthropology*. Cheltenham: Edward Elgar, pp. 547–57.
'Property', in James G. Carrier (ed.), *A Handbook of Economic Anthropology*. Cheltenham: Edward Elgar, pp. 110–24.
'"Religia obywatelska" a postsocjalistyczne społeczeństwo obywatelskie: jak powiązać skalę mikro i makro w antropologii społecznej?' in J.S. Wasilewski, A. Zadrożyńska and Instytut Etnologii i Antropologii Kulturowej Uniwersytetu Warszawskiego (eds), *Horyzonty antropologii kultury: Tom w darze dla Profesor Zofii Sokolewicz*. Warsaw: Wydawnictwo DiG, pp. 329–44.
'Tradition, sozialer Wandel, Evolution: Defizite in der sozialanthropologischen Tradition', in Hansjörg Siegenthaler (ed.), *Rationalität im Prozess kultureller Evolution: Rationalitätsunterstellungen als eine Bedingung der Möglichkeit substantieller Rationalität des Handelns*. Tübingen: Mohr Siebeck, pp. 283–301.
'Über Kulturen, Wissenschaftskulturen und die Biographien einzelner Ethnologen', in Katja Geisenhainer and Katharina Lange (eds), *Bewegliche Horizonte: Festschrift zum 60. Geburtstag von Bernhard Streck*. Leipzig: Leipziger Universitätsverlag, pp. 445–58.
'Utóparasztok a Futóhomokon: Az "egyszerűbb" mezőgazdasági szövetkezetek bonyolult társadalmi öröksége', in Gyöngyi Schwarcz, Zsuzsa Szarvas and Miklós Szilágyi (eds), *Utóparaszti hagyományok és modernizációs törekvések a magyar vidéken*. Budapest: MTA Néprajzi Kutatóintézet/MTA Társadalomkutatóintézet, pp. 19–36.

2004

'The Cartography of Copyright Cultures versus the Proliferation of Public Properties', in Erich Kasten (ed.), *Properties of Culture – Culture as Property: Pathways to Reform in Post-Soviet Siberia*. Berlin: Reimer, pp. 289–304.
'Die Kosten der neuen Zivilgesellschaft im ländlichen Osteuropa', *Sociologus* 54(1): 79–95.
'Endlich Eurasien!', *Berliner Debatte Initial* 15(3): 60–68.
'In the Church of Civil Society', in Marlies Glasius, David Lewis and Hakan Seckinelgin (eds), *Exploring Civil Society: Political and Cultural Contexts*. London: Routledge, pp. 44–50.

'Két tudományág összemosódása? Néprajz és szociálantropológia a szocialista és posztszocialista időszakokban', in Balázs Borsos (ed.), *Fehéren, feketén: Varsánytól Rititiig. Tanulmányok Sárkány Mihály tiszteletére I*. Budapest: L'Harmattan, pp. 45–63.
'Le regard éloigné: Eurasia in the Perspective of Jack Goody', *Archives Européennes de Sociologie* 45(3): 91–98.
'Landwirtschaftsgenossenschaften, Langfristrechte und Legitimation: eine Fallstudie aus Ungarn', in Julia M. Eckert (ed.), *Anthropologie der Konflikte: Georg Elwerts konflikttheoretische Thesen in der Diskussion*. Bielefeld: Transcript, pp. 217–30.
'Wine, Sand and Socialism: Some Enduring Effects of Hungary's "Flexible" Model of Collectivisation', in Martin Petrick (ed.), *The Role of Agriculture in Central and Eastern European Rural Development: Engine of Change or Social Buffer?* Halle/Saale: IAMO, pp. 192–208.

2003

'Civil Society: The Sickness, Not the Cure?', *Social Evolution and History* 2(2): 55–74.
'Creeds, Cultures and the "Witchery of Music"', *Journal of the Royal Anthropological Institute* 9(2): 223–39.
with Mihály Sárkány. 'The Great Transformation in Rural Hungary: Property, Life Strategies, and Living Standards', in Chris Hann and the 'Property Relations' Group, *The Postsocialist Agrarian Question: Property Relations and the Rural Condition*. Münster: LIT Verlag, pp. 117–42.
'Introduction: Decollectivisation and the Moral Economy', in Chris Hann and the 'Property Relations' Group, *The Postsocialist Agrarian Question: Property Relations and the Rural Condition*. Münster: LIT Verlag, pp. 1–46.
'Is Balkan Civil Society an Oxymoron? From Königsberg to Sarajevo, via Przemyśl', *Ethnologia Balkanica* 7: 63–78.
'Modell der Toleranz und Ökumene?', *Ost-West Gegeninformation* 15(4): 3–9.

2002

'All "Kulturvölker" Now? Social Anthropological Reflections on the German-American Tradition', in Richard G. Fox and Barbara J. King (eds), *Anthropology Beyond Culture*. Oxford: Berg, pp. 259–76.
'The Development of Polish Civil Society and the Experience of the Greek Catholic Minority', in Peter G. Danchin and Elizabeth A. Cole (eds), *Protecting the Human Rights of Religious Minorities in Eastern Europe*. New York: Columbia University Press, pp. 437–54.
'Fieldwork in East-Central Europe and Fieldwork Among the Ethnowissenschaftler', in Konrad Köstlin, Peter Niedermüller and Herbert Nikitsch (eds), *Die Wende als Wende? Orientierungen Europäischer Ethnologien nach 1989*. Vienna: Institut für europäische Ethnologie, pp. 122–34.

with Caroline Humphrey and Katherine Verdery. 'Introduction: Postsocialism as a Topic of Anthropological Investigation', in Chris Hann (ed.), *Postsocialism: Ideals, Ideologies and Practices in Eurasia*. London: Routledge, pp. 1–28.

'Political Ideologies: Socialism and Its Discontents', in Jeremy MacClancy (ed.), *Exotic No More: Anthropology on the Front Lines*. Chicago: University of Chicago Press, pp. 86–98.

'Understanding Postsocialism: New Property Relationships and Their Consequences', in Bojan Baskar and Irena Weber (eds), *MESS, Mediterranean Ethnological Summer School* Ljubljana: Filozofska Fakulteta, pp. 49–68.

2001

'Być Ukraińcem w Polsce: Głosy z podzielonego miasta', in Aldony Jawłowskiej (ed.), *Wokół problemów tożsamości*. Warsaw: Wydawnictwo LTW, pp. 182–207.

'From Volksgeist to Radical Humanism: Culture and Value in Economic Anthropology', *Reviews in Anthropology* 30(1): 1–30.

'Gellner, Ernest (1925-95)', in Neil J. Smelser and Paul B. Baltes (eds), *International Encyclopedia of the Social & Behavioral Sciences* Vol. 9. Amsterdam: Elsevier, pp. 5899–901.

'Gellner's Structural-Functional-Culturalism', *Czech Sociological Review* 9(2): 173–81.

with Ildiko Bellér-Hann. 'Mazlum olan kim? Rize'de cay üreticeleri örnegi', *Toplum ve Bilim* 88: 55–68.

'Problems with Religion and Nationalism in Przemyśl, in Michał Buchowski (ed.), *Poland Beyond Communism: 'Transition' in Critical Perspective*. Freiburg: Universitätsverlag Freiburg, pp. 71–92.

2000

'Culture and Civilization in Central Europe: A Critique of Huntington's Theses', in Werner Konitzer and Kristian Bosselmann-Cyran (eds), *Ein erweitertes Europa verstehen: Die Rolle der Geistes-, Sozial- und Wirtschaftswissenschaften – Understanding an Enlarged Europe. The Role of the Humanities, the Social Sciences and Economics*. Frankfurt am Main: Peter Lang, pp. 99–120.

'Echte Bauern, Stachanowiten und die Lilien auf dem Felde: Arbeit und Zeit aus sozialanthropologischer Perspektive', in Jürgen Kocka and Claus Offe (eds), *Geschichte und Zukunft der Arbeit*. Frankfurt am Main: Campus, pp. 23–53.

with Stanisław Stępień. 'Preface', in Christopher Hann and Stanisław Stępień (eds), *Tradycja a tożsamość: Wywiady wśród mniejszości ukraińskiej w Przemyślu*. Przemyśl: Południowo-Wschodni Instytut Naukowy w Przemyślu, pp. 8–10.

'Problems with the (De)Privatisation of Religion', *Anthropology Today* 16(6): 14–20.

'Zivilgesellschaft oder Citizenship? Skeptische Überlegungen eines Ethnologen', in Manfred Hildermeier (ed.), *Europäische Zivilgesellschaft in Ost und West: Begriff, Geschichte, Chancen*. Frankfurt am Main: Campus, pp. 85–109.

1999

'Introduction: On Nation(alitie)s in General, and One Potential Nation(ality) in Particular', in Paul R. Magocsi (ed.), *Of the Making of Nationalities – There Is No End: Vol. 1; Carpatho-Rusyns in Europe and North America*. New York: Columbia University Press, pp. xiii–xxxvii.

'Lifting the Lid on Local Politics in Przemysl, S-E Poland', in Birgit Müller (ed.), *Power and Institutional Change in Post-communist Eastern Europe*. Canterbury: Centre for Social Anthropology and Computing, University of Kent, pp. 169–85.

with Ildikó Bellér-Hann. 'Peasants and Officials in Southern Xinjiang: Subsistence, Supervision, Subversion', *Zeitschrift für Ethnologie* 124: 1–32.

'Peasants in an Era of Freedom: Property and Market Economy in Southern Xinjiang', *Inner Asia* 1(2): 195–219.

'Die Bauern und das Land: Eigentumsrechte in sozialistischen und postsozialistischen Staatssystemen im Vergleich', in Hannes Siegrist and David Sugarman (eds), *Eigentum im internationalen Vergleich: (18.-20. Jahrhundert)*. Göttingen: Vandenhoeck & Ruprecht, pp. 161–84.

1998

'Drama postkomunizmu: Rozvytok pol'skoho hromadjan'skoho suspil'stva j dosvid hreko-katolic'koï menšyny', *Ljudyna i Svit* (4): 9–14.

'Foreword', in Susan Bridger and Frances Pine (eds), *Surviving Post-socialism: Local Strategies and Regional Responses in Eastern Europe and the Former Soviet Union*. London: Routledge, pp. x–xiv.

'Grekokatolicy w Przemyślu i regionie w świetle antropologii społecznej', in Stanisław Stępień (ed.), *Katolickie unie Kościelne w Europie środkowej i wschodniej: Idea a rzeczywistość*. Przemyśl: Południowo-Wschodni Instytut Naukowy w Przemyślu, pp. 425–50.

'Introduction: The Embeddedness of Property', in Chris Hann (ed.), *Property Relations: Renewing the Anthropological Tradition*. Cambridge: Cambridge University Press, pp. 1–47.

with Ildikó Bellér-Hann. 'Markets, Morality and Modernity in North-East Turkey', in Thomas M. Wilson and Hastings Donnan (eds), *Border Identities: Nation and State at International Frontiers*. Cambridge: Cambridge University Press, pp. 237–62.

'Nationalism and Civil Society in Central Europe: From Ruritania to the Carpathian Euroregion', in John A. Hall (ed.), *The State of the Nation: Ernest Gellner and the Theory of Nationalism*. Cambridge: Cambridge University Press, pp. 243–57.

'Postsocialist Nationalism: Rediscovering the Past in Southeast Poland', *Slavic Review* 57(4): 840–63.

'Proper Peasants in the "Longue Durée"', *Budapest Review of Books* 8(3–4): 145–48.

'Przedmowa: Studiów z dziejów polsko-ukraińskiego sąsiedztwa tom czwarty', in Stanisław Stępień (ed.), *Katolickie unie Kościelne w Europie środkowej i wschodniej: Idea a rzeczywistość*. Przemyśl: Południowo-Wschodni Instytut Naukowy w Przemyślu, pp. 7–8.

'Religion, Trade and Trust in South-East Poland', *Religion, State and Society* 26(3–4): 235–50.

'Ukrainian Epiphany in Southeast Poland', *Ethnologia Europaea* 28(2): 151–67

1997

'Ethnicity in the New Civil Society: Lemko-Ukrainians in Poland', in László Kürti and Juliet Feldman (eds), *Beyond Borders: Remaking Cultural Identities in the New East and Central Europe*. Boulder: Westview Press, pp. 17–38.

'Ethnicity, Language and Politics in Northeast Turkey', in Cora Govers and Han Vermeulen (eds), *The Politics of Ethnic Consciousness*. Basingstoke: Palgrave Macmillan, pp. 121–56.

'The Nation-State, Religion, and Uncivil Society: Two Perspectives from the Periphery', *Daedalus* 126(2): 27–45.

1996

'Class', in Alan Barnard and Jonathan Spencer (eds), *Encyclopedia of Social and Cultural Anthropology*. London: Routledge, pp. 98–99.

'Ethnic Cleansing in Eastern Europe: Poles and Ukrainians Beside the Curzon Line', *Nations and Nationalism* 2(3): 389–406.

'Europe: Central and Eastern', in Alan Barnard and Jonathan Spencer (eds), *Encyclopedia of Social and Cultural Anthropology*. London: Routledge, pp. 203–6.

'Gellner on Malinowski: Words and Things in Central Europe', in John A. Hall and Ian Jarvie (eds), *The Social Philosophy of Ernest Gellner*. Amsterdam: Rodopi, pp. 45–64.

'Introduction: Political Society and Civil Anthropology', in Chris Hann and Elizabeth Dunn (eds), *Civil Society: Challenging Western Models*. London: Routledge, pp. 1–26.

'"It's Out There, Like Mount Everest": Thoughts on the Gellner Legacy', *Cambridge Anthropology* 19(2): 35–49.

'Land Tenure', in Alan Barnard and Jonathan Spencer (eds), *Encyclopedia of Social and Cultural Anthropology*. London: Routledge, pp. 321–23.

'Land Tenure and Citizenship in Tázlár', in Ray Abrahams (ed.), *After Socialism: Land Reform and Social Change in Eastern Europe*. Providence: Berghahn Books, pp. 23–49.

'Mode of Production', in Alan Barnard and Jonathan Spencer (eds), *Encyclopedia of Social and Cultural Anthropology*. London: Routledge, pp. 375–76.

'Property', in Alan Barnard and Jonathan Spencer (eds), *Encyclopedia of Social and Cultural Anthropology*. London: Routledge, pp. 453–54.

'Sharecropping', in Alan Barnard and Jonathan Spencer (eds), *Encyclopedia of Social and Cultural Anthropology*. London: Routledge, pp. 764–65.

1995

'Ferenc Erdei and Antal Vermes: The Struggle for Balance in Rural Hungary', in David A. Kideckel (ed.), *East European Communities: The Struggles for Balance in Turbulent Times*. Boulder: Westview Press, pp. 101–14.
'Intellectuals, Ethnic Groups and Nations: Two Late-Twentieth-Century Cases', in Sukumar Periwal (ed.), *Notions of Nationalism*. Budapest: Central European University Press, pp. 106–28.
'Philosophers' Models on the Carpathian Lowlands', in John A. Hall (ed.), *Civil Society: Theory, History, Comparison*. Cambridge: Polity Press, pp. 158–82.
'Subverting Strong States: The Dialectics of Social Engineering in Hungary and Turkey', *Daedalus* 124(2): 133–53.

1994

'After Communism: Reflections on East European Anthropology and the Transition', *Social Anthropology* 2(3): 229–49.
'Fast Forward: The Great Transformation Globalized', in Chris Hann (ed.), *When History Accelerates: Essays on Rapid Social Change, Complexity and Creativity*. London: Athlone, pp. 1–22.
'Sources of Identity in the Laz Region', *Turkish Studies Association Bulletin* 18(1): 54–57.

1993

'Culture and Anti-culture: The Spectre of Orientalism in New Anthropological Writing on Turkey', *Journal of the Anthropological Society of Oxford* 24(3): 223–43.
'Elvtársaktól jogászokig: Szociálantropológiai jegyzet a rendszerváltásról', *Valóság* 36(3): 26–37.
'From Comrades to Lawyers: Continuity and Change in Local Political Culture in Rural Hungary', *Anthropological Journal on European Cultures* 2(1): 75–104.
'From Production to Property: Decollectivization and the Family-Land Relationship in Contemporary Hungary', *Man* 28(2): 299–320.
'Introduction: Social Anthropology and Socialism', in Chris Hann (ed.), *Socialism: Ideals, Ideologies, and Local Practice*. London: Routledge, pp. 1–26.
'Property Relations in the New Eastern Europe: The Case of Specialist Cooperatives in Hungary', in Hermine De Soto and David G. Anderson (eds), *The Curtain Rises: Rethinking Culture, Ideology, and the State in Eastern Europe*. Atlantic Highlands, NJ: Humanities Press, pp. 99–119.
'Religion and Nationality in Central Europe: The Case of the Uniates', *Ethnic Studies* 10(1–3): 201–13.
'The Sexual Division of Labour in Lazistan', in Paul Stirling (ed.), *Culture and Economy: Changes in Turkish Villages*. Huntingdon: Eothen Press, pp. 126–39.

1992

'Civil Society at the Grass-Roots: A Reactionary View', in Paul G. Lewis (ed.), *Democracy and Civil Society in Eastern Europe: Selected Papers from the Fourth World Congress for Soviet and East European Studies, Harrogate, 1990.* London: Macmillan, pp. 152–65.

'Market Principle, Market-Place and the Transition in Eastern Europe', in Roy Dilley (ed.), *Contesting Markets: Analyses of Ideology, Discourse and Practice.* Edinburgh: Edinburgh University Press, pp. 244–59.

'Radical Functionalism: The Life and Work of Karl Polanyi', *Dialectical Anthropology* 17(2): 141–66.

with Ildikó Bellér-Hann. 'Samovars and Sex on Turkey's Russian Markets', *Anthropology Today* 8(4): 3–6.

1991

'Ethnic Games in Xinjiang: Anthropological Approaches', in Shirin Akiner (ed.), *Cultural Change and Continuity in Central Asia.* London: Kegan Paul International, pp. 218–36.

'Europe Centrale et Orientale', in Pierre Bonte and Michel Izard (eds), *Dictionnaire de l'ethnologie et de l'anthropologie.* Paris: PUF, pp. 261–62.

'Notes on the Transition in Tázlár', *Cambridge Anthropology* 15(3): 1–21.

1990

'Introduction', in Chris Hann (ed.), *Market Economy and Civil Society in Hungary.* London: Cass, pp. 1–20.

'Introduction', *Journal of Communist Studies* 6(2): 1–20.

'Second Economy and Civil Society', in Chris Hann (ed.), *Market Economy and Civil Society in Hungary.* London: Cass, pp. 21–44.

'Second Economy and Civil Society', *Journal of Communist Studies* 6(2): 21–44.

'Second Thoughts on Smallholders: Tea Production, the State and Social Differentiation in the Rize Region', *New Perspectives on Turkey* 4: 57–79.

'Socialism and King Stephen's Right Hand', *Religion in Communist Lands* 18(1): 4–24.

1988

'Christianity's Internal Frontier: The Case of Uniates in South-East Poland', *Anthropology Today* 4(3): 9–13.

1987

'The Politics of Anthropology in Socialist Eastern Europe', in Anthony Jackson (ed.), *Anthropology at Home.* London: Tavistock, pp. 139–53.

'Worker-Peasants in the Three Worlds', in Teodor Shanin (ed.), *Peasants and Peasant Societies: Selected Readings*. Oxford: Blackwell, pp. 114–20.

1986

'Notes from a Medical College', *Cambridge Anthropology* 11(3): 104–8.

1985

'Rural Transformation on the East Black Sea Coast of Turkey: A Note on Keyder', *Journal of Peasant Studies* 12(4): 101–10.

1983

'Progress toward Collectivized Agriculture in Tázlár, 1948–78', in Marida Hollos and Bela C. Maday (eds), *New Hungarian Peasants: An East Central European Experience with Collectivization*. New York: Brooklyn College Press, pp. 69–92.

1982

'Kisüzemi gazdálkodás Tázláron a hetvenes években', *Ethnographia* 93(1): 33–72.

1980

'Rural Change in Hungary and Poland', *Cambridge Anthropology* 6(1–2): 142–50.
'Tázlár: The Frontier Community since 1945', *New Hungarian Quarterly* 21(78): 139–47.

1979

'Tázlár: The Frontier Community on the Great Plain', *New Hungarian Quarterly* 20(74): 116–21.

Index

Africa, 55, 58, 124–25, 216. *See also specific countries*
The Age of Surveillance Capitalism (Zuboff), 113
agriculture, 53, 55–57. *See also collectives*
  cooperatives for, 56, 59–60, 65–67, 71–72, 170
  in Czech Republic, 73
  EU for, 70–71
  in France, 186
  in Hungary, 59–60, 64–73
  in Kenya, 56
  in labour, 65–66
  in pre-Ottoman Southwest Arabia, 128–30
  rice, 219–27
  rituals in, 210–13
  ritual technologies in, 223–24, 228n6
  in Russia, 164
  in socialism, 59–60
  solidarity for, 78
  subsidies for, 70
  swidden, 219–27
  in Turkey, 194–203, 204n11
Allen, Richard, 269
Amsden, Alice, 68
Anderson, Bridget, 165

anthropology. *See also specific topics*
  anthropological scholarship, 1, 105, 145–47, 153–54
  of civil society, 107–12
  economies in, 25–29
  employment in, 8–9
  Eurasia in, 3–5, 12–13, 35–43, 42–43
  Hann for, 106–7, 130, 136, 145, 154, 240
  historical regions in, 36–43
  language in, 149–50
  moral dimensions of, 157–65
  Open Anthropology Cooperative, 151
  open science in, 149–53
  peasant societies in, 52–60
  Polanyi for, 3–5, 8–10, 12, 26–31, 58, 105–12, 121, 130, 136, 147, 182–85, 191–92
  religion in, 216–17
  social, 41–42, 105–6
anti-communism, 79–80
anti-neoliberalism, 84
Appadurai, Arjun, 243
Arabia. *See* pre-Ottoman Southwest Arabia
Arnason, Johann P., 5–6, 33, 40
Arthurs, Harry, 134

Ascherson, Neal, 38
Asia. *See also specific countries*
　Africa and, 124
　Buddhism in, 232–33
　East, 24, 55
　Europe compared to, 11, 42–43
　kinship in, 3–4
　labour in, 94–95
　South, 55, 147, 255–63
　Southeast, 219–27
　for Weber, 24
Atatürk, Mustafa Kemal, 194
Austrian School of Economics, 26, 97–98
Ayyubid dynasty, 125
Azerbaijan, 162

Balcerowicz, Leszek, 77, 86n4, 166n3
Balkans, 35, 38, 46, 111. *See also specific countries*
Bauman, Zygmunt, 77
Beckmann, Keebet and Franz von Benda, 171
Bellér-Hann, Ildikó, 3, 10, 52, 157
Berufsmensch (Weber), 24
Biernacki, Richard, 95–97
Black Sea Region, 35, 38–39, 46, 195. *See also specific countries*
Bloch, Ernst, 45
Borderlands of Western Civilization (Halecki), 36–37
Bourdieu, Pierre, 238
Bradbury, Michael, 44
Brătianu, Gheorghe Ion, 38
Braudel, Fernand, 38
Brumann, Christoph, 11, 14n2, 240
Bru people, 219–27, 228n1, 228n3, 228n8
Buchowski, Michał, 7, 85–86, 146, 149–50
Buddhism, 11, 232–40

Calic, Marie-Janine, 46
Cannon, Isidore Cyril, 135–36
CAP. *See* Common Agricultural Policy
capitalism
　history of, 20–21

　in Hungary, 72
　labour in, 91
　for Marx, 30–31, 56, 90
　in Marxism, 209
　modern, 21, 24
　for neoliberalism, 7, 73, 79–80
　Smith for, 90
　social, 215
　socialism compared to, 8, 170
　for social justice, 85
　surveillance in, 113
　theories on, 97–99
cash crops, 56–57, 194–203
caste system, 256–63, 264n5, 264n7
Çaykur (Turkey), 197–202, 204n9
Central and Eastern European (CEE) scholarship, 149–50, 155n7
Central Europe. *See* East-Central Europe
Chandra, Vijaya, 247
child sex ratio (CSR), 187
China, 261
　Buddhism in, 234–35
　Confucian social ethics in, 28
　Europe compared to, 3
　Global South for, 45
　India compared to, 19–20, 32–33
　kinship in, 268–69
　research on, 157
　socialism in, 52
　surveillance in, 114
　Tibet and, 236–37
　USSR with, 55
civilizations
　economies and, 19–21
　modernity in, 22–25
　scholarship on, 25–29, 35–36
civil society, 107–12
class, 83, 96, 100n2
CNRS. *See* National Center for Scientific Research
Cold War, 19, 55, 76–78
collectives, 137, 174–76, 179n9, 180n10
Colombia, 212, 214
colonialism, 12, 55, 256, 267–76
commodities, 183–91, 194–203, 203n1, 243–44, 272–73

Common Agricultural Policy (CAP), 70
communism, 77–80, 103
Confucian social ethics, 28
cooperatives, 151
  in Hungary, 6, 64–73, 108, 170
  in Kenya, 6, 53–60
  in Poland, 159–60, 166n4
COVID-19, 86n4, 110, 113
Crab Antics (Wilson), 274–75
creativity, 211
credit, 100n3
Creole people, 269–76
CSR. *See* child sex ratio
Czech Republic, 4, 73

Dalits, 255–63, 264n5, 264n7
Dashi-Dorzho Itigelov (lama), 236
Daston, Lorraine, 147–48
Davies, Norman, 45
Delanty, Gerard, 41
Disappearing World (film), 91
discrimination, 83, 90, 92–93, 98–99
Domains and Divisions of European History (Halecki), 40–41
Dresch, Paul, 128–29
Dukes, Ruth, 8–9, 142
Durkheim, Emile, 19–20, 24–25, 31–32
Durst, Judit, 92

East Africa, 58, 124–25
East Asia, 24, 55. *See also specific countries*
East-Central Europe, 35–37, 43–45, 55, 68, 78. *See also specific countries*
Eastern Europe
  communism in, 103
  EU for, 69–70
  gig economy in, 106
  globalization for, 68
  Orthodox Church for, 36–37
  postsocialism in, 2, 178–79
  racism in, 107–8
  research on, 102–3, 149–50, 170–71
  Western Europe compared to, 9
The East in the West (Goody), 46
economic anthropology. *See specific topics*

economic sociology, 27
economies. *See specific topics*
Eidson, John, 14n3
Eisenstadt, S. N., 20, 22
The Elementary Forms of Religious Life (Durkheim), 20
elitism, 82–83
embeddedness, 121, 130, 136, 157–65, 275–76
employment, 8–9
Endres, Kirsten W., 13, 14n2
Erdei, Gerence, 56
Eriksen, Thomas Hylland, 12, 276
Ethiopia, 125–26
ethnicity, 271–72
ethnography, 32–33
EU. *See* European Union
Eurasia. *See also specific countries*
  in anthropology, 3–5, 12–13, 35–43
  for Hann, 6, 36, 42–43, 46, 184–85, 268, 275–76
  research on, 182–83, 191–92
  resilience in, 102–5, 114–15
  surveillance in, 105, 113–15
Europe. *See also specific countries*
  Asia compared to, 11, 42–43
  Balkans for, 46
  China compared to, 3
  European Commission, 148
  history of, 36, 39–42, 54
  modernity in, 21
  nationalism in, 7
  postsocialism in, 275
  Romania for, 110–11
  socialism in, 10
  Socialist Bloc in, 164
European Union (EU), 67–71, 86n3
  for moral economies, 163
  for neoliberalism, 106–7
  for Poland, 80–81, 86n3
  politics of, 105
exchange systems, 121, 130
exchange value, 173–79
exploitation
  in Hungary, 89–90
  in Marxism, 93–97
  usury as, 91–93, 97–99

Facebook, 113
Fassin, Didier, 147
France, 56, 152–53, 155n9, 186

Gati, Charles, 43
Gauchet, Marcel, 23
GDR. *See* German Democratic Republic
Gellner, David N., 12, 105, 263
gender, 157–66, 188–91
geopolitical terminology, 43–44
German Democratic Republic (GDR), 2–3
Germany, 13, 95–96, 99
The Gift (Mauss), 32
gig economy, 106
Gingrich, Andre, 8, 130–31
globalization
  Cold War related to, 76
  after colonialism, 12
  for Eastern Europe, 68
  economic anthropology in, 8–10
  neoliberalism in, 67–68, 84–85
  resources in, 129–30
  for Russian Federation, 46
Global South, 45
goddesses, 243–51, 252n5
Godelier, Maurice, 85
Gomułka, Stanisław, 86n4
Goody, Jack, 2, 5, 46, 89
  for Hann, 105, 182–83
  legacy of, 114, 268
  Polanyi compared to, 183–85, 192
Google, 113
goulash socialism. *See* socialism
Gramsci, Antonio, 79
The Great Transformation (Polanyi), 54, 183, 275
Gregory, Chris, 10, 192
Griaule, Marcel, 155n10
Ground Down by Growth (Shah), 263
Gudeman, Stephen, 11, 217–18, 244
Gypsies. *See* Roma

Habeck, Otto, 14n1
al-Hadi Yahya, 121
Halecki, Oskar, 36–37, 40–41

Hann, Chris
  academic journey of, 1–5
  agriculture for, 220
  for anthropology, 106–7, 130, 136, 145, 154, 240
  class for, 100n2
  with colleagues, 64–65, 89–90, 146, 149–50, 244–45, 263
  embeddedness for, 157–65
  Eurasia for, 6, 36, 42–43, 46, 184–85, 268, 275–76
  Goody for, 105, 182–83
  Hart with, 25–27
  Harvey, David, 78
  Hungary for, 6–7, 273
  legacy of, 114–15, 140, 155n7
  for moral economies, 8–10, 157–58, 160–61
  morality for, 255
  for MPI, 13, 109–10
  on nationalism, 68
  NGOs for, 108
  Polanyi for, 94, 103, 106, 121, 147
  for postsocialism, 5–7, 102–5, 107, 163
  property relations for, 169–73, 178–79
  religion for, 233
  research by, 61n2, 105–6, 165, 178–79, 209–10
  Schlee with, 14n1
  scholarship of, 12–13, 52–53, 61n1
  for sociology, 56
  Turkey for, 194–203, 204n9
Harris, Rosemary, 98–99
Hart, Keith, 25–27, 105
hegemony, 79, 83
Heintz, Monica, 9, 154
Hijra settlements, 123–24, 126–28, 131n4
Hinduism, 12, 186–90, 245–51, 268–76
The Hindu Jajmani System (Wiser), 256–57
Historical Atlas of (East) Central Europe (Magocsi), 43–44
historical regions
  in anthropology, 36–43

historiography of, 35–36
transregionalism in, 43–46
'The Historical Regions of Europe' (Delanty), 41
historiography, 35–36
history
    of capitalism, 20–21
    of civil society, 107–12
    of Europe, 36, 39–42, 54
    of France, 56
    of human autonomy, 22–23
    of India, 267–69
    of Industrial Revolution, 53
    of Marxism, 147
    of meso-regions, 38–39
    of Poland, 76
    of pre-Ottoman Southwest Arabia, 121
    of Romania, 103–4
    trends in, 44–45
    of wealth, 29–33
Hivon, Myriam, 164
homo oeconomicus, 19, 22, 24–25
homo Sovieticus, 82, 84
Honeysett, Bethany, 153
household
    economy, 59–60, 69, 159–61, 163, 174–78
    land, 59, 67, 174–78, 179n9, 180n10
    oikos, 28, 32
human autonomy, 22–23
human economy, 8, 147, 184, 275–76
human rights, 93
Hungary, 4
    agriculture in, 53–60, 64–73
    capitalism in, 72
    exploitation in, 89–90
    for Hann, 6–7, 273
    Hungarian Forints, 93
    labour in, 58–59
    Poland and, 102–4, 160, 164–65, 195–96
    postsocialism in, 64–73
    religion in, 37
    research on, 52–53, 61, 64–73, 89–90, 111, 158
    Romania compared to, 115
    socialism in, 64–73, 110, 160–61, 164
    usury in, 91–93, 97–99

Iberoamérica, 45–46
Ibn Battuta, 125
L'Idéel et le Materiel (Godelier), 85
ideology, 86n8
immigration, 165
Imperial Chemical Industries, 98–99
India, 12
    caste system in, 256–57, 260–62, 264n5, 264n7
    China compared to, 19–20, 32–33
    East Asia for, 24
    history of, 267–69
    Kondagaon, 185–91
    Orissa, 243–51
Industrial Revolution, 53, 55–56
industry
    in East-Central Europe, 78
    industrial sociology, 134–42
    in Rize, 200
    in socialism, 68–69
    of tea, 204n4, 204n7, 204n9, 204n11
integration, 121, 130, 155n6
International Monetary Fund, 166n3
International Typographical Union, 135–36
Italy, 59–60

Jajmani system, 255–63, 264n5, 264n7
Japan, 53, 232–33, 235–39, 261
Juhász, Pál, 68

Kaczyński, Jarosław, 86n4
Kádár, Janos, 103
Kaneff, Deema, 9–10, 13–14, 179
Kaser, Karl, 46
Kenya, 53, 56, 58–59
Khe Sanh (Vietnam), 219–27
King, Charles, 38
kingship, 243–51, 252n8
kinship, 3–4, 10, 157–66, 182–91, 268–69
Kochanowicz, Jacek, 68
Kondagaon (India), 185–91
Koselleck, Reinhart, 44–45

labour
  agriculture in, 65–66
  in Asia, 94–95
  in capitalism, 91
  as commodities, 187–91, 272–73
  discrimination in, 98–99
  food and, 57
  household land related to, 179n9
  in Hungary, 58–59
  laws, 134–42
  for Marx, 29–30, 95–96
  in Poland, 161–62
  in postneoliberal political economies, 134–42
  psychology of, 32, 209–17
  research on, 98–99
  in socialism, 162–64
  solidarity in, 142n2
  in United Kingdom, 106
  value of, 183–84
land, 183–87
language, 149–50, 221, 224, 228n3, 257
Latin America. *See specific countries*
Latin Americans, 216
legal norms, 134–42
Lévi-Strauss, Claude, 30–31, 148
Lewandowski, Janusz, 86n3
The Limits and Divisions of European History (Halecki), 36
Lipset, Seymour Martin, 135
Locke, John, 94
longue durée, 21, 38–39, 42–43, 45

Magdeburg Law, 37
Magocsi, Paul R., 43–44
Malaysia, 261
markets, 126–28, 255–63
marriage
  arranged, 274
  in Hijra, 124, 127–29, 131n6
  intermarriage, 122, 271
  kinship and, 183, 188–92
  religion and, 258–59
Marx, Karl, 24
  capitalism for, 30–31, 56, 90

  commodities for, 183
  credit for, 100n3
  labour for, 29–30, 95–96
  modernization for, 53–54
  neoliberalism for, 23
  Polanyi compared to, 58
  on sociology, 94
Marxism, 7, 29, 93–97, 147, 172, 209
Marxist-Leninist-Maoist (MLM) socialism, 42
Maurel, Lionel, 155n9
Mauritius, 267–76
Mauss, Marcel, 19, 31–32
Max Planck Institute for Social Anthropology (MPI), 105
  Hann for, 13, 109–10
  research for, 3–4, 9–10
  resilience for, 107
  scholarship from, 169–71
  science for, 2–3
mercantilism, 38–39
meso-regions, 38–39
Metcalfe, Charles, 255
Mill, James, 255
Mittal, Lakshmi, 189–90
MLM socialism. *See* Marxist-Leninist-Maoist socialism
modernity, 21–25, 52–60
money, 232–40
  expoloitation with, 94–97
  usury, 91–93, 97–99
Mongolia, 55, 235, 239
moral economy
  of anthropological scholarship, 145–47, 153–54, 155n5
  Buddhism in, 232–40
  of Creoles, 274
  domestic, 188
  ethnography of, 166n2
  EU for, 163
  Hann for, 8–10, 157–58, 160–61
  Hungary as, 69
  open access in, 149–51
  open data in, 151–53
  open science in, 147–49
  of theft, 245
moral embeddedness, 136

Index

MPI. *See* Max Planck Institute for Social Anthropology
Müller, Michael G., 44
Mundy, Martha, 128–29
Murawska-Muthesius, Katarzyna, 44
Muslims, 121–26, 128–30, 131n6, 246

Nagoya Protocol, 147, 152, 154n4
National Center for Scientific Research (CNRS), 153
nationalism, 7, 68, 76, 85
neoliberalism, 6
   anti-neoliberalism, 84
   capitalism for, 7, 73, 79–80
   EU for, 106–7
   in globalization, 67–68, 84–85
   Marx for, 23
   for Poland, 84–85
   in politics, 86n4
   populism compared to, 76–80
   postneoliberal political economies, 134–42
   in postsocialism, 86n6
   poverty for, 72
   reform for, 78–79
Nepal, 256–63
New Institutional Economics, 28–29
NGOs. *See* nongovernmental organizations
nongovernmental organizations (NGOs), 108, 112, 149
nostalgia, 6, 84

OECD. *See* Organisation for Economic Co-operation and Development
Open Anthropology Cooperative, 151
open science, 146–54
Organisation for Economic Co-operation and Development (OECD), 81
Orissa (India), 243–51
Orthodox Church, 36–37
Osterhammel, Jürgen, 39
Ottoman Empire, 38
Özal, Turgut, 198
Özveren, Eyüp, 38
Özyürek, Esra, 194

Panama, 210, 214
Paulmann, Johannes, 39–40
peasant societies, 52–60, 147, 222
The Philosophy of Money (Simmel), 25
Piketty, Thomas, 186
Pine, Frances, 9, 165–66
Plan S, 148, 151, 153, 155n9
Poland, 4
   EU for, 80–81, 86n3
   history of, 76
   Hungary and, 102–4, 160, 164–65, 195–96
   labour in, 161–62
   neoliberalism for, 84–85
   politics in, 166n3
   populism in, 82–83, 82–84
   postsocialism in, 77–80, 108–9, 158–59
   socialism in, 2, 166n4
Polanyi, Karl, 5, 8, 26–30
   for anthropology, 130, 182–83
   criticism of, 209
   double movement for, 114
   economics for, 52
   Goody compared to, 183–85, 192
   The Great Transformation by, 54, 183, 275
   for Hann, 94, 103, 106, 121, 147
   labour for, 96
   legacy of, 157
   Marx compared to, 58
   Mauritius and, 267–68, 272–76
   reputation of, 89–90
   scholarship on, 105–6
politics
   after Cold War, 77–78
   discrimination in, 90, 92–93
   of EU, 105
   geopolitical terminology, 43–44
   hegemony in, 79
   neoliberalism in, 86n4
   nostalgia in, 84
   in Poland, 166n3
   political economies, 243–51
   postneoliberal political economies, 134–42
   of religion, 21

politics (*cont.*)
  religion in, 82–83
  in Turkey, 196–97
  in USSR, 27–28
popular law, 140
populism, 7, 76–85, 86n8
Portugal, 45
postcolonialism, 267–76
postcommunism, 77–80
postneoliberal political economies, 134–42
postsocialism
  for East-Central Europe, 45
  in Eastern Europe, 2, 178–79
  in Europe, 275
  Hann for, 5–7, 102–5, 107, 163
  household land in, 180n10
  in Hungary, 64–73
  nationalism in, 76
  neoliberalism in, 86n6
  in Poland, 77–80, 108–9, 158–59
  research on, 42
  as resilience, 106–7
  socialism related to, 105–6
poverty, 72, 191–92
pre-Ottoman Southwest Arabia, 121–30
property
  relations, 3, 169–73, 178–79
  transmission, 182–83, 186, 191, 210
Protestant Ethic (Weber), 22, 214–15
psychology, of labour, 32, 209–17

racism, 72, 107–8, 271–72
Raheja, Gloria Goodwin, 258–60
Rasulid dynasty, 125
Rates of Exchange (Bradbury), 44
Reagan, Ronald, 77
Realising Eurasia (research project), 4, 182–84
Red Flag cooperative, 66–67
reform, for neoliberalism, 78–79
religion. *See also specific religions*
  in anthropology, 216–17
  for economies, 11–12, 211
  goddesses in, 243–51, 252n5
  for Hann, 233
  hierarchies in, 271

  in Hungary, 37
  kinship in, 10, 182–91
  in law, 130
  in politics, 82–83
  politics of, 21
  scholarship on, 20
  in Vietnam, 220–27, 228n8
  wealth in, 186–88
  for Weber, 214–15
Repatriating Polanyi (Hann), 103, 106
resilience, 7, 102–7, 111–12, 114–15
resources, 129–30, 170–79
rice, 219–27
Rigby, Peter, 212
rituals
  in Buddhism, 232–33, 239
  economy as, 209–17
  gifts, 260
  ritual technologies, 223–24, 228n6
  in Zaydism, 128–30
Rize (Turkey), 196–203, 204n9
Robbins, Lionel, 26
Roma, 72, 90–93, 97–99, 110, 113–14, 164
Romania, 7, 103–4, 110–15
Rostovtzeff, Mikhail, 38
Rostowski, Jan-Vincent, 86n4
royalty, 243–51, 252n8
Russia, 42, 46, 164, 179n6
Rydzyk, Tadeusz, 82–83

Sachs, Jeffrey, 86n4
sacred economies, 10–12
Sampson, Steven, 7, 115
Sárkány, Mihály, 6, 61
Saudi Arabia, 123. *See also* pre-Ottoman Southwest Arabia
Scandinavia, 38
Schenk, Frithjof Benjamin, 44–45
Schlee, Günther, 14n1
Schmale, Wolfgang, 44–45
Schnepel, Burkhard, 11–12, 251–52
scholarship
  anthropological, 1, 105, 145–47, 153–54
  CEE, 149–50, 155n7
  on civilizations, 25–29, 35–36

after Cold War, 19
of Hann, 12–13, 52–53, 61n1
MPI, 169–71
on religion, 20
Schorkowitz, Dittmar, 14n2
science, 145–54, 155n6
Scott, James, 9, 147, 159
second economies, 111–12
secular economies, 10–12
Shah, Alpa, 263
Siberia, 14n1
Siegrist, Hannes, 39
Simmel, Georg, 25
slavery, 269
Slovakia, 4
Smith, Adam, 90, 94, 97–98, 147, 215
social anthropology, 41–42, 105–6
social capitalism, 215
social change, 169–70, 173–79
social inequality index, 86n7
socialism
  agriculture in, 59–60
  capitalism compared to, 8, 170
  in China, 52
  during Cold War, 55
  for Durkheim, 24–25
  in Europe, 10
  goulash, 64–73
  in Hungary, 6, 64–73, 110, 160–61, 164
  industry in, 68–69
  labour in, 162–64
  MLM, 42
  in Poland, 2, 166n4
  populism and, 7
  postsocialism related to, 105–6
  religion in, 10–11
  surveillance in, 103–5
  trade in, 97–98
  in USSR, 27, 82, 179n7
  usury in, 91–92
social justice, 85, 93
The Social Life of Things (Appadurai), 243
social norms, 134–42
sociology
  economic, 27

Great Transformation in, 54
Hann for, 56
industrial, 134–42
Marx on, 94
rural, 68
social anthropology, 41–42, 105–6
Weber for, 21, 268
soft nationalism, 68
solidarity, 78, 135, 137–39, 142n2, 147, 210
Sombart, Werner, 53
South Asia, 55, 147, 255–63. *See also specific countries*
Southeast Asia, 219–27. *See also specific countries*
South Korea, 261
Soviet Union (USSR)
  with China, 55
  hegemony of, 43, 45
  household land in, 174–78, 180n10
  modernization for, 54–55
  politics in, 27–28
  Russia compared to, 179n6
  socialism in, 27, 82, 179n7
  Soviet Bloc, 37
Spain, 45
special commodities, 183–91
Sri Lanka, 235, 238–39
stereotypes, 72, 82–83
Stewart, Michael, 7, 100
Stiglitz, Joseph, 77
Strathern, Marilyn, 94
Streeck, Wolfgang, 8–9, 142
Sundhaussen, Holm, 38
suq (market), 126–28
surveillance, 103–5, 113–15
Swain, Nigel, 6–7, 73
swidden agriculture. *See agriculture*
Szűcs, Jenő, 37

Tanzania, 212
Taylor, Lance, 68
Tázlár (Hann), 2
tea (Turkish), 194–203, 204n4, 204n7, 204n9, 204n11
Thailand, 235–36
Thatcher, Margaret, 77

A Theory of Moral Sentiments (Smith), 97
Thompson, E. P., 9, 147–49, 158–60
Tibet, 236–37
Todorova, Maria, 38, 45–46
totalitarianism, 2
Toynbee, Arnold, 38
trade, 97–98, 126–28
transregionalism, 43–46
Troebst, Stefan, 6, 46
Turkey, 2, 10, 53, 194–203, 204n11

Ukraine, 174–78
UNESCO. *See* United Nations Educational, Scientific and Cultural Organization
Union Democracy (Lipset), 135
United Kingdom, 77, 95–96, 106, 113, 165
United Nations Educational, Scientific and Cultural Organization (UNESCO), 146
United States, 45, 77, 214
Us and Them (Anderson), 165
use value, 173–79
USSR. *See* Soviet Union
usury, 91–93, 97–99
Utopian projects, 145–54

value, 173–79, 183–84
Váradi, Monika, 72

Vargyas, Gábor, 11, 227
Verdery, Katherine, 104
Vietnam, 11, 219–27, 228n6, 228n8, 228nn1–2
A Village without Solidarity (Hann), 2

Wage Labour and Capital (Marx), 95–96
wealth, 29–33, 86n7, 186–91
The Wealth of Nations (Smith), 97
Weber, Max, 11, 19
  Asia for, 24
  modernization for, 53
  Protestant Ethic by, 22
  religion for, 214–15
  for sociology, 21, 268
Western Europe, 9, 55
Why Come to Slaka? (Bradbury), 44
Wilson, Peter J., 274–75
Wiser, W. H., 256–58
World Bank, 166n3

Yalçın-Heckmann, Lale, 10, 14n2, 203
Yemen. *See* pre-Ottoman Southwest Arabia

Zaydism, 121–26, 128–30, 131n6
Zeitlyn, David, 152
Zeitschichten (Koselleck), 45
Zuboff, Shoshana, 113

www.ingramcontent.com/pod-product-compliance
Lightning Source LLC
Chambersburg PA
CBHW070910030426
42336CB00014BA/2350